Harvard Historical Studies 142

Published under the auspices
of the Department of History
from the income of the
Paul Revere Frothingham Bequest
Robert Louis Stroock Fund
Henry Warren Torrey Fund

The Battle for Children

World War II, Youth Crime, and Juvenile Justice in Twentieth-Century France

Sarah Fishman

Harvard University Press

Cambridge, Massachusetts, and London, England | 2002

Library of Congress Cataloguing-in-Publication Data

Fishman, Sarah, 1957–
  The battle for children : World War II, youth crime, and juvenile justice
in twentieth-century France / Sarah Fishman.
    p. cm.—(Harvard historical studies ; 142)
  Includes bibliographical references and index.
  ISBN 0-674-00755-7
    1. Juvenile delinquency—France—History—20th century.   2. Juvenile
justice, Administration of—France—History—20th century.   3. France—
History—1945–   I. Title.   II. Harvard historical studies ; v. 142.

HV9154 .F57 2002
364.36'0944'0904—dc21   2002022916

*To the memory of Bonnie B. Boyd
and Kathleen Marie Wendt*

Contents

Acknowledgments

It is a great pleasure finally to thank the many people whose generosity and support have sustained this endeavor. I should first like to express my deepest appreciation to two people of tremendous intellectual and personal importance in my life, Patrice Higonnet and Dominique Veillon, not only fabulous scholars but also incredible human beings. In the field of juvenile delinquency, both Jacques Bourquin and Michel Chauvière generously shared their time, expertise, and even materials with an American they barely knew. Undertaking the archival work for this book required figuring out which archives to check for documents. For her indispensable help directing me to all the right places, thanks to Chantal de Tourtier-Bonazzi, retired director of the Section contemporaine of the Archives nationales. Thanks also to her equally helpful, knowledgeable, and kind successor, Paule René-Bazin; to Alain Erlande-Brandenburg, director of the Archives nationales for help with permissions; and to the provincial archival directors who helped me gain access to their holdings, Claudine Wallart at the Archives départementales du Nord, Florence Beaume at the Archives d'Indre-et-Loire, and Lise Carretero at the Archives départementales du Gard. The Archives départementales de Paris proved indispensable to this study; my heartfelt thanks to the director, Jean-Marie Jenn, as well as to archivists Philippe Grand and Roger Cousin from the ADP's annex at Villemoison. Most especially I must thank Brigitte Lainé, a remarkable archivist who has courageously insisted on archival access and honesty about France's past. I should also like to thank Mademoiselle Poinsotte at the Public Assistance Archives in Paris, and Françoise Bosman and Madame Etienne-Magnien at the archives of the Ministry of Labor and Social Affairs. Jeanne Decker, *attachée du directeur* at the Association Olga Spitzer (formerly the Service social de l'enfance) not only made available the association's holdings from the era but also was instrumental in helping me find a publisher for a French version of my first book on prisoner-of-war wives, so I thank her for her help in both areas. As a result of a happy accident, Georges d'Heucqueville kindly agreed to an interview about his wartime activities in the field. In August 1991, the person who delivered his book to my table at the Bibliothèque nationale mentioned that the author was his father, then telephoned him to arrange the meeting. Jean Donnedieu de Vabres was kind enough to share his own experiences as well as those of his late father, the renowned jurist Henri Donnedieu de Vabres. Catherine Cléré at La Documentation française helped me locate relevant photographs.

For most excellent, thought provoking, and always welcome suggestions, thanks to Robert Zaretsky, Bailey Stone, Karl Ittmann, Kathleen Nilan, Richard Blackett, Pamela Cox, Kenneth Mouré, and Martin Alexander. Thanks to Sharif Gemie and Barry Bergen for essential information about schooling; to Brett Bowles for help with Vichy's Hollywood policies; to Alain Bancaud for information about judges; to Simon Kitson for information about the police; to Claudine Giacchetti, Roger Wiesenbach, and Irene Rosenberg for help understanding legal issues; to Charles Closman and Paulette Hernandez for help with translations. For more general intellectual and moral support, I should like to acknowledge Irene Guenther, Tom O'Brien, Miranda Pollard, Paula Schwartz, Geneviève Dermenjian, Bert Gordon, Dan Sherman, Yves Durand, Philippe Burrin, John Sweets, Richard Jobs, and my partners in the Gang of Four: Leonard V. Smith, Laura Lee Downs, and Ioannis Sinanoglou. I have benefited, as have so many, from the towering intellectual influence of Robert Paxton, Stanley Hoffmann, Henri Rousso, and Rod Kedward. For an incredible job correcting factual errors, my thanks to Bernard Sinsheimer, and to Julie Ericksen Hagen for her respectful and precise editing. The University of Houston Research Council, College of Liberal Arts and Social Sciences, and History Department have provided both grants and leaves of absence that made possible the research and writing of this book. I should like especially to express my gratitude to my colleague Joe Pratt, who generously funded departmental leaves of absence that benefited me and other colleagues. At Harvard University Press, thanks to Elizabeth Suttell and Kathleen McDermott.

This book required many trips to France and quite a bit of travel while there. For their kind hospitality, thanks to Florence Perronin, Isabelle and Christophe Alasseur, Alain and Germaine LeCoufle, Thierry Zabal, Edith Giacchetti, Kay and Jean-Marie Panterne, Laurence Doubinsky, Jacqueline and Philippe Lebert, and Annette Becker. Thanks to Katy and, especially, Alex for putting up with my absences. And of course without someone willing to take over full-time household and child-care duties, I could never have made those trips. I can hardly express the depth of my gratitude, for everything that he does, to my husband, Andy Boyd.

Some material in Chapters 1, 3, 4, and 6 appears in different versions and is reprinted with permission. "Juvenile Delinquency as a 'Condition': Social Science Constructions of the Child Criminal, 1936–1946," Western Society for French History, *Proceedings* 24 (1997): 92–100; copyright 1997. "Youth in Vichy France: The Juvenile Crime Wave and Its Implications," in Sarah Fishman et al., eds., *France at War: Vichy and the Historians,* copyright 2000 by Berg Publishers. "Crisis and Change in the Juvenile Justice System, 1934–1945," in Kenneth Mouré and Martin S. Alexander, eds., *Crisis and Renewal in Twentieth-Century France,* copyright 2002 by Berghahn Books. "Absent Fathers and Family Breakdown: Delinquency in Vichy France," in Pamela Cox and Heather Shore, eds., *Becoming Delinquent: British and European Youth, 1650–1950,* copyright 2002 by Ashgate Publishing.

Abbreviations

AEMO   *Action educative en milieu ouvert,* educational action in an open
       setting
ARSEA Association régionale de sauvegarde de l'enfance et de l'adolescence
       déficientes et en danger moral, Regional Association for Safeguarding
       Deficient and At-Risk Children and Adolescents
CAP   Certificat d'aptitude profesionnelle, Certificate of Professional
       Aptitude
CEP   Certificat d'études primaires, Certificate of Primary Education
CFLN   Comité français de la libération nationale, French Committee of
       National Liberation
CJD   *Centre de jeunes détenus,* center for young detainees
CGF   Commissariat générale à la famille, General Commission on the Family
IPES   *Institution publique d'éducation surveillée,* public institution for
       supervised education
ISES   *Institution spéciale d'éducation surveillée,* special institution for
       supervised education
JAC   Jeunesse agricole chrétienne, Christian Agricultural Youth
JEC   Jeunesse étudiante chrétienne, Christian Student Youth
JOC   Jeunesse ouvrière chrétienne, Christian Working-Class Youth
JOCF   Jeunesse ouvrière chrétienne féminine, Female Christian Working-
       Class Youth
POW   Prisoner of war
SOL   Service d'Ordre légionnaire, Service of the Legionnaire Order
SSE   Service social de l'enfance en danger moral, Social Service for Children
       in Moral Danger
STO   Service du travail obligatoire, Obligatory Labor Service
TEA   Tribunal pour enfants et adolescents, Court for Children and
       Adolescents

The Battle for Children

Introduction

Across Europe, nearly every country involved in World War II experienced a similar social phenomenon: a rapid and large increase in juvenile crime. The 1947 report of the International Committee of Criminal Police cited examples from Germany, Czechoslovakia, Denmark, Great Britain, and France.[1] Concerned experts and officials studying the problem listed a wide variety of causes: death and destruction, social breakdown, economic disruption, and black markets.

Despite complaints by various historians about the death of traditional political-diplomatic history, this study clearly highlights the intersection of social history and political, even geopolitical, history. From a social history perspective, World War II had a major impact on one of history's most silent groups, children. And one form of children's behavior, delinquency, certainly had a major political impact at high levels of the French government. The French state's response to children's behavior in this instance demonstrated that people at the time viewed children as critical to national survival and to France's global status.

Most French scholars and officials firmly believed they knew exactly why juvenile crime increased so rapidly in France during the war. In March 1945, Henri Frenay, minister of prisoners, deportees, and refugees, reported to the postwar provisional government, "Alas, children of the prisoners of war made up a considerable proportion of juvenile delinquents."[2] Research for my earlier book on the wives of French prisoners of war during World War II turned up this fact: of the nearly 1.6 million French soldiers captured in 1940 who were transferred to POW camps in Germany, about 60 percent were married and 40 percent had children. Had Frenay found information proving that these were the very children clogging the juvenile courts? Did he base his remarkable statement on studies that linked the increased incidence of juvenile crime during the war with POW

1

children? Unable to devote more than a brief search to those questions at the time, I found several scholarly studies of juvenile delinquency published during and just after the war, including a report issued by the Ministry of Justice. However, the studies simply attributed the increase in juvenile crime to the absence of so many fathers during the war—primarily POWs, but also deportees and forced laborers. Yet none of the books or articles documented the connection or even noted how many minors charged during the war were POW children.

My curiosity aroused, I began searching further to see if any scholar or expert in the field had in fact proven, statistically, even a correlation between POW families and juvenile delinquency. It turned out that literally hundreds of books and articles had been written during the war on the topic of juvenile crime, a subject of great concern owing to the alarming increase in the number of minors appearing in court, yet a topic about which the popular press remained surprisingly subdued. However, I found no study that proved that absent POW fathers caused rising juvenile crime statistics. Why then did all of these authors not only assume a causal relationship but assume it so strongly they felt no need to prove it?

Undoubtedly that assumption rested comfortably on strongly held patriarchal beliefs about family life and the nature of men and women. Mothers and fathers, nearly everyone who wrote on the topic insisted, played different roles in the family, the mother nurturing and encouraging, the father directing and disciplining the children. According to this view, mothers by nature did not have the authority to discipline their children properly. Sons, especially, needed the strong arm of the father as they reached puberty.

Given those assumptions, contemporaries believed it could hardly be an accident that the sudden absence of nearly 600,000 fathers taken as POWs was followed by a threefold increase in the number of minors appearing before the courts. Such an assumption was bolstered by the prewar work done by many leading experts in the field. Without considering how a temporary absence, neither chosen by either parent nor connected with social stigma, might differ from divorce in its impact on children, studies during the war simply extrapolated from prewar studies.

The fact that specialists during the war pointed so quickly to the POW problem and family causes in general became even more puzzling, notwithstanding deeply held patriarchal ideas, given the agenda of most writers on the topic. Although they quickly pointed the finger at families, their proposed remedies, observational centers, medico-psychiatric examinations, and reeducational institutions directed virtually no attention to the family. Thus, clearly, juvenile delinquency in France in this period raised complex issues extending far beyond my initial question about the relationship between wartime captivity and juvenile crime statistics.

History of Childhood

To some extent, the history of juvenile delinquency forms one chapter in a broader history of childhood. Most scholars agree that Western ideas about childhood have changed dramatically over time. In the premodern era, the church viewed children as tainted by original sin and in need of constraints to repress sinful urges. Aside from the few privileged children of the nobility, the vast majority of children began to enter the adult world around age seven. Historian Hugh Cunningham convincingly locates the origins of a new vision of childhood in the Enlightenment. Writers like John Locke and Jean-Jacques Rousseau denied that children were inherently evil and insisted on the critical importance of early childhood training. Nineteenth-century romanticism simplified and magnified Enlightenment ideas, resulting in the concept of children as inherently good and childhood as a time of carefree innocence. Cunningham argues that the historical conjunction of this idealized notion of childhood with an industrial revolution that propelled huge numbers of children into factories and mines gave rise to a group often labeled the "child savers."[3] Nearly everywhere in the West people began to press for laws limiting child labor, requiring education, and protecting children from abusive families. Among those children considered in need of rescue, child savers eventually turned their attention to those who seemed least deserving of public sympathy, child criminals.

History of Crime and Punishment

Michel Foucault's seminal work *Discipline and Punish* has strongly shaped the historiography of crime and punishment in France.[4] Foucault discredited the positivist view that changes in systems of punishment from the medieval to the modern era revealed rising humanitarian impulses, calling attention, rather, to the ways in which courts and punishments reflected and served political and economic structures and power relations. Robert Nye, based on more strenuous historical research and looking at a more precise period, followed Foucault's lead in viewing reactions to crime and deviance, the rise of psychology, and the development of such systems of punishment as relegation, as profoundly political.[5] More recently, Christian Debuyst and Laurent Mucchielli have focused on the development of criminology in France.[6] These scholars emphasize the system's treatment of adult criminals, but Jacques Donzelot and Philippe Meyer extend the method to juvenile crime, considering how the development of a separate system to deal with child criminals empowered medical doctors at the expense of priests and gave the state an entrée into working-class and poor families.[7]

Not rejecting Foucault so much as shifting the focus from broad systemic factors and elite writings to specific institutions or fields, another body of work on crime in France takes a more pointillist approach. Patricia O'Brien's study of French prisons and Henri Gaillac's classic work on public correctional houses for youth both consider the long-term development of incarceration starting in the nineteenth century. A group of researchers coming from the justice sector in France have focused on the impact of the war years on aspects of juvenile justice or children's protection. Michel Chauvière wrote about what he labels the "maladjusted children's sector." Jacques Bourquin heads a group of scholars researching and publishing extensively on the history of public and private institutions for delinquent minors.[8] Béatrice Koeppel's research centers on the institutional treatment of delinquent and wayward girls.[9] From a different vantage point, Vichy specialists, moving beyond leaders at Vichy and translating broad national policies to various specific governmental realms, have begun to explore Vichy's prisons, the police, and the administration of justice, focusing primarily on adults.[10]

This book is a hybrid of the discourses-on-crime approach and the pointillist approach. Starting with the broad trajectory of juvenile justice in twentieth-century France in comparison with other places, I ask why, counter to both what we might expect and to what most people in France today believe, the Vichy years laid the critical foundation for France's existing therapeutic system for juvenile offenders. This question would not have clearly emerged without careful study of the period. Thus the book narrows in on the war years, a careful archival study of which forms its core. Focusing on the war years uncovered critical unexplored aspects of the Vichy regime, revealing and explaining in this policy area the continuities that much of the French public would prefer to overlook. Archival material on delinquency further addressed the vexed question of war and social change in twentieth-century France, opening a new and revealing window onto French society during the traumatic years from the Battle of France through the liberation.

Concentrating on a restricted period also allowed me to combine a "top-down" political, intellectual, and even military history approach—looking at state policy, elite writings, the war, and the creation of the Vichy regime—with a "bottom-up" social history approach, exploring the impact of broad political events on people's lives as well as examining the motives driving the behavior of the small fry, the children and adolescents who found themselves in court. Many studies in the history of crime remain in the realm of theory and discourse. Very often the actual people involved—accused criminals, judges, social workers, prison officials—function solely as objects of social concern and political rhetoric. Because crime is a social construct, because attempts to "explain" why people commit crimes can be naively positivist, because, as Foucault has noted, most sources about criminals are generated by repressive institutions, we have stripped the actors of their voices, of their agency. While admitting all these problems, rather than perpetuating the silence this book looks at the real people involved, presenting their contacts with the system as a two-way interaction. Although the bottom-up analysis relies almost entirely on documents generated by a judgmental system, I do not agree with those scholars who argue that the system's distortions completely drown the voices of the repressed. The minors in court and their families could and did manipulate the systems they faced. They were not entirely powerless objects of state authority.

To place the 1936 juvenile justice system into historical context, this volume briefly details the evolution in France, from Napoleon I to the eve of World War II, of laws relating to minors and also of evolving elite conceptions and public views of the child criminal. By the twentieth century, France's child savers began linking child crime to a broader family crisis. Combining their efforts with a press campaign in the 1930s, reformers finally, by the end of the decade, gained public sympathy for a previously scorned group. The juvenile justice system, in considerable flux by the mid-1930s, then faced the crisis of war. Since a number of works now present rich and nuanced pictures of daily life during the war, especially Dominique Veillon's *Vivre et survivre en France,* this book examines more specifically the impact of the war and occupation on French children and adolescents, and then turns to exploring youth crime and the administration of justice at the lowest level, in four juvenile courts. Next I analyze books and articles published in the 1940s to discern the war's impact on expert approaches to delinquency. (Comparing the picture of juvenile crime contained in court records with expert reactions and analyses uncovered a number of revealing gaps and blind spots.) I also consider the impact of the creation of the authoritarian state at Vichy. The regime's muted reaction to youth crime and the deep continuity of policy set the stage for understanding why Vichy's existence enabled juvenile justice reformers to succeed in reaching some of their goals. Finally, the system that operates in France today continues to rest on the critical law of 2 February 1945. In the last chapter, I compare the 1945 law with a Vichy law of 1942, and then consider how the 1945 law set in motion changes that created the current deinstitutionalized, therapeutic, and extremely intrusive system, which is occasionally challenged but still widely supported in France.

The study of juvenile crime enlightens our understanding of the process of war and social change in twentieth-century France. Several broad questions shape this study of war, delinquency, and the juvenile justice system: Why was this decade critical in the formation of the French juvenile justice system? What can we learn about Vichy France from studying juvenile delinquency? What does juvenile delinquency teach us about French society as it went through the crisis of the Second World War? What long-term impact did the war have on French politics and society? Why did the number of minors appearing in court triple by 1942? How did contemporary observers, journalists, judges, psychiatrists, social scientists, and social workers explain what was happening, and why did they explain it that way? How well did their views correspond to the reality of the situation? What can court records tell us about juvenile crime, the children and adolescents involved, and the impact of the war and occupation on French society, family life, youth, schooling, and work life?

Court records reflect the great events of the period, the Battle of France in May and June 1940, the exodus of refugees, German occupation, internal strife, the liberation, and the postwar "purification," demonstrating in minute detail the impact such events had on average people and the variety of ways people attempted to cope. The tripling of juvenile crime statistics by 1942, combined with the conservative, authoritarian French State at Vichy, might well have inspired social fears and resulted in a conservative crackdown, a "get tough" policy. (In contrast, Nazi Germany tried hard to subdue its unruly youths by sending them to labor camps.) But neither the pubic nor the state advocated tougher, more punitive policies. Rather, various groups promoted a series of liberal, therapeutic reforms similar to many of the prewar Popular Front's initiatives. The Popular Front's reform efforts had run out of steam by the late 1930s as France moved closer to war. But following the defeat of June 1940 the system continued to move in the same direction, not in spite of Vichy but with the regime's blessing and active support, coming to final fruition in the immediate postwar period. In other words, the decade from 1936 to 1946 proved critical to the establishment of the juvenile justice system currently functioning in France, from laws to court procedures to institutions and personnel. Attempts to shift courts away from punishment to protection, to render state and private institutions rehabilitative and therapeutic rather than penal, increased in speed during the war and were definitively encoded in 1945 and 1946.

The study of juvenile crime, delinquency, and the justice system reveals a great deal about the German occupation and the Vichy regime. Chapter 3's examination of four juvenile courts, their functioning over time, their procedures, and their personnel, exposes both breaks and, more often, continuities between Vichy and the Third and Fourth Republics. It also provides an interesting case study in the relationship between the German occupiers and French public officials, from high-level ministers and regional judges to local police officers.

In addition to describing the justice system's operation, I address some big questions about the nature of the Vichy regime. My interpretation falls solidly into the post-Paxtonian model, denying that the French State at Vichy was either a puppet of Germany or a caretaker regime. Juvenile policy, rather, highlights Vichy's independent activity. I do not deny the basic racist, authoritarian, and partisan impulses behind Vichy's creation and operation. However, as recent works reveal for Nazi Germany (studies of cancer research or environmental policy, for example), some issues seem to float above politics, rather than instantly arousing divided responses from left and right. In France, policies on children and the family exhibited strong continuities, despite certain profoundly authoritarian, intrusive, repressive manifestations of Vichy's approach to both. Fundamental motivating fears of family breakdown, demographic decline, and the degeneration of France's population continued throughout the entire era, allowing policymakers after the war to rescue many of Vichy's initiatives, most often by covering up any continuity with Vichy.

Vichy produced no drastically new ideas about or approaches to juvenile delinquency. Many juvenile delinquency experts active in the 1930s continued to work, study, and advocate reforms. However, Vichy's nature as an authoritarian system that did not have to bother with parliamentary oversight and approval proved crucial to the implementation of many reforms. First, power within the inner corridors of the regime shifted, owing to the bias of those at the top. Distrust of the Ministry of National Education, considered a hotbed of radical republicanism, demoted that ministry in importance, allowing administrators from the Justice Ministry and the Ministry of Family and Health finally to create "schools" outside Education's control. Second, the seemingly unbridgeable gap between Catholic activists, scholars, and administrators and secular medical, psychiatric, pedagogical experts began to close. By the 1930s, a great many Catholic thinkers were rejecting sin-based interpretations and adopting more technical approaches to the problem of juvenile crime. Vichy's clerical outlook thus empowered many Catholic activists and forced secular experts to include them, setting the stage for the major effort represented by the 1942 law.

Although the new legal procedures in the July 1942 law were never implemented and eventually its more authoritarian aspects were discarded, institutional changes that the 1942 law encouraged began to take shape right away. At the end of the war, despite its repudiation of the 1942 law, the provisional government's 1945 law would bear many similarities to it. Together with several other legal, institutional, and administrative changes, the 1945 law represented the fruition of long-standing demands for reform. Why was the decade from 1936 to 1946 critical to the series of reforms—legal, intellectual, procedural, institutional, structural, and human—that created the system still in place? Reformers had been pressing for change from the early years of the century.

On the eve of the war, the governing laws still reflected nineteenth-century notions about children who commit crimes, strongly influenced by the romantic vision of innocent childhood. As Kathleen Nilan's work explains, if children were innocent, then most children who committed crimes had been corrupted by misery or abuse at home or in the workshop. Some small percentage of children, however, seemed to challenge the very foundation of childhood innocence. Their attitude in court indicated no remorse. They were somehow not really children; they had been precociously perverted and could be treated like adult criminals. Thus the penal code's treatment of children rotated around the concept of "discretion" *(discernement)*. The judge, having determined that the minor committed the act, then decided whether the minor acted with or without discretion. The court decision followed that determination.

By the time it came into effect, the 1912 law was already out of line with views of childhood developing since the late nineteenth century. Sigmund Freud's work seriously undermined the notion of childhood innocence. Meanwhile, people interested in childhood were elaborating a new age category, adolescence, a transitional period between childhood and adulthood. New fields, such as psychology, sociology, and especially neuropsychiatry, had begun to explore childhood development, to classify normal and abnormal development, and to develop a series of subcategories to understand abnormal children. By the 1930s that trend was in full swing, and juvenile delinquency was considered a manifestation not of immorality, sin, or perversity, but of a medical-psychiatric condition. Thus it was thought that the courts should no longer divide minors on the basis of discretion into innocent children deserving lenience and perverted sinners deserving punishment. Rather, it was believed that the state should diagnose the condition and then treat it. Courts were seen as the first step in a series of exams. A judge was to have recourse, once a minor had been diagnosed, to institutions that would not punish but would treat and rehabilitate juvenile offenders.

The Popular Front of 1936 ushered in the first attempt to reshape two public institutions for delinquent boys. The attempt was neither entirely successful nor a complete failure. However, the war years proved a much more fruitful period, and this book explores why the war proved to be the key to unlocking the doors to reform.

My research rests on two very different kinds of sources. I used writings on juvenile delinquency, mostly books and scholarly articles, as primary sources. A variety of people with diverse backgrounds—judges, lawyers, doctors, psychiatrists, social workers, educators, social activists from various arenas (Catholic social movements, scouting, even the Quakers)— studied and wrote about juvenile crime. While their approaches diverged in many ways, they also converged at a number of points. The popular press before the war devoted much attention to the abuse of children and adolescents in public and private institutions for delinquent boys. During the war the media exhibited some concern about rising delinquency rates, yet remained surprisingly subdued on that score, reserving hysterical diatribes for countercultural youth, known in France as the *zazous*.

Government documents in France's National Archives, primarily Justice, Penal Administration, Youth, and Education records, helped me sketch out public policy and its peculiarities. Unfortunately, records relating to the critical ordinance of 2 February 1945 could not be located, with the exception of a few brief letters. I also amassed a large database from court records and case files from the Seine Department and three regional departments outside Paris: the Nord, Indre-et-Loire, and Gard.

The court records proved to be extremely rich sources, illuminating day-to-day operations and allowing me to discern regional variations, change over time, and local court responses to the Vichy government and to the German occupation authorities. Court case files, with their arrest reports, criminal complaints, police and judicial investigations, letters and attestations by neighbors, schoolteachers, and local authorities, provided valuable snapshots of society. The police and judicial investigations were sometimes supplemented by social and medical reports that presented very detailed (and clearly biased) information about the minors and their families, where and how they lived.

What juvenile justice system existed in France in the early twentieth century? Why did the clamor for change intensify in the 1930s? What did experts at the time think was wrong, and what did they want to do differently? Why in this instance did the war prove critical to social change? To understand the war's impact on children, adolescents, youth crime, and the juvenile justice system, Chapter 1 examines developments up to the eve of the war.

1

From Child Criminals to Juvenile Delinquents, 1810–1939

So long as there are children who break the law, people will try to understand why they do so. Explanations of why children commit crimes are fluid, changing in response to political concerns, ideas about childhood, new theories about crime, and research in such fields as medicine, psychology, sociology, criminology. Furthermore, the prevailing social anxieties of an era are reflected in the responses to crime, to children, and especially to children who commit crimes. Sociologist Francis Bailleau points out that for adults, children and adolescents function both as subjects of their hopes for the future and as objects of their fears about threats to adult values. Symbolically the child criminal represents perceived threats to the social order. How a system deals with child criminals thus reflects as much about the deeper social issues as it does about the "objective" reality of juvenile crime.

Paul Griffiths, historian of early modern England, vigorously criticizes historians who describe juvenile delinquency as a modern phenomenon that came into being in the nineteenth century. His research on youth and authority in sixteenth-century England uncovered clear evidence of both youthful misbehavior and adult concern about that misbehavior.[1] However, legal systems that define criminality and deviance have changed over time and place, as have ideas about childhood and appropriate behavior, as have the actual things children do, as have adult society's interpretations of and responses to various child and adolescent misbehavior. We ought not take people completely at their word that particular kinds of behavior really are unprecedented and call for a new response; nor should we take the ahistorical, essentialist approach that because children always misbehave and break the law, nothing ever changes. Embedding this study carefully in its historical context helps us avoid both pitfalls.

In early nineteenth-century France, the recently ended Revolution and its aftermath—twenty-five years of civil and international war—aroused deep social fears and anxieties in elite circles. Many leading citizens thought of popular revolt and criminal activity as two sides of the same phenomenon, feeding the notion that "dangerous classes" posed a threat to the social order. Their anxieties about the future focused inward more than outward. While France was twice defeated, in 1814 and 1815, it had taken a coalition of Europe's leading powers to stop Napoleon. Even after the defeat, thanks to Talleyrand's wiliness, France maintained a seat at the Congress of Vienna and continued to play an important role in the European power system. The surprising absence of widespread European warfare in the first half of the nineteenth century, in comparison to the previous century, allowed France the luxury of assuming a leading international role. The French elite's preoccupations centered on the more immediate threat of renewed revolutionary upheaval.

By the end of the nineteenth century, the focus of anxiety and ideas about France's global position had shifted as a result of two trends many French observers viewed as interrelated: a declining population growth rate reflected in census reports, and France's international decline, confirmed by Prussia's rapid and shocking defeat of France in 1870–1871. After that defeat, a new set of anxieties centered less on the threat of internal social upheaval and more on what demography and military defeat seemed to reveal about the health of the social body undergoing the pernicious effects of modernization. France had already fallen from being the most populous nation in Europe to a middle rank, owing to the decline in the birth rate over the nineteenth century. Doctors and demographers worried about that phenomenon, which they labeled denatality (*dénatalité*), and its effects on France's international stature.

However, only a fairly small circle of experts shared the sense of crisis about population. In frustration, Dr. Jacques Bertillon, leading worrier about French population trends, founded in 1896 the National Alliance for the Increase of the French Population to try to break the official silence on France's demographic crisis.[2] By the 1920s Bertillon's efforts paid off. Nearly fifty years of demographic warnings on the declining birth rate, combined with the tremendous loss of life during World War I, finally aroused widespread social and official concern. Eventually, fears about French depopulation reshaped the public's reaction to child criminals. France could no longer afford to waste a single child, and increasingly the child criminal, considered a victim of conditions beyond his or her control, aroused more pity than fear. It was believed that with proper treatment and rehabilitation, nearly every child could become a productive member of society.

The power of demographic goals to motivate public policy at every level had important implications for the French state's approach in the twentieth century to children who broke the law. In France, public opinion and state policy toward delinquent minors evolved in a direction almost completely opposite to that of the United States during the twentieth century, from a punitive response at the turn of the century, based on fear of child criminals, to a protective, therapeutic, rehabilitative response by the end of the century, based on the assumption that child criminals suffered from factors beyond their control. The evolution from a punitive to a therapeutic system hardly represents the simple triumph of humanitarian progress over a primitive drive for revenge. The therapeutic approach, which accepts that most criminals can be rehabilitated, entails an extremely intrusive system that intervenes extensively in people's private and family lives. Nevertheless, the punitive trends seen in the United States since the 1980s temper somewhat the sinister view of the therapeutic model, for all its social control, for surely it is preferable to the American "get tough" attitude that has led to boot camps for juvenile offenders, lowered certification ages for trial in adult court, and, in some states, capital punishment for minors.[3]

The juvenile justice system—a combination of age-specific laws and procedures and separate courts and institutions for juvenile offenders—came to be a system in France only in the late nineteenth and early twentieth centuries. By the 1920s, many experts considered the existing laws and institutions out of date with new ideas about childhood and adolescence and developments in such fields as psychology, psychiatry, and sociology. The period surrounding World War II functioned as a watershed for France, the culmination of a century of legal, institutional, conceptual, and social developments.

Origins of Juvenile Justice in France

As with all discussion of the French legal system, the Napoleonic Code represents the starting point for the modern period. The 1810 Penal Code's provisions for legal minors were written in response to a set of questions: Why do young people commit crimes? To what extent should their age be taken into consideration? Should the state respond with punishment or rehabilitation? At what point do minors become adults? Article

66 of the Penal Code defined sixteen as the age of penal majority (civil majority was set at twenty-one) and not only differentiated children from adults but also, within the population of children, created a second distinction based on the notion of *"discernement."* Roughly translatable as discretion, *discernement* corresponds to our notion of penal responsibility. A minor acted with discretion if he or she understood that the action was illegal and understood the potential consequences of the action when it was committed. If the judge determined that a minor acted without discretion, then he or she could be either returned to parents or taken to a correctional house *(maison de correction)* for a period of time left to the judge's discretion, although the minor was not to remain there beyond the age of twenty-one. Article 69 stated that if the minor was found to have acted with discretion, he or she could receive a correctional sentence (penalty for a minor offense), which could not exceed one-half the adult sentence for a similar conviction. While the Napoleonic Code acknowledged that the law should treat minors differently from adults, it did not establish separate courts or procedures for minors, nor did it mandate separate institutions where they could be held in preventive detention before their court appearance or sent to if convicted or found to be in need of correction.

Because Napoleon was obsessed with reinforcing the father's authority in the family, his 1803 Civil Code granted fathers the right to "paternal correction." A father, without having to provide justification, could order the courts to imprison his child for a period of one month if the child were under sixteen, six months for children over sixteen. The Code placed no limit on the number of times paternal correction could be invoked. The courts were required to order such an arrest without investigation (Articles 375–383).

Also relevant to minors, *vagabondage*, roughly equivalent to vagrancy, was a misdemeanor. Articles 270 and 271 of the 1810 Penal Code defined vagrants as "those who have neither a fixed abode, nor means of subsistence, and who do not habitually exercise either a career or a profession." Adults found guilty of vagrancy could be sentenced to three to six months in jail. Minors, however, fell under Articles 66 to 69 of the Penal Code, which allowed judges the flexibility to determine discretion and the appropriate response. Minors arrested for vagrancy tended to be runaways and street kids. A large percentage of minors in the justice system were charged with vagrancy even when other illegal activities accompanied vagrancy, because courts considered petty theft and other misdemeanors committed by street kids secondary to the vagrancy.[4] Ironically, adolescent girls engaged in prostitution did not meet the vagrancy criteria, as they usually had a domicile and exercised a profession.

The Napoleonic Code dealt in a minimal, authoritarian way with the criminal activity of children. Over the course of the nineteenth century many people became increasingly dissatisfied with Articles 66 and 69. Nineteenth-century thinkers were torn by conflicting impulses. On the one hand, despite the 1789 Revolution, Catholicism remained the religion of the majority of French people. Christian doctrine interpreted crime as an expression of original sin, a surrender to universal evil human impulses. Concupiscence, the Catholic tenet that we are all born prone to sin, applied equally, even especially, to children, who needed strict supervision and punishment to overcome such impulses.

Enlightened thinkers developed a competing view of crime; many of their ideas were codified after the 1798 Revolution. The key Enlightenment text on childhood, Jean-Jacques Rousseau's *Emile,* elaborated on John Locke's concept of the mind as a blank slate. Human beings, rather than tainted by original sin, were shaped by their experiences. To create virtuous adults, Rousseau believed society must focus on the proper education of children. Enlightenment thinkers rejected the notion that humans were sinful by nature. Because human reason and rationality allowed humankind to differentiate right from wrong, every individual had a personal responsibility to do the right thing. Should that sense of responsibility not be strong enough, it could be reinforced by a punishment proportional to the crime, advocated by such Enlightenment thinkers as Cesare Beccaria. The real focus, therefore, was ensuring the proper education of children, without which reason and rationality withered.

In addition to Catholicism and the Enlightenment's diametrically opposed views of the sources of crime and appropriate reactions to it, in the early nineteenth century another set of contrasting views emerged. Kathleen Nilan argues that people living in early nineteenth-century France inhabited a moral universe shaken to its foundations by the Revolution and the ensuing twenty-five years of international warfare. Continuing political upheavals through 1848 intensified fears aroused by such ongoing processes as modernization, urbanization, and the spread of capitalism. Public opinion perceived criminal activity as rising in frequency and as a serious threat to the social order. Solid citizens feared what they called "dangerous classes." Owing to the young age at which some people began their debauchery, many social observers came to believe that the corruption of an entire generation of working-class children heralded a future of political anarchy. They feared an evil criminal class, discernable at youth. This view contrasted starkly with romanticism, another nineteenth-century school of thought. Distinct from both Catholic and Enlightened ideas, romanticism idealized childhood as a period of natural innocence. Children who misbehaved were seen as innocent, trusting victims of unscrupulous adults.[5]

These conflicting views—the universal sinfulness of the human condition, the personal responsibility of rational beings, the fear of the criminal child as harbinger of revolution, the goodness and innocence of childhood—could all be resolved with a bipolar explanation for the criminal activity of children. Most children were innocents who resorted to vagrancy, begging, and stealing food because they were led astray by adults or corrupted by the pressures of poverty and abuse. But some children flouted the idealized image of the innocent victim, and thereby ceased to be true children. Such "precociously perverse" children, lazy, cunning, immoral, even at times monstrous, lost any claim to sympathy or lenience.[6] The division of child criminals into "innocent sheep" or "perverse lambs" corresponded nicely to the discretion distinction set out in Articles 66 and 69. A minor who acted with discretion was precociously perverse and required the repression of penal sanctions. Hapless victims of circumstance, however, deserved indulgence. The use of discretion allowed judges both to ease public fears of a rising criminal class through repressive measures taken against "perverted" minors and to remain charitable to criminal children considered innocent victims.

Nineteenth-Century Correctional Institutions for Young People

The Napoleonic Code stipulated that minors acquitted as acting without discretion could be sent to correctional houses, but it did not mandate the creation of separate institutions for minors. During the Restoration (1815–1830), Louis XVIII expressed concern about the mixing in prisons of young offenders with hardened adult criminals.[7] Starting in the 1820s the larger prisons began to set aside separate quarters for minors. In 1836, under the July Monarchy, the first prison specifically for minors, La Petite-Roquette, opened in Paris.

Run by Gabriel Delessert, prefect of police, La Petite-Roquette took boys ages six to sixteen. La Roquette's philosophy rested first on the notion that young criminals were the most susceptible to reform and therefore should be shielded from corrupt adults. La Roquette also adopted what was known as the Philadelphia system, named for a Quaker-run penitentiary in Philadelphia that pioneered a number of elements, including individual jail cells designed to prevent the corruption of one prisoner by others and to enable each inmate to make a total break with both his own past and with society. Because the Quakers believed that only a complete break allowed a person to confront and reform the self, the Philadelphia system required total isolation. Rather than sharing common workshops and eating and recreation areas, inmates worked, ate, and slept in their cells. Any movement outside the cell required covering the inmate's head with a hood to prevent contact with other inmates.

La Roquette adopted the Philadelphia system for its minors—a radical enough system for adult inmates—instituting twenty-four-hour isolation for all inmates, with disastrous results. Even before psychologists developed theories of adolescence highlighting the critical importance of social contacts in this transitional phase, a disturbing trend noted in the 1840s led to criticism of the cell confinement of children. For example, a study by Dr. Chassinate, a surgeon attached to the Ministry of the Interior, revealed that child mortality rates at La Roquette were double those in regular prisons. Dr. Fourcault of the Academy of Medicine in Paris found children suffering from illnesses he attributed to the "influence of the prison."[8] Other experts attributed increased mental derangement of young inmates to the system. By 1847, 90 percent of the attendees of the International Penitentiary Congress in Brussels opposed La Roquette's system of total isolation for minors.[9]

Two years after La Roquette was established, another institution opened that provided a much more influential model for the treatment of juvenile offenders. In the nineteenth century, many observers believed that France's growing cities were breeding social upheaval, revolution, and crime. The unhealthy urban environment was the explanation for why so many youthful offenders came from cities. Therefore, it was believed that young criminals should first be removed to the countryside. The agricultural youth colony was designed to correct the pernicious influence of city life, reform young criminals, and teach them good work habits by exposing them to the hard but healthy rigors of rural life.[10] Under the direction of Frédéric-Auguste Demetz, a former criminal court judge, France's first such institution, Mettray, opened in 1838, funded not by the state but by private interests. In 1842, Fontevrault, another agricultural colony, was opened. A medical inspector's 1844 report on Fontevrault, confirming the era's hopes for such colonies, concluded that "every face breathes out an air of vivacity and health."[11]

In 1840 the July Monarchy mandated the creation, for young offenders, of central houses of correctional education *(maisons centrales d'édu-cation correctionnelle)*, which came to be called *maisons de correction,* or correctional houses. While it represented a private effort, the success of Mettray, which, together with a similar institution opened in Hanover in 1833, quickly became the model for work farms for children across Europe, inspired legislation to create public versions of the agricultural youth colony.[12] Even before he came to power, Louis Napoleon Bonaparte advocated a system of national work farms (for people of all ages) to eliminate poverty. Not surprisingly, he looked with favor on Mettray, and during his presidency of the short-lived Second Republic, he successfully sponsored the law of 5 August 1850 on the education and patronage of youthful prisoners that created public agricultural colonies *(colonies pénitentiaires)* for delinquent boys.

The 1850 law could be interpreted in the context of the history of childhood in France. The terror aroused by crime in general and crimes committed by minors in particular coexisted with a growing concern about the condition of children and a new sense that the state had a duty to intervene on their behalf. A number of laws in the nineteenth century directed attention to the lives of France's most vulnerable children, including the first child labor law, in 1841, and several laws that attempted to reduce abandonment and to improve the lot of abandoned children.[13] To a certain extent, the 1850 law followed the trend toward children's protection. It rested on the principle that incarcerated minors should be separated from adult prisoners and should receive education in specialized institutions. However, Henri Gaillac, in his work on correctional houses for minors, places the 1850 law in a strictly political context. The period from Louis Napoleon Bonaparte's December 1848 election as president of the Second Republic to his December 1851 coup establishing the Second Empire ushered in a series of conservative laws, including the Falloux Law, which reestablished religious schools, the institution of press censorship, and restrictive electoral laws. Although the 1850 law prescribed an approach that combined punishment and rehabilitation, Gaillac points out that Interior Minister Jean Gilbert, duc de Persigny, who was a conservative henchman for Louis Napoleon and a firm believer in hereditary criminality, implemented the 1850 law in such a way as to limit its liberal impulses and emphasize its repressive ones.

The first article of the 1850 law decreed that all minors of both sexes incarcerated for misdemeanors, offenses, serious crimes, or paternal correction, would, during preventive detention, receive "moral, religious, and professional education."[14] Minors acquitted under Article 66 but not returned to their parents, and those convicted under Article 69 and sentenced to more than six months but less than two years, could be taken to a penitentiary colony to be raised with "harsh discipline" *(discipline sévère)* and to perform agricultural labor. Although "penitentiary colony" remained the official designation for public institutions for delinquent minor boys until 1927 (when they became *maisons d'éducation surveillée*), people who wrote about the juvenile justice system continued to refer to them as correctional houses or reform houses *(maisons de correction, maisons de redressement)*.

Late Nineteenth-Century Views of Children and Crime

The Second Empire collapsed in the midst of France's 1870 defeat by the Germans. The Third Republic, which replaced it, focused more attention on children than perhaps any other regime in France's history. The Third Republic created France's national education system, which ensured free, secular primary schools for every child and mandated schooling until age thirteen. The Ferry laws, creating France's public educational system, passed in the 1880s, represented the republic's effort to mobilize the youth of France on its behalf. The Third Republic also passed its own child labor law in 1874.[15]

During the early decades of the Third Republic, connected to the humiliating military defeat that gave it birth, prevailing social anxieties shifted from those of the early and middle nineteenth century. The 1870 defeat inspired much hand-wringing about France's decline as a great power, and the search for causes directed attention to France's population and its evidently weakened state. Less often viewed in terms of domestic political upheaval, crime was increasingly feared as one of many signs of the rising degeneracy of the French population. Here evolutionary theories and the rise of psychiatry profoundly influenced thinking about crime and delinquency.

By the end of the nineteenth century, new medical models of deviance had profoundly reshaped public debates about crime.[16] A number of theories circulated internationally. Sociologist Cesare Lombroso, founder of the Italian positivist school, initially gained a wide following for his theory of the born criminal. However, French sociologists, anthropologists, and criminologists never completely accepted Lombroso. As Gabriel Tarde, a criminal judge and sociologist, explained, "Even accepting as certain the new [Italian] school's anthropological data, a sociological interpretation would seem highly preferable to the too exclusively biological interpretation that its founders have formulated."[17]

French thinkers on crime elaborated a competing "social milieu" approach, which stressed the interaction of inherited traits and the environment. However, the French and Italian schools both clearly reflected Western medicine's late nineteenth-century obsession with degeneracy. The French particularly privileged the neo-Lamarckian theory that bad traits created by the environment in one individual could be passed down to the next generation, eventually resulting in a degenerate population. Rising criminality signaled such a decline into degeneracy, but, happily, restoring a healthy environment could reverse degeneracy. According to Robert Nye, the medical theory of degeneracy, by the turn of the twentieth century, permeated political and journalistic discourses about crime.[18] The impulse to prevent the spread of degeneracy and protect the social body expressed itself in a desire to rid France of dangerous criminals through expulsion. The result: an 1885 relegation law stipulated transportation to a penal colony for the recidivist criminal, defined as any person convicted of seven offenses of which two carried sentences of at least three months.[19]

Interestingly, from the 1880s on, just when fear of degeneracy began to saturate the popular media, a number of French psychiatrists began to distance themselves from the notion of degeneracy, according to Christian Debuyst, a psychologist and an expert on the history of criminology. French medicine separated prenatal traumas that could cause developmental problems for children from truly hereditary maladies, leading to new optimism in France about the treatment of mental illness. However, Debuyst notes that hereditary theory did not disappear in France. Rather, in the early twentieth century Dr. Ernest Dupré, chief doctor at the Paris Police Prefecture, took it up in developing his theory of instinctive perversions, a return to an extreme, organic vision of degeneracy. Despite French psychiatry's growing rejection of degeneracy, Dupré's theory of constitutional perversion strongly shaped the study of juvenile delinquency well into the twentieth century, largely owing to Dupré's tremendous influence on his star student, Georges Heuyer, who applied these ideas to children.[20]

Although Dupré and Heuyer theorized about constitutionally perverse children, they assumed that such children represented a small minority. In general, experts believed that most children heading down the wrong path could be redirected. In fact, childhood presented the best opportunity to intervene and reverse the degeneracy of not just the individual but also of future generations of French people. Thus some observers urged the state to seek out neglected, abused, and other children "in moral danger" and, with proper measures, prevent them from becoming criminals.[21]

The notion that the state's interest in protecting the life and safety of children can supersede parental rights forms the foundation of all modern child protection systems. The law of 14 July 1889 "on the protection of ill-treated and morally abandoned children" allowed the state to terminate parental custody of abused children by declaring "termination of parental rights" *(déchéance de puissance paternelle)*. The 1889 law, together with the law of 19 April 1898 "on the suppression of violence, assault and battery, acts of cruelty and attempted murder committed toward children," represented a move beyond indulgence for child victims pushed into crime by unfortunate circumstances, to active intervention to remove children from what the authorities considered dangerous family environments. Sylvia Schafer's book *Children in Moral Danger* analyzes the multiple contradictions that the 1889 law entailed. To pass a law enabling public authorities to intervene in families, legislators had to work against three strong tendencies: first, a liberal state; second, an era that elevated a romanticized picture of ideal family life; third, a culture and legal system that promoted paternal control over family life. Only growing political fears about the future health of France's population, social peace, and foreign threats justified moving beyond the established laissez-faire system. However, Schafer astutely points out the state never defined exactly what behavior would trigger intervention, which meant that the mechanisms created to intervene in families' lives and to care for the children removed from homes raised as many problems as they resolved. Schafer rightly labels the period she studies, the 1880s through 1914, a transitional era.[22] First, the nineteenth-century's moral rhetoric, reflected in the label "children in moral danger," was being replaced by medical-psychiatric language. Second, fears about the future in the 1880s were also shifting. Although the horrible year of 1870–71 included both military defeat and revolutionary upheaval, the perceived weakness of France's population came increasingly to be viewed as a threat to France's global rather than domestic status.

Thus a number of new concerns about childhood and youth had arisen by the late nineteenth century. The Napoleonic Code, which set penal majority at age sixteen, reasonably reflected the facts of life when it was written; most young people would have been well on their way in a trade by that age. By the turn of the twentieth century, however, the lives of young people and ideas about age were changing. In particular, the transitional stage of life that formerly fell under the vague rubric of "youth"—anywhere from age twelve to age thirty—attracted the attention of child psychologists. Eventually the narrower and more behavioral-physiological concept of adolescence as a distinct and universal transitional phase replaced "youth" in psychological circles. Kathleen Alaimo's research reveals that the theories of adolescence pulled together and articulated by American sociologist Stanley Hall were disseminated in France by a number of influential scholars, such as Gabriel Compayré, pedagogical expert and primary school inspector-general, and psychologists Marguerite Evard and Pierre Mendousse. In comparison to American approaches to adolescence, French experts tended to downplay the physiological changes of puberty in favor of the emotional and intellectual aspects of adolescence.[23] Compayré, Evard, and Mendousse all considered adolescence a period of new mental abilities as well as new and unstable emotions linked to sexuality. Adolescents experienced a series of conflicts between their need for courage, friendship, logic, and faith, on the one hand, and their sense of uncertainty, emotional instability, and tendency for excess, on the other. In other words, adolescence, a concept eventually accepted by experts and the larger public, represented a phase of "physical and mental anarchy."[24]

What worried many experts and officials about this phase was that France's educational system did not extend to most adolescents. The Third Republic's national system of secular schools made schooling compulsory, but only until a primary school certificate had been earned or to the age of thirteen, whichever came first.[25] The school leaving age corresponded to the point at which most adolescents would have entered an apprenticeship, but the practice of apprenticeship was declining rapidly by the late nineteenth century. Only about 5 percent of adolescents, nearly all from the middle and upper classes, attended secondary school.[26] Many child psychologists and municipal authorities worried that, given their state of mental and emotional anarchy, working-class adolescents, neither in school nor serving as apprentices, received adequate adult supervision. Alaimo's article clearly outlines the fear surrounding the notion of unsupervised adolescents, the assumed need for vigilance, and the attempts by the state and reformist individuals and organizations to remedy the need for supervision. Various groups opened superior primary schools, postscholastic groups, and adolescent classes to try to keep working-class adolescents in an educational setting for a few more years. However, such unofficial efforts to extend schooling met with only limited success, as the majority of working-class youth expected, and were expected by their families, to contribute to the family income at the end of their official schooling.[27]

The concept of adolescence required a new language and way of thinking about young offenders. First, the term *child* no longer properly described minors over the age of thirteen, when adolescence began, and so the term *juvenile* was used increasingly by institutions and laws to merge the categories of child and adolescent while keeping them distinct from adults.[28] Second, the new theories of adolescence had implications when it came to explaining why young people committed crimes, and particularly why most delinquent minors were between thirteen and sixteen, for the mental anarchy of adolescence was seen to spawn rebelliousness and such related behavioral problems as stealing, sexual promiscuity, and running away from home.[29]

Children in the Justice System

By the late nineteenth century, a growing number of people worried not only about abused or neglected children and adolescents, but also about the fate of young people in the courts and in public correctional institutions. If a minor landed in court because of behavior resulting from abuse or neglect, did he or she not deserve protection as well? Children's reformers, including Henri Rollet, France's first juvenile judge and founder in 1888 of the French Union for the Rescue/Salvation of Children (Union française pour le sauvetage de l'enfance), and Paul Flandin, associate justice of the Paris Court of Appeals, took up the cause of children in the criminal justice system. In 1890, Rollet and Flandin created the first Committee to Defend Children in the Justice System (Comité de défense des enfants traduits en justice). The committee, under the presidency of politician Paul Deschanel, drew its inspiration largely from developments in America, where separate juvenile courts with specialized judges and simplified procedures were first established. Chicago opened its first juvenile court in July 1899, Philadelphia in 1901, and many more American cities followed.[30] Rollet, Deschanel, and Flandin wanted France to follow the American lead. They also advocated, through books, articles, and Rollet's review *L'Enfant*, the replacement of prisons or penitentiary colonies for children with specialized, rehabilitative institutions, and the adoption of a probation system. The Committee to Defend Children in the Justice System in Paris spawned a number of committees in such cities as Marseilles (1893); Grenoble and Caen (1895); Bordeaux (1896); Toulouse, Angers, Le Havre, Lille, Montpellier, and Rouen (1898). Each committee oversaw local courts, guided judges, and kept an eye on conditions in local public and private institutions, and once a committee was instituted, its members often served as probation officers for minors *(délégués à la liberté surveillée)*.

In the meantime, frustrated by the system and wanting to give judges options for the placement of minors, in 1890 Rollet opened a Paris residential center for minors in the justice system, the Patronage des enfants et adolescents. Judges could send minors to the Patronage, which usually functioned as a transitional center. If the judge granted custody to the Patronage, after a short stay there the minor was placed on a farm or apprenticed in a shop. Eventually the Paris Patronage developed into a beehive of activity for leading specialists in a variety of fields. An American social worker, Chloe Owings, who came to Paris in 1917 to study the juvenile court system, brought Rollet together with Olga Spitzer, who was from a wealthy banking family. Owings then persuaded Spitzer to bankroll the creation of the Social Service for Children in Moral Danger (Service social de l'enfance en danger moral, or SSE).[31] In addition to running a number of homes for wayward children, the SSE developed a cadre of social workers to assist judges by conducting social case studies of minors in the court system. The SSE set up shop at the Patronage in 1923. Two years later, Georges Heuyer opened a pediatric neuropsychiatry clinic at the Patronage.

Although adolescence represents a transitional phase of life that gradually merges into adulthood, by the early twentieth century most specialists did not consider the transition complete by age sixteen. A new law of 12 April 1906 raised the age of penal majority to eighteen, but also stipulated that minors between sixteen and eighteen found to have acted with discretion would receive no reduction of penalty. Many judges and lawyers who pushed for that change also argued that minors under sixteen should be presumed to have acted without discretion and minors sixteen to eighteen presumed to have acted with discretion. Yet the 1906 law did not spell out that distinction, allowing judges to adjust their verdicts in petty offenses so as to provide for treatment or to avoid saddling a young person with a criminal record that could harm employment prospects.[32]

Although specialists and professionals in the field, for the most part, considered children in the justice system to be victims, the broader public continued to manifest fear of child criminals and reacted negatively to the 1906 law. *Le Petit journal* ran a photo on 17 November 1907 with the caption "Too many lazy young people . . . too many young criminals." By then, the public was also reacting negatively to a new urban phenomenon, gangs of unruly youths, nicknamed "apaches." Press sensationalism magnified fears of male youth gangs, drumming up hysteria out of proportion to the reality.[33] A July 1908 report, "Crime's Conscripts," that appeared in the popular review *Lecture pour tous,* blamed the perceived crime wave on the rising number of delinquent youth gangs, who were responsible for a veritable "tidal wave of muck and blood . . . We can hardly imagine how far these precocious gangs can push immorality and cold cruelty."[34] In contrast to public hysteria however, the state continued to favor increased lenience, greater state supervision of adolescents involved in delinquent behavior, and earlier intervention in their families.

Most discourse on delinquent youth in France, whether fearful or reformist, implicated male youths. Whether depicted in fearsome gangs or as poor, victimized thieves, the image of the young offender was that of a boy. Although girls committed crimes too, concerns about female misbehavior typically centered on sexuality.[35] Fathers could invoke paternal correction against promiscuous daughters, but commercial sexuality of minor girls remained beyond the state's reach because in France prostitution, while heavily regulated, did not constitute an offense.[36] The growing public concern about youth and the future of the French population rendered the prostitution of minor girls increasingly problematic. Minors engaged in prostitution could not be arrested for vagrancy, since they usually had a domicile and means of support, the absence of which defined vagrancy. A law passed to address those concerns on 11 April 1908 did not criminalize the prostitution of minors but allowed courts to intervene and order rehabilitative measures *(mesures de redressement).* In effect, judges could send prostitutes who were minors either to private institutions, most commonly one of a network of church-run institutions called Bon Pasteurs, or to public institutions for delinquent girls. Significantly, as indicated by their different designation, such public institutions for girls blurred the line between delinquency and promiscuity for girls. While public institutions for boys were designated penitentiary colonies, the designation for girls, *écoles de préservation,* or preservation schools, clearly suggests a different goal: girls needed to be preserved from immorality and for marriage.

The Law of 22 July 1912

The efforts in France of administrators, judges, and activists in the field to reform the Penal Code for juvenile offenders finally met with success on the eve of the Great War. A bill Ferdinand Dreyfus and René Béranger presented on 7 June 1910 represented the partial fulfillment of ideas that had developed over the late nineteenth and early twentieth centuries about children who commit crimes; it aimed to render the system protective and therapeutic. Yet some legislators balked at removing the possibility of punishment and others objected to the implications of a therapeutic system. Paul Beauregard, for example, reacting to the interventionism contained in the notion of protection, stated, "I am a bit worried about this authority interposed between the family and the child."[37] Thus, the resulting law of 22 July 1912 reflected a certain ambiguity. It attempted to accommodate both the public's punitive desires and the protective concerns of children's activists. It also balanced the desire to intervene and protect children with the desire to maintain paternal authority over the family. To reconcile punishment and protection, the required determination of the child's discretion, under Articles 66 and 69, remained in effect.

The law of 22 July 1912 declared that all minors under age thirteen would automatically be considered to have acted without discretion, and their cases, decriminalized, would be handled by the civil court's Advisory Chamber (Chambre de conseil). Minors under thirteen could not be sent to penitentiary colonies but could be returned to parents, placed in private or public institutions, or placed with Public Assistance (Assistance publique), the agency given custody of abandoned children as well as abused or neglected children removed from their homes. Minors between thirteen and eighteen would fall under the jurisdiction of a Court for Children and Adolescents (Tribunal pour enfants et adolescents, or TEA). In each judicial region the District Court (Tribunal de première instance) "[would make] itself into a Court for Children and Adolescents to judge, in a special hearing," minors thirteen to sixteen charged with offenses (*délits*) or felonies (*crimes*) and minors sixteen to eighteen charged only with offenses.[38] A TEA included three judges (one presiding, two associates), a representative from the public prosecutor's office, and a court clerk. The law indicated that the judges, if possible, be specialists in juvenile law, and that one of the investigating magistrates (*juges d'instruction*) should also specialize in juvenile cases. The court had to appoint a defender for every charged minor.

The 1912 law severely restricted public access to TEA sessions, and strictly limited publicity about cases involving minors. Names, photographs, and descriptions of offenses or crimes involving minors could no longer be published, ending the sensationalized accounts of child criminals that until then had regularly appeared in the *Gazette des tribunaux*.[39]

The 1912 law required, alongside an investigation of the crime, a social investigation of the minor's personality, school performance, work habits, friends, activities, family situation, and neighborhood. Most often, investigating magistrates sent a form for the local police chief to fill out, although the judge could appoint an outside party, officially designated a *rapporteur*, to conduct the social investigation. Eventually in the Paris region the court came to rely on three private agencies that employed social workers to conduct the investigations. Judges could use information from the social investigation in making their final decisions. The investigations required by the 1912 law did not focus at all on the minor's maturity and legal responsibility, relevant to the determination of discretion. Rather, the additional social and environmental information reflected new ideas and theories about delinquency, and opened the way for outside experts to exert some influence over the legal system.

However, the law still stipulated that for defendants thirteen to eighteen, courts had first to decide discretion. Minors who acted with discretion would receive the appropriate adult penalty but benefited up to age sixteen from the attenuating excuse of youth, which meant shortened jail sentences that could be served in juvenile penitentiary colonies or separate sections of adult jails. Minors thirteen to eighteen, if acquitted as acting without discretion under Article 66, could be sent to private institutions or public juvenile penitentiary colonies until they reached the age of 21, or returned to their parents.

The 1912 law also formalized a new practice judges had taken up, copied from the American system of probation. Minors sent to private institutions or returned to their parents could be placed on probation or, as the French put it, under supervised liberty *(liberté surveillée)*. A delegate, chosen from an approved list of willing and upstanding volunteers, would be appointed to supervise the minor and report back to the court regularly. A new sensitivity and awareness of adolescence, and the desire to maintain greater vigilance and supervision, provided the context for formalizing probation, a process that allowed courts to continue supervising even minors released to their families.[40]

Twentieth-Century Pediatric Neuropsychiatry

Although it rested on the Napoleonic Penal Code's fulcrum of discretion, the 1912 law recorded the significant shift in worldview that was under way. Continuing developments quickly surpassed the 1912 law. The early twentieth century saw the rise of a new subfield of psychiatry, neuropsychiatry, and the attempt by the human sciences to apply scientific methodologies to the study of the human mind. French scientist Alfred Binet was at the international forefront in the development of intelligence testing. Michel Chauvière points out that neuropsychiatry sat at the crossroads of Benedict Morel and Valentin Magnant's theories of degeneracy, Alexis Carrel's eugenicism, Cesare Lombroso's constitutionalist theories, Emile Durkheim and Henri Joly's sociological or environmental theories, Pavlovian models of conditioning, and Freudian theory. I would add to that mix Dupré's theories of constitutional perversity. After all, his disciple, Georges Heuyer, more or less created the field of pediatric neuropsychiatry. In 1914 Heuyer began comparing children at a mental hospital, La Bicêtre, juvenile delinquents at La Roquette, and children in "special education" classes. According to Heuyer, these three groups of children shared certain similarities in appearance, character, heredity, and family structure, leading him to coin a new, unified designation, "abnormal children." Despite the scientific facade of Heuyer and his colleagues' studies, with their theories, observations, and testing, in fact pediatric neuropsychiatry involved, as Chauvière puts it, considerable "tinkering" (he describes it as *"bricoleuse"*).

Neuropsychiatric articles stressed almost exclusively the diagnosis, observation, testing, and categorizing of various sorts of abnormal children. Neuropsychiatry, however, devoted barely any attention to the treatment of these disorders. Determining what category they fit into outweighed interest in rehabilitating so-called abnormal children. As increasingly sophisticated methods of testing and observation developed, the reeducation of delinquent or abnormal minors remained arbitrary, haphazard, almost completely unconnected to any diagnostic process. Chauvière argues that neuropsychiatrists in part abandoned attempts to follow up after diagnosis because opening new treatment and reeducational institutions aroused the fierce opposition of powerful people connected to the public educational system, youth movements, and scouting. Nevertheless, Chauvière argues that pediatric neuropsychiatry functioned as a key mobilizing and organizing force as France developed systems for screening and treating abnormal and delinquent children.[41]

The neuropsychiatric worldview rejected the notion that a criminal act committed by a young person resulted from evil tendencies or precocious perversity. Even in cases involving misery or abuse, it was held that the criminal behavior of children and adolescents most often resulted from a neuropsychiatric condition. The criminal act itself signaled a potential mental or emotional condition, and thus the required response was neither punishment nor rehabilitation but observation and testing.[42] Some experts took an optimistic, if alarmingly interventionist, view: since the delinquent act manifested a condition, then that condition should be apparent even before the act. Neuropsychiatrists thus advocated screening for "predelinquent" children.

The existence of a public education system gave the state access to and experience with supervising France's children. Adding to the greater possibilities for intimate knowledge of France's children, the new profession of social work provided educated, middle-class women with direct access to working-class families. Courts increasingly called on social workers to conduct case studies of arrested minors.

As a result, some authorities in child psychology called for removing juvenile delinquents from the judicial and penal systems altogether, and merging delinquent youth into a broader category, that of "abnormal" or "maladjusted" children. Many children's advocates hoped to create a coordinated system involving public elementary schools, family doctors, and social workers, to screen, treat, and protect all maladjusted children and adolescents, whether mentally retarded, abused, or "predelinquent." It was hoped such screening could reveal those children "at risk" of delinquent behavior. Then experts could test, observe, and diagnose the child and family. Based on the assumption that a minor's delinquent act is nearly always caused by a personality flaw or condition that can be detected, and not by a spur-of-the-moment response to temptation or peer pressure, such an approach could thus prevent delinquency.

With minors who committed crimes placed on the far end of a spectrum of children with various disorders, nineteenth- and early twentieth-century terminology needed revision. Historian Françoise Tétard explains that nineteenth-century writings referred to "young criminals," a term that indicated lawbreakers who differed from adult criminals only in their age. Early twentieth-century specialists often used the term "guilty children" *(enfance coupable)* as half of a binary concept separating them from "victim children" *(enfance victime)* suffering from abuse or neglect. However, as the twentieth century progressed, more and more children's reformers found the term "guilty children" unsatisfactory. The guilty/victim dichotomy no longer sufficed in an era when more and more people considered minors who committed crimes to be victims too. Meanwhile, in 1904, a Dutch scholar, G. L. Fries, coined the term "juvenile delinquency" to refer to children and adolescents who broke the law. By the 1930s "juvenile delinquency" was gaining wider acceptance.[43] Not only does the word *juvenile* incorporate both children and adolescents while still separating them from adults, the word *delinquent,* less pejorative than *criminal,* also more accurately reflected the fact that most minors committed petty offenses and misdemeanors, or *délits,* and not felonies or serious crimes. In 1934 the journal *Pour l'enfance "coupable"* (For "Guilty" Children) first appeared and resolved the terminology dilemma by placing quotation marks, to suggest doubt, around the word *guilty*.[44] As *Pour l'enfance "coupable,"* edited by Quaker activist Henry Van Etten, became critically important in the effort to reform the juvenile justice system, the title became increasingly problematic, and in June 1946 the editorial board rebaptized it *Sauvons l'enfance*.[45]

Studies of juvenile delinquency in the 1920s and 1930s worked toward building a taxonomy of conditions that predisposed minors to delinquency. Criminologists, jurists, judges, social workers, psychologists, and psychiatrists interested in juvenile delinquency solidified into a virtual establishment through a series of meetings and congresses, and in the expanding number of journals, such as *Pour l'enfance "coupable," Défense de l'enfance malheureuse,* and *Voix de l'enfant.* Specialists in juvenile crime hardly spoke with a unanimous voice. Some experts stressed medical or hereditary causes, some focused on the family, and others on the personality. Some experts advocated rural camps, others favored apprenticeships that would meet practical needs, and one group advocated scouting as a way to reform minors. However, nearly all juvenile delinquency experts believed that minors, whose young minds and habits were more susceptible to change, could be treated if properly diagnosed. Their coalescence into an interest group was signaled by the unification of local committees to defend children in the justice system that had formed in many French cities.

Renewed Efforts to Reform Juvenile Justice

A decree of 8 June 1927 instituted the National Committee for the Defense of Children in the Justice System, to study and propose legislation concerning the judicial, administrative, and institutional treatment of minors. The committee, which included many leading activists, doctors, and jurists, such as Joseph Barthélemy, Henri Rollet, Louis Rollin, Georges Paul-Boncour, and Georges Heuyer, first met on 21 May 1928 to coordinate efforts to rehabilitate minors and formulate suggestions for improvements in the system.[46] The committee's creation and makeup indicated a new desire to bypass turf quarrels between public institutions and private charities, and between legal and psychiatric approaches.[47] One group excluded by anticlericalism from the emerging synthesis, the Catholic church, undertook a parallel effort and created in 1928 the National Secretariat of Catholic Sanitary and Social Charities, to ensure itself a voice in the coordination of services.[48]

While not yet included in the dialogue, religious activists in the field had for the most part abandoned the sin-punishment paradigm for boys by the 1930s.[49] However, the misbehavior of girls continued to be seen in moral terms, in both religious and secular circles. In fact, courts were very likely to remand girls who appeared in the courts to religious institutions, like the Bon Pasteurs, where they received large doses of morality in a strict, conventlike setting. The small number of public institutions for girls, the preservation schools, copied practices of religious institutions, mandating short "Joan of Arc" haircuts, shapeless black monastic-style robes, and heavy doses of penitence and moral instruction.[50] Scholarship on the treatment of wayward and delinquent girls in a variety of countries clarifies how gendered notions shaped court and institutional treatment of girls. Across the West, the public perception of delinquent youth portrays boys as thieves and girls as prostitutes. While noncriminal behavior, commonly called "status offenses" in the United States, such as truancy and running away, could land boys in the court system in France, the sexual activity of boys was highly unlikely to trouble authorities, in contrast to that of girls. In France, both paternal correction and the 1908 law on prostitution could be invoked to control girls considered promiscuous. In the general atmosphere of growing concern about population decline, such girls presented a threat to more than their family's reputation.

Alongside changing ideas about childhood and adolescence and fresh theories about crime, the early twentieth century witnessed a major reorientation in prevailing social concerns. A new set of social and political fears began to crowd out older social anxieties about the connection between child criminals and either political upheaval or degeneracy. Nationalist concerns were strengthening at the same time that France's population began to reflect the decline in the birth rate that started in the mid-nineteenth century. France experienced the demographic transition to low birth rates earlier than either of its rivals, England and Germany. If, as was commonly assumed in France, national strength could be measured by the size and vigor of a nation's population, then the relatively slow growth of France's population could endanger its world position. The opinion spread that France needed babies and a healthy population, eventually easing attitudes toward children and adolescents who commit crimes. Rather than portraying juvenile delinquents as fearful, evil, precociously perverted children destined for a life of crime unless firmly repressed, children's activists eventually redefined the problem in demographic terms. France needed the contribution of its entire population and could no longer afford to waste a portion of its youth. Articles and books in the field emphasized that a large majority of the children who found themselves in trouble with the law came from broken or otherwise "defective" families. The media echoed experts' ideas, denying that society could distinguish between "victim children" and "guilty children." Most minors who broke the law were troubled and in need of protection rather than repression. "The young delinquent, in effect, is not just guilty, he is also, most often, a victim."[51]

While fairly successful in redefining the terms of the public debate, juvenile delinquency experts became increasingly frustrated with their inability to reform the system in France, which they compared unfavorably, time and again, to more enlightened and modern systems, especially in the United States and Belgium. The United States pioneered the use of juvenile courts and rehabilitative institutions. Belgium had passed a juvenile code the same year as France, 1912, but according to French experts, the Belgian system went considerably further in a therapeutic direction. French books and articles asserted that Belgium successfully rehabilitated a much greater proportion of its delinquent youth. Although the reality of the situation in both American and Belgian institutions may not have matched the reputation, to French observers certainly these efforts looked very promising, more modern and scientific than what France was doing.[52] In France, some juvenile delinquency activists simply sidestepped the inability to reform state institutions by creating private institutions, Patronages, schools, clinics, and diagnostic centers. They worked hard both within and outside the system to reform it.

Although it represented an improvement, the 1912 law attracted much criticism. First of all, many people involved with the system believed that determining whether a minor was an innocent victim acting without discretion or a perverted criminal acting with discretion was unimportant and diversionary. Adolescence represented precisely a period in which no one has full discretion, when notions of right and wrong are developing, and thus critics said it was wrong to use discretion to determine repressive or lenient responses. In fact, most judges no longer took the distinction seriously. More often they used Article 66 to justify the response they determined best to fit the situation, acquitting under Article 66 even minors who clearly knew they were breaking the law, if they felt reeducation and supervision would be useful, convicting them under Article 69 if they felt the crime did not indicate any serious psychological problem, and, if the crime were not serious, passing down suspended sentences. Eric Schneider's study of Boston's juvenile courts found similarly that the laws creating juvenile courts only systematized existing practices.[53]

A minority of truly "perverted" children, delineated no longer by their discretion but through scientific, psychiatric testing, needed a strict disciplinary system, it was agreed. However, most experts asserted that the vast majority of minors in the justice system needed protection and rehabilitation, not punishment. Focusing on discretion did not answer the real question: What condition caused the minor to misbehave? They believed the court's response should be based not on the minor's discretion but on a series of examinations, physical, mental, and social, of the minor. Once innocence or guilt had been decided (and a small percentage of cases were dropped or resulted in normal acquittals, not acquittals owing to action without discretion), the courts should determine what condition caused the behavior. "The offense matters less than the delinquent. The offense represents the past, the delinquent, the future."[54]

Under the 1912 law, minors who had been arrested could be returned to their parents' custody while the investigation proceeded, or, if they represented a danger to the community or were likely to disappear, placed in preventive detention. While some minors were sent to Patronages, many minors were held in separate quarters in adult pretrial detention jails *(maisons d'arrêt)*, where they might spend a month or more. Despite the separate quarters, most juvenile delinquency experts viewed preventive detention as unnecessarily punitive and dangerously corrupting.

To address the two critiques, namely the need for appropriate information about the minor and the evils of the preventive detention of minors, juvenile delinquency experts began to advocate a completely new solution, observation centers where minors awaiting hearings could be observed and receive medical, intelligence, and psychological testing. Judges could then use the information collected by the centers to make better decisions about placement and treatment. Several observation centers were developed in the private sector before World War II, the most famous being the one created under the initiative of neuropsychiatrist Heuyer and funded by Olga Spitzer, operating out of Rollet's Patronage in Paris.[55] Experts hoped that every jurisdiction would open an observation center for minors, preferably located near the court.

Critics of the system established by the 1912 law pointed out that not every jurisdiction developed a truly separate Court for Children and Adolescents, or TEA. Given its size, the Department of the Seine dedicated the Fifteenth Chamber Court to cases involving minors, but most provincial jurisdictions did not have a separate chamber for minors. The same chamber would hear cases involving adults, then designate itself a TEA and hear cases involving minors. As a consequence, most judges hearing cases involving minors had no special training in child development or adolescent psychology. More and more, legal, medical, and even religious activists pushed for truly separate courts run by specialized *juges des enfants*, children's judges, trained to understand test results and make the proper determinations.[56] The 1912 law recommended that judges order a case study by a social worker or medical-psychiatric testing of the minor, but experts like Luaire noted that in rural regions and even in smaller cities, courts rarely if ever ordered such tests. The law needed to extend and regularize the procedures for all jurisdictions.

Experts called for trained judges, separate juvenile courts, and observation and testing centers to improve the judicial process. As for the penal side of the equation, nearly everyone in the field, even people who worked in the penal administration bureaucracy, condemned existing public institutions for delinquent youth as ineffective and cruel. Books and articles consistently referred to state-run correctional houses or penitentiary colonies for minors as *bagnes d'enfants* (children's penal camps), making explicit the comparison with adult penal labor camps *(bagnes)*, which were renowned for their harsh conditions and cruel wardens.[57] Sending young people to such institutions represented a waste of people France could no longer spare. Under conditions of demographic crisis, throwing away children could have disastrous consequences.

Nevertheless, juveniles continued to languish in miserable institutions even though many legislators across the political spectrum agreed that France's demographic situation warranted action. The nature of the Third Republic, its continual changes in government and resulting legislative stalemates, made any bold legislative reform regarding delinquency difficult. Even administrative institutional reforms that did not require legislative approval were stymied by resistance at every level, from the cabinet to the staff at public institutions.

Frustrated by their inability to get results, reformers took their story to the media. Press campaigns starting in the 1920s described in vivid detail the horrors of life in these "children's penal camps." Slowly, by the mid-1930s, the media succeeded in creating public sympathy for juvenile delinquents. Then, with the newly compassionate public opinion in place, the system received a jolt.

State institutions for minor boys were rocked by scandals in the 1930s. Probably the best-known scandal took place at the correctional school on Belle-Ile, an island off the Brittany coast. On 2 August 1934 wardens badly beat a young inmate for having begun to eat his dinner before the signal bell rang. In the midst of the ensuing riot, all the boys managed to escape. Over the next few days, the local police offered townspeople and vacationing tourists a reward of 20 francs for the return of any fugitive, and all the boys, trapped on the island, were recaptured. Widely publicized, the *Oliver Twist* nature of this incident aroused public pity for the boys. Jacques Prévert eventually wrote a poem about the Belle-Ile incident, "Children's Hunt" ("La chasse aux enfants"), which Paris cabaret singer Marianne Oswald popularized in song.[58]

In 1935 *Détective,* a crime magazine not known for its coddling attitude toward criminals, titled a story about state juvenile institutions "Martyred Children."[59] The theme was echoed by the *Journal de la femme*—"Child Martyrs: Enough!"—and finally taken up in the conservative mass-circulation paper *Le Figaro* by the Catholic thinker François Mauriac.[60] Expressing the new view, the socialist paper *Le Populaire* ran a story entitled, "Guilty Children? No, Guilty Society!"[61]

France's most influential children's reformer, journalist Alexis Danan, wrote for *Paris-Soir,* Paris's largest-circulation daily.[62] In response to the loss of his five-year-old son to illness, Danan dedicated his life to improving the lives of unhappy children and took up the campaign against children's correctional institutions. Active well into the 1950s, Danan began his children's crusade by reigniting the press's interest in correctional schools, which had begun to flag by 1936. In 1937, Danan unsheathed his biggest "sword of scandal" involving a correctional school: the "Eysses Affair." Danan published a front-page article about the death of Roger Abel, a nineteen-year-old inmate at the Eysses penitentiary colony subjected to

150 days (six months) of "harsh regime" *(régime sévère)*, a program combining total isolation with a severely restricted diet. On three separate occasions Abel's restricted diet was further reduced to eight days of dry bread and water.[63] The medical report concluded that Abel died of tuberculosis resulting from the physical strain of his punishment. As Gaillac points out, the medical report clarified that Abel did not die at the hands of rogue, overzealous, brutal guards, who could be fired.[64] Danan's coverage stressed repeatedly that a law passed on 15 February 1930 limited the solitary confinement of minors to a maximum of eight days. Abel's treatment meant either that those running Eysses had violated the rules, in which case the director and doctor should be fired, or that they had had special permission from the authorities in Paris, in which case the director of Penal Administration should be fired. Anything else, Danan wrote, would be "idle chatter, weakness and complicity."[65]

Early in 1937, Danan publicized another death at another public institution. At Saint-Hilaire a boy suddenly died after having been forced to work all day in a water-filled ditch, even though he had complained of a cold. Danan skillfully orchestrated his media campaigns. *Paris-Soir* ran huge headlines and front-page photographs of these scandals, and usually the other Paris dailies and papers across France followed suit. The press campaigns made it impossible for the government to ignore the situation. Danan's rhetoric and coverage of these incidents also fostered a new, more benevolent public image of the inmates in juvenile correctional houses. Danan used the rhetoric of childhood, referring even to older adolescents as children, denying that they were cold-blooded future criminals and insisting that they were most often victims of unfortunate circumstances.

Even aside from the fact that the correctional houses were often cruel and abusive, most people in the juvenile delinquency establishment considered them fundamentally flawed. Juvenile delinquents needed treatment, education, rehabilitation, counseling, and job training, not punishment and meaningless labor designed to break them. In a counterargument to the Mettray philosophy of removing children from the cities, experts began to point out the irrelevance of the skills adolescents gained through rural labor and their need for urban occupational skills that would allow them to earn a living after their release.[66]

In addition to calling for severing juvenile courts from the rest of the judicial system, some experts began to advocate that the Penal Administration, the bureaucracy that ran prisons in France, cede control of state institutions for juveniles. Severing ties would both indicate a new philosophy and have an important practical effect, as institutions for minors would no longer be required to hire personnel from the ranks of prison wardens. Experts decried the lack of specialized personnel in juvenile institutions, as they had the lack of specialized judges in juvenile courts. So long as those who staffed juvenile institutions had been hired and trained by the Penal Administration and risen through its civil-service ranks, juvenile institutions would retain their punitive and repressive atmosphere. Hiring a few teachers or occupational therapists to come in weekly could hardly mitigate, much less eradicate, the basic punitive nature of the setting. Experts believed state institutions needed to shift their focus away from punishing offenders to providing education, training, and rehabilitation. Most admitted that some minors, the truly perverted, might require a strict disciplinary regime, but they believed the majority of minors would benefit from a new approach. And replacing Penal Administration personnel with specialized educators for juvenile institutions would require the creation of centers and programs to train people interested in working with delinquent minors.

Despite the level of alarm in the 1930s, reforms had already begun in the late 1920s. For example, while of little immediate import, on 31 December 1927 the designation of state institutions was formally changed. Penitentiary colonies were instantly transformed into supervised education houses, *maisons d'éducation surveillée*. While changing names proved as effective as pretending to wave a magic wand in altering actual practice at these institutions, it articulated the desired outcome. In another move toward reform, the National Committee to Defend Children in the Justice System first met on 8 June 1928. Also, La Roquette, the first prison built for minors, stopped taking minors in 1930, becoming a women's prison. Minors from La Roquette were transferred to Fresnes Supervised Education House, really a separate quarter of the Fresnes jail. Therapeutic initiatives for juveniles had already been instituted at Fresnes under the leadership of neuropsychiatrists Jacques Roubinovitch and Georges Paul-Boncour.[67]

One key change in the Penal Code also occurred prior to the Second World War. Minors in France could find themselves in court for two reasons beyond committing an offense: paternal correction and vagrancy. Paternal correction had been slightly modified by the 1889 law on paternal power and by a 1904 law that provided for new ways, short of paternal correction, of dealing with minors with behavioral problems. While uncommon, a much higher percentage of girls were in both public and private correctional institutions for paternal correction than boys.[68] In contrast, a large fraction of minors who found themselves in court were charged with vagrancy. According to Lepointe's 1936 study, the charge of vagrancy accounted for 30 to 40 forty percent of all juveniles who appeared in the courts, approximately 5,000 to 6,000 minors a year in the late 1920s and early 1930s, 400 to 600 in the Paris region alone.[69]

By 1934 and 1935 the outcry against cruelty in public correctional institutions generated the corresponding idea that it was not fair to treat as criminals vagrant minors who may have been abandoned or who were escaping abusive parents or employers. Minors charged with vagrancy had not necessarily committed any actual offenses. If they had, such behaviors as theft clearly resulted from their vagrant status, which required them to survive on the streets. Thus many children's advocates argued most vagrant minors did not have criminal tendencies and needed protection, not punishment. Jurist and child activist Louis Rollin wrote, in his proposal to decriminalize the vagrancy of minors, that such minors were unhappy and should not be sent to prison, where they would establish a criminal record, or to a youth correctional facility. Vagrant minors were in "an unfortunate state of affairs."[70]

Rollin's ideas eventually formed the basis of the law of 30 October 1935 that decriminalized the vagrancy of minors. Under this law, TEAs could review the situations of minors under eighteen who had left their parents, were abandoned or orphaned, and had no job or domicile and were "earning their living from debauchery or from prohibited trades," alluding to girls engaged in prostitution.[71] After investigating the children, their families, and their social milieux, judges could either return minors to their parents or guardians, or send them to a charitable institution, to a public preservation school, or to Public Assistance, the agency that handled children abandoned or removed from their homes. The cases did not appear in a criminal court, and therefore no criminal records resulted. Minors and their families could appeal placement decisions. During an appeal a minor waited in a "special jail" *(dépot spécial)* while the judge weighed further options. Judges could also decide in vagrancy cases to send minors before the TEA, where they would fall under Penal Code Articles 66 and 69 and the 1912 law.

The 30 October 1935 law, which addressed the plight of abandoned children as well as minors brought in for paternal correction, mandated only rehabilitative measures *(instruments d'amendement)*. However, rehabilitative measures included placement in supervised educational houses, or preservation schools for girls, so the difference to minors handled under the 1935 law must have been nearly invisible.[72] In practice, the law on vagrancy meant that vagrant minors no longer could be found responsible and given adult prison sentences. Yet short of prison, which was rarely used under any circumstances, the range of options for judges remained quite similar to those in effect before 1935.

The Popular Front's Effort to Reform Juvenile Justice

The 30 October 1935 law represented the only legal reform of the interwar period, but institutional reforms for boys originated during those years. The Popular Front's victory in the spring 1936 elections ultimately had the most profound impact on juvenile institutions in the interwar wars. An antifascist coalition of radicals, socialists, and communists, the Popular Front is well known for its attention to labor-related issues: settling of a wave of strikes with the Matignon accords, decreeing two-week paid vacations for all employees, imposing the eight-hour day, and so on. Major controversies erupted in response to Minister of Education Jean Zay's attempt to unify the school system, ending the strict separation that prevented talented children educated in public primary schools from entering elite public secondary schools, the lycées. Also, a law of 9 August 1936 raised to fourteen the age for leaving school.[73]

However, little has been written about the Popular Front's desire to overhaul the juvenile justice system. Several efforts to rewrite the 1912 law failed.[74] Archival documents indicate that both Minister of Finance Vincent Auriol and Marc Rucard, the Popular Front's first minister of justice, proposed bills. In 1937, radical deputy César Campinchi presented two bills that together constituted a complete overhaul of the system. His plan included systematizing medical and social examinations of young delinquents, setting up triage centers, transforming public institutions into truly reeducational centers, and severing Supervised Education from Penal Administration. As one recent study concluded, Campinchi's bill pulled together the full range of contemporary demands. However, nothing came of any of the proposed legislative reforms.[75]

As in so many arenas, the Popular Front's bold and ambitious plans for juvenile justice came undone owing to a combination of internal and external circumstances. To begin with, the three parties that made up the Popular Front coalition, while all left of center, did not really share a vision. Rather, they had come together defensively against the threat of the far right. Thus socialist prime minister Léon Blum and his cabinet could rarely count on legislative support. Externally, France faced a number of excruciating choices. Almost immediately after coming to power, the unity of the Popular Front coalition was tested by the outbreak of the Spanish Civil War, in addition to difficulties dealing with France's allies and with the rising menace of Nazi Germany. In the end, the Popular Front's early flurry of legislation quickly gave way to the usual Third Republic stalemates.[76]

Still, the Popular Front did initiate institutional reforms in two supervised education houses. While he was minister of justice, Marc Rucard met at the Sorbonne in 1936 with Sir Robert Baden-Powell, founder of the modern scouting movement. Baden-Powell advocated scouting to remedy the evils modern urban life posed for young people. Scouting could prevent misbehavior by inculcating correct moral values in a natural setting, and its group methods and discipline could also retrain youth heading down the wrong path. Many interwar French reformers, in particular Henri and Fernand Joubrel, were quite excited about the possibility of introducing scouting methods in juvenile correctional houses.[77]

Officially, Rucard, Minister of Public Health Henri Sellier, and Minister of National Education Jean Zay signed a law on 13 August 1936 concerning the reorganization of the Saint-Maurice Supervised Education House. Work implementing that law began in May 1937, and in July of that year a similar law passed to reform Saint-Hilaire. The reformers intended to shift the focus at supervised education houses away from punishment and toward rehabilitation, education, and job training. First, educators replaced prison wardens in the rehabilitation of the wards. Second, new workshops at Saint-Maurice provided apprenticeships for minors in useful fields.[78] Hoping to draw staff from a new pool, with the cooperation of the National Education Ministry, Rucard recruited students attaining their Certificate of Pedagogical Aptitude (Certificat d'aptitude pédagogique) to work at Saint-Maurice, promising them specialized training in the field and guaranteeing that their training and work experience would entitle them to salaries and tenure provisions comparable to those of regular schoolteachers.[79]

Despite the shared desire to undertake serious reforms, territorial battles developed between the three main government bureaucracies involved in rehabilitating minors, the Ministries of National Education, Justice, and Public Health. National Education, for example, hoped eventually to take control of all school-related measures for all minors, whether they were delinquent or had mental or emotional disorders or physical disabilities. The ministry felt empowered by the law of 15 April 1909, which gave Education, then named Public Instruction, control over so-called deficient children *(enfants déficients).*[80] Minister of Public Health Sellier advocated a joint committee to coordinate the often contradictory and overlapping efforts of the Justice Ministry's Penal Administration with the Ministries of Public Health and National Education.

The competition among ministries was the least of many factors that undermined the Popular Front's attempts to reform the two supervised education houses, Saint-Maurice and Saint-Hilaire. Ferocious resistance came from within the institutions. After a little more than a year, the first team of reformers sent to Saint-Maurice wrote to Marc Rucard indicating the problems they had encountered. Signed "the educators of Saint-Maurice," the writers, preferring to remain anonymous, identified themselves as among the twenty interested young teachers Rucard had recruited for a training session at Fresnes in December 1936 and January 1937. At Fresnes, they had attended lectures by leading members of the juvenile delinquency establishment, Heuyer, Paul-Boncour, and Spitzer. They learned to think of the young people in state institutions not as born criminals but as troubled youth in need of treatment. They traveled to Belgium to observe its world-renowned institutions. They had arrived at Saint-Maurice in January 1937 filled with enthusiasm, only to be shocked by the dirt and disorder and the lamentable state of the buildings. In theory, a triage center examined all entering minors; two teachers were to be assigned to every twenty-four students; students were to spend their days attending classes and learning a trade in the workshops. None of this was being done. The new staff had been promised sports facilities, a theater, greater freedom of movement to take the boys out, and an end to barred windows, locked doors, and corporal punishments. They advocated the creation of a self-governing body at the school to facilitate the relationship between students and teachers. By May 1938 the reformers, "very discouraged and very weak," had been reduced to this anonymous appeal to "their minister" Rucard, the "father of the reform." They asserted that contrary to Saint-Maurice director Risbourg's promise to Rucard to institute new methods like scouting, Risbourg had undermined all the reformers' efforts. The letter writers claimed Risbourg took sadistic pleasure in abusing the students, favoring such humiliations as public head shavings and the use of leg irons. The reforming teachers claimed that Risbourg referred to them variously as "an insignificant group of pimps, thieves, puppets."[81] This group of teachers speculated that the Penal Administration, which had never fully supported the reforms, had allowed the new teachers into Saint-Maurice only to calm public opinion, hoping by sabotaging their efforts to prove that reform was a chimera.

Rucard, who had left the Justice Ministry to become minister of public health, apparently took this letter seriously and forwarded it to the Justice Ministry with a personal note asking the minister to act quickly to ensure the success of the reform "that proves indispensable at the present time." In a 1937 report, Penal Administration inspector Jean Bancal recommended appointing a new director to Saint-Maurice for a transitional period, someone from education circles. In early 1938, Andrieux, director of Penal Administration, took Bancal's advice and appointed a new director, Hourcq, and an assistant director, Courtois. They inaugurated a slow evolution. Hourcq introduced serious professional training at Saint-Maurice, installing in previous disciplinary quarters new industrial workshops equipped with the latest machinery. Even before putting in the workshops however, in July 1938 Hourcq had all the students considered likely to pass take the final exam for either a Primary Education Certificate (Certificat d'études primaires, CEP) or a Certificate of Professional Aptitude (CAP), which education officials agreed to administer at Saint-Maurice. All twenty of the boys who took the exams passed, a spectacular success that, according to Gaillac, had instant and important psychological effects on both the wards and their educators. Thus, after a rocky start, the reform process made some headway at Saint-Maurice before the war.[82]

A similar effort at Saint-Hilaire at first met similar resistance from that school's director. After more than a year of upheaval, a new director, François Dhallenne, was named in September 1938. He accepted the position on the condition that he would be allowed to choose his own team. He brought with him a new assistant director, Marquette, a new educational director, Buzenac, and a new overseer and physical education instructor, Nantier. Dhallenne described conditions at his arrival: "The establishment appeared to be in a state of complete disintegration . . . How can I describe the ruins everywhere? In the dormitories, no glass panes in the windows . . . An obstructed sewage collector near the kitchen produced in that area a putrid and nauseating muck . . . refuse everywhere. In the dormitories, fancy word to designate such "squalor"—swarming with regiments of bugs—the beds were in a lamentable state . . . the bedding infested . . . The wards are deplorably dressed."[83] Dhallenne immediately began the reconstruction of the facility, refurbished the refectory, replaced sleeping cages with open dormitories and individual rooms, initiated new activities and pedagogical methods including physical education, sponsored soccer and basketball teams, and established training in advanced agricultural methods. Although Dhallenne did not have the facilities to set up an industrial training section like the one at Saint-Maurice, he created a workshop to train the boys for rural artisanal trades like shoe repair, iron work, and electrical work. Rather than physical punishment and confinement, discipline rested on the use of progressive sections through which the students moved, each one entailing more comfort and personal freedom.

The Popular Front took another decisive action in reforming juvenile justice. Mettray, the very first agricultural colony for boys, emulated in the nineteenth century as a model of the latest techniques, finally came to be seen for the stark and brutal labor camp it was. Public Health Minister Henri Sellier, hoping to avoid "incidents concerning children's penal camps like the ones that recently have been the main topic in the scandal press," sent a general inspector from Children's Services to Mettray, whose honorific administrative board was under the direction of the dean of the Paris law faculty and the future Vichy minister of justice, Joseph Barthélemy.[84] Meanwhile, journalist Alexis Danan had compiled a thick folder on Mettray, replete with cases on children who had died from mistreatment and administrators who had pocketed the sums of money Mettray received for each ward. Danan sent his folder to then Justice Minister Rucard on 4 June 1936, inducing Rucard to send his own inspectors. Sellier withdrew all wards of Public Assistance from Mettray and prohibited placement there. Rucard also withdrew all minors sent by the courts and notified juvenile court judges to stop placing minors at Mettray. Several months later, the absence of wards and stipends forced Mettray to close its doors. Ironically, Danan and *Paris-Soir* faced two lawsuits, one by the Mettray board of directors, one by Barthélemy, for a total of 350,000 francs in damages.[85] The court, in a judgment filled with unflattering comments about Mettray, dismissed all charges brought by Mettray's board, which was also directed to pay all legal costs. Joseph Barthélemy won his libel suit, but the court, clearly sympathetic to Mettray's critics, ordered *Paris-Soir* and Danan to pay Barthélemy only a symbolic sum, 1 franc, in damages and refused to order the paper to publish an apology, as Barthélemy had demanded.[86]

The Popular Front, facing severe domestic and international crises, did not last long enough to oversee fundamental legal reforms, or to initiate reforms at other state institutions, and the reformist impulse of the mid-

1930s stalled by 1938. The general mobilization and the outbreak of war on 3 September 1939 dealt the final blow to institutional reform. Military mobilization removed most of the younger, reform-minded directors and personnel from supervised education houses, with occasionally disastrous consequences. However, after the initial disruption during the summer and fall of 1940, the trend toward institutional and legal reforms continued during the Vichy years and beyond. By 1946, serious reform was well under way at boys' institutions and just starting at girls' institutions, which had finally attracted the attention of reformers. Before we explore the impact of World War II and the German occupation on the juvenile justice system, the next chapter will examine their impact on children and adolescents in general.

2

The Experience of World War II for Children and Adolescents

For many young people in France, the war, which really began in May 1940, despite its official declaration nine months earlier, meant being uprooted, facing the terror of separation from family, and seeing death first-hand. The trauma started with the "exodus" of millions of people who fled their homes as the bombs began to fall and the German army advanced into France. Raymond Ruffin, eleven in 1940, described refugees from the Battle of France passing through his small village: "Long columns of refugees flood into town, hanging on to ill-assorted and eccentric harnesses. Behind the heavy wagons pulled by big red horses with long blond manes, led by Belgians or people from the north of France, follow convoys of every sort of vehicle; from carriages and carts to asthmatic jalopies, the whole accompanied by bikes, baby carriages, handcarts, wheelbarrows, trailing behind or pushed by worn-out, panting, tattered pedestrians. The crowd seethes with shouts, curses, insults, crying babies."[1]

Although published many years after the war, Ruffin's description reveals a number of traits common to children's descriptions of traumatic events. In particular, the memory is entirely visual and aural. The vehicles, described first, and the people connected to them, simply flood in, like a natural disaster. The fact that the carriages were led by (note the passive voice) Belgians and people from the North was probably an accretion, information adults added to Ruffin's memory. Noise, disorder, and a vague sense of threat shape his reaction, and not, as in adult accounts, an overarching sense of despair about how the flood of miserable humanity foreshadowed a horrible outcome for the war.[2]

Children and adolescents experience warfare differently from adults, owing to a number of factors. Physically and mentally, children have not yet fully developed; their place in the world is not yet fixed. Younger children, especially, have a limited ability to place traumatic events into a

45

broader context that would make sense, although adolescents often can and do. Both children and adolescents, however, are dependents, not in charge of their own destinies. In 1940s France, their occupation involved attending school. After age thirteen or fourteen, most adolescents gained a greater measure of independence, by earning an income, for example, and spending time apart from their families with other young people, in either organized or spontaneous groups. Yet most adolescents remained fundamentally dependent for basic necessities on adults. Thus children and adolescents experienced the same great events connected with World War II as adults did, but from a very different perspective.

The war does not represent a shadowy backdrop to this study of juvenile delinquency. It must be in the foreground, for without the war, defeat, and occupation, there would have been neither a Vichy government nor a dizzying rise in juvenile crime statistics. Understanding what happened in juvenile courts, why the war years represented a critical turning point in the juvenile justice system, why contemporary experts stressed the factors they did, requires knowledge of the war and how young people lived through and responded to it. This chapter attempts to correct the tendency of many observers writing at the time to privilege the absence of so many fathers as the primary difficulty French children experienced during the war; it examines the multiple ways the war reshaped children's lives and the variety of reactions it produced. Children's lives in wartime France varied over time; their age and sex, their families' social class and ethnic or national background, and their geographic location all shaped their experiences. Further, delinquent minors were a subset of France's youth; their behavior represented one response to wartime conditions. This chapter outlines the war's events in France and analyzes government policies directed at young people. Using accounts produced by children and adolescents—diaries, memoirs, and school essays—the chapter pinpoints how various children reacted at the time, how they later remembered the war, and what those reactions reveal about the differential effects of the war on young people.

The Battle of France and the Exodus

For most people in France, World War II, although declared in September 1939, really began when Germany launched its blitz against the west on 10 May 1940, signaling the start of the Battle of France. After nine months of waiting—a period known as the phony war—in just five days

German tanks crossed the Meuse River, took three key cities, Monthermé, Dinant, and Sedan, and opened up a 90-kilometer gap in the front through which poured massive numbers of German units, trapping the French soldiers in Belgium and pushing hundreds of thousands of French and British soldiers to the coast at Dunkirk.[3]

The war hit France like a tidal wave. The fighting in 1940 took place primarily in the north and east of France, but it was accompanied by the exodus of civilians, first from the Netherlands and Belgium, then from the Nord and Pas-de-Calais, then from other areas in the war's path. Eventually, some 6 to 8 million people, anywhere from one-third to one-half of them children, fled the warring armies. Families packed up their belongings and left their homes by car, bicycle, cart, and even on foot. According to one estimate, of the 400,000 people living in the industrial regions of Lille, Roubaix, and Tourcoing, only 40,000 remained by the end of May 1940.[4]

For millions of children in France, the exodus represented their first direct experience of war. Like young Ruffin, the children of 1940 who either took part in or witnessed the exodus retained vivid memories of that period. François Pakonyk, eight years old in 1940, left with his parents and five siblings. He describes the miseries of those weeks, seeing wounded soldiers, starving refugees from Belgium, pillaged shops, and almost being separated from his family nearly a dozen times. "I have been marked for life by the month of June 1940."[5] One fifteen-year-old boy from Lille was not so lucky. In May 1940 his family joined the exodus out of Lille. His mother and uncle rode on a cart with the boy following behind on his bicycle. In the midst of the confusion, he became separated from his mother's wagon, lost sight of her, and wandered aimlessly until July 1940 before returning home. One year later his mother had "not yet returned home."[6]

Alfred Brauner interviewed 250 children shortly after the war. He notes that younger children asked about the exodus usually reported a strictly personal episode, whereas older adolescents spoke more about more general conditions, the sounds of bombing raids and machine-gun fire, hunger, fatigue, fear, and death. Few reported witnessing any acts of solidarity. Brauner found that "nothing in these accounts reveals anything other than regret for well-being gone by."[7]

Some 90,000 children were temporarily separated from their families during the exodus, according to historian W. D. Halls. After the armistice of June 25, 1940, newspapers across France were filled with notices from families searching for their lost children. Most of them were eventually reunited.[8] René Clement's classic film *Les Jeux interdits (Forbidden Games)* beautifully renders the trauma of the exodus for children. The film centers on Paulette, a young girl of five or six, whose parents are killed by air strafing as they flee Paris to the south during the Battle of France. Paulette, taken in temporarily by a peasant family, manifests an intense preoccupation with death through her construction of an elaborate cemetery for dead animals and insects.[9]

As the German army proceeded toward Paris, panic hit on 10 June when the government declared the capital an open city and left town, spurring hundreds of thousands of Parisians to join the exodus over the next week. Parisian children who did not leave also faced extraordinary circumstances. One student, after witnessing German air raids directed at the factories east of Paris, showed up at his lycée, Jean-Baptiste Say, the next day. "I finally get to school: very few students, only one professor and a director in a panic, having received instructions to close the establishment, which seems to me, this morning, in keeping with the logic of events. Good! Let's go home . . . The streets are deserted."[10]

Court records provide another glimpse of the chaos in Paris. Despite the calamities, the courts struggled on with their dockets of petty theft cases and other misdemeanors. Court records from the Seine Department, which includes Paris and its closest suburbs, began to show signs of unusual circumstances in May 1940. For the Fifteenth Chamber, the number of cases declined from about twenty a day to ten a day. But the deepest impact was felt in June, when the Fifteenth Chamber heard an average of four cases a day and, on 24 June, none. All eleven of the cases scheduled for 24 June were postponed to a later date because those involved were "unavailable owing to the circumstances," as the court clerk dutifully recorded eleven times.

Some adolescents took advantage of the situation, by looting, for example. In one of the more unusual cases that reflects the chaos and confusion of June 1940, twenty-eight people, including several minors, were charged with the theft of equipment from a military warehouse. After investigating, the judge dropped all charges. It turned out the people had not taken the items from the building, but from the street. Some five hundred people had taken part, as soldiers had tossed military equipment and office furniture out a window and urged passersby to take it, hoping to prevent it from falling into the hands of the advancing Germany army.[11]

Not surprisingly, many cases involved looting of abandoned buildings or cars. For example, two brothers, both minors, were charged with entering an abandoned factory on 14 June and stealing two bicycles, a spare tire, and a motorcycle. Also on 14 June, two adolescent boys stole an abandoned horse cart, filled it with various objects, tools, jewelry, household items, and food they had gathered from the train station in Malesherbes. They returned to Paris, where they were promptly arrested.[12]

The French government moved first to Tours, on the Loire River. Tours proved to be an unhappy choice, as its suburb Saint-Pierre-des-Corps, one of the major hubs of the French rail system, drew heavy air attacks. The flood of refugees also passed through Tours, and eventually the German army entered the city on 21 June. Abandoned goods and vehicles tempted some of those who chose not to leave Tours. One young man found an abandoned car on one of the river quays (Quai Portilla in Saint-Cyr). From it he removed and hid a suitcase and a radio, returning at night to collect his loot, which included clothing, shoes, and six silver place settings. He gave the women's clothing to his sister and her friend, telling them he had saved it from a burning house. When caught, he received a fairly light penalty, but his sister's friend, a minor, was sent to a Catholic reform school for two years for receiving the stolen property.[13]

As the Germans advanced, the French government abandoned Tours and moved on to Bordeaux, near the Atlantic coast in southwestern France, where it agreed to the armistice on 22 June 1940. Under its terms, Germany was to occupy the entire Atlantic coast, including Bordeaux, so the French government finally moved to a town in unoccupied France, the mineral spa city of Vichy. Although southern France experienced little in the way of air raids or fighting in 1940, the tidal wave of war washed up in the south. Millions of refugees from the north, Belgium, Luxembourg, and the Netherlands found themselves in southern France, destitute, desperate, and, at least initially, prevented from returning home by a new set of borders, including the demarcation line separating occupied from unoccupied France. Many refugees were adolescent boys without their families. The court in the southern city of Nîmes was inundated in the late summer of 1940 by cases involving teenage boys, mostly Belgians who could not speak French, warehoused in refugee camps, who were charged with theft, usually of food. The case files suggest that starvation probably motivated these minors to steal. For example, one of two Belgian boys who each stole 20 kilos of potatoes and stashed them away to eat as needed, insisted, "It was because of lack of provisions that we, my buddy and I, committed this misdeed." The friend agreed, "Hunger obliged me to [behave that way] because our ordinary provisions are not enough." They returned what was left of the potatoes to the farmer, and both received two-month suspended sentences.[14]

Surprisingly few children responded to the extreme situation of June and July 1940 in violent ways. Out of 153 case files in four departments, I found only one adolescent charged with murder during the war.[15] However, France's rapid defeat in 1940 produced one unintended effect. The police, at least temporarily, suffered a loss of status in the eyes of young people, some of whom felt empowered to mock them as shirkers when they intervened in local situations. For example, on 9 June 1940, a seventeen-year-old Parisian, charged with insulting an officer, had yelled at a group of mobile guards, "They're doing very well here! But they don't want to get themselves killed up there [at the front]." The court decided he had acted with discretion and fined him twenty-five francs.[16] Another case in October 1940 involved two adult men and a seventeen-year-old boy. Inspired by the men's taunting of a guardian of the peace, the minor dropped his pants and exclaimed, "When the Germans arrived, this is what you did." The judge fined him fifty francs.[17]

The Armistice and the Creation of the French State at Vichy

The rapid crumbling of France's defensive strategy and the military leadership's inability to regroup set off a major governmental crisis with profound consequences for France. Decisions made in June 1940 created the political situation that governed children's material lives and that shaped the institutions that integrate children into society, schools, youth organizations, and youth culture. After a disaster like a military defeat, leaders often turn to future generations with both fear and hope. Adults may be too far corrupted by existing systems, but children represent limitless future possibilities. However, contrasting policy with reality in wartime France points up the wide gap between what officials wanted to accomplish and what they settled for. Despite their many efforts, children did not prove to be empty vessels into which the regime could pour a ready-made set of values.

The French governmental crisis that erupted in Bordeaux in mid-June over whether to go into exile and continue the war from North Africa or seek terms from Germany left power in the hands of the defeatist group led by Marshal Philippe Pétain and Pierre Laval.[18] Pétain, a World War I hero, became prime minister and initiated armistice negotiations, announcing over the radio on 17 June 1940, "The fighting must stop." The armistice entered into effect one week later, 25 June 1940.[19] Many people in France reacted, understandably, with relief, saddened by the defeat but hoping that, for France, the war would be over. While the armistice did stop the fighting and temporarily stopped air raids, it hardly ushered in normality.

The terms of the armistice were harsh. Germany was to occupy three-fifths of France, including the entire North Sea and Atlantic coasts. A demarcation line divided the occupied zone from the unoccupied, or southern, or free zone, establishing a frontier that could be crossed by French citizens (including public officials) only with a special pass. The armistice limited mail sent across the demarcation line to 300 letters a day and divided France into five zones in addition to the occupied-unoccupied demarcation: Alsace-Lorraine was annexed by Germany; the zone including the Nord and Pas-de-Calais departments was detached from the German military command in Paris and reattached to the Germany military command in Belgium; the area next to Alsace-Lorraine became the reserved zone; next to those zones lay the forbidden zone (so called because refugees from the region were forbidden to return); Italy occupied at first a small zone along its border with France, but in November 1942 extended its zone east into the Alps. In response to the Allied landing in North Africa, on 11 November 1942 the German army occupied the southern zone but maintained the demarcation line between north and south.

The armistice also required France to turn all war materials over to Germany and restricted France to an armistice army of 100,000 troops. The 1.6 million French soldiers captured in June 1940 would remain POWs in Germany until the conclusion of a peace treaty. Finally, France was to pay occupation costs of 20 million marks a day, which at the artificially inflated rate of 20 francs per mark meant 400 million francs a day. After the November 1942 Allied invasion of North Africa, occupation costs, briefly lowered to 300 million francs a day, were raised to 500 million, where they stayed through the liberation.[20] Occupation costs totaled some 65 billion francs and soaked up nearly 60 percent of the national budget over the four years of Vichy's existence, causing currency depreciation and rapid inflation.[21]

Pétain became prime minister in June 1940 and took advantage of the crisis to destroy the Third Republic, which he considered an evil system whose weakness and inability to lead France were confirmed by her defeat. On 10 July 1940, the National Assembly voted full powers to Pétain, who then passed four constitutional acts that established a new government, officially named the French State, with its capital, in theory temporarily, in Vichy. Pétain became the head of state *(chef de l'état)*, and initially Pierre Laval became the head of the government. Vichy's laws applied to all zones of France (except Alsace-Lorraine, incorporated into Germany) unless contradicted by the German authorities. The French State maintained some offices in Paris, where it hoped eventually to return. Most important, the corps of civil servants, France's administrative carapace justly renowned throughout the world for truly governing France through two hundred years of political upheaval and numerous changes of regime, also continued to exercise its functions throughout France, even in the zone attached to the Belgian military command. Court records clearly show that for day-to-day, petty operations, the Germans strongly favored allowing French authorities to govern, and intervened only in matters of military or political importance to them.

Given the draconian nature of the armistice, why did some French leaders consider it preferable to exile? Men like Pétain and Laval argued that accepting the defeat, negotiating with Germany, demonstrating the two governments' mutual interests, and offering collaboration would gain France concessions. In 1940, the leaders in Vichy hoped to gain real benefits for France, a reduction in the burden of occupation costs, for example, or the return of the POWs; after the war they claimed to have at least spared France the worst, "Polandization." However, work by Robert Paxton, Michael Marrus, Jean-Pierre Azéma, and André Kaspi has decisively dismissed the assertions of leaders like Pétain and Laval that they softened the blows or acted as a shield to protect France. Comparing France not to Poland, as German treatment of occupied areas varied from east to west, but to such other western occupied countries as Belgium, Denmark, and the Netherlands, historians have found that France gained no significant benefit from having a collaborationist government.

Material Conditions and Children's Lives in Wartime France

Children's lives were profoundly marked by the material conditions that Vichy hoped but failed to ameliorate. To start with, Vichy proved unable to spare France the heavy human toll taken by the German occupation. Germany captured nearly two million soldiers during the Battle of France, the largest number ever captured in such a short period of time.[22] After the initial chaos of the summer of 1940 subsided, the Germans began transferring French POWs to Germany under the terms of the armistice. It had always been part of Germany's plan to use POWs to remedy its own labor shortages without mobilizing German women's labor. Germany put 95 percent of the 1.6 million French POWs to work in agriculture and industry. Leaders at Vichy claimed they would get the POWs home through continuing negotiation with Germany. Laval initially pressed Germany to return the POWs, promising that French people would express their gratitude by volunteering to work in Germany. But German leaders had no desire to exchange not only a labor force but also a potential fighting force for the dubious promise of voluntary French labor.[23]

Eventually not even POWs provided enough manpower to remedy German labor shortages, causing Germany to institute forced labor across occupied Europe. Vichy only delayed the imposition of forced labor in France for several months. By war's end, France had provided proportionally as many POWs and forced laborers as Belgium or the Netherlands.[24] The human toll hit children through the loss of fathers and other older male friends and relatives.

The costs of the German occupation of France went beyond the human drain and heavy occupation payments. Germany treated France as a source of booty to feed the German war machine, requisitioning massive amounts of agricultural and industrial production and purchasing more with inflated marks. A rich agricultural producer, France proved to be a valuable prize. The German delegate to the Armistice Commission at Wiesbaden, Franz Richard Hemmen, admitted, "No other European country contributes nearly as high a balance for German armaments and even goods imports."[25]

At least some children were aware of the connection between the occupation and shortages. One group of elementary school students, assigned to write an essay about clothing in 1943, explained clothing shortages: "When the Germans arrived in France, they bought clothing and shoes, because they decided that one mark was worth twenty francs, and they sent all that stuff to their families in Germany, and we, poor French people, we have to deprive ourselves for these nice gentlemen. They, the Germans, are well dressed and have good shoes, we French people have to wear mended and ragged clothing."[26] These children do not write about the lack of clothing in terms of frustrated personal desires for particular items but interpret the issue in childlike political terms, as us against them. The German team wins by cheating the French. The children do not point at German policies but at individual German soldiers who, in their view, bought things for their families. The correctly noted currency exchange rate suggests a bit of tutoring by the instructor.

In addition to the lack of clothing, food shortages created by German demands for French agricultural production were a constant, nearly universal, and exhausting feature of life in France during the war. By the time they left, the German occupiers had taken 2.4 million metric tons of wheat, 891,000 metric tons of meat, and 1.4 million hectoliters of milk.[27] In fact, caloric intake in France during the war was lower than in all of Western Europe except Italy, remarkable given that France had been Western Europe's richest agricultural producer. Food shortages were worst in large cities and in the Midi region of the south. The northern half of France had always produced most of France's food, including some 70 percent of the wheat, 85 percent of the butter, 65 percent of the beef, and all the sugar. Southern France produced three-fourths of France's wine; however, wine was of marginal value to southerners under the circumstances.[28]

An obsession with food took hold of people of all ages. Micheline Bood, fifteen years old in 1941, wrote in her diary for 17 January 1941, "I was weighed on Tuesday and I've lost 2.5 kilos since October. Restrictions! I filched a jar of jelly . . . I never would have done that before because I don't like jelly, but nowadays we eat so poorly that I'm always hungry."[29] Interestingly, Micheline reported as new not her willingness to pilfer but her willingness to eat something she did not like. Janine Roux, thirteen, wrote an essay in June 1941 on how people in her town got by. "As soon as it rains, you can see nearly all the people from the village go outside looking for snails. Some families eat snails for three straight days."[30]

On an individual basis, people could mitigate the shortages if they had relatives in the countryside, extra cash, or access to provisions that could be traded on the black market. Even with access to the black market, Paxton estimates that caloric intake in France averaged 1,500 calories a day (a weight-losing goal today). One report in 1945 estimated that in the winter of 1942–43, official rations dropped below 1,200 calories a day. Bread rations varied from 275 to 350 grams a day. In September 1940, meat rations were set at 360 grams a week (about 13 ounces), but from January 1942 on they averaged 120 to 180 grams (4 to 6 ounces) a week.[31] Ration entitlements did not necessarily guarantee availability, as one group of schoolchildren in Tournissan explained. In December 1943, even though children six to thirteen had the right to a quarter liter of milk a day, the milk was simply not available. "The dairyman brings 20 to 30 li-

ters of milk every other day, but it would take 100 liters at least to fill all
the official rations. So, children over six years old have not had a single
drop of milk since the month of August."[32]

In addition to food shortages, France suffered shortages of fuel, rubber,
and metals. In response, the government established a Ministry of Provisioning (Ravitaillement) with the power to issue regulations and to requi-
sition food and other goods for distribution. Food rationing began gradually, starting on 3 July 1940 with a regulation limiting to one the number
of lumps of sugar restaurants and cafés could serve with beverages. On 2
August 1940 rationing extended to noodles, rice, and soap, and by October nearly everything, including meat and bread, was rationed.[33]

A critical aspect of the World War II experience, food rationing clearly
had a differential impact on children. The Ministry of Provisioning divided France's population based on a combination of age and utility. For
rationing purposes, individuals fell into one of eight categories, E for children under three; J1, J2, and J3 covered juveniles ages four to twenty; A
for adults twenty-one to seventy; T for workers in strenuous jobs (a category eventually extended to pregnant and nursing mothers); C for farmers; V for those over seventy.

Shortages and the complicated rationing system rendered shopping for
food an all-consuming daily challenge. Several scholars have written about
the impact of shortages on women in France, who primarily faced that
challenge.[34] Older children at least were aware of the hardships rationing
and shortages posed for their families. Raymond Ruffin, writing in November 1941, described what his mother went through to obtain food for
the family. "Up at 5:00 a.m., she left an hour later for the local markets,
going off to feed the line of housewives standing in front of still empty
stalls . . . The morning passed like that, in interminable hours of standing
around in front of shops . . . In the afternoon, she had to start all over
again."[35]

Under the circumstances, new kinds of personal qualities gained value,
subtly changing moral calculations in ways that many adolescents keenly
sensed. The French devised a term for the combination of ways of cop-
ing with the hardships: the *"système D."* The D stands for the verb *se
débrouiller,* which means to manage, to get by. The noun *débrouillardise*
translates as "smartness, resourcefulness," clarifying the subtext of the
"système D, which implied not hard work to get by so much as wiliness,
clever resourcefulness.[36] The *système D* thus covered a wide variety of cop-
ing mechanisms, from legal means—receiving packages from relatives in

the countryside, growing food in small plots, raising animals on balconies in the city—to illegal means, such as trading ration tickets on a friendly basis, selling ration tickets, making trips out to the countryside to buy directly from farmers, and, naturally, having recourse to the black market, which eventually permeated the entire French economy. The black market involved both large-scale distributors and small shopkeepers. The Ministry of Provisioning's regulations and inspectors could hardly keep up. To discourage both trade and theft of ration coupons, the ministry made it illegal to use another person's ration cards or tickets. Inspectors visited food shops, testing milk for the addition of water, for example. The police also routinely stopped arriving passengers in urban train stations to inspect bags for food, and stopped people out in the countryside who looked suspicious. Almost everyone over a certain age who lived in wartime France was involved in the *système D;* for the most part lack of opportunity more than lack of desire kept some people out: those with no goods to exchange, no family in the country, or low disposable incomes. Thus a huge number of people, under normal circumstances law-abiding citizens, became involved in activities that blurred the line between legal and illegal. The combination of new infractions and vigorous policing contributed its share to the rising crime statistics during and immediately after the war.

However, state policy indirectly encouraged such infractions. The Ministry of Provisioning set rations below minimal caloric needs, based on the hypocritical assumption that everyone would be able to supplement rations with nonrationed goods, which begs interpretation as a cynical wink at the black market. Further indicating that government turned a blind eye to black market *consumers,* the law of 15 March 1942, which penalized rationing infractions with penalties of two to ten years and 2,000 to 10,000 francs, stated: "Not subject to the dispositions of the present law are infractions committed solely for the direct satisfaction of the personal or family needs of the delinquents."[37] The 15 March 1942 law directed attention to providers and away from consumers, acknowledging the recourse many families had to the black market. The increasing fines courts imposed on black market infractions committed by sellers, in the thousands of francs and higher compared with fines for other infractions that hovered in the 16-to-50-franc range, signaled an attempt to crack down on black market profiteers.

Brauner's immediate postwar study of children noted that the *système D* implicated even young children. Family members who went off to the countryside in search of food returned home and recounted with pride their successful fraud. "Children were mixed up in these daily lies. Trickery had become a necessity, deception a merit."[38] Not surprisingly, older children and especially adolescents were hardly immune to the temptations the black market presented, and were further encouraged to partake, even if their parents forbade it, by their keen eye for adult hypocrisy. Roger-Fernand's play *Les J3*, named after the rationing category for adolescents, satirizes adult doublespeak about the black market.

> *The Principal:* Today's youth knows no law other than that of its own pleasure . . . that's all there is.
>
> *Mr. Lany:* Have we given birth to monsters? . . . But you, as Principal, still must have some authority over these young people?
>
> *The Principal:* In theory, yes. In fact, none . . . Look, Mr. Lany, what we've come to as the year 2000 approaches . . . Can you imagine, just yesterday my own son said to me, "If you let Barbarin leave the school grounds on Sunday, he'll bring you back a ham and a case of champagne . . ." Does that surprise you?
>
> *Mr. Lany:* Not at all. Gabriel offered me a fur-lined jacket and some chocolate in exchange for a liter of 90-proof alcohol. And I would have to pay 5,000 francs on top of that.
>
> *The Principal:* What did you do?
>
> *Mr. Lany:* And you, about the ham?
>
> *The Principal (with a gesture of helplessness):* What do you think?
>
> *Mr. Lany (same gesture):* Me too![39]

While everyone suffered from food shortages, their physiological impact differed with age. Ironically, some of the period's dietary restrictions proved beneficial to adults. For example, the limits on wine consumption greatly reduced the incidence of alcoholism. However, dietary restrictions were anything but benign for developing children and adolescents. A 1942 study of five urban industrial centers in the unoccupied zone found that the average weight of both boys and girls was anywhere from 1 to 7 kilograms lower, depending on age, than it had been in 1938. Similarly, boys were found to be 1 to 5 centimeters shorter on average and girls 1.5 to 2 centimeters shorter than the 1938 averages.[40] Widespread weight loss among developing children is a clear sign of undernourishment. In Paris the situation may have been worse. Already in June 1941, a study of students aged fourteen to sixteen found that 20 percent were developing normally and gaining weight, 60 percent were stable, and 20 percent had lost weight.[41] A 1943 study of children in Montpellier revealed that over half exhibited vitamin A deficiencies.[42] Adolescents suffered more from food restrictions, given their high nutritional requirements, than the rest of the population. Just after the war, the Red Cross, based on a study by the National Hygiene Institute, found that the group showing the most signs of malnutrition was that of adolescents aged thirteen to twenty-one.[43]

Thus, although the Ministry of Provisioning attempted to mitigate food shortages for children, their developing bodies suffered disproportionate effects. Writings both during and since the war express the resulting obsession with food. For example, in July 1942 a newspaper posed a question to its young readers that would normally evoke a fantastic response. "If the fairies granted you one wish, what would you ask for and why?" But in this case, a schoolgirl from the Nord responded, "Never to be hungry . . . Already when I have not eaten and I'm hungry, it hurts, but to die of hunger must be terrible."[44] A question about fairies and wishes in this instance evoked thoughts of starvation.

Poor nutrition has a serious impact not just on children's physical health but also on their mental development. Hunger reduces attention span and impedes learning, and at the limit can have a permanent effect on intellectual development. At first, Vichy's desire to create a stronger, healthier population led it to impose a greater emphasis on physical education in the schools, to mold "a strong youth, healthy in mind and body."[45] Notwithstanding Vichy's goals for the educational system, schools in France were eventually forced to adjust to the effects of fatigue and poor nutrition on their students. In November 1941, the Ministry of Education shortened the school day by one hour and lowered physical educational requirements. In March 1942, Minister of Education Jérôme Carcopino issued a circular to all teachers urging them to avoid overtaxing the children, many of whom suffered from lack of food and heat. He recommended further shortening the school day and adopting less strenuous exercises.[46]

In addition to shortages, the economic situation created a serious wage-price gap for working-class families. German requisitions and mass purchases using overvalued marks created inexorable inflationary pressures that Vichy could not contain. The black market thwarted the government's ability to enforce controls, leading to price increases of 200 percent and more during the occupation. At the same time, Vichy maintained tight control over wages and deliberately kept them low. Already in 1942 a German study noted that prices had risen 70 percent since the beginning of the war but wages had risen only 30 percent, and this gap widened every year.[47] Alfred Sauvy, prominent French economist and demographer, calculated the cost of food sufficient to cover basic nutritional needs as a percentage of average family income during the war. For a couple without children, food took up 95 percent of an average family income if the wife was not employed but 55 percent if she was. Children under six received additional rations, but if the family included two children over the age of six, with two salaries food took up 91 percent of an average family income; with only one salary, it took up 126 percent.[48] Working-class families, with wages frozen and unions banished, were the hardest hit. One group of children expressed an awareness of the differential hardships. The school-children of Tournissan wrote: "For the four years that our country has been suffering, food for people and livestock, clothing, shoes, transportation, tools, wood for heating, lighting, all are very expensive. But the poor workers only earn very sorry wages and cannot manage to pay all their debts."[49] As Chapter 3 highlights, nearly all minors arrested during the war came from working-class families.

For nearly everyone, survival required the entire family's effort. The difficulties families faced in making ends meet prompted many married women either to work outside the home or to take in work like laundry and sewing. In addition, hundreds of thousands of wives had to cope with their husbands' absence. My research shows some 800,000 prisoner-of-war wives, about 600,000 of them with children, had to take charge of their household for up to five years. Over half of the prisoners' wives in my study worked for wages, another 30 percent took over a family shop or farm.[50] In addition, a great many of the adolescents who did not continue past primary school also had to contribute financially to their household. While working for wages benefited their families, it also presented the adolescents with many temptations and opportunities for theft, as court records clarify.

As just mentioned, approximately 600,000 of the French soldiers captured in June 1940 and transferred to German POW camps were fathers. Their captivity increased the material hardships for most prisoners' wives and had a direct impact on their children as well. Interviews and correspondence with former prisoners' wives revealed that while most of the women report having had no serious problems with their children, a significant number of women felt their children had been more anxious, fearful, or depressed during the war. Still, only one of the nearly seventy-five former POW wives with whom I corresponded in the mid-1980s reported that her son had suffered severe psychological disturbances. Young children, some of whom had no prewar memories of their fathers, had a hard time comprehending why their fathers were gone and what it meant to be a prisoner of war. Older children could correspond with their fathers, and they also contributed items to send in care packages. Although some mothers felt this made the absent father more real to their children, other mothers noticed growing resentment in children regularly asked to sacrifice their own goodies. However, most children adjusted to the long absence in a variety of ways. Prisoners' wives reported that the most difficult period for children was the period just after the father returned. Family relationships constructed over a period of up to five years without the father at home had to be renegotiated. Older adolescent sons seemed to have the most trouble accepting what some of them considered intrusive authority figures.[51]

The Work of Children: Schooling and the Vichy Regime

Children from age six to about age fourteen attended school during the war, but in addition to temporary interruptions in June 1940 and again over the summer of 1944, France's public schools underwent many changes. The French State at Vichy had a domestic program that revolved around a renunciation of the Third Republic and all it had stood for, democracy, individualism, liberalism, capitalism, and egalitarianism. Vichy was hardly monolithic, and various factions continually clashed; nonetheless, more traditional, Catholic conservatives like Georges Lamirand and Paul de la Porte du Theil controlled Vichy's youth and education policies. They believed France suffered not just from having the wrong political system but also from what that system had created: a population rendered soft by a too-easy life, accustomed to too much leisure, debilitated by drink and dissolute activities like dancing, jazz, and movies. Conservatives considered this factor critical in explaining the debacle of 1940. Impressionable children and adolescents represented the best hope for reshaping national values, and France's youth ranked high on Pétain's list of priorities. In a December 1940 "Message to Youth," Pétain explained: "The unwholesome atmosphere your elders grew up in slackened their energies, weakened their courage . . . You who have committed yourselves from the youngest age to take the steep paths, you will learn to prefer the joy of difficulties overcome to easy pleasures."[52] A children's magazine summarized Pétain's 1941 "back to school" speech to children at an elementary school in Perigny: "After having told you many times he was counting on you to 'rebuild,' the Marshal asked you today to go to the head of a great campaign of loyalty and tenacity he is launching among the schoolchildren of France."[53]

Through the public schools, the French State had direct and sure access to a very large proportion of France's children. Not surprisingly, Vichy quickly directed its attention to reforming public schools. Conservative educational thinkers, such as Albert Rivaud, René Benjamin, Abel Bonnard, and Alexis Carrel, agreed with Pétain. Although they had the Third Republic to thank for France's national network of public elementary schools, conservatives surrounding Pétain blamed the public schools for corrupting France's youth. Their goal was to emphasize traditional morality, obedience, hierarchy, and respect for authority, to restore the Catholic church's influence, to counteract secularism, and especially to inspire reverence for Pétain. As one historian of education, Jean-Michel Barreau, explains, "Schools under the Vichy government were 'Marshal, here we are' schools where children in classrooms sang, 'Before you, savior of France, we, your boys, swear to serve and to follow in your footsteps.'"[54]

Jacques Chevalier, minister of national education from December 1940 until February 1941, added "duties to God" to the moral instruction required in public elementary schools. Jérôme Carcopino, his successor, set aside free time in the school day for children who wished to receive religious instruction.[55] The Ministry of Education also revised school manuals and purged certain texts.[56] According to historian Gilles Ragache, some twenty instructional manuals were stricken from the lists, including six history books. The criteria for exclusion included unfavorable treatment of Germany and, ironically, the promotion of pacifism. Ragache notes that while French texts directed at children celebrated the glories of the French race and denigrated colonial peoples, such representations hardly differed from those in the prewar era. In contrast, anti-Semitism surged in Vichy-approved publications intended for young children, including explicit and even violent attacks on Jews.[57]

Vichy's education reforms involved both the attempt, with dubious success, to inculcate its values, and a more successful attempt to remove certain people from the education system. Vichy leaders blamed Third Republic schoolteachers for instilling such values as secularism, free thought, a cult of science, and faith in progress, not to mention republicanism and pacifism, all of which had supposedly laid the groundwork for the 1940 defeat. Thus Vichy from the start conducted a strongly repressive policy against public schools and especially against teachers.

One of Vichy's earliest laws, that of 17 July 1940, allowed the state to fire any civil servant considered to be an "element of disorder."[58] Since France's education system was entirely administered by the national government, all teachers were civil servants. While the law was directed against all state employees, teachers—especially primary schoolteachers— bore the brunt of the resulting purge. In another policy directed against public schoolteachers, enacted on 18 September 1940, Georges Ripert closed what he and others at Vichy considered hotbeds of republicanism, the normal schools created by the Third Republic to train schoolteachers.[59] Under a law closing all civil service jobs to Freemasons, some 1,328 teachers lost their jobs.[60] The Alibert anti-Semitic laws of 3 October 1940 purged some 1,100 Jewish teachers.[61] Schoolteachers who remained on the job were required to sign a declaration that they were neither Jewish nor Freemasons, which some of them found demoralizing.[62] Simone de Beauvoir describes returning after the exodus to her school in Paris in the fall of 1940. "At the Camille Sée lycée, as at every lycée, they made me sign a paper affirming under oath that I was neither affiliated with Freemasonry nor Jewish; I found it repugnant to sign, but nobody refused to do it: most of my colleagues and I had no way to avoid it."[63] Marcel Ophuls's documentary *The Sorrow and the Pity* included an interview with a schoolteacher and a school librarian in Clermont-Ferrand, who claimed they had tried to find private tutoring for fired Jewish colleagues. Ophuls asked, "Ultimately you could have offered a collective resignation from the lycée, couldn't you?" The response: "Well, that was out of the question. You don't have any understanding of teachers . . . collective resignation, come on!"[64] Giolitto describes just such a heroic refusal and resignation by Gustave Monod, inspector of the Academy of Paris.

Shortly after the purge of Jews, many female public schoolteachers were hit by another measure, the law of 11 October 1940 decreeing that married women whose husbands could support them were to be fired from public service jobs. A great deal of conservative anxiety focused in the interwar years on the evil effects of rising female employment rates on family life, on women, and on France's birth rate.[65] Linda Clark's research highlights the fact that public service provided a fruitful avenue for many career-minded women in the interwar era, resulting in a fairly high percentage of women in this sector. Thus, although it only applied to the public and not the private sector, the 11 October 1940 law threatened a relatively high proportion of female employees, including and especially teachers.[66]

Vichy's attempt to reshape the public schools was thus primarily expressed by repressive attacks on teachers and certain institutions. Unfortunately, little evidence alludes to schoolchildren's reactions to Vichy's exclusionary policies against teachers. One schoolmistress described how Fanny Salmon, a Jewish schoolteacher fired in 1940 (who eventually died at Auschwitz-Birkenau), in the midst of her personal distress, consoled a young child in tears.[67]

Despite the fact that only true conservative allies ran the National Education Ministry, the deep distrust Vichy leaders felt for an institution so closely affiliated with the Third Republic led to a demotion of National Education's status within the central corridors of power at Vichy. This would have interesting if unintended repercussions on the development of policies directed at delinquent youth.

Schools and teachers were attacked by more than Vichy conservatives. Notwithstanding its prochild rhetoric, Vichy could not shield France's youth in schools from the harsh realities of war, any more than it shielded the rest of France. A postwar study produced for the United Nations Educational, Scientific, and Cultural Organization (UNESCO) claims that in France, 1,500 elementary schools and 82 secondary schools were destroyed or badly damaged during the war.[68]

Adolescents after Schooling: Vichy's Youth Initiatives

Despite the availability of public schools as a vehicle to reach children, their impact was limited because, by law, children attended school only until age fourteen. Only 5 to 7 percent of French schoolchildren attended secondary school.[69] If they could, given the high rates of unemployment, many young people went to work for wages after primary school, as agricultural laborers, in small shops, in apprenticeships for skilled trades if they were lucky, in factories, and in domestic service.

To extend socialization and adult supervision beyond the school years, Vichy both created and encouraged the creation of certain kinds of youth movements for boys. Some people at Vichy hoped to create a single, unified youth movement like Germany's Hitler Youth, but Vichy's secretary general for youth, Georges Lamirand, could not overcome the opposition of both France's Catholic church, unwilling to allow its youth groups to be integrated into other movements, and the German occupying authorities, wary of regimenting France's youth.[70]

Lamirand's main accomplishment, the Chantiers de la jeunesse, was set up quickly by La Porte du Theil to try to capture the army class of 1940. A law of 31 July 1940 relieved all young men who would normally have reported for duty on 8 and 9 June 1940 of their military obligations but required them to spend six months in a youth group that eventually became the Chantiers de la jeunesse. In the unoccupied zone only, all twenty-year-old men were required to serve at first six then, as of January 1941, eight months in the Chantiers, which combined elements of an army boot camp and scouting. One-fourth of a young man's time in the Chantiers would be spent in physical education, one-fourth in professional training. For the remaining half of the time, men in the Chantiers undertook a variety of locally determined public works projects, such as building roads and helping with harvests. The young men lived in rural camps, their days starting with flag ceremonies and other rituals, their evenings spent singing at campfires.[71]

However, the Chantiers only took twenty-year-old men, leaving open the question of what to do with boys in the six years between leaving primary school and joining the Chantiers. Henri Dhavernas, a finance inspector, created and led the second Vichy-sponsored youth movement, the Compagnons de la jeunesse. Dhavernas hoped to attract unemployed youth, no longer in school but not old enough for the Chantiers, to a movement that included a mixture of military and scouting activities modeled on the Chantiers program. The Compagnons were similarly organized in companies and undertook public works projects in their local areas. Unlike the Chantiers, joining the Compagnons was voluntary. Through hard work combined with elaborate rituals and ceremonies, both the Chantiers and the Compagnons endeavored to virilize boys and young men, and to inculcate the virtues preached by Vichy, obedience, hierarchy, respect for authority, patriotism, and strength.[72] Estimates of the number of boys who joined the Compagnons range from 25,000 to 33,000.[73]

Vichy directed another, little-known initiative at adolescents who no longer attended school. Adolescent unemployment was high, and many young people were not adequately trained for adult occupations. In 1940, the secretary-general of youth began opening up Youth Centers (Centres de jeunesse). These residential centers provided occupational training and apprenticeships for unemployed youth. In this case, for once, "youth" referred to both boys and girls. The residents spent their first month in orientation, the next six months completing apprenticeships in six different occupations, and the last four months apprenticing in their chosen occupation. Boys were offered metallurgy, carpentry, and other artisanal and mechanical trades, while girls received training in trades considered suitable for women: sewing, dressmaking, making silk flowers for hats and clothing. Both sexes also received heavy daily doses of "moral education" during their stay. Children's Court judges placed some delinquent minors in the Youth Centers. By 1942 there were 600 Youth Centers in the northern zone.[74] According to children's book author René Duverne, by 1944 there were 897 centers with 85,000 clients. After the liberation, the Youth Commission was folded into National Education. The Youth Centers became Centers for Professional Training, and they abandoned moral education. Duverne, for one, regretted that shift, as well as the move away from broad recruitment of personnel to work at the centers in favor of hiring only people with formal diplomas. "As evil as it might be from certain points of view, can a government not have some good ideas and set up some happy innovations?"[75]

Alongside state-sponsored movements like the Chantiers, the Compagnons, and the Youth Centers, a wide variety of unofficial movements also flourished during the war. In the occupied zone the Germans allowed only overtly collaborationist groups, like Pierre Clementi's *Jeune front* and Marcel Déat's *Jeunesses nationales populaires,* or confessional groups for young people. So long as they stayed under the aegis of the church, young people could also join one of the many Catholic youth movements available to them, such as the Association catholique de la jeunesse française, or the Jeunesses ouvrières chrétiennes (JOC; Young Christian Workers), which spawned a similar group for young women, the JOCF, and parallel groups for other social milieux, the Jeunesses étudiantes, agricoles, maritimes, and indépendantes chrétiennes (JEC, JAC, JMC, and JIC). Protestant youth had the Conseil protestante de la jeunesse.[76] In addition, scouting groups attracted ever-increasing numbers during the occupation. One source estimated that the number of young people in scouting groups rose from 42,000 before the war to 120,000 by 1942 and 160,000 in 1944, dwarfing the 30,000 or so boys who joined the official Compagnons.[77] Typically, France had no national Boy Scout movement in the interwar years. Rather, a variety of scouting movements competed for membership, including the Eclaireurs de France, open to all boys, and the Fédération français des éclaireuses, open to all girls, the Eclaireurs unionistes for Protestant boys, Eclaireurs israélites for Jewish boys, and two Catholic scouting movements, the Scouts de France and the Guides de France.[78] In September 1940, under Vichy prodding, five scouting groups agreed to form a loose federation, Scoutisme française, led by General Lafond.[79] Interestingly, Lafond shielded the Jewish Eclaireurs israélites from Commissariat général aux questions juives leader Louis Darquier de Pellepoix's attack, but could not prevent its eventual disbanding in November 1941.[80]

Germany's Plan for France's Youth: Forced Labor

To remedy the labor shortage that persisted despite the use of huge numbers of POWs and forced laborers from Eastern Europe, Germany finally turned west to Belgium, the Netherlands, and France. Vichy briefly deflected Germany's imposition of forced labor with an ill-starred plan, the Relève. This agreement, announced in June 1942, set up an exchange. For every three skilled workers who volunteered to go to Germany, one French prisoner of war would be repatriated. Despite a massive propaganda campaign for the Relève, it was far from a resounding success, and in September 1942 France passed a law requiring all male workers eighteen to fifty and unmarried women twenty-one to thirty-five to register for a labor draft and began using coercion to keep up the quotas of "free laborers." The police raided entire factories and accompanied the workers to the trains. In February 1943, this ruse was ended when Vichy, under German pressure, enacted the Obligatory Labor Service (Service du travail obligatoire, or STO). Young unmarried men faced the greatest risk of being requisitioned. Eventually nearly 800,000 French laborers were forced to go to Germany, including many older adolescent boys.

The STO created a dilemma for older adolescent boys and young men. Should they go to Germany or try to evade the labor draft? Some significant number of men went into hiding to avoid the STO. Those who refused to go to Germany, the *réfractaires* (objectors), usually hid in rural areas, on farms or in the woods. Some of the men in hiding subsequently joined the maquis, armed bands of rural resisters.[81] Kedward points out that while not all *réfractaires* joined the maquis, young men already living outside the law provided a pool of potential recruits. The STO touched the lives not only of the workers but also of their entire families. Many people in France previously barely touched by the war and the occupation suddenly confronted a painful dilemma: they could illegally send their offspring into hiding, or send them to a war zone to produce goods for the enemy. When governments enforce policies that are widely hated, those who resist are often glamorized as popular heroes. By the end of 1943, widespread public hatred of the STO in France turned more and more people against the regime and increased public acceptance of certain kinds of illegality. Avoiding the labor draft was already illegal, hiding out in the woods and raiding farms for food were required to survive. Going from this to carrying out acts of sabotage became a smaller step than it had been. Thus, historian H. R. Kedward argues, the STO spawned a "cult of the outlaw" around the young men avoiding the labor draft; they took on an aura of mystery, and their outlaw status, because it expressed popular views, met widespread approval. The cult of the outlaw also legitimized the move to active resistance and inoculated many people in rural France against the authorities' attempt to portray young men in the maquis as terrorists.[82]

Youth Counterculture and the Limits of Vichy Propaganda

Long before the STO drove large numbers of young men to disobey the Vichy authorities, an urban youth counterculture sprang up in France. Although the behavior of these young people was rebellious and defiant, it was usually not, strictly speaking, illegal. Interestingly, however, the fascist and collaborationist press in Paris could not distinguish between the two types of behavior. The brunt of the growing frustration over the failure of youth policies thus fell on a group called the *zazous,* connected to the swing jazz movement in France.

Unexpectedly, after France's defeat in 1940, the small audience for jazz in France underwent explosive growth. While there had been only a few jazz concerts a year in prewar Paris, the number increased to nineteen jazz concerts in Paris in the last quarter of 1940 and sixty-one Paris concerts in 1941. Radio Paris went from carrying 3 hours 50 minutes of jazz weekly in September 1940, to 24 hours a week in December 1941, to 35 hours 20 minutes of jazz a week in April 1941. The southern zone's Vichy-controlled Radio nationale went from 9 hours 15 minutes of jazz weekly in May 1941 to 38 hours 40 minutes by January 1942.[83] In addition to a number of big hits by such French swing artists as Johnny Hess and the internationally renowned Hot Club of France with Django Reinhardt and Stéphane Grappelli, Richard Pottier's film *Mademoiselle Swing* came out in June 1942.

The German occupation and the Vichy regime provided the context in which young swing admirers began to develop a sense of collective identity and a designation, the *zazous.* The term itself refers to Cab Calloway and the Cotton Club Orchestra's 1933 hit, "Zag Zuh Zag." A 1939 hit, "Je suis swing" (I am swing), sung by French swing star Johnny Hess, united the terms swing and zazou with the lyrics: "Je suis swing / Je suis swing / Za-zou, za-zou, za-zou, za-zouzé."[84]

The *zazous*, young men and women of seventeen or eighteen, engaged in behavior that rejected Vichy's moral order. Their appearance and clothing symbolically expressed their animosity to Vichy. Contrary to the clean-cut look favored in Vichy propaganda, the young men grew thin mustaches and wore long jackets and pants with big baggy knees and legs that tapered to narrow ankles over white socks, an outfit that flaunted the textile industry stipulation that clothing should use the least fabric possible. The young women wore short pleated skirts, blouses or jackets with large padded shoulders, and heavy, flat shoes, all of which defied the conservative, feminine look promoted by Vichy and most women's magazines at the time. Worse yet, in opposition to the desire for a healthier, "natural" look, the young women dyed their hair blond and used large quantities of makeup.[85] For both sexes, dark sunglasses and a "Chamberlain umbrella," nicknamed for former British prime minister Neville Chamberlain, functioned as the ultimate trademarks.[86] The rebellious youth also listened to jazz, music associated with degenerate American culture, spent time in cafés in the Latin Quarter or along the Champs-Elysées (the Pam-Pam, the Soufflot, the Grand and Petit Cluny, the Colisée). *Zazous* developed their own ironic terms, such as calling the Paris Metropolitain subway system the *"Pétain mollit trop,"* which translates, "Pétain is getting too soft." The youth counterculture clearly repudiated both the moralism of Vichy and the austerity of the era.[87]

However, the *zazous'* cultural rejection of Vichy did not necessarily represent a resistance stance politically. Some *zazous* favored the Allies and de Gaulle, but for most, swing represented a youthful rebellion against parental authority, which included father figures like Pétain. As Rioux explains, many *zazous* seemed unaware of the political implications of their behavior, which she eventually labels resistance with a small *r*. A *zazou* who joined the Resistance would have had to stop dressing as a zazou to avoid attracting attention. Rioux concludes that being a *zazou* was "above all a way of amusing oneself in an era where the political regime sought rather to make youth aware of its responsibilities."[88]

Nevertheless, the collaborationist press complained bitterly about the *zazous*, whose defiance of clean living and hard work led *La Gerbe* journalist Pierre Ducrocq to offer his assistance to fellow theater critic André Castelot, who recommended a "public spanking on the Champs Elysées."[89] *Au Pilori* printed a poem in September 1942 that picked up on the same theme: "We are going to spank the *zazou*."[90] What collaborationists' obsession with spanking bad boys indicates about their own ambivalent sexuality I leave others to speculate. From the time of Pierre Laval's return to power in 1942, Vichy became increasingly authoritarian and repressive, a shift reflected in its youth policies. The press campaign against *zazous* peaked in 1942, at the moment of supreme frustration with the failures of the National Revolution. As Jean Bosc lamented, rather than fulfilling youth's mission of carrying the torch, *zazous* adopted an attitude of "indifference to the country's misery, of ferocious selfishness and a total incomprehension of the problems the defeat has posed to our consciences." He found their "extraordinary 'I don't give a damn' attitude" shocking.[91] The conservative press never made a distinction between delinquent youth and the *zazous,* who may have usefully deflected conservative attention.

In part the *zazous* constituted an easy target because they so visibly thumbed their noses at Vichy's values. The music they liked was not just American but African-American; the clothing was borrowed from Chicano zoot suits; their language and rhetoric teemed with anglicisms.[92] Many conservative critics, in a typical trope about degeneracy, saw something Jewish about the *zazous*. They were egotistical, unwholesome, lazy, idle, snobs, slackers, daddy's boys who cared nothing about family life. *Gringoire* celebrated the fact that the police, in July 1942, had put an end to the eccentricities of "perverted kids and idle little girls who haunt the cafés and brasseries of the Champs-Elysées and the Latin Quarter and who have adopted the slogan: A swing France in a *zazou* Europe."[93]

Even the German occupying authorities exhibited some curiosity about France's *zazous*. An article in *Pariser Zeitung,* a paper intended for Germans in France, reassured them that the *zazous* favored the English, Americans, and de Gaulle primarily out of a contrarian spirit. If England had occupied France, the article contended, the *zazous* would have been pro-German.[94]

Neither German nor Vichy nor Paris press hostility destroyed the *zazou* phenomenon. Rather, it died with the introduction in France of forced labor in Germany in late 1942 and early 1943. Making oneself noticeable could land a young man in a labor convoy to Germany. While some *zazous,* like young men of all persuasions, went into hiding and even joined the Resistance to avoid the labor draft, Rioux points out that as such, they were no longer, by definition, *zazous*. Not only did being a *zazou* imply a different dress code from the maquis, but joining the Resistance meant abandoning disinterested *zazou* cynicism.

The End of the Occupation

The Fate of Jewish Children

After the chaos of the Battle of France subsided, France enjoyed two years of relative calm so far as the war was concerned. However, 1942 represented a turn for the worse for conditions in France, with Pierre Laval's return to power in April 1942 and the deterioration of Germany's position in the war. The Allied invasion of North Africa in November 1942 set off a chain of events, starting with the German army crossing the demarcation line on 11 November to occupy France's southern zone (Italy also extended its zone to include the French Alps). Rather than taking total occupation to signal the end of any reasonable expectation for autonomy and dismantling itself, the leaders at Vichy accepted the total occupation, and most of southern France finally experienced a direct German presence. Faced with Allied successes, Germany took an increasingly hard line in France, intensifying its relentless demands for money, labor, and material, escalating its repression of resisters and persecution of Jews. France experienced new threats, intensified hardships, and deepening trauma. With total occupation, Germany extended the Final Solution to the entire country.

In October 1940, long before the Germans began to pressure France, Vichy had enacted its own anti-Semitic policies of isolation, exclusion, quotas, and expropriation known as the Alibert laws (Raphaël Alibert was minister of justice at the time). While the Alibert laws were not equivalent to extermination, ultimately the fact that the French State had conducted a census of Jews living in France, revoked French citizenship granted to immigrant Jews as far back as the 1920s, and rounded up "foreign" Jews in camps made it easier for the Nazis to carry out the Final Solution when they turned to France. Furthermore, the persecutions of the early years, while less drastic, took a heavy toll on Jewish families. The businesses and other property lost to Aryanization and the firings required by quotas deprived many families of their livelihood. Jewish children and adolescents found themselves barred from public parks, movie theaters, and, eventually, schools. Official anti-Semitism made the open public expression of anti-Semitism widespread and acceptable.

Non-Jewish children noticed the racism directed against their schoolmates. Raymond Ruffin, who entered secondary school during the war, discovered that one of his friends was Jewish when she was refused entry to a public swimming pool. "I don't know what to say, I stand there, stunned. I look at her, her delicate face tenses . . . With a sudden irrational impulse, I stand up and embrace her on her two cheeks, as we always did whenever we met. I probably should not have done that, because this time she really starts to cry. I stand there stupidly, crushed by her sorrow, too awkward to know how to console her."[95]

On 7 June 1942 the Germans signaled their shift to a more radical racist policy with the imposition in the occupied zone of the Jewish star of David. Maurice, a Jewish boy, credits both his mother and his entire local community for subverting the humiliating intent of the yellow star he and his family were required to wear. Maurice remembers his mother sewing the star on his school jacket: "The star stood out marvelously. I never felt it was something humiliating, rather like a kind of decoration I was the only one who got to wear in my class. The children at school never treated me like a 'dirty Jew.'"[96]

However, Maurice's experience, while not unique, was hardly universal. Other Jewish children faced intensified prejudice rather than understanding and compassion. Lazare, a schoolboy of eight, admits he was a difficult child, but says the yellow star made life miserable for him. "During every recess, every time we left the classroom, I was insulted; I did not put up with it, I fought to the death . . . I was subjected to harassment by the teachers, volleys of slaps . . . Fortunately I was always a sturdy kid. None of them ever made any humane gestures. If someone called me a 'dirty Jew' I did not put up with it, I would land on him."[97] Raphael had similar experiences, except that he was too small to defend himself when the other children attacked him at recess. "The teachers watched without intervening . . . but I made one friend, a true friend. I found him again after the war. He always defended me; he could not stand those 'all against one' gatherings, as he called them. And yet he was only eight years old."[98]

The Jewish star law was only part of a series of anti-Semitic measures that culminated in mass roundups and deportations. In the end some 75,000 Jews suffered deportation from France. Only 2,500 Jewish deportees survived. The sole benefit of the existence of Vichy was that Jews in the southern zone did not have to wear the yellow star.[99]

Laval's return in April 1942 coincided with the beginning of German pressure for Jewish deportations from France.[100] In the summer of 1942, in a dubious attempt to maintain French administrative autonomy and sovereignty, Laval insisted that French police carry out Nazi racial policies. He explained, "What I wish to see is that the French police, whose task has never been so hard, technically and morally, can in the full expression of its independence, which is the most striking sign of the sovereignty of its government, pursue with a fierce energy the struggle against all the enemies of French internal security."[101]

The stage was set for the first big roundup of Jews in Paris on 16 and 17 July 1942, targeted at 28,000 Jews in the Paris region. Some 7,000 people, including 4,000 children, were crammed for five days into a Paris sports stadium, the Vélodrome d'hiver, with no water, food, or sanitary arrangements. From there they were transferred to a French concentration camp in Drancy and eventually deported to concentration camps in the east. The police arrested a total of 12,884 Jews in this one operation. Still, approximately 16,000 Jews escaped arrest in this operation, owing to the assistance of neighbors, friends, concierges, and even some officials. Some French police officers, on an individual basis, forewarned threatened Jews.[102] Maurice recalls that "the morning of the big roundup, in July 1942, two police inspectors came over very early in the morning to warn us that they would be back looking for us an hour later."[103] A neighbor assisted Madeleine's family. "The morning of the big roundup at the Vel d'Hiv . . . (we had been warned by my dad's organization that the roundup was imminent) someone knocked on our door, heavy, repeated knocks . . . We had been told not to answer, to shut ourselves in, not to move. The neighbor across the hall came out and told the police that the husband had been taken to a camp and the wife and two children had left for relatives in the countryside a long time ago already." Their neighbor then brought provisions, and eventually helped them find a place to hide until they escaped to Switzerland.[104]

Although spared the wearing of the yellow star, Jews in the southern zone faced roundups and deportations beginning in August 1942. Despite the regime's idealization of youth, once the Final Solution began, Vichy did nothing to protect Jewish children who faced arrest, deportation, and death.[105] Serge Klarsfeld estimates that in 1942 alone, 1,032 children under the age of six, 2,557 children ages six to twelve, and 2,464 ages thirteen to seventeen were deported to Auschwitz from France. In fact, the German SS officer responsible for Jewish affairs in France, Theodore Dannecker, tried to exclude Jewish children from the early convoys, but the French authorities pushed the SS to deport the children. In Paris during the July 1942 roundups, French police under orders from Vichy arrested Jewish children the Germans had not requested, on the dubious grounds that arrest and deportation were preferable to separating children from their parents.[106] Marrus and Paxton soundly disproved the claim, advanced after the war, that Laval had attempted to help some 5,000 Jewish children escape France. On the contrary, Laval delayed exit visas to the United States for a group of Jewish children that had been arranged by the American Friends Service Committee, the Jewish Joint Distribution Committee, the YMCA, and the U.S. State Department. Including children in the convoys helped Laval to meet German quotas.[107]

Jewish parents tried desperately to protect their children. Many parents, making what historian Deborah Dwork rightly described as one of the hardest choices a parent faces, accepted their inability to protect their own children and sent them away into hiding, either with other families, in religious boarding schools, or with a rescue operation like the American Friends or the Oeuvre de secours aux enfants (OSE) that spirited children into Switzerland and other safe places.[108] With choices starker than those facing other children during the war, those Jewish children who survived did so only through a variety of deceptive practices: lying about their religion, using a false, less Jewish-sounding name, concealing their identity.

The deceptions generated by Nazi persecution continue to generate controversy fifty years after the event. Recently, two complicated cases have emerged that highlight the long-term repercussions of concealed identity. The first is former U.S. secretary of state Madeleine Albright's public discovery of her Jewish ancestry and of family members lost to the Holocaust, information her parents had carefully hidden. In the second case, the *New Yorker* magazine covered the furor over the supposed memoirs of Swiss clarinetist Binjamin Wilkomirski, who claims to have been a Jewish Holocaust survivor, an assertion recent fact checking called into serious doubt.[109] During the war, however, failure to deceive meant deportation for many Jewish children, virtually a death sentence for the youngest children. Because the Nazis saw no labor value in keeping young children and babies alive even temporarily, the Nazi selection process in the camps represented a nightmarish mirror image of the common social norm of protecting babies and young children. Of the Jewish children deported from the Indre-et-Loire Department, none of the twenty-nine children under the age of fourteen survived the war. Of the sixteen children between the ages of fifteen and seventeen deported from Tours, only eight returned.[110]

Even those Jewish children who avoided or survived the camps were profoundly marked by the war. After the war, psychologists who worked with adult Holocaust survivors developed the concept of survivor's guilt as an explanation for the ambiguous and even negative reactions to having survived. Jewish children experienced their own version of survivor's guilt. Many children experienced the sudden, usually inexplicable disappearance of one or both parents. The inability to truly comprehend the broader events left some children puzzled. Lazare, whose father was deported to Auschwitz, explains, "I knew he would not come back. But from the Liberation on, I listened every night to the list of survivors . . . if only, by chance . . . It was exhausting." Lazare points out that his father went to the police station when he was summoned because the police threatened reprisals on his family. His fate forewarned the rest of the family not to answer the door when the police later came for them. The rest of the family went into hiding and survived, but Lazare was left with a burden of guilt. "To a certain extent, he sacrificed himself so that we could live."[111]

Paul also recalls the day his father was summoned and went to the police station fearing reprisals against the family. "So in the end, it's intolerable, you see: he sacrificed himself for us!" His mother, devastated by her husband's departure, went into a deep depression and stopped eating and responding to her son, causing Paul to fear losing his mother as well. However, eventually she revived and arranged false papers and a hiding place on a farm for her son.[112] Some children expressed a projected version of survivor's guilt, hating, even blaming the deported parent. Madeline, ten when her father was deported, confesses, "I am going to admit something atrocious. I hold it against my father, I blame him for letting himself be deported without trying to escape his fate."[113] Rather than feeling anger, Samuel honestly admits, "I was ashamed to tell anyone that my dad had been deported. Before my eyes I could see images of those cattle cars, then the striped pajamas and shaved heads of the deportees, their grotesque appearance. I was ashamed." He told his friends that his father had been arrested for resistance and shot by the Germans.[114] Even when parents did return from the camps, deportation usually had serious long-term effects on postwar family life. Both of Raphael's parents had been deported but his father survived Auschwitz. However, after returning, his father "never opened his mouth, he never laughed any more, he did not speak to anyone. I was afraid of him, I no longer recognized him."[115]

In France, Jewish children had a critical impact on broader public opinion toward the Vichy regime. Widespread prewar anti-Semitism in France and the growing discussion in the 1930s of a so-called "Jewish problem" inured many people to the rights violations perpetrated under the October 1940 and January 1941 anti-Semitic laws. Many non-Jewish French people did not care about Vichy's policy of quotas, exclusion, and the expropriation of property, and some anti-Semites even applauded it. However, as France took part in the Final Solution, the cruelty of French police officers toward 'innocent' Jewish children began to break down the widespread apathy. Scenes of children being arrested or separated from their parents took place in the midst of French cities, profoundly disturbing quite a number of people in France. The roundups finally inspired a number of key religious leaders to criticize Vichy, including Monsignors Jules Saliège of Toulouse and Pierre Théas of Montauban, and Pastor Marc Boegner, leader of the Reformed Churches of France.[116]

For many ordinary, non-Jewish people, including children, the roundups proved to be a personal turning point. Monique D. wrote an essay after the war about her memory of the day when Jewish families living in her apartment building in Paris were arrested. "A half hour passed, filled with the heartbreaking cries of women and children being taken away, barely awake, hastily dressed, with only a light suitcase for everything . . . Children hanging on to their sobbing mothers' skirts, and the mothers imploring the immobile and powerless onlookers. A rumor spreads that one of the unhappy women threw herself out the fourth floor window with her baby."[117] All but two prefects' reports from across France mentioned that the public had been moved and shocked by such events.[118]

Adolescents Take Sides

As repression increased, the public, shocked by the arrests of Jews, by the total occupation of France, by the STO, increasingly distanced itself from the Vichy government. The Resistance increased in size and expanded from primarily small urban cells to a large rural movement—the maquis—that became an embryonic army conducting military-style operations. Not just adults but also children of all ages got involved in the Resistance, facing threats like arrest, deportation, and execution. The search for meaning, idealism, and taste for adventure common in adolescence made quite a number of teenagers receptive to Resistance propaganda. Furthermore, youth provided some measure of invisibility, as the authorities were less likely to suspect a ten-year-old child of being a resister and more likely to respond leniently. Some resistance groups therefore used children to carry messages. Brauner claims his experience in the Resistance demonstrated "the idealizing spirit of children, who were always the most zealous and the most reliable messengers." According to Brauner, because children and adolescents in the Resistance were motivated by political ideals, in spite of the strict illegality of their actions they were less likely to be "corrupted by black market habits and by individual *débrouillardise.*"[119]

Children whose parents were in the Resistance, even if they themselves were not, also felt the impact of involvement. According to Brauner, locked doors, secret meetings, forbidden printed tracts, and late-night comings and goings made it impossible to hide such activity from children; like Jewish children, they had to learn secrecy and deception. Laurence Doubinsky remembers that every unexpected knock on the door caused her father's face to go white. Some children were profoundly marked by the experience of witnessing the police arrest a parent or search their home.[120] One boy, who was five when the police searched his apartment, two years later continued to hide under the table every time anyone, friend or stranger, came to visit the family.[121] Also like Jewish children, many children of resisters learned to use false names, or were sent away to boarding schools or to live with rural families for their protection. Although he came across one young adolescent boy who could not give up habits of deception adopted during the war because his father was in the Resistance, Brauner argues that "in many cases, children undeniably profited in their personality development from their parents' resistance activity, because the children had faith in the 'just cause' their parents defended."[122]

Like adults, the vast majority of children and adolescents stayed aloof from political activism. However, the sympathies of some politically active young people ran not to the Resistance but to fascism and collaboration. In addition to joining youth fascist groups, many of which predated the war, procollaborationist adolescents and young men eventually had another option. To counter the threat of the Resistance, which the authorities labeled terrorism, Vichy created a paramilitary group. Joseph Darnand, a notorious fascist and collaborationist, formed and ran the Service d'Ordre légionnaire (SOL), originally as an offshoot of Vichy's organization for veterans, the Légion française des combattants. In 1943, the SOL became the Milice française (French Militia), commonly known as the Milice. As Darnand's star began to rise he became secretary general for the maintenance of order, and in January 1944 he replaced René Bousquet as minister of the interior. Like the German SS, the Milice was a political paramilitary police force designed to carry out the ideological convictions of its leader. Renowned for its brutality, the Milice took the lead in fighting the Resistance and pursuing Jews, using tactics that included torture and summary execution.

The Milice, which claimed in June 1943 to have 30,412 troops, was nearly universally hated.[123] Student Raymond Ruffin recounts in his journal an incident he witnessed in Paris in May 1944. A young mother with three children refused to get off an overcrowded bus. A group of Milice soldiers, verifying identification cards nearby, came to investigate the commotion and ordered the woman off the bus. One Milice soldier grabbed her arm to force her down, causing her to stumble and the baby to start crying. Her son then attacked the Milice soldier, who slapped the boy in return. By now, the crowd had grown furious and began yelling insults—"Bastards, Sell-Outs, Shits, Trash, Assassins!"—at the Milice soldier. Raymond's friend pointed out to him two French policemen across the street rapidly exiting the scene, leaving the Milice soldiers alone to face the angry crowd.[124]

What kind of older adolescents and young men chose to join the Milice? Louis Malle's film *Lacombe Lucien,* whose antihero joins the Milice after the local Resistance leader rejects him as too young, suggests that a random desire for action and excitement, combined with a certain level of chance, determined which side a young man might choose. (Obviously the Milice did not accept young women as fighters, whereas the Resistance, primarily its urban groups, welcomed both sexes. A small number of women even engaged in armed combat, as Paula Schwartz's research has uncovered.[125]) However, serious historical or sociological studies of the rank and file of the Milice have yet to be carried out. Shortly after the war a psychiatrist, Simone Marcus-Jeisler, examined Milice fighters. Her work reinforced one postwar myth of this widely detested group: that the Milice recruited thugs, delinquents, and psychopaths. Marcus-Jeisler reported that the young men she studied were "nearly all of weak character and below average intelligence, very suggestible, and found themselves caught up in the system. The Germans flattered their sadistic penchants or their greed. Or they were unstable, or again, paranoid . . . Very few sincere and normal young men accidentally found themselves in the pro-German ranks." The young Milice fighters, Marcus-Jeisler asserts, eventually realized the odious nature of the role they were called upon to fulfill, and many of them resigned or fled.[126]

The accuracy of these two versions, that members of the Milice were naive adventurers or psychopathic sadists, is difficult to gauge. However, one case from the Paris courts corresponds to the negative stereotype. In February 1942 the courts first heard the case of a seventeen-year-old boy charged with trafficking in ration cards. He was returned to his parents with probation. Later, however, the probation officer's report to the court raised serious concerns about his behavior, which left much to be desired. "Rude and insolent" with his family, he had hit his mother and tried to choke his stepfather. In July 1942 the police stopped him for insulting a woman in public—he was yelling "Go fuck yourself!" at her. But despite such continuing extreme behavior, at his followup hearing the court noted that he had signed an enlistment contract with the Milice, which was considered a positive step that allowed the court to leave him with his family on probation.[127]

Rising tension between the Resistance—empowered by Germany's falling fortunes and the Allies' rising ones—and the increasingly savage occupation and collaborationist forces took its toll. Historians have argued for years about whether the final phase of the war for France, the period from the Allied landing on 6 June 1944 through the liberation, can be called a civil war. Unquestionably the French people were severely divided, and in some but not all regions the court records suggest that the term *civil war* would not be an exaggeration. In the southern region around Nîmes, the Gard Department, records from 1945 show a sudden increase from January 1944 through the liberation in unsolved homicide cases. In the four years from 1940 to 1944, my search uncovered one murder case in the Gard, but in the four months from January to April 1944, case files included three attempted homicides, two murders, twenty-eight voluntary homicides, six death threats, seven cases of destruction of property, five explosions, and twelve unspecified "terrorist acts" in and around Nîmes.[128] This is especially surprising, since the total number of murders in all of France averaged about 220 a year before the war and dropped during the war to an average of 110 a year.[129] According to Robert Zaretsky, by the spring of 1944 the maquis had taken control of the northern and western areas of the Gard. The authorities lived under a state of siege.[130]

Children and Adolescents during the Liberation

The massive Allied bombing raid on the Renault factory in Boulogne-Billancourt on 3 March 1942 signaled an escalation of Allied air raids. Children's writings about the events of the final year of war in France reveal again how differently children experience and understand such events. Air raids aroused fear among adults, but they also divided adult opinion politically. For collaborationists and the few loyal pro-Vichy types left, the bombs confirmed Vichy's most rabid anti–Anglo-American propaganda. A surprising number of people, while not necessarily pro-Vichy, still believed that since France had signed the armistice in 1940, it was no longer involved in the war and therefore did not constitute a legitimate target for Allied attacks. Finally, many letter writers, including POWs worried about their families back in France, expressed both fear and hope, taking the bombs to signal the beginning of the end for Germany.[131]

Children experienced fear too, but many had no broader context of understanding. Thus, air raids emphasized children's general sense of powerlessness and dependency in an unpredictable and dangerous world. Bernadette, nine years old at the time, wrote in 1948, "The wartime memory that is still the most precise in my mind is that of the bombing of the Renault factory, the first one I went through." Her family lived nearby in Issy-les-Moulineaux. When the explosions began, she and her brother jumped into their parents' bed for protection. When the attack ended two hours later, "Stupefied by the infernal din, my eyes shut, tightly squeezing my little brother's hand while he cried and moaned, I fell asleep, with the noise still ringing in my head."[132]

German and Allied bombing caused wide-scale destruction in France during World War II.[133] Allied air raids in 1941 and 1942 had targeted precise strategic objectives, such as ports and factories producing war material for Germany. Allied bombing intensified in 1943 and began targeting train hubs, most of which were just outside of major cities. The American B-17 bombers, "flying fortresses," which flew at high altitude to avoid antiaircraft fire, were notoriously inaccurate and caused much of what the military today euphemistically labels "collateral damage."[134] Many of the bombs meant for the train hubs fell in crowded urban areas, and many civilians, including children, died in the raids, which explains the excess of civilian deaths in France, 360,000, over the 250,000 military deaths.[135] By the war's end, an estimated 1.3 million French children had been left homeless.[136]

However, in France as a whole, the situation varied dramatically from region to region, with some areas hardly touched by the fighting and destruction. Megan Koreman studied three towns in 1944 and 1945. One town, Saint-Flour, owing to geographic luck, avoided destruction and trauma because the Germans there simply packed up and left. The other two towns she studied suffered more directly from the final battles for France's liberation.[137]

The final phase of World War II began with the Allied invasion of France on the beaches of Normandy, D-Day, 6 June 1944. The fiftieth anniversary celebrations of D-Day reinforced the mythic portrayal of the events as heroic and liberating, the beginning of the end of Nazism. However, local populations paid a heavy price. Jill Sturdee presents a vivid picture of the terror the incessant Allied bombing produced in children who lived in target cities like Caen. She cites the diary of sixteen-year-old Janine Espiasse, "As I sit on a mattress in the cellar of the Petites Soeurs des pauvres convent, I begin here the account of the dreadful events of June 1944 . . . I can remember every single hour of anguish which we have already suffered. I await those to come."[138] The fiercest fighting in June was localized to the coastal areas. Sturdee points out that although the experience terrified adults and children equally, adults at least could comprehend the broader significance. Some adults considered liberation from German occupation sufficient to justify their suffering. Most young children, however, could not comprehend the broader significance of events that seemed to bring only total chaos and terror. As with the exodus in 1940, children's accounts highlight the assault on the senses, lending their versions an almost dreamlike quality. Jean-Paul Corbasson remembers the June 5 bombing that preceded D-Day: "The night before the 6 June and the morning were very noisy. I didn't go to school. Lots of people were queuing early at the baker's." As he walked across town, "houses were still standing on both sides of the street . . . Things jumped in flames from the window holes . . . these minutes remain today the most dramatic picture of war in the eyes of the nine-year-old I was."[139]

Once the attempt to repel the Allied landing failed, the German army retreated. Paris was liberated on 25 August 1944. In contrast to the fear and suffering evoked by children in Normandy during the Allied landing, when asked about the liberation, the Parisian children whom Brauner studied mostly described it in heroic, romantic, and celebratory terms. The final fight to liberate Paris in August was much less intense than the experience of Normandy in June 1944. While some fighting did take place in Paris, much of the action had a highly theatrical quality. Crowds of last-minute resisters participated in pulling up cobblestones, playacting in an old Paris script. Some children's accounts pick up on this atmosphere. Yvette K. wrote, "Everyone got involved . . . Men, women, children rushed in, carrying sand bags . . . They cut up trees, pulled up cobblestones. On every side barricades went up; the FFI [Free French] took up positions behind the barricades . . . they were not afraid. France's grandeur is all they wanted!"[140]

During the German retreat a number of bloody battles erupted between the Germans and the maquis. Some resistance attacks were countered with atrocities like the 10 June 1944 massacre of the people of Oradour-sur-Glane. German soldiers from the SS Das Reich division shot all of the men from the village, then herded the women and children into the local church, which they then barricaded and set on fire.[141] Across France the German retreat spawned similar if less well-known incidents, in towns like Maillé in Indre-et-Loire. When Jacqueline B., born in 1933, was assigned an essay after the war describing "a scene that struck you during the war or the Occupation," she wrote about the April 1944 reprisal in her Perigord town for a maquis attack on a German convoy. She was sick the day of the maquis action, and her friend Micheline came to visit. "I did not know when I embraced her at the end of her visit, that it would be a final adieu I was saying without realizing it." Several days later, German soldiers entered the town, took hostages, and burned down houses. "People were arrested. Micheline and her mom were taken prisoner. Micheline was burned to death, she was thirteen years old." Twenty-three people were killed.[142] Children were not spared the atrocities of the war, and sometimes they were even targeted.

In general, younger children in France during the war had difficulty making sense of events that surrounded them, communicating a child's-eye view of the world as chaotic, arbitrary, and incomprehensible. Some older children and adolescents better understood the broader context of the events. A number of observers by the end of the war noted that many older children seemed too mature for their age, having been forced to grow up quickly. Clearly children experienced the war differently from adults. But like adults, not all children and adolescents reacted in the same way to the war's conditions, owing to individual circumstances, family situations, developmental levels, and personalities. Some children became cynical and inured to suffering, some grew combative, some were fearful and anxious, some cynically enriched themselves, some risked their lives in the Resistance. And a very small but growing proportion of minors broke the law. Thus delinquency represented only one manifestation of the many and complicated ways children and adolescents reacted to the disruptions the war caused in their lives.

3

The Wartime Juvenile Crime Wave as Manifested in the Courts

Although every European country directly involved in World War II witnessed rising juvenile crime rates, France experienced an especially dramatic upsurge.[1] By 1942, the number of minors appearing in court was triple the prewar averages. In the 1930s, the number of minors appearing before juvenile courts each year hovered between 10,000 and 12,000. In 1937, 11,917 minors appeared in juvenile court. In spite of the disruption caused by the Battle of France, the number rose to 15,911 in 1940, and it peaked in 1942 at 34,751, a 192 percent increase from 1937.[2] A 1946 Justice Ministry report, explaining the increase, concluded: "Lack of education, of supervision, and of authority often results from the absence of fathers, either captive or laboring in Germany; the mother who takes over as head of the family does not have the necessary authority and, in many cases, the time she otherwise would to devote to her children, as she often must work outside the home."[3]

However, a number of facts cast doubt on that conclusion, universally shared at the time, which rested on assumptions about family roles rather than statistical studies. Most contemporary observers mentioned but did not emphasize the critical fact that the overwhelming percentage of juvenile trials involved petty theft. This was true before the war. In 1937 for example, 59 percent of all juvenile cases involved theft and only 79 of 11,917 cases involved serious crimes, defined as arson, rape, assault, murder, and grand theft. As the absolute number of juvenile cases increased in the 1940s, so did the proportion of cases involving theft. In the peak year, 1942, some 75 percent of all juvenile cases involved theft; only 56 juveniles were charged with serious crimes in that same year, fewer than in 1937. The fact that small-scale petty theft acted as the leading edge of juvenile crime, alone accounting for the overall increase, strongly suggests the importance of economic hardship, shortages, and the black market in driving both juvenile and adult crime statistics. Another highly revealing fact rarely mentioned in the voluminous writing on juvenile crime equally indicates the importance of economic factors—adult crime statistics followed an almost identical curve to juvenile crime statistics (see figure). Between 1937 and 1942, theft trials increased 267 percent for juveniles and 245 percent for adults (see table).[4] Rising adult crime rates could hardly be attributed to the absence of fathers.

More important than emotional disturbances resulting from absent fathers, wartime economic factors drew a greater number of young people into petty crime, existing studies indicate. For example, a study of recidivism in Lyons during the war concluded that the actual number of recidivists, who usually committed the more serious crimes, stayed the same during the war. In the context of nearly doubled juvenile cases, the recidivism rate actually declined from 8 to 4 percent.[5] The Lyons data again point away from deep-seated personality factors, which should have increased recidivism, and toward short-term economic factors.[6]

Confirming the importance of the material situation requires more detailed information about the circumstances surrounding the delinquent acts. Yet studies produced in the 1940s about juvenile crime are frustratingly vague about the actual offenses committed by young people. At the time, experts who studied delinquent youth had shifted their focus from the crime to the criminal. Consequently, the studies provide only general information about the category of the offense, leaving out details, for example in theft cases, about what had been stolen, or where, or how. Even information about the minor's background is spotty. The era's obsession with family structure, for example, led researchers to blur the distinctions between families separated by divorce, the death of a spouse, or war captivity; all were lumped together as "broken" families.[7]

In a 1994 review essay, sociologist Philippe Robert argued that, given the shortcomings of existing criminal statistics, scholars should undertake the slow, painstaking archival work needed to build our knowledge of smaller cohorts. He further urged those studying crime to go beyond the existing studies of penal institutions and their discursive structures and of professions like policing and the magistracy to focus on what he labels the "authors" of the behavior. Robert describes penal systems as an instrument, played more or less skillfully by the various parties.[8] For this study of juvenile courts in wartime France I undertook the two tasks Robert recommended.

Filling the gap in information about crime left by scholarly studies from

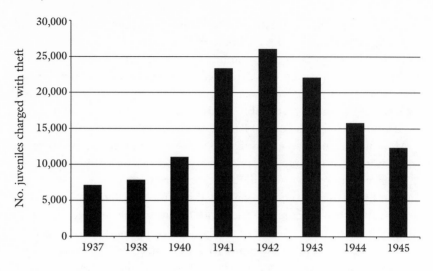

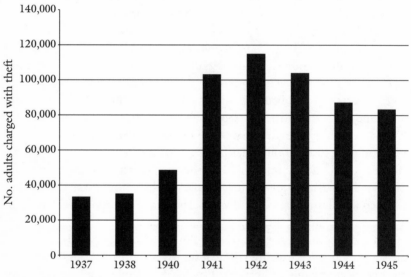

Juvenile and adult theft cases in the French courts, 1937–1945. Although the number of minors charged with theft varies from the number of adults by an order of magnitude, the two curves follow very similar patterns.

Murder and theft cases in the French courts, 1937–1947

Year	Adults		Juveniles	
	Murder	Theft	Murder	Theft
1937	225	33,237	8	7,088
1938	227	35,029	3	7,820
1940	121	48,481	2	11,003
1941	133	103,046	1	23,327
1942	102	114,905	4	26,035
1943	77	103,856	7	22,057
1944	73	87,090	3	15,754
1945	148	83,268	9	12,301
1946	272	102,853	23	20,704
1947	254	92,474	29	15,395

Source: Ministère de la Justice, *Compte-générale de l'administration de la justice civile et commerciale et de la justice criminelle: Années 1944 à 1947* (Melun: Imprimerie administrative, 1953), pp. xix, xx, xxiii.

the 1940s and the Justice Ministry's aggregate crime statistics required work in juvenile court records from several regions. A study of individual cases supplies more complete information about the kinds of offenses committed and the circumstances surrounding them. The detailed exploration of case files also opens a window onto the operation of the juvenile justice system, making possible an evaluation of such factors as race, national origin, gender, and the severity of the crime. Most important, court records reveal a great deal about the adolescents who found themselves in the courts, the families they came from, and how they, their families, and their communities responded to the difficult circumstances in which they found themselves. Such information, when combined with aggregate data, allows me to go beyond speculation in understanding individual motives and the overall crime statistics.

On the other side of the bench, court records also expose administrative and policy matters critical to this study. Did either the creation of a new government in 1940 or its demise in 1944 change the day-to-day court operations? Did the French police, the courts, or the German occupation authorities intensify the repression of crime, contributing to increased crime rates?[9] Wartime court cases document low-level German interactions with French courts, thus allowing for some generalizations about Germany's impact on the system.

Court Records from the Seine Department

Beginning in the Paris records generated by the Fifteenth Chamber, Department of the Seine, a region that includes all of Paris and its surrounding suburbs, I examined two kinds of documents, penalty registers (registres de peines) and case files. The penalty registers, bound, handwritten volumes, record, day by day, every case heard by the Fifteenth Chamber. Each volume, numbered by date, covers about one month. Every case description includes the names of the judges, prosecutors, other officials present, the lawyer or parents if present, and each person accused. The register notes each defendant's vital statistics: date of birth, profession, parents' names and addresses, the person with "civil responsibility" for the minor. Then follows a formulaic statement of the charges and minimal details about the actual crime. For example, a typical entry would read, "On 15 April 1942, in the city of Paris, John Doe fraudulently subtracted a bicycle to the prejudice of the lady Jane Roe. This constitutes the crime of theft, a violation of Penal Code Article X expressed in these terms," and here the law is restated.

The entries end with the court's decision. If the police or the investigating magistrate did not find enough evidence of guilt, the judges could declare the minor not guilty *(relax)*. If the investigation concluded that the minor was guilty, then the judge next pronounced on whether the minor acted with discretion. If the minor acted with discretion, then the judge convicted and sentenced *(condamné)* the minor to an attenuated penalty: prison, a fine and court costs, or both. The penalty could be suspended, which would also be noted. If the minor acted without discretion, then the judge acquitted the minor as acting without discretion under Article 66. The judge did not have to release the minor as in a simple acquittal, however, but could choose from a range of options. He could either return the minor to his or her parent(s), with or without probation, or he could place the minor with a charitable person or institution, specified by name, for example the Patronage des enfants et adolescents for boys or a Bon Pasteur home for girls. Judges could also send minors acquitted under Article 66 to a state-run institution for juvenile offenders, designated after 1927 a supervised education house *(maison d'education surveillée)* for boys or a preservation school for girls.

For the fifty-two months from the outbreak of fighting through the liberation of Paris, May 1940 through August 1944, the Fifteenth Chamber generated sixty-five registers containing some 100 to 300 cases each. The court clerks' daily tallies of judgments allow for a rough count of 13,500 judgments over that time period. Given this large number of cases, which were handwritten and difficult to decipher, I realized I could not generate a sample that would satisfy a statistician. Instead, I created a database of 667 cases that includes some from every one of the sixty-five registers for the war years, as well as several pre- and postwar registers. I consulted several registers from before and after the war so that I could compare court operations across time.[10]

While not randomly generated, my database of 667 cases reassuringly mirrors national statistics. For example, the gender breakdown, 80 percent boys and 20 percent girls, is consistent with Crémieux's wartime study of 2,964 delinquent minors, which found 85 percent were boys and 15 percent were girls.[11] The breakdown of charges also reflects national figures. Theft cases made up 72 percent of the total, which corresponds with the Justice Ministry report that 75 percent of all juvenile offenders were charged with theft.[12] Two additional wartime studies similarly reported 70 to 72 percent of the minors arrested were charged with theft.[13]

Information in Individual Case Files

I was able to supplement the general information compiled from the penalty registers with information gleaned from a different set of records, the actual case files. For the Fifteenth Chamber, Seine Department, only case files from 1943 are available. The Paris Departmental Archives decided to keep one year as a sample and destroyed all other case files for the rest of the war and occupation years. In comparison to the Seine's penalty registers, which contain only summary information, court case files include a huge amount of information about the minors, their families, and the circumstances of the crimes, arrests, and investigations. For the Seine Department, I compiled information from forty-six full case files.

The case files provide a complete written record of a minor's journey through the system. Starting with either a victim's initial complaint or the police arrest report, a dossier includes the police investigation report, the *procès verbal,* which in the French system becomes part of the official body of evidence. Police reports include testimony from victims, questioning of witnesses and of the accused minor, and confessions. A case file also includes material evidence, such as falsified ID cards, phony ration tickets, prostitute registration cards, Communist Party cards, even shards of metal from an explosion. Case files contain the investigating magistrate's records, which might involve a social worker's report, any medical or psychiatric reports, additional questioning of the parties involved, and questioning of and statements given by the parents or guardians, teachers, and even employers. Letters received from any of the parties, parents, victims, employers, teachers, and even occasionally pastors (I saw no letters from priests), also found their way into the files.

Under the 1912 law, the investigating magistrate was required to investigate not just the crime but also the minor's background. In most cases in Paris (67 percent) and nearly always in provincial courts, the investigating magistrate sent out a blank informational sheet *(bulletin de renseignement)* to be filled out by an appropriate person—most often the local police commissioner; sometimes, in small towns, the mayor (see sample in Appendix). These sheets posed a series of questions about the minor and his or her family—parents' names, ages, marital status, profession, income, rent, the harmony of the marriage, morality, alcohol consumption, ability to supervise the children adequately, local opinion of the family. The informational sheets included questions about the minors and their habits, friends with whom they spent time *(fréquentations)*, their schooling and work history. Questions also explored whether the minor had "bad tendencies" *(mauvais penchants)* or other signs of perversity, if she or he was capable of "improvement" *(amendement)*, and whether or not the parents wanted the child to be returned to them. The sheets ended with the category "Justified Opinion" *(Avis motivé)*, where the information about the minor and family was summarized in a sentence or two and a final recommendation was made about whether the minor should be returned to the parents, placed in a charitable institution, or sent to a supervised education house.

In the Seine Department, for one-third of the case files investigating magistrates supplemented informational sheets by ordering a social worker's report and even sometimes a medical-psychiatric examination. Judges relied on social workers from four private agencies in Paris: Moral Assistance to Youth (L'Aide morale de la jeunesse), Social Godmothers (Les Marraines sociales), Safeguarding Adolescence (Sauvegarde de l'adolescence), and the Social Service of Children in Moral Danger (Service social de l'enfance en danger moral, or SSE, founded by Olga Spitzer).[14] My forty-six case files include reports from three social workers (whose first names could not be ascertained), Miss Zwiller for Social Godmothers, Miss de Loustal for Moral Assistance, and Miss Demoisy for Safeguarding Adolescence. There are no reports in these files from an SSE social worker, in part because the SSE specialized in minors under thirteen. Since the

1912 law decriminalized all offenses committed by minors under thirteen, they generated no criminal case files.[15] The pediatric neuropsychiatrists discussed at length in Chapter 4 conducted most of the medical-psychiatric examinations.

Provincial Court Records

While approximately one of every four juvenile cases originated in the Seine Department, juvenile crime in the Paris region might have differed widely from other parts of France. The Seine Department, which was entirely occupied by Germany throughout the war, included Paris and its ring of large working-class and industrial suburbs. The Seine's urban population of about 2.8 million dwarfed that of every other large city in France. For adult and juvenile crime alike, the Paris area presented both more opportunities and more temptations; it also permitted more anonymity and invisibility. Extending my study to France in general thus required work in court records outside Paris. Based on available holdings, I chose three departments that contrasted in various ways with Paris, attempting to inject as much variety as possible into my research.[16] Fortunately, case files are available for the entire war period in the three provincial departments I visited: the Nord, which includes courts in Lille, Douai, and Cambrai; Indre-et-Loire, which includes courts in Chinon and Tours; and the Gard, which includes courts in Nîmes and Uzès. My provincial findings rest on 107 case files, 45 from the Nord, 34 from the Gard, and 28 from Indre-et-Loire.[17]

Several peculiarities made the Nord Department interesting for the purposes of this study. With one of France's heaviest concentrations of industry and mining, it was a densely populated region with a large urban area that had a higher than average number of juvenile cases. Unlike Paris, however, the Nord received special treatment during the war. While French administrative structures, including the courts, remained in place and answered to the French State at Vichy, the region's military command was detached from Paris and reattached to the German military command in Belgium, part of a German ploy to incite Flemish ethnic separatism.[18] Given the critical importance of the region's industrial output to the German war effort, the Germans maintained a heavy presence there from the start. Finally, incongruous military boundaries rendered the frontier between the Nord and Belgium more fluid, with Belgians entering France easily to work in French factories and vice versa.

The second provincial department, Indre-et-Loire, a region in France's heartland, presented several interesting factors. A major national railroad hub was located in Saint-Pierre-des-Corps, a suburb of the department's capital city of Tours. As a result, the area around Tours experienced very heavy bombing in 1940 and again in 1943–44. The demarcation line separating the occupied north from the unoccupied south of France cut through the department, dividing it into its own occupied and unoccupied zones. Stories of resisters and refugees secretly crossing the line, which bisected the famous chateau of Chenonceaux set atop arches spanning the Cher River, are legendary in the area. The department included a fairly large urban population in Tours and many small farming communities.

Finally, the Gard provided me with one department entirely in the southern, unoccupied zone. For two years the Gard experienced no German presence. The agricultural economy of this predominantly rural region centered almost entirely on winegrowing, so the food situation in the department ironically approached the misery of most cities, despite the Gard's rural nature. According to one resident, the inhabitants of Nîmes suffered from hunger even with storehouses "flooded with wine."[19] The Gard was also unusual in that it had a significant Protestant minority with a strongly anchored memory of historical persecution in France. Robert Zaretsky argues that the Protestants in the Gard distanced themselves from the Vichy regime more quickly than many people because they were offended by Vichy's intolerant Catholic rhetoric and practice. The region's Protestants also identified more readily with the local Jewish population when persecution began.[20] Even before the war, the Gard was home to an unusually large population of immigrants. The only cases involving gypsies in my database originated in the Gard.[21] After 1940, refugees from northern France and Belgium who left during the exodus of 1940 flooded into the region.

The fact that departments outside the Seine did not compile penalty registers with summary information about the charge and the court's decision prevented my collecting a large provincial sample for statistical comparisons. Thus my statistical generalizations—about what was stolen, the gender breakdown, and so on—rest primarily on Paris information, with only tentative extensions to the provinces. Fortunately, however, case files were constructed in the same way across the country, because the 1912 law required courts to collect background information on the minor's social milieu in all cases. Thus although there are fewer cases than from the penalty registers, each case file contains much more information than the penalty registers' summaries. The 107 case files from these three regions allowed for empirical comparisons and clarified how the regions outside the capital differed from Paris and from each other. As expected, the centralized national justice system varied in practice from place to place, shaped by the nature of the region and, during the war, the nature of the occupation in each area.

Three critical differences from Paris quickly emerged in the provincial court records. First, there were only two social workers' reports in the 107 provincial files. Most investigating magistrates contented themselves with the informational sheet filled out by a local official. Like case reports, the informational sheets include a great deal of information about the minor and his or her schooling and lifestyle, family background, rent, housing, income, and so on. But the answers are usually stated in only a few words. In comparison, the social workers developed each category in a case report as a mini-essay and included personal impressions. In other words, the informational sheets reveal the income, housing, rent, parents' occupation, health status, schooling, and much more about the minor involved, but do not offer the wealth of detail that social workers included.

Second, the 107 provincial case files contained only four medical-psychiatric examinations. The different level of recourse to both social workers and doctors substantiates differences between Paris and much of the rest of France. In part, provincial regions simply had fewer social workers and psychiatrists. Provincial judges also would have felt less need for outside "professional" advice. In contrast to Paris, a large, anonymous city, judges in the three provincial departments could still count on some local authority figure, the police commissioner or mayor, to have personal knowledge of minors from their areas.

Finally, out of 143 cases for which I have the information, the provincial courts sent only five boys and did not send any girls to public juvenile institutions.[22] In other words, supervised education houses were populated almost entirely by adolescents from Paris, a fact never stated by contemporaries who wrote about these institutions, despite the implications about what training would be most appropriate for urban youth shaped by Paris street culture.

How the Police Operated

A minor's contact with the justice system started with the police. Given the specificity of policing in France, some background is in order. Although policing originated in Old Regime France, the upheaval of the 1789 Revolution, combined with Napoleon's authoritarian desires, profoundly shaped French policing. Fear of social unrest created a police system whose top priority was maintaining public order. By the twentieth century, France had developed a variety of police forces. The largest contingent of French police, the gendarmes, a branch of the military, operated in the rural areas and small towns that constituted 95 percent of French territory and where the vast majority of the French population still lived in the 1940s. The gendarmes performed both administrative and judicial police functions. In addition to the gendarmes, provincial cities and towns had their own local, municipal police forces. From 1851 on, the central government began extending control over these municipal police forces, starting with the one in Lyons. Over the next ninety years, France slowly merged the various municipal police forces into the centralized National Police, with recruitment, training, pay, and advancement controlled by the Ministry of the Interior. In April 1941, Vichy quickly completed what had been a leisurely process, passing a law that made the state responsible for policing in all towns with more than 10,000 people.[23] Yet even Vichy proved powerless to override the autonomy of the Paris Municipal Police, a force entirely separate from all the others that bypassed the National Police and reported directly to the Ministry of the Interior.[24] Municipal police forces were divided into the uniformed administrative police who handled public order, intelligence, traffic control, and administration, and the plainclothes judicial police who investigated crimes.[25]

According to historian Jean-Marc Berlière, various practices connected to the maintenance of order, such as opening mail, listening in on telephone conversations, stopping and searching people based only on vague suspicions, were part of police practice even before the war and the authoritarian Vichy regime. The police could always stop and check any person's identity. In "flagrant" cases, in the midst of the crime (in flagrante delicto, or *délit flagrant*), which in France included a day or two after notification of the crime, the police could search the home and personal effects of any suspect, without a warrant. Under Article 77, the police could place anyone under suspicion in police detention for a period of twenty-four hours, extendable to forty-eight.[26] Although Vichy did not institute new police procedures, Berlière argues that it perpetuated and amplified them. Further, historian Simon Kitson points out that during the war the police searched for evidence not just of theft but also of resistance activity, labor draft evasion, and hidden Jewish identity.[27] According to Berlière, "different 'economic police' services to hunt down the black market and the trafficking provoked by penury and the difficulties of provisioning proliferated as rapidly as economic misdemeanors did."[28] Thus the police took an unusually active role in repressing minor misdemeanors, for example by setting up "control" points on the roads and in subway or train stations to stop people and search their personal effects, briefcases, sacks, suitcases.

The police caught a number of minors by using such methods. For example, D.'s parents had given him money to travel to a job. After failing to get the job, D. returned, broke, to Paris, checked into a hotel, and took the sheets from his bed to the flea market at Clignancourt to sell them. The police officer reported that, "passing through the flea market on Vache Street," he and his partner noticed "two young suspicious-looking people, one of whom was carrying a small suitcase in his hand and a package wrapped in newspaper under his arm." When he noticed the police, the suspect turned and walked rapidly in the other direction. The police caught him, searched his suitcase, and found the sheets, embroidered with the hotel logo.[29] The police at the Odéon Metro Station searched C's suitcase and found 200 francs worth of preserves which C. admitted stealing from his employer.[30]

The Vichy regime's surveillance of mail exchanged in France also expanded the authorities' ability to uncover crimes. For example, a seventeen-year-old seamstress was tried for having an abortion after police got the information from a letter her fiancé had written to a doctor, requesting the abortion. The Postal Control Service had opened the letter and turned it over to the police.[31]

Even before the war, Paris had created a new force that further increased vigilance over young people. In 1935 the Paris police hired two social workers as police assistants, to supervise the city streets especially near schools, public parks, and subway stations, looking for runaways, truants, prostitutes, and minors breaking the law. By 1943 a team of twelve police assistants, headquartered on the rue Monge, kept an eye on young people in Paris and its suburbs, with the number set to increase to twenty.[32] In the short term, more vigorous policing often causes the crime rate to increase, not so much because the number of crimes increases, but because more crimes are uncovered.

One question about police procedures remains unanswered, although the evidence is suggestive. Very often in the official police crime reports minors deny guilt when first questioned. Later, without explanation, many reports simply state that the minor "made a confession" *(il a fait ses aveux)*. The fact that so many minors confessed to their crimes after initial denials raises questions about what took place between the denial and the confession. Did French police commonly beat minor suspects to force a confession?[33] Three cases suggest that some policemen at least slapped kids around, and one suggests even greater brutality against very young suspects.

G., a shepherd in the tiny town of Uzès, was accused of stealing three ewes from his employer. According to the police report, after thirty minutes of questioning, G. finally admitted having sold the sheep to German soldiers at 200 francs apiece and reporting them missing to his boss. The file then contains a lawyer's letter insisting that G. confessed only "following blows administered by the gendarmes in the presence of the rural policeman, Mr. X." When questioned, the rural cop could not understand the fuss. "The gendarmes gave him a couple of slaps before he made his confession, nothing more." The slaps, he insisted, were not violent. The court finally dropped the case against G., not because of the police tactics, but because a skin from one of the missing sheep, identifiable because of the distinctive mark on its right ear, turned up in someone else's garden, and that person was eventually convicted of the theft.[34]

A second case involved M., a seventeen-year-old boy who worked on his family's farm. Neighbors accused him of public indecent behavior *(outrage public à la pudeur)*, claiming that out in the fields they interrupted him committing sodomy with a mare, which another neighbor had loaned him for plowing. Although the case ranks among the more unusual in the nature of the crime, eventually it became clear that it had erupted out of a long-standing rural family rivalry. The young man denied the accusation to his mother, later confessed to the police, and finally retracted his confession. He claimed that when the neighbors saw him, "I had just relieved myself and was buttoning up my pants." Questioned again, he continued to deny the charges and insisted that he confessed to the gendarmes only "because they were hitting me." He provided a written doctor's report verifying that he had been struck. The police recommended a psychological evaluation of the minor, but the investigating magistrate instead solicited a letter from a veterinarian. Based on the description in the accusation and an examination of the harness and plow, the vet stated unconditionally, "It would have been physically impossible to accomplish the act charged . . . under the circumstances as described." After retaining the services of a lawyer, the minor finally got the case dismissed.[35]

The last case of reported brutality took place in Beaucaire, near Nîmes. A thirteen-year-old boy confessed to stealing bicycles with several of his friends. His mother then accused the police of beating the confession out of him. The Nîmes public prosecutor investigated the mother's charge. The police commissioner insisted that while questioning the group of boys, he had simply raised his voice and struck the table to impress them. However, another local official whose office adjoined police headquarters corroborated the boy's version. The Justice of the Peace's court clerk claimed that on entering his office on the day in question, he overheard crying, appeals for help, slaps, and a child's voice calling for his mother. His secretary complained that the abuse had been going on for two hours. Finally, the court clerk intervened to stop the beating. Two additional office employees confirmed the court clerk's version. On the one hand, it was more than two hours before anyone intervened to stop the beating. Still, the reaction of those in the adjoining office indicates that they found the police behavior both unusual and unacceptable, as does the prosecutor's quick investigation and his handwritten note stating that this was a "serious matter."[36] Still, the file does not indicate any sanctions against the police officers involved. Given that the use of corporal punishment against children was acceptable in other spheres, in the public schools, for example, the police probably used a certain level of violence, which the public usually accepted. In this case, both the level of violence and the young age of the boys aroused indignation. However, without outside corroboration the investigation probably would have ended with the police denial.

Social Workers and the Case Reports

In the Paris region, about one-third of the minors who appeared in court would have had contact with a social worker before their final hearings. Social workers prepared studies and made recommendations that became a part of the case files. The social workers involved in the juvenile justice system came from a profession that developed in the early twentieth century. Like nursing and teaching, social work represented a field thought to build on "natural" female instincts of nurturing, educating, caregiving. Women had long been active in private charitable and religious efforts to mitigate the effects of poverty, and social work professionalized and secularized such impulses. Social workers visited poor families, conducted scientific investigations to determine their needs, and reported back to their agencies, but they also interacted with the families, providing advice, suggestions, instruction, and, in theory, inspiration. Because social work was considered both a respectable profession for middle-class women who were unlikely to marry and a mission they were called on to fulfill, the majority of social workers in France in the 1940s were single, middle-class women. Answering the objection that single women with no children of their own were unsuited to intervene in the family lives of others, children's protection legal specialist Pierre Waquet argued, "This task is a vocation that requires total devotion; few fathers or mothers with families could fruitfully participate in it." Even the class differences between social workers and the families they visited were all for the best, according to Hyacinthe Dubreuil. Her essay on the mission of the social worker argued that the industrial revolution had pulled women out of their homes, causing them to loose their desire and aptitude for motherhood. An educated social worker, by substituting herself for the mother and reconstructing the family, served as a living example of the good homemaker. To Dubreuil, contact with a cultivated person only increased the benefits of the exchange for the working-class families.[37]

The case reports for the Paris TEA in the 1930s and 1940s provide ample evidence both of the time and energy the social workers put into their task and of the class, gender, and professional biases they shared. The case studies are remarkable documents, usually eight to ten single-spaced pages of information broken down into various categories, such as antecedents, description, schooling, character. About the minor, social workers went far beyond simple date of birth to include such information as birth weight, whether or not the child was breastfed and for how long, when the first tooth appeared, when the child began to walk. For example, B. had a normal delivery, weighed 3.3 kilograms, was breastfed to twenty-two months.[38] The reports list every childhood illness and accident, and summarize school records and performance, usually based on interviews or letters from teachers: for example, A.'s "teachers were always satisfied with his work."[39] However, most of the teachers interviewed were not particularly satisfied. One teacher described C. as a "student below the average, regular under duress—about average in work habits . . . very minimal education."[40] D.'s teacher reported, "passable work—not very talented student, shifty, liar, a bit rough, dirty, completely without upbringing."[41] The social workers always indicated if minors had completed their Certificate of Primary Education (CEP), which 41 percent of the minors in the forty-six case files from the Seine Department had. The CEP required passing an examination at the end of primary school, and many adolescents left school without passing the test.

Under the rubric "description," the social worker discussed physical appearance, mannerisms, and notable features, with a distinct emphasis on attitude and cleanliness. Interestingly, social workers frequently used two phrases to describe minors: "of good appearance," and "is polite and calm" *(se présente bien; est poli et calme)*. An example of a social worker's description of a minor: "of good appearance . . . 1 meter 56, 54 kilograms, dark brown hair, brown eyes . . . good facial expression, responds quietly, polite and calm, sufficient cleanliness." The description of D.: "of suitable appearance . . . facial expression a bit wild, not nasty, polite, not shy, is calm." Commonly social workers mentioned for girls that they used "no vulgar language" *(pas de vilaines expressions),* which would have indicated sexual promiscuity to the interviewers. Often the social worker's description contrasts disagreeable features, malicious or wild facial expressions, with politeness and good behavior during the interview: R. "has a pretty stiff appearance . . . not very agreeable facial expression, pale coloring, speech a bit dry and not very polite, not shy, no vulgar language . . . Personal hygiene, washes up morning and evening, goes to the showers every Saturday."[42] Another social worker wrote of S.: "of good appearance . . . Slightly malicious facial expression. Not very talkative. Polite, calm. Goes to the swimming pool twice a week, brushes her teeth daily."[43]

While tooth-brushing habits would hardly seem relevant to criminal tendencies, the social workers' middle-class preoccupation with hygiene strongly shaped their impressions and colored their descriptions. The limited time working-class families had for housework, the frequent lack of indoor plumbing, and the unavoidable overcrowding prevented nearly all these families from attaining middle-class standards of cleanliness. To social workers, however, an adolescent's level of hygiene within the limits of the situation represented an external manifestation of the family's internal order.

Another section of the report, entitled "character," indicated the minor's habits and activities. Three issues that delinquency experts had long emphasized preoccupied social workers: films, dances, and detective or crime novels. Reports also noted how late the minor stayed out alone and whether or not he or she consumed alcohol. For example, G. "seems to have a certain attachment to his family, stays home a lot, Sundays goes to the movies with friends."[44] P., "sufficiently clean, polite and calm . . . goes to the movies with his parents. Reads little, only the newspaper."[45] W. said her preferred leisure activities were walks in the countryside and "the flicks" *(le cinéac).*[46]

The most common reading materials, according to the case reports, were detective or crime novels. A social worker described one adolescent: "of good appearance . . . slightly severe facial expression. Answers a little too sharply. Polite enough, more or less calm, sufficiently clean—rarely goes to the movies, does not like that. Reads little, maybe a few illustrated magazines or police novels."[47] Another minor "reads detective novels in the *Junior* series and other publications of doubtful morality. Loves tobacco, hangs out in cafés."[48]

Most reports were neither entirely positive nor negative. The social workers' judgmental tone about facial expressions, habits, and lifestyles contrasted with the favorable image they presented of most of the minors as at least polite and calm. Some clients, however, rubbed the social workers the wrong way, particularly those not deferential enough. V., for example, "has a haughty appearance . . . A cold and distant expression. Responds without expanding, with reticence. Totally external politeness. A bit agitated. Very well groomed appearance . . . Arrogant and dishonest child, seems to be an inveterate thief . . . Uncommunicative and cold, recalcitrant."[49] In another case, a seventeen-year-old girl was described: "unbalanced minor, habitual liar, morbid tendency it seems for the melancholy . . . very withdrawn, dirty, untidy, lazy." Yet in this case the social worker concluded that the young woman had "a big heart. Indelicacies committed to satisfy her need to give."[50]

Social workers rarely spared the rest of the family from such critical scrutiny. The case studies summarize information extending back to both sets of grandparents, aunts, and uncles, what they did, how old they were, and the cause of their death, if relevant. Case studies documented both parents' professions and salaries. They described the family's lodging in great detail, from the amount paid in rent to whether the apartment was well ventilated *(bien aérée)*, dark, clean, or dirty. Social workers listed the furniture, including the number of beds in relation to the number of people, and the furniture's condition. T., for example, lived with his family in a "factory district, two wardrobes, a mirror broken 'by the kids'—three beds [for the parents and four children], running water, electricity, outside toilet." "Interior," according to the social worker, "is neither very nice nor very comfortable, but they are happy with it."[51] One case, involving the child of Spanish immigrants, brought out the social worker's ethnic bias. The parents, who had immigrated to France in the late 1920s, had married after two years of cohabitation. The social worker described the mother's facial expression as "good enough" but noted critically that the mother "says 'yes' to everything. Spanish type. Calm, not made-up, no accent.

Gentle speech—clothing—without affectation or eccentricities, hands and fingernails clean."[52] No other reports in this study mention a mother's clean fingernails, which in this case must have defied the social worker's expectations.

Social workers always commented on the appearance, clothing, and manner of the mothers, who could hardly please their observers. Social workers described mothers who were too well groomed as affected or arrogant, and commented negatively about a shabby appearance too. The social worker described P.'s mother as "a woman with a very tired appearance, hair permed and dyed, slightly monkeylike face."[53] G.'s mother was "very simply dressed, clothing in bad shape. Very 'woman of the people,' not well-groomed."[54] J.'s mother must have annoyed her social worker. Despite her poor health, anemia, and the fact that she was nearly blind, the social worker described her as "fairly arrogant . . . far from making a very favorable impression."[55] In contrast, the social workers exhibited not the slightest interest in the physical appearance of fathers. Rather, they focused on three other concerns: the fathers' drinking habits, their ability to provide for the family, and whether or not they were abusive.

The social workers' process of visiting a juvenile's home and interviewing the entire family as well as neighbors, teachers, and employers raises a number of points. First, a clear class difference between the middle-class social workers and the working-class families they investigated colored every aspect of the encounter, as the social workers' obsession with cleanliness and aversion to so-called arrogance on the part of the working class reveals.

Second, the social workers represented an intrusive presence for these families, who were already under scrutiny by the police and the judicial system. The minors and their families surely were aware of the social prejudice of the middle-class women investigating their lives, yet the stakes were apparently high enough that few objected. I found only one protest against a social worker's intrusion. In this case the protest was lodged not by the father, who objected most strenuously to the visit, but by his wife, who bore the brunt of his objections. Afterward, the woman wrote the judge that when her husband learned of a social worker's recent visit, he "was very angry with me about the visit and he made a violent scene, taking it out on me and responding to my replies with insults and vulgarities to the point of threatening to give me a good thrashing, because to please Mr. D. the father I should have nicely tossed this lady out the door. And my husband let me know that he would not accept other people sticking their noses into his son's affairs."[56] The file suggests that the wife passed along Mr. D.'s objections not only in hopes of sympathy but also hoping to draw the social worker into a family dispute, for she and her husband differed profoundly in their estimation of her stepson. Other families may very well have resented a social worker's intruding, but no other explicit objections appeared in the case files I examined.

Third, although the case files, and especially the social workers' reports, provide a huge amount of information about the children and adolescents involved, it hardly needs to be pointed out that the information is all filtered through a system that is by definition judgmental. On the one side, those observing or interrogating the minors and their families most often came from different social backgrounds, and what they saw or chose to describe was deeply colored by their biases. On the other side, people often dissimulate when faced with police, courts, and social workers, especially when their future and the future of their child could be at stake. Minors likely tried to make themselves presentable and put on their best manners for the social workers. The signed statements by either the minor or family members include formulaic expressions that suggest coaching by the police officer, social worker, or investigating magistrate.[57] Occasionally someone wrote an unsolicited letter to a judge, revealing something of a person's real voice, handwriting, spelling, and syntax. But of course the letter writer often had something critical at stake. Still, case files bring us closer to the people involved in the system than either aggregate statistics, other studies, or even the Paris penalty registers, in spite of the strong coloring provided by the social workers.

The three social workers whose names appear on the reports I studied focused on certain types of information, in response to general ideas about criminality and deviance. These reflected widely held beliefs about the contributions to juvenile delinquency of heredity, of alcoholism or syphilis in parents, and of the family's adherence to bourgeois conventions—for example, whether the parents were legally married or lived together out of wedlock *(en concubinage)*. The reports also reflected concerns about so-called *mauvaises fréquentations* (keeping bad company) and the evils of the cinema, dancing, and detective novels for youth.

Historically, these files have two useful aspects. Winnowing out the judgmental language, the reports do provide a picture of where and how the families lived: how many rooms the dwellings had, what rent they paid, what amenities they had or lacked, and so on. And they also allow us to "watch" these fascinating past encounters, if only from one side. Both social prejudice and definite echoes of the discourse on juvenile crime figure strongly, providing evidence that normative and literary sources did have an impact on belief systems, at least among social workers. Using clipped phrases and dry language, the social workers nevertheless write in strongly judgmental, brutally blunt, even harsh terms about people mostly from a lower social class than themselves.

However, a surprising aspect of these case reports is the strong contrast between the negative tone of the reports and the positive tone of the final recommendations. As it turns out, judges relied heavily on social workers' reports to help determine their course of action, namely whether to be punitive or lenient, leave the child with the family, or send him or her to an institution. In nearly every case, the social workers favored lenient treatment of minors, most often recommending release to the family with or without probation. The only exceptions to favoring the family involved cases of minors who requested placement or whose families had entirely disintegrated (such as orphans living with someone who did not want the responsibility). Thus the social workers' biases had little, if any, impact on their recommendations.

Occasionally the courts ordered one last element for the case files, a medical-psychiatric evaluation. Psychiatric examinations did not focus on the minor's level of maturity, knowledge of right or wrong, and ability to weigh consequences. (This and case file evidence confirm that judges no longer took seriously the legal requirement that they determine discretion in a case. Rather, they used discretion only to apply the measure they felt best fit the minor's situation.) Interestingly, the one-page psychiatric reports merely summarized intelligence and personality test scores. For information about the family or even about character, the medical reports paraphrased the social workers' reports. The doctor's final recommendation also invariably echoed that of the social worker. Thus, although the psychiatrists were professional men with scientific degrees, the female social workers wielded much greater influence within the juvenile justice system.

Who Appeared in Juvenile Courts?

Although experts in the 1940s rarely discussed social class, it played a major role. Both in the Paris area and in the provinces, the minors overwhelmingly came from working-class backgrounds. Although the Paris penalty register sample of 667 cases did not always indicate a profession for the minor or the parents, their addresses could be ascertained in 599 cases. Of the 255 cases from Paris proper, 223 of the adolescents involved, or 87 percent, lived in working-class districts.[58] Of the 344 cases from suburban municipalities, two suburbs had 15 cases each, Montreuil-sous-Bois and Drancy. Aubervilliers had 13, Saint-Denis had 10, and Boulogne-Billancourt had 11, all "red belt" working-class suburbs.

The case files substantiate the evidence of geographical location for the Seine and the other departments. Case files indicate the minor's job (if he or she had one), both parents' professions, and the family's income. In cases in the Paris area, most parents were solid working class. A number of fathers worked for the railroad, the Société nationale des chemins de fer, or SNCF. There were factory workers, electricians, toolmakers, metal or wood turners, plumbers, and gardeners. A few parents, usually mothers, had marginal, very low-paid, employment, as ragpickers, for example, cleaning ladies, or concierges—the women who lived in small ground-floor apartments in nearly all Paris apartment buildings, who supervised the buildings, distributed mail, performed minor maintenance, and so on. A number of the minor girls worked as domestic servants. In the Paris area only one potentially middle-class family appeared in the case files, that of a minor whose mother, listed as a professor of English (a high school or university teacher), at the time held a low-paying clerical job. One family had owned a small café but had been forced to sell it for unspecified reasons. Typical monthly incomes hovered at or below 2,000 francs a month. A few of the skilled adult men earned as much as 4,000 francs a month; working mothers usually earned considerably less than 2,000 francs.

The provincial records echo those of Paris. Most minors and their parents were listed as manual laborers *(manoeuvres),* tradespeople like carpenters or masons, factory workers, employees of the SNCF. There were also a few ragpickers and one family of gypsies who recaned chairs *(rampailleuses de chaises).* Several minor girls or mothers worked as domestic servants or cleaning ladies. In rural areas, most minors came from the landless rural proletariat. Seven minors in the Gard Department were listed as agricultural day laborers. Only three or four parents could be considered middle class: a transportation entrepreneur earning 4,000 to 5,000 francs a month, a mother listed as a dockyard manager, a doctor. One father was listed as the proprietor of a small vineyard.

The working-class background of most accused adolescents is hardly surprising. Beyond their modest backgrounds, the detailed information in the case files revealed the severe economic stresses these families faced during the war. Many families lived on the edge, their resources barely keeping up with their expenses. For example, one girl's father, who died in the 1930s, had been deaf, alcoholic, and abusive. Of the six children in the family, three were deceased. The mother worked at a private school cafeteria, earning 550 francs a month, which was supplemented by 150 francs in monthly family allowances. The family lived in a one-room apartment in an old, run-down building without running water, gas, or electricity. The social worker described the apartment as "a bit poor but clean and well-maintained" and closed by observing "precarious material situation."[59] Another boy's mother, a ragpicker, earned 120 francs a month. His father was deceased. His stepfather brought in 672 francs a month in unemployment. A charity provided them with an extra 100 francs a month in assistance.[60] One father wrote to the judge in the case from Germany, explaining that he was a POW, his wife had been killed in an air raid "at the time of the events of May 1940," and his child had gone to live with an aunt.[61] Another boy's father had died prematurely as a result of having been gassed during World War I. The mother had remarried but the stepfather had disappeared. She worked as a concierge for 500 francs a month, supporting three children without family allowances. The social worker wrote, "One wonders what this family lives on."[62] A. was an agricultural day laborer earning 35 francs a day. His parents, also agricultural laborers, supported four children on 60 francs a day. C.'s father, a laborer, supported three children on 45 francs a day (1,350 a month).[63]

Even families living less precariously would have found themselves seriously strained by the wartime economic problems of shortages, stagnant wages, and rapid inflation. Despite rationing, families, except those on farms that produced food, found it difficult to meet their basic nutritional or clothing needs without recourse to the very expensive black market. These families could barely afford basic necessities. Although they were not, strictly speaking, starving, or even malnourished, many of the people in these families surely went hungry at least occasionally.

So far as family structure is concerned, a small but notable number of the families would have been considered "irregular" by contemporary bourgeois observers like social workers and judges. Of the 107 provincial cases for which information was available, 8 minors had been born out of wedlock (7.5 percent), with one parent listed as "unknown" or "unnamed."[64] Six of the 46 Paris case files and 7 of the 107 provincial cases (13 percent and 6.5 percent, respectively) involved separated or divorced parents. The case files also note unmarried parents cohabiting. In some cases the parents simply took their time before marrying, like B.'s parents, who lived together eight years before marrying.[65] Some parents had separated but not divorced their first spouse and were living with their second partner out of wedlock. C.'s parents had married a year after her older brother was born, had been separated for six years, and now her mother was living with another man. The social worker noted that the minor had been well behaved and unproblematic until his "stepfather," who happened to be Jewish, "had to leave Paris" for reasons unspecified (since the incident dated to October 1942, he could have been deported or gone into hiding).[66] D.'s parents were divorced and he himself was living out of wedlock with his pregnant girlfriend.[67] These situations might not strike us as unusual today, but to the middle-class judges and social workers of the 1940s, they would have seemed highly irregular.

Nearly everyone in the 1940s assumed that the war's sudden removal of POW fathers explained rising juvenile crime rates. Unfortunately the Paris penalty registers hardly ever noted a father's captivity. Only 2 of the 667 cases mentioned fathers who were POWs. The case files provide more reliable information on that score. The low numbers—4 of the 46 Paris region case files involved POW children (8.7 percent), as did 9 of the 107 provincial cases (8.4 percent)—refute the era's widely held belief.

In general, the number of "broken" families in these files falls far short of the 50- to 80-percent level asserted by contemporary experts (see Chapter 4). Barring a comparable study of family structure for the working-class population as a whole, we cannot determine whether such "irregular" situations were more common in the families of accused minors than among working-class families in general. In any case, notably, neither the social worker's recommendation nor the court's decision varied depending on the marital status of the parents. Furthermore, most irregular family situations were independent of, rather than created by, the war.

The Judicial System

The question remains about the impact on the court system of the war, German occupation, and the Vichy regime. In mid-June 1940, as the war reached Paris, the Fifteenth Chamber of the Seine Department had a difficult time remaining operational. Otherwise, however, court documents reveal no sudden changes in the judges, the procedures, or the overall operation of the courts with the advent of the Vichy government, either in Paris or in the provinces. Nor did dramatic changes occur in the courts after most of France was liberated in late August through early September 1944. Rather, a slow evolution took place over the four years of the occupation.

In late 1941, two changes became apparent in the Paris penalty registers. First, although Vichy passed the first rationing law on 17 September 1940, rationing cases began to appear only fourteen months later, in November 1941. The series of new regulations to violate might well have contributed to rising juvenile crime rates. The government, however, directed its enforcement efforts against suppliers, not consumers. As a result, the number of rationing cases is surprisingly small. My database of 667 cases includes three rationing cases from November and December 1941, nine cases from 1942, thirteen from 1943, and only six rationing cases from 1944. These figures are hardly significant in comparison to the overall number of juvenile cases.

The second change was the disappearance from the Fifteenth Chamber in Paris of cases involving communist propaganda. In 1940 and 1941, nine minors were charged—under the Third Republic's law of 26 September 1939 passed in reaction to the Hitler-Stalin pact—with disseminating communist propaganda. However, the last such case in the Paris records appeared in August 1941. According to historian Alain Bancaud, German pressure and threats to take over the repression of communism in France led Vichy to pass the law of 14 August 1941 that created Special Sections (Sections speciales), panels combining civilian magistrates and military judges, to combat communism. Unaware of the Special Sections, the commander of German military forces in France wrote a letter on 19 August 1941 to the French delegate in the occupied zone, instructing the authorities to communicate to German military tribunals all denunciations, procedures, and dossiers concerning communist activity. A week later, on 25 August, the German commander cancelled this demand, noting that the 14 August law provided French courts with an effective tool against communism. Nevertheless, the German authorities continually threatened to take over such prosecutions.[68]

In cases that did not involve communism or resistance, evidence reveals in most instances minimal German interference. If anything, the German occupation authorities preferred to let the French authorities handle petty crimes. For example, in Cambrai, G., fifteen, stole an unattended bicycle. The owner returned in time to see G. riding off on the bike and yelled, "Thief!" whereupon three cyclists intercepted him. At this point a German officer appeared and took custody of the boy. Shortly thereafter, a French policeman appeared, and the German officer immediately handed over the boy.[69] Another case involved P., a seventeen-year-old boy working for the Todt Organization, Germany's organization for the construction of roads and other infrastructure. In October 1942, the *Feldgendarmerie,* having held P. for twelve days, turned him over to the French police for trafficking in bread ration tickets.[70] The German authorities preferred not to handle the matter, even though the infraction had been committed under their jurisdiction.

Even D., a young boy who, with his older brother, stole a briefcase directly from a German worker, was turned over to the French authorities. In this case, the German district commandant sent a letter to the French police. He was not concerned with punishing D. so much as cracking down on his older brother: "It is in no way acceptable for a lazy young man to lead children to illegal dealings and to ruin them morally." The commandant requested "that the responsible French authority send me a thorough report regarding this person and forward me the court's final decision."[71] The informational sheet in the case file reports very favorably on both the boy and his family. But indeed the older brother had been convicted of theft in another case, and D. himself had already been questioned about two thefts and warned many times, according to the police, who also claimed that he and his big brother regularly begged in German military quarters. The French authorities apparently agreed with the commandant that the elder brother's behavior signaled a poor family environment, because in June 1942 the court placed D. in a Patronage for Morally Abandoned Children rather than following the informational sheet's recommendation that he be returned to his parents.[72]

Even more interesting for its political overtones was the case of M., a seventeen-year-old boy charged with death threats, possession of a weapon, and carrying a prohibited firearm. His job-training instructor filed a complaint after receiving a handwritten death threat that read: "While waiting for your hour to come, because it's very near, here's [*voici*] for your celebration, you informing rat and dirty cuckold—soon you'll be bumped off." He signed the note only with a large *V* and drew small Gaullist resistance symbols, the Croix de Lorraine, in the middle of both the *v* of *voici* and the signature. When arrested, M. was carrying a concealed revolver. Yet, in spite of the Churchill *V* for victory, the Gaullist Croix de Lorraine, the gun, and the similarity of the threat to resistance practice, the Germans apparently decided this was a youthful prank pulled by someone of no consequence. The local police commissioner explained to the judges that he had forwarded the case to the German police but, "given the nature of this case," the Germans had decided to give the French courts the "trouble of prosecution."[73]

In other cases of suspected resistance activity, however, even those involving minors who committed extremely petty acts, the Germans hardly hesitated to take over prosecution. One teenage girl persisted, despite several warnings, in wearing a broach with the French and English flags crossed. A case notation reads: "The delinquent youth will be prosecuted with a direct summons; the file has been sent on to the German authorities." In another case, seventeen- and nineteen-year-old boys were caught drawing a Gaullist Croix de Lorraine in a public place. The documents do not mention the ultimate outcome in either the English flag or the Croix de Lorraine cases, except that they were turned over to the German authorities.[74]

The archival records reveal that French judicial authorities found many German demands excessive and troublesome. In response to complaints he had received from several judges, Minister of Justice Barthélemy wrote to François Darlan, then head of the government, protesting "abusive" and "unjustified" German interference in French judicial matters. Barthélemy asked how to respond to such German "illegal interference." In a letter of 12 November 1941, Darlan replied that he would lodge a protest with the Armistice Commission at Weisbaden. He instructed Barthélemy "not to conform spontaneously to illegal German orders" and to "resist abusive demands to the full extent possible." When constrained to give in, he wrote, "only do so protesting."[75] Historian Alain Bancaud notes that, fearing serious local incidents, Barthélemy decided not to circulate Darlan's instructions. Maurice Gabolde, who replaced Barthélemy as minister of justice in March of 1943, recommended in a circular of 4 July 1943 trying to avoid direct contact with the occupiers. If contact was unavoidable, the French were not to be intransigent but to cede in cases where German interests were clearly at stake. However, Gabolde also ordered French judges to start their own investigations in every case they handled, as a way of asserting their authority and improving their bargaining position with the German authorities.[76]

The above instructions might suggest that French judicial authorities resisted German demands, yet such attempts to fend off interference could hardly be considered Resistance with a capital *R*. Nor did they indicate that the French authorities hoped to protect those accused of resistance. Rather, Barthélemy, Darlan, and Gabolde were engaged in a struggle to maintain French jurisdiction, seeing the ability to handle matters themselves as a sign of sovereignty. In other words, this was a territorial battle, one that went badly for France, as German interference and pressure only increased over time. Bancaud notes that as the number of resistance attacks increased from late 1942 on, the Germans seized more of the important cases and left the French courts with the rest.[77] Still, from the German point of view, allowing the French police and courts to handle petty crimes proved to be a cheap and laborsaving way of maintaining order over the large occupied territory.

While weakly trying to fend off German interference in the courts, some evidence suggests that French police and courts took their own initiative to reduce rising crime rates in 1942. A Justice Ministry study in 1946 explained, "Faced with the increase in juvenile criminality, the courts exercised a clearly more severe repression."[78] Adult criminal statistics support the notion of a more repressive judiciary, perhaps even an attempted crackdown in 1942. The criminal court conviction rate for adults hovered at about 75 percent prior to the war and even in 1941 attained only 76 percent, but it jumped to 92 percent in 1942 and remained at or above 90 percent through 1947.[79] Contemporary reformer Henri Joubrel found two indications of greater severity in the Paris juvenile courts during the war. First, the percentage of juveniles who faced trial after an initial appearance before the court rose from 33 percent in 1938 to a high of 43 percent in 1942.[80] Second, according to Joubrel, the number of juvenile delinquents returned to their families without probation, 25 percent before the war, declined to 17 percent in 1943.[81]

As to the system's harshness, another notable change took place. Both Paris and provincial courts handed down increased penalties in abortion cases. Vichy's so-called 300 Law of 15 February 1942 made abortion a capital offense that could be tried by the new Tribunal d'état. But the Tribunal heard only forty-two abortion cases during the war. The vast majority of abortion cases were handled, as before the war, by district courts. While far from the severe punishments the Tribunal d'état handed down —two death sentences, fourteen life sentences, and twenty-six sentences of twenty years' hard labor—even at the lower, less visible end of the scale, punishment in abortion-related cases increased.[82] Until 1942, the Fifteenth Chamber, when it convicted either minors or adults, generally handed down short sentences of fifteen days, one month, or three months, often suspended. Starting in 1942, the Fifteenth Chamber handed down a number of one- to five-year sentences for abortion. In addition to the harsher penalties, starting in 1940 there was a massive increase in the pros-ecution of abortion. The French courts prosecuted about 200 abortion cases a year before the war. By 1940, that number nearly tripled, to 599, and in 1943 it peaked at a tenfold increase, 1,995 cases. Although I found one instance of postal surveillance uncovering an abortion, the massive increase in the number of cases probably owed more to heightened anti-abortion propaganda and increased denunciation than to increased polic-ing. An abortion involves a woman with an unwanted pregnancy, an abor-tion provider, and possibly a father, creating many potential denouncers in a situation that often aroused anger, shame, humiliation, and a desire for revenge. Interestingly, even after France's liberation, the repression of abortion dropped only slightly in 1945, and then the number of cases climbed even higher, to 2,232, in 1946.[83]

Another critical factor contributed to rising crime rates during the war. Under the circumstances of rationing, shortages, and inflation, victims of petty theft were much more likely to report their losses. Justice Ministry statistics count criminal complaints, police crime reports, and denuncia-tions in a single category. Not surprisingly, the total number of com-plaints, denunciations, and crime reports nearly doubled nationally during the war, from around 650,000 annually in the 1930s to more than 1 mil-lion in 1941 and 1.2 million in 1942.[84] The increase partly reflects the citi-zens' disturbing tendency to turn in neighbors for violations like failing to black out windows, harboring an escaped POW, or hiding a Jew. Vichy au-thorities, overwhelmed by the rising tide of anonymous denunciations, eventually passed a law punishing them.[85] However, based on information from the case files, we should not attribute too large a share of the rising crime statistics to the denunciatory practices encouraged by an authoritar-ian state. Of the forty Seine case files that involved theft in my sample, there were no random denunciations by third parties.

Nevertheless, circumstances of rationing and severe material shortages rendered theft victims more likely to report even minor losses. Twenty-one of forty theft arrests resulted from complaints filed by the victims of theft.[86] Before the war, a small amount of cash stolen might not have been worth the trouble of reporting to the police. But the loss of ration tickets or a food package from the countryside meant loss of access to basic provi-sions, making a theft report necessary. For example, E. took a package de-livery notice that protruded from someone else's mailbox and used it to claim the package, which contained three cheeses and two packs of butter that E. shared with her family. The true recipient filed a complaint after receiving a letter from the sender inquiring about the package. The Post Office investigation uncovered E.'s signature on the receipt.[87] Penury and the difficulty of obtaining food made it even more likely that minor thefts of food would be reported during and after the war. During the war, several farmers filed complaints about people stealing small amounts from their fields. One complaint involved a minor who stole ten pears from the farm where he worked.[88]

While there were no sharp discontinuities at either end of the war, over time the kinds of crimes prosecuted in the courts slowly changed in minor ways. New violations connected with rationing laws appeared in the records; other crimes, those connected to the Resistance or communism, found their way into different special courts after 1941. Intensified surveillance, by both the police and by civilians of each other, increased the number of criminal complaints and denunciations. Nationally the number of prosecutions connected with abortion rose tremendously. However, aside from the politically sensitive issue of abortion, for the most part delinquency cases reflected the extremely hard economic situation of both the perpetrators and the victims.

Treatment of Minors in the Juvenile Courts

Two general conclusions about the treatment of young offenders emerge from court records. First, although by the 1930s nearly every reformer criticized the required determination of a minor's discretion in committing a crime, actual practice in juvenile courts had subverted the system from within. Juvenile judges simply pronounced minors to have acted with or without discretion, depending on the solution they felt best fit the situation—short prison sentence, reeducational measure, or return to the family. Second, the juvenile courts ran a relatively lenient system. A realistic scale from least to most repressive can be fairly easily determined. The most lenient, least repressive response of the juvenile courts, aside from outright acquittal or dropping charges, would be to acquit a minor as acting without discretion and return the minor to his or her parents. The next most lenient response would be returning the minor to the parents with probation. The question becomes a bit more complicated in moving to the next harsher alternative. It could be argued that finding that a minor acted with discretion and then handing down a jail sentence, fines, or both was the harshest decision a juvenile judge could make. But when considering the actual time spent incarcerated, conviction was nearly always less harsh than certain kinds of acquittals. First of all, most convicted minors received suspended sentences. Although a conviction would be entered on the criminal record, no time would be served. Even when sentences were not suspended, they were attenuated by law for minors and tended to be very short, almost always less than three months, often only fifteen days. I hardly ever saw sentences of six months or more in the records. Furthermore, time spent in detention prior to the hearing would be subtracted from the time to be served.

However, while judges had complete discretion over the length of a minor's stay in a supervised education house, judges in the court records I examined, with one exception, always sent minors to a supervised education house until the age of majority, twenty-one. Such a decision could be invoked for any minor after the thirteenth birthday. In other words, a thirteen-year-old minor could spend up to eight years in a state-run supervised education house. Although most juveniles involved in the system were older than thirteen, even for minors age seventeen, the oldest to fall under the juvenile court's jurisdiction, a supervised education house placement could mean four years in the institution. Juvenile judges were well aware of this discrepancy in length of incarceration.

Judges also nearly always placed minors in private charitable institutions until age twenty-one. But in practice, it was easier to revise a private placement and restore custody to the parents, and for boys, the regime in such institutions may have been less severe than in public ones. In fact in most cases, after a brief stay boys were sent out of private institutions to work on a farm or for a business. In my view, therefore, acquitting a minor as acting without discretion and sending him or her to a supervised education house represented the system's harshest response. The following list presents the possible judgments, from least to most repressive.

Acquit as not guilty, or drop charges
Acquit/return to parents
Acquit/return to parents with probation
Acquit/place in private charitable institution
Convict, sentence suspended
Convict, sentence not suspended
Acquit/send to supervised education house

Based on the 593 Paris cases in my sample that involved first appearances (some 58 cases involved violations of probation or of the 1935 law) only 9 minors (2 percent) were acquitted outright, but 286 minors (48 percent) were returned to their parents, 103 (17 percent) of them without probation. In other words, half of the minors received one of the three most lenient responses. Another 111 minors (19 percent) were sent to private charities. While 114 (19 percent) were convicted, 49 of the 114 sentences were suspended. Only 11 percent of the 593 minors served prison sentences. As for the harshest treatment, 73 (12 percent) were sent to supervised education houses.[89]

In the provinces, the figures are quite similar, except that conviction was more likely, placement in a supervised education house less. Among the 143 provincial cases in my sample (including Chinon), 8 minors, or 6 percent, were acquitted outright—a low rate but higher than the 2-percent acquittal rate in Paris—45 percent were returned to parents, 22 percent were sent to private institutions, and 25 percent were convicted (half with suspended sentences). Hardly any minors who appeared in courts outside of Paris were sent to a supervised education house. Only 5 of the 143 minors for whom information is available were sent to a supervised education house, or 4 percent of the total. All 5 sent to supervised education houses were boys, 4 from Indre-et-Loire and 1 from the Gard.

Why were provincial courts more likely either to acquit outright or convict, and less likely to send minors to supervised education houses? First, provincial judges might have deemed such institutions too harsh for the less urban adolescents they encountered. The above figures strongly suggest that supervised education houses consisted almost exclusively of adolescents from Paris and its working-class suburbs. Second, in smaller communities judges relied more on their own authority and moral power to dissuade minors from misbehaving again. The personal contacts of a small town, the shame of a court appearance and a "severe admonishment" from a judge, and the community's knowledge and disapproval of a conviction would have been more effective in small towns and villages than in a large and impersonal metropolitan area like Paris. Finally, in provincial courts the judge might even know the family or the local authorities who would oversee the minor.

What determined how the system treated a particular minor? The nature of the charge itself played a relatively minor role, shaping the court's response only in the most serious case, involving murder. Interestingly, in the vast majority of juvenile cases, those involving theft, the value of the item stolen did not influence the courts' decisions. To a certain extent, the circumstances surrounding the theft—in particular, stealing from an employer—could inspire a somewhat firmer response from the judges.

But by far the clearest factor determining the courts' overall range of responses was the offender's sex. There was less middle ground in the treatment of boys. More often the courts handed out either the most lenient or the harshest option to boys. In contrast, girls often fell in the middle range of the scale. For example, in comparison to girls, the courts were more likely to return boys to their parents. The Seine Fifteenth Chamber returned 47 percent of the boys but only 38 percent of the girls to their parents. In the provinces, the figures are nearly the same: 45 percent of boys but only 35 percent of girls were returned to their parents. However, courts were also much more likely to send boys to a supervised education house than girls. In the Paris area, the Fifteenth Chamber sent 15 percent of boys and just 10 percent of girls to supervised education houses.[90] The provincial courts did not send any of the girls in the case files studied to a public preservation school.

Girls, if unlikely to be sent to a public preservation school, were more likely than boys to be placed in private religious or charitable institutions. In the Paris cases, 27 percent of the girls but only 17 percent of the boys were sent to private institutions.[91] Provincial courts sent even more girls, 33 percent, to private institutions, as compared to 18 percent of the boys. One social worker explained her recommendation to place R. in a Catholic Bon Pasteur. "It is to be hoped that a stay at the BP will help her straighten herself out."[92] Many judges and social workers equated criminality with immorality in girls. The courts, reflecting widely held views, often considered a crime committed by a boy the result of ceding to a momentary temptation. Some forms of young male misbehavior, fistfights and bicycle theft for example, were even to be expected. In such cases a severe warning sufficed, and the boy could be sent home.

In contrast, courts viewed the girls who appeared, even though they were usually charged with petty crimes like theft, as fundamentally depraved and in need of strict supervision and remoralization. State institutions, both prisons and supervised education houses, were rumored to be hotbeds of immoral behavior, more likely to corrupt than to straighten out an errant girl. Nuns, however, could provide the proper moral rehabilitation needed to erase the threat posed by female adolescent criminality to the patriarchal order. Most private institutions for girls were religious, and their regime was stricter than that of most private institutions for boys. Most girls remained at the institution under careful supervision; they were rarely placed in outside jobs. Inside the institution, they worked at a variety of tedious tasks—lace making, for example—less for the value of such labor as training for a future career but because it was considered salutary. In general, while many reformers questioned making boys perform useless labor aimed at "breaking them in," rather than providing them with useful skills, few raised similar concerns about girls. Even though the vast majority of the girls in public institutions and charities came from working-class backgrounds, few reformers advocated occupational training for young female offenders, perhaps because of the reformers' class- and gender-based assumptions about marriage and domesticity.

While the offender's sex proved to be the strongest factor shaping juvenile court responses, two other factors, the judge and the age of the minor, also influenced the severity of the Paris courts. In the Fifteenth Chamber, judges varied day by day. In relative terms, I found one "hanging judge" in my sample. While seven of the eight judges who regularly served in the Fifteenth Chamber sent an average of 11 percent of the minors before them to supervised education houses, one judge sent 18 percent. His name began to appear in the records in 1942, which suggests he may have been appointed as part of a crackdown. The second factor, the minor's age, strongly influenced the court's likelihood of conviction with discretion. Juvenile judges for the most part did not use the discretion determination as it was originally intended, instead applying it in a praetorian manner to obtain the desired outcome. However, judges' decisions reflected the prevalent view that juveniles over age sixteen, approaching adulthood, could more readily be treated as adults. From the 667 Paris registries, only one fourteen-year-old was convicted with discretion, as were three fifteen-year-olds, thirteen sixteen-year-olds, and forty-six seventeen-year-olds.[93]

The impact of race or ethnicity proved more difficult to ascertain, first because race proved troublesome to determine with certitude. If the minor was born outside France, a nationality would be listed, but race per se was not listed. Among the 667 cases, 11 minors either violated Vichy's anti-Semitic legislation or had both Jewish first names—such as Sarah, Benjamin, Solomon, Abraham, Israel—and common Jewish family names. Of those 11, 4 were sent to supervised education houses (1 for violating the anti-Semitic laws). However, while 4 out of 11 is a higher ratio than that of the general delinquent population the Fifteenth Chamber sent to supervised houses, the numbers are simply too small to determine with certainty whether judges treated Jewish minors more harshly than non-Jews. Even if the judges meant to be harsh, ironically, during the occupation, Jewish minors in a state supervised education house were likely to be safer than nearly anywhere else, as the Germans did not interfere with those institutions. A small number of other foreigners appear in the records: nine Poles, nine Italians, four with Arabic last names. Of those twenty-two, four were sent to supervised education houses—none of the minors with Arabic names, but three Italians. Again the total number is too small to allow any sure conclusions.

When we shift focus from the overall range of court responses to the narrow category of those minors sent to supervised education houses, by far the best predictor of the court's decision to send a minor to a supervised education house was whether the minor or the parents, or both, actually appeared in court for the hearing. A parent's failure to appear often meant bad news for the minor. And if the minor did not appear (which usually meant the parents were not there either), he or she was very likely to be sent to a supervised education house. Of my Paris sample of 667 cases, 47 of the 96 minors sent to a supervised education house, or 49 percent, were listed as absent.[94] From another angle, the 47 cases in which an absent minor was sent to a supervised education house represented 64 percent of all cases involving a minor who did not appear for his or her hearing (74 cases). Another 19 percent of the absent minors were convicted as acting with discretion, the next harshest alternative. Some 49 minors who did appear for their hearings were sent to a supervised education house, but 21 of them were already being detained, either preventively or for some other offense. I conducted sample tallies for random days that confirmed my general observations. On any given day, never fewer than 50 percent—and on some days 100 percent—of the minors sent to a supervised education house had failed to appear for their hearings.[95] Judges likely considered failure to appear at a court date at least a sign of disrespect, if not a rejection of the court's authority. Perhaps Irene Rosenberg's research findings on contemporary juvenile courts in the United States apply to 1940s France. Rosenberg has determined that so-called throwaway kids, those whose parents do not appear, are more likely to receive harsh treatment by the system.[96]

To some extent, the offenses varied by region. The Gard, my most rural region, had the most crop thefts *(vol de récoltes)* and hunting violations (carrying a weapon without a permit, illegal traps, hunting out of season). Nîmes had a number of cases involving gypsies, referred to as "nomads" or *romanichelles*. In France, not surprisingly, even nomads had to carry a card. Several gypsies were charged with not carrying their nomad cards *(cartes de nomade)*. Nîmes also had more Protestants (the informational sheets indicated religion), and Protestant pastors occasionally intervened on behalf of particular minors by sending a letter to the judge. (In contrast, none of the files in my sample contained letters from priests, even though most of the minors were listed as Catholic.)

Reports from an observation center on the rue de Crimée began to appear in the Paris case files in 1942. These centers began opening in response to Justice Minister Barthélemy's circular of 21 March 1942 strongly urging juvenile judges to avoid sending minors in need of preventive detention to county jails *(maisons d'arrêt)*. Instead Barthélemy urged the courts to work with local private groups to set up welcome centers or observation centers *(centres d'accueil, centres d'observation)* for minors awaiting their hearings. The juvenile delinquency law of 22 July 1942 mandated the same solution. While the law's procedural changes never entered into effect, financial credits immediately became available to open observation centers.[97] Centers also began to appear in the provinces. By the end of the war there were five observation centers serving Paris, at Tourelles, Villejuif, Charenton, the rue de Crimée, and the rue de Madrid, set up in collaboration with the General Secretariat for the Family (Secretariat Général à la Famille).

What Kinds of Illegal Acts Did Minors Commit?

The registries and case files reveal that most minors were accused of committing extremely petty crimes, nearly all property crimes. Sixty-nine percent of the minors in the Paris region, 458 of the 667 cases in my sample, were charged with theft *(vol)*. Another 36 infractions could also be counted as property crimes: 29 infractions of rationing laws, usually involving selling ration tickets or using false tickets, and 7 infractions of railroad regulations, which involved either riding the train or subway without a ticket or selling goods in a station without a permit. In addition, 5 fraud *(escroqueries)* and 13 breach-of-trust *(abus de confiance)* charges involved property crimes like keeping the errand money an employer had given the minor, falsifying receipts to skim off part of a delivery, and altering invoices to procure additional goods. Thus there were 512 property crimes, which represented 77 percent of the total.

As to what minors stole, most frequently in the Seine Department minors stole money. Of the 458 theft cases, 107 involved stealing money, most often small sums as low as 10 francs, with a few cases involving sums of 10,000 francs or more. Of the 107 minors charged with stealing money,

88 were boys (82 percent). Judges sent 12 (11 percent) of them to super-vised education houses (sending only one girl). The second and third most frequently stolen items were food, which 83 minors were charged with stealing, and bicycles, in 82 cases. Stealing-food charges involved 72 boys (87 percent). Nine of the food thieves (11 percent)—8 boys and 1 girl—received the harshest response, placement in a supervised education house. By far, boys made up the highest proportion of those charged with bicycle theft, 77 of the 82 cases, or 94 percent. Yet only 6 of the 82 bicycle thieves, or 7 percent (no girls), were sent to supervised education houses.

There was a fairly steep drop to the next most frequent category, shop-lifting, with 53 cases. Here again, the data seem to confirm gendered as-sumptions about criminal proclivities: girls made up a much larger propor-tion of the cases of shoplifting. Of the 53 shoplifters, 28 (53 percent) were girls, whereas for the three categories above, money, food, and bicycles, girls represented 6 to 13 percent of the total. This could indicate that girls really did shoplift more often than boys and stole money, bicycles, or food less often than boys. Or the discrepancy could have resulted from what is currently labeled "profiling," where the police focus their attention on a group assumed to commit the majority of certain kinds of crimes, girls in department stores, for example. Six of the 53 shoplifters (11 percent) were sent to a supervised education house, and 5 of those 6 were boys. Note that the 1 in 28 girls sent to supervised education houses for shoplifting represents only a 3.6 percent rate, meaning judges were not harsher on girls who shoplifted (10 percent of the girls who appeared in the Fifteenth Chamber were sent to supervised education houses). On the whole, about 11 percent of the minors in theft cases received the harshest treatment, a figure that does not vary by category except for bicycle theft. There, the slightly more lenient treatment, only 7 percent sent to public institutions, might suggest that judges viewed stealing bicycles as a normal youthful prank.

What motivated adolescents to steal? Based on my careful reading of the case files in both Paris and the provinces, two factors—situational tempta-tion and pressure from other people—led most of the minors to commit their crimes. One clear example of peer pressure involved the only minor in my entire sample living in the sixteenth arrondissement, Paris's wealthi-est district. This boy stole a briefcase worth 4,000 francs off a table in a shop. He claimed, "I committed this act following a bet I had with my friends, who claimed that I was incapable of stealing something without getting caught." His friends turned out to be right.[98] The judge acquitted him as acting without discretion and returned him to his mother. More often teenagers persuaded each other to commit a particular crime together.

Adolescents, most of whom left school for work by age fourteen but received very low wages, were easily tempted by materials at hand on the job. One-third, 15 of the 46 relevant Paris case files, involved minors who stole from their employers. D. stole lead pipes from the job. G. stole wine, washers, electric wire, and screws from his workshop—worth 15,000 francs, according to the complaint. He considered these items to be a perquisite of the job, and his mother disputed the valuation, insisting that what he brought home was of such small value that she felt it was not important.[99]

Working around food presented powerful temptation. One seventeen-year-old boy stole four liters of cooking oil and three packets of margarine from the cooking oil refinery that employed him, but he insisted that the oil was "meant for cooking potatoes for my personal consumption."[100] P., who worked for a biscuit maker, stole forty kilograms of flour and was arrested with several young coworkers as they were dividing it up. The boys claimed that "if they got enough to eat" thanks to biscuits provided on the job, "their parents didn't have enough bread."[101]

While theft from employers could have served to satisfy either personal or family needs, a few cases clearly involved minors who stole in order to sell goods on the black market. In some cases the theft involved expensive and rare materials. For example, D., a sixteen-year-old working at a factory, together with a nineteen-year-old coworker, tried to steal a six-kilogram lead plaque.[102] A delivery boy for a soap factory altered a receipt to read that twenty kilos of soap had been paid for instead of twenty-nine, and sold the extra nine kilos "under the table" *(sans ticket)* for fifty francs.[103] P. stole meat, oil, noodles, and cheese from a warehouse in Paris over a period of several months. He sold it to several people, including his own mother, who claimed not to have known it was stolen. The father in this case admitted that his son routinely brought home extra food, but since the boy worked at a cafeteria, the father indiscreetly explained, "I figured that he was involved in little black market activity like everyone else these days."[104]

On a small scale, an eleven-year-old boy plotted with his fourteen-year-old friend to steal a rabbit. One boy distracted the owner while the other ran off with the rabbit. After they got caught, they explained that they had hoped to make a deal, to sell the rabbit and split the proceeds.[105] A sixteen-year-old boy placed at a transit center for young French labor volunteers on their way to Germany took his work jumpsuit and sold it at a café for 400 francs "to get myself a little pocket money."[106] Several teenage girls who worked (for abysmal pay) as domestics or maids stole money or jewelry from their employers. W. took clothing, a watch, and some jewelry; R. took 40 francs and jewelry worth 15,000 francs; M. took 1,600 francs to buy herself a bicycle.[107]

Less clear was the case of T. In 1942, police near Le Bourget stopped T., a sixteen-year-old apprentice metalworker, and his twenty-year-old friend and found twenty-five kilograms of apples in each one's bicycle sack. When questioned, T. used the oldest excuse in the book: everyone else was doing it. He claimed he and his friend had just gone out for a ride in the country when they saw other people gathering apples in a field and decided to "gather some up for our brothers." His adult companion thought up a more compelling reason, "I didn't know we weren't allowed to take apples, because I thought they belonged to the whole world."[108] Fifty kilos of apples would have been a lot to share with their brothers; however, there is no way to know whether they intended to eat the apples or sell them on the black market.

Other case files present less ambiguous situations, for example, several bicycle-theft rings that relied on boys to steal the bikes. In one case, the police learned from an eighteen-year-old butcher's assistant accused of stealing three bicycles about "traffic in stolen bicycles" regularly taking place at a café in Boulogne, just outside Paris. The boys stole the bikes and were paid by the café owner, who disguised and then resold the bikes, often for double what he paid the boys. L. sold one men's bicycle he had stolen to the café owner for 1,500 francs, three-fourths of a month's wages for an adult man. Another of L.'s victims, a fourteen-year-old apprentice seamstress, helped break up the ring. Several days after her bike was stolen, she saw another young woman riding it. She approached the rider, who explained that she had purchased the bicycle from a local garage, proudly pointing out that she had bargained the garage owner from 2,200 down to 1,800 francs. The garage owner, when questioned, claimed that a local café owner had asked him to repair a tire and then offered to sell him the entire bicycle for 900 francs. The garage owner claimed ignorance of its origins and refunded the purchaser's money.[109] Another ring operated in Tours. C., age seventeen, stole nine bicycles in Tours during his career as a thief. He sold them all to a mechanic the police described as a well-known "disguiser of bicycles."[110]

Other kinds of theft rings also developed. In Saint-Ouen, a Paris suburb, B., fourteen, and his stepbrother were part of a gang that stole coal, clothing, food, and alcohol from packages stored in shipping facilities of the national rail service, the SNCF. B. admitted to stealing from the SNCF for about a year, and explained that he sold the goods at the Paris flea market (at Clignancourt). According to the social worker in the case, "an entire, organized gang stole from the warehouses, even from POW care packages."[111] I found eight cases from the Paris region and two from the provincial courts that unambiguously indicated minors involved in opportunistic theft for sale.

More often, a sense of deprivation created the temptation to steal, as several of the cases already cited reveal. For example, one seventeen-year-old girl who worked as a packer in a pastry shop for 6.60 francs an hour was accused of shoplifting two blouses and some makeup from La Samaritaine, a Paris department store. Her father worked irregularly as a plumber to support a family of four on 1,600 francs a month. Her mother, a housewife, wrote, "I admit I am not rich and cannot satisfy my children's needs, but I never would have stood for my daughter's doing such a thing!"[112] The items stolen strongly suggest that the girl wanted nice things she could not afford.

Some of the minors claimed to have been hungry or even starving. C., an eighteen-year-old ironworker, stole a suitcase from a hotel room and sold the contents in local cafés. The police report stated dubiously, "He claimed to have acted in the grip of hunger." C. himself insisted, "It's because I had not eaten for two days that I was pushed to commit this theft." He said he spent the proceeds at a restaurant. Since he had a reasonably well-paid job, he might very well have been lying about starving.[113] More believable were the claims of starvation made by the Belgian refugees who had fled the war zone in 1940 and found themselves warehoused in refugee camps in the Gard (see Chapter 2).

Some contemporary observers after the war linked the rising curve of juvenile crime during the occupation to the Resistance. However, determining whether theft or other felony cases involved Resistance activity proved difficult. Indeed, rural resistance groups did steal food from farms. But resisters caught stealing food would most likely have been tried in the special courts set up to repress the Resistance, not charged with theft. Furthermore, the food theft cases contained no indications of Resistance activity. Nevertheless, several of the cases indicated strong anti-Vichy sentiments, whether or not the individuals involved carried such feelings over to organized Resistance activities. One office boy, seventeen, was charged in 1942 with insulting a police officer, violence, and drunkenness after yelling obscenities at police he claimed represented the "new order."[114] Another seventeen-year-old boy, charged in 1943 with insulting an officer, drunkenness, rebellion, and "insulting the Head of State" had called the police "Pétain's manure."[115] Although the disrespect for authority such cases expressed may not have been related to the actual regime in power, the one boy's reference to the "new order" denotes his awareness of the regime's politics. Moreover, insulting Philippe Pétain by name took on a more radical meaning in the context of the authoritarian Vichy regime, as this boy's arrest and prosecution attest.

In general, cases unambiguously tied to the Resistance were, at an increasing rate, turned over to special French tribunals or German military courts. Aside from the communist propaganda cases, only one incident in the sample studied clearly revealed Resistance sympathies. The police in a small town in the Gard arrested H., a seventeen-year-old student, and accused her of making "remarks liable to exert an unfortunate influence over the public state of mind" and listening to BBC radio. A specific incident had provoked the arrest. In March 1942, an altercation broke out among a group of women standing in line for milk. One woman, reacting to a recent British air raid near Paris, commented sarcastically, "Here's what our English 'friends' are doing to us." This comment aroused the ire of another woman, a fifty-three-year-old housekeeper who replied, "You'd have to be awfully stupid to believe such printed lies. The Marshal is not governing! The radio and the newspapers follow orders from the Germans." H. joined the fray, claiming that, if she could, she "would happily go with the English." The investigating magistrate's report on the minor raved about the good qualities of the parents. He noted, however, that the family was Protestant, possibly to explain her anglophilia, and added, "The H. family is considered to profess Gaullist ideas." One member of the family had already been convicted of antinational propaganda. However, in this case the court dropped all charges against H.[116]

Extremely rarely, cases indicating serious mental or emotional problems appeared in the case files. I found five such cases, three in Paris, two from the provinces. One case was tragic in every aspect. It involved a mentally retarded fifteen-year-old boy who had murdered a woman riding her bicycle. She turned out, more tragically, to have been a prisoner-of-war wife. The psychiatrist in the case reported that the boy had explained that he "got the idea of killing a woman from reading books." Also, one of his friends had supposedly told him that "to get yourself some money, you need to attack women to burglarize them." The accused minor explained that he had killed his victim "the way I read about it in gangster books; the way I had seen it done in the movies." This case could be seen to confirm the era's prevalent fears about the evils of the cinema and gangster novels. But in fact this was the only case in which an accused minor so much as mentioned books or movies. Furthermore, in addition to the boy's mental retardation, which could have made him more suggestible and certainly made it more difficult for him to understand the consequences of his actions, another tragic factor enters the picture. This boy's mother had been accidentally separated from him as they fled the advancing German army in May 1940 and was never seen again. According to the psychiatrist, when questioned about his mother, "the accused boy tensed up and shed a few tears." The doctor concluded that the boy was retarded—not perverse *(pervers)* but perverted *(perverti)* by friends, books, and movies. Yet the doctor insisted that the boy knew right from wrong and could be held responsible for his actions. He was convicted as acting with discretion and was sent to a penal colony in 1941 for fifteen years, was released in 1948, and was pardoned in the mid-1950s.[117]

Another pathetic case involved a seventeen-year-old agricultural worker accused of sexually assaulting a three-year-old girl. His mother had been concerned about him for years and requested a psychiatric exam, which found him to be mentally retarded. However, according to the medical report, until the assault he had never shown any sign of "perverted instincts" and the court followed the doctor's recommendation to return him to his family with medical treatment.[118]

One Parisian girl who worked as a domestic servant stole money and jewelry from her employer. The file revealed that her father, deceased, had been abusive and alcoholic. The social worker described her as an "ugly girl, liar, of difficult character. She tried to stand up to me for the entire interview, then ended up crying." After her arrest, she attempted suicide by drinking iodine but changed her mind about the suicide quickly enough to drink several glasses of water. She then admitted she had been seeing a married man who had already seduced and then abandoned one of her friends before doing the same to her. After her attempted suicide, she requested immediate placement in a Catholic Bon Pasteur. The mother seconded that request, the social worker quickly notified the judge, and the minor was placed the same day.[119]

Another Paris domestic servant, a seventeen-year-old girl, stole clothing and jewelry from her boss. The investigation uncovered a sad story. She had lived with her aunt since the age of six, when her father had abandoned the family and her mother had been stricken with polio. Eleven years later, shortly before the theft, her mother died. Apparently the mother and aunt had been on bad terms, and despite the fact that she had taken care of her from the age of six, the aunt displayed little affection for her niece, requesting that the court not return her: "My niece is a depraved girl and I can no longer keep her in my home." The social worker noted that the niece had been "shunted around from place to place" and described the aunt as "very strict, not very understanding." The judge placed this minor at Saint-Michel de Chevilly-Larue, a private institution, in February 1943.[120]

Finally, there was the case of a fifteen-year-old boy who continuously turned up at train stations offering to carry bags for money. He was found sleeping on a bridge platform in Paris. By the time the file opened, he had already run away from home six times, even though his parents tried never to let him leave the house without them. Apparently he had caused his parents no trouble until after June 1940, when the running away began, but the court did not look into possible connections with the traumatic war events of that month. The court first placed him with Public Assistance. By March 1941 he had run away ten times, and the judge sent him to an Observation Center. His mother wrote the judge claiming that he had become ill and anemic as a result of his stay at the Observation Center and requested his transfer to a private institution, Frasnes-le-Chateau, or back to Public Assistance, where the material conditions were better. By February 1942 he had run away seventeen times and been placed in several different kinds of institutions, including a Youth Center to learn auto mechanics. While at the Youth Center, he stole ten work uniforms. Finally the court sent him to a supervised education house.[121]

These details provide a glimpse of the few cases that indicated serious emotional, family, or psychiatric disorders. Yet these five cases were truly exceptional. The other 148 full case files from all four departments read more like the stories on *People's Court*. The crimes were petty, usually poorly executed, and often resulted from temptation created by opportunity, a sense of deprivation, or the influence of friends. The black market clearly represented a magnet in such hard times. Not only did it provide an opportunity to make quick money but the black market also profoundly altered France's entire culture of legality—that is, the generally accepted sense of what should be legal or illegal. Trading on the black market was illegal, but most people considered it entirely justified. As A.'s father stated, everyone was trading on the black market, adults as well as minors. The line between right and wrong, legal and illegal, blurred during the war. Most people did not condone making large profits at others' expense, but a mother buying food for her family? There was a case in September 1942 of a mother, a ragpicker, who sent her fifteen-year-old daughter to buy two kilos of bread with false tickets.[122] The minor was acquitted as acting without discretion and returned to her parents.

The contemporary attribution of the rising juvenile crime rate to the absence of prisoner-of-war, deportee, and STO fathers distorted the reality. In the few cases where the absence of a POW father proved to be a factor, the problems arose not because prisoners' wives proved incapable of disciplining and exerting adequate authority over their children. Rather, problems arose when the prisoners' absence resulted in extremely unstable situations. For example, in one case, in addition to the father's captivity, the mother had been killed in an air raid in 1940. In another case the parents had long been divorced, and when mobilized, the father, who had custody, left his children with his common-law wife and then was taken prisoner. One POW had left his daughter in the custody of an uncle and aunt, who then both died. Surprisingly, the death of a parent was rarely discussed as a factor in juvenile delinquency, yet it was common among the minors both in my database and in several other studies, even more common than separation or divorce. About one-third of the minors in my database had one or both parents deceased (see Chapter 4).[123] The chances of losing a parent probably increased significantly during the war, although few cases of deceased parents in my study involved war-related deaths.

Juvenile crime during the war was a response to an interlocking set of complicated factors. The stresses of the wartime economy—deprivation, shortages, frozen wages, inflation, and the black market; the creation, with rationing laws, of new crimes; increased police, judicial, and social vigilance; and the shifting notions of legality under such circumstances all contributed to the phenomenon. Every society defines acceptable behavior and thereby creates categories of unacceptable behavior. Under normal circumstances, at least prior to the late twentieth century, the line dividing legal from illegal, moral from immoral, good from bad, was fairly clear and broadly accepted. However, conditions in wartime and occupied

France blurred all those distinctions, creating confusion, ambiguity, and hypocrisy.

One sign of the confusion was the blurring of distinctions between various youth populations that could broadly be defined as antisocial, although for very different reasons: resisters, the *zazous,* and juvenile delinquents. The harsh response by both French and German authorities to resisters bore little relation to the person's age. Interestingly, public anxiety about rising youth crime rates was deflected by the confusion between delinquent and countercultural youth. The conservative press reacted with near hysteria to the *zazou* urban youth counterculture (see Chapter 2). Yet in absolute numbers not that many young people took part and, while defiant, most of their activities were not strictly illegal. At one end of the spectrum, some *zazous* carried defiance over the edge of what could be labeled resistance. For example, a group of *zazous,* mocking the law requiring all Jews to wear the yellow Star of David, were arrested and deported to Auschwitz for wearing yellow stars inscribed with the word *swing.*[124] At the other end, some *zazous* certainly trafficked on the black market or stole items. However, *zazou* culture defined itself through consumption, and the working-class minors, barely scraping by, who ended up in court could not have afforded the trappings of *zazou* life. While some of the young people who turned up in court may have been *zazous,* the police could not arrest and the courts could not charge a young person with having the wrong attitude or wearing undesirable clothing. The very different social backgrounds of *zazous* and juvenile delinquents indicates two different groups. Yet note how juvenile judge Jean Chazal's description of Paris youth gangs during the war blurs the distinction between defiant and delinquent behavior. Chazal wrote, "They divide their time between the movies, fun fairs, neighborhood pools, and dancing parties held in abandoned waste yards. Their conduct is almost always antisocial. They pilfer. They plunder. They traffic. They burgle. At thirteen they already seek out the company of loose women."[125]

The rising rate of delinquency (from about 2 delinquents per 1,000 young people before the war to 5 per 1,000 in 1942), the very small number of truly serious cases in the juvenile courts, and the low recidivism rate suggest that wartime conditions drew a much larger group of adolescents into illegal acts. I would argue that adolescent misbehavior, if not always well planned or executed, was to a large extent a rational response to the circumstances and did not differ significantly from adult misbehavior. However, the attention paid to children victimized by the absence of

POW fathers, the anxiety aroused by youth counterculture, and the blurring of distinctions between *zazous* and delinquents all, ironically, served the purposes of reformers hoping to transform the system. With public anger deflected onto the *zazous,* experts could continue to portray delinquent minors as victims. The contrast between information found in the penalty registries and case files and expert opinion in the field of juvenile delinquency in the 1940s opened up a space for change.

4

The Juvenile Delinquency
Establishment during the War

Although France's defeat in 1940 divided the Third Republic from the Vichy regime, there were no parallel breaks in the field of juvenile delinquency. While some certainly experienced personal tribulations, for the most part specialists concerned with juvenile crime continued to undertake research projects, study, publish, attend conferences, work with state ministries on policy, run societies, edit journals, and work with juvenile delinquents at public and private institutions, clinics, and schools. However, the war without doubt intensified their activity, promoting a convergence of experts from a wide variety of fields around ideas long in the air. Thus prewar developments progressed and intensified, notwithstanding France's defeat, the collapse of the Republic, and the rise of an ultraconservative, authoritarian, repressive regime.

First, the war years saw a convergence of people, both experts and lay activists in the field, into a juvenile delinquency establishment. In fact, this trend paralleled a similar movement in a related, overlapping field, the creation of what Michel Chauvière, in his seminal work *Enfance inadaptée: L'héritage de Vichy* names the "maladjusted children" *(enfance inadaptée)* sector.[1] Chauvière analyzes the ideas, debates, areas of agreement, and recurring divisions in this sector, which originally hoped to include juvenile delinquents. Juvenile delinquency, however, retained its separate intellectual and institutional status after the war.

Who Was Who in Juvenile Delinquency

The experts who wrote about juvenile delinquency in the 1930s and 1940s included several masters surrounded by circles of apprentices. The most prominent specialist was pediatric neuropsychiatrist Georges Heuyer who, together with doctors Georges Paul-Boncour, Jacques Roubinovitch, and Paul Dublineau, ran the pediatric neuropsychiatric enterprise in the Paris region. They operated three neuropsychiatric clinics for children that conducted medical-psychiatric examinations for the Seine Children's Court.[2] Heuyer also trained many students, supervising doctoral theses by Georges Menut, Guy Néron, Simone Marcus-Jeisler, and Georges-Dominique Pesle. In the 1940s, Lyons, which had played a key role in the development of the French "social milieu" school ever since Alexandre Lacassagne had been a professor at the medical school there, continued to exert a critical influence in the field.[3] Two doctors, Paul Girard and Pierre Mazel, directed neuropsychiatric clinical work and research. Mazel, on the faculty of the Lyons Medical School, trained André Gamet and Guy Rey. Girard advised legal specialist André Perreau.

The nonmedical approach to understanding personality included child psychologists. In Paris, Henri Wallon, an internationally renowned child psychologist and a professor at the Collège de France, wrote about juvenile delinquency and served on a number of committees. Before the war he had written a critique of state institutions, *Une plaie de la société: Les bagnes d'enfants*.[4] Other psychologists in the field included Dr. Daniel Lagache, professor of psychology at the University of Strasbourg, and René Le Senne, professor of educational psychology at the Sorbonne.[5]

Circles of legal experts on juvenile and criminal law contributed another perspective to the field. Juvenile judges Jean Chazal, Georges Epron, Robert Chadefaux, and Erwin Frey wrote about delinquency. In Paris, Henri Donnedieu de Vabres, professor of criminal law at the University of Paris, published the *Dalloz* commentary on reforms of juvenile law in both 1942 and 1945. Donnedieu de Vabres also served on the editorial board of *Pour l'enfance "coupable"* and trained at least one student in the field, Geneviève Mazo, who published her doctoral thesis on Observation Centers in 1944.[6]

Another circle of lawyers concerned about juvenile justice developed at the University of Rennes Law School. Its founder, Henri Joubrel, served on the editorial board of *Pour l'enfance "coupable"* and copublished his brother Fernand's doctoral thesis, completed at Rennes. Pierre Waquet also completed a thesis on children's protection at Rennes. In Toulouse, Joseph Magnol, dean of the law school there and an expert on juvenile law, created the Institut pédotechnique together with a Catholic activist Abbot Jean Plaquevent, founder of L'Essor occitan, a remedial institution for "at risk" and delinquent youth. The field of juvenile law attracted a number of women. Attorney Hélène Campinchi regularly served as appointed defender for the Seine Children's Court and contributed articles to *Pour l'enfance "coupable."*

Social work provided women with another avenue for activism in the field. A number of social workers who worked with troubled minors published regularly in *Pour l'enfance "coupable,"* including Raymonde Gain, director of the Social Service for Children in Moral Danger (SSE) and Miss Barbizet, director of the Service for the Protection of Minors (Service de la protection des mineurs), a female police unit that surveyed the streets of Paris looking for minors in danger.[7] Mrs. Guichard, the director, and Miss Demoisy, a social worker for Safeguarding Adolescence (Sauvegarde de l'adolescence), produced many case reports for the Seine Children's Court and also published articles, as did Anne-Marie de la Morlais, director of the Social Service Safeguarding Children and Adolescents in the Ile-et-Vilaine (Service social de Sauvegarde de l'enfance et de l'adolescence d'Ile-et-Vilaine).[8] Social worker S. Cotte published a study of her city, Marseilles, in 1945 and, together with Albert Crémieux and M. Schachter, coauthored a highly influential and widely cited study that pulled together information on 3,000 cases culled from a variety of smaller studies. In addition to their critical role in the Seine Children's Court and their publications, one or two social workers were often included in conferences and on policy teams, although minutes from one meeting reveal that the social workers' comments were mostly ignored during the committee's debates.[9]

Finally, there were activists. The Joubrels, for example, were known both for their published work in the juvenile law field and for their advocacy of scouting programs in reform schools. Henri Joubrel, commissioner of the Eclaireurs de France, one of France's main scouting groups, and his brother Fernand formed a pro-scouting circle in Brittany that also included Dr. Pierre Bianqui, regional director of health and assistance in Brittany, Georges Bessis, a Christian activist, and Charles Péan, a major-general in the Salvation Army, a reformer of the penal colony in Guyana, and an eventual reformer of Ker-Goat, the private boys' institution.

As the names on the above list suggest, activists involved with delinquent youth came from every religion. Reflecting the paradigm shift that had taken place in religious thinking about children and adolescents who commit crimes, religious activists no longer interpreted youth crime in moral terms, as a manifestation of sinfulness. Nearly every religious activist in the field had by 1940 adopted the new, social-scientific language and approach. For example, Abbot Philippe Rey-Herme, in his book on delinquent youth, outlined Catholicism's historical approach to juvenile delinquency within the theology of sin and punishment. But Rey-Herme argued that the "progress of child psychology" required society to abandon punitive solutions in favor of pedagogical ones. A reformed juvenile justice system, he insisted, should reflect the "rapid progress in the science of childhood."[10]

The war and the German occupation had a profound personal impact on some key people in the field. Alfred Brauner, for example, joined the Resistance in 1943 but managed to complete a dissertation on the effects of the war on children in France at the Faculté des lettres in Paris in 1946. Psychiatrist Albert Crémieux was deported in 1944, but I could determine neither why nor whether he survived.[11] The book he coauthored only mentioned that his deportation interrupted the study of 3,000 dossiers his team had undertaken in 1942. Olga Spitzer, a banker's wife and patron of the SSE, apparently went into hiding or left France. She contributed no signed articles to the SSE's publications between 1940 and 1945. Although the Vichy government appointed her to an advisory council on juvenile law in September 1941, Spitzer was "excused" from attendance. Meanwhile, her husband, Edmond, director of the Banque franco-polonaise, had been anonymously denounced as Jewish in August 1941. Public prosecutor and future Vichy minister of justice Maurice Gabolde pressed his superiors to prosecute Spitzer for violation of the requirement to report himself as Jewish. However, in January 1942 the chief prosecutor at the Paris Court of Appeals intervened with then justice minister Joseph Barthélemy on behalf of Spitzer, citing not only his high standing in the world of finance but most especially the two medals Spitzer had earned for valor during the Great War. Barthélemy quietly signed off on dropping the charges. The fate of the Spitzers after January 1942 remains murky, although at least Olga Spitzer survived the war. A 1945 report makes veiled reference to the fact that the SSE had been "deprived of Mrs. Spitzer's support while she feared for her personal safety."[12]

One of the SSE's social workers was not so lucky. Miss Silz died in deportation. The SSE's 1945 report also hinted that the organization tried, without endangering its primary mission, to help "families being hunted down" and saved a certain number of Jewish children and their families.[13] Georges Bessis, appointed in the spring of 1942 to run the private boys' rehabilitative institution the Centre du Hinglé at Ker-Goat in Brittany, was deported and died in Germany. After the war the center was renamed after Bessis.[14]

Finally, for reasons unclear, publication of the journal *Pour l'enfance "coupable"* was suspended in November 1942, after a special double issue devoted to neuropsychiatrist Georges Heuyer's study of 400 dossiers from his clinic at the Patronage. The study contained nothing overtly political, and *Pour l'enfance "coupable"* survived as the *Internal Information Bulletin* (*Bulletin intérieur de l'information,* with, in parentheses, *Pour l'enfance "coupable"*) of the Study and Action Committee for Diminishing Crime (*Comité d'étude et d'action pour la diminution du crime*).[15] For most specialists, the war intruded primarily through economic disruptions that curtailed funding and raised the expenses of running institutions and conducting research, but such hardships had no effect in reducing the number of publications during or after the occupation.

In spite of continuing disagreements, experts had begun in the 1930s to converge on certain fundamental beliefs about why children or adolescents committed crimes. The areas of agreement ultimately manifested themselves in real legal and institutional changes. The continuing disagreements, intellectual divisions, and territorial jealousies limited the universalizing impulse, however, leaving juvenile delinquency as a separate sector.

France's Place in the World

Nearly everyone in France who wrote about the problem of juvenile crime in the 1940s agreed that the country had fallen seriously behind the rest of the world. French experts compared their system unfavorably to glowing reports from other countries and to what they saw of accomplishments elsewhere. Many of them went on pilgrimages to Belgium's renowned juvenile facility at Moll, reputed to rehabilitate some 80 percent of its delinquent minors. In his research on the series of European Congresses on Penitentiary Reform, first held in Frankfurt in 1846, Chris Leonards underlines the growing interest of specialists across Europe in the treatment of juveniles. Discussion time spent on children peaked at the 1895 Congress in Paris. In the twentieth century the Congress met in 1900 in Brussels, 1905 in Budapest, 1910 in Washington, 1925 in London, 1930 in Prague, and 1935 in Berlin.[16] French experts attended regularly, learning about foreign initiatives from reports by specialists from around the world.[17]

France's apparent failure to keep up with the latest technical developments represented a significant concern for scholars in a country that prided itself on its intellectual and cultural superiority. While the humiliating defeat of June 1940 severely tested national confidence, people active in the juvenile justice field continued to appeal for reform on that basis. They insisted that France's treatment of delinquent minors in the courts and in institutions needed to equal its intellectual achievements. Raymond Valet, for example, wrote in 1942, "If our country is the fatherland of the founders of reeducational methods, French achievements seem quite modest compared with certain foreign achievements."[18] Some experts noted that even Germany surpassed France in this arena. They also pointed to superior systems in Italy, Switzerland, and the United States, and most admiringly, those created by "our Belgian neighbors," who, according to Geneviève Mazo, "by working patiently at reeducation, manage now to create honest men out of 80 percent of their delinquent minors." Why, Mazo asked, had France not taken advantage of modern scientific methods?[19] Heuyer, Pesle, Perreau, and Joubrel also described the Belgian system in glowing terms, noting with shame that Belgium had established a much more advanced system in 1912 than France had that same year. In spite of the improvements brought about by the 22 July 1912 law, France's juvenile justice system continued to rest on the notion of punishment rather than rehabilitation. France had yet to adopt the new methods in treating delinquents that Belgium's system, they insisted, proved effective: observation centers, specialized courts, reeducation institutions. Perreau clarified why this galled him and his compatriots: "It is regrettable that the country that gave birth to Descartes should have let itself be outdistanced in the application of Cartesian principles by countries like England, the United States, Belgium, and Italy."[20]

The French Social Milieu School

France was not just the homeland of Descartes and other founders of modern scientific methods; in the nineteenth century French scholars had been in the forefront of criminological debates. In fact, French thinkers went to great lengths to define what came to be considered a French school of criminal anthropology, the "social milieu" school. The French school addressed the perennial debate about the relative importance of nature and nurture, heredity and environment, in explaining deviance and criminal behavior: Are character, personality, and behavior biologically determined at birth, dictated by a person's physical state? Is character innate and preprogrammed? Or are humans born blank slates, entirely shaped by the environment in which they spend their childhood?

In particular, a French doctor of legal medicine, Alexandre Lacassagne, challenged the then-dominant Italian school of criminal anthropology.

Italian sociologist Cesare Lombroso's studies of the "born criminal" and the stigmata of degeneracy rested on biological determinism. Lombroso, based on his work in prisons, asserted that criminals, in contrast to the insane, represented a step back in the evolutionary process. The theory of atavism proposed that in some individuals, older, more primitive traits suddenly reappear. The atavistic man thus represents an earlier stage, the so-called infantile phase of human evolution. Nineteenth-century anthropologists believed that "savages" were at an earlier phase, for example; that primitive humans lived subject to basic instincts and drives, unconfined by society. Thus atavism could explain the criminal's violence, aggression, and failure to conform to social norms.[21]

To oppose Lombroso, at the First International Congress of Criminal Anthropology in 1885, Lacassagne coined an aphorism, insisting, "Societies have the criminals they deserve." In fact, recent scholars, such as Marc Renneville and Laurent Mucchielli, have pointed out that Lacassagne and subsequent scholars have overplayed the differences between Lacassagne's French social milieu school and Lombroso's Italian positivists.[22] They note first that Lombroso, while insisting on the biological determinants of criminal behavior, also wrote about a wide variety of environmental and social factors, including climate, alcoholism, education, race, and economic factors. Second, they note that the French social milieu school, under the sway of Lamarckian views of evolution, countered Lombroso's theory of the sudden, unpredictable eruption of atavism with the theory of degeneracy. They believed that a bad social environment could cause lesions to the brain, resulting in insanity or criminal behavior. Such acquired traits, if the environment continued to favor them, would be passed down. Rather than individualistic primitivism, an unhealthy social milieu caused the slow, pathological degeneracy of entire populations.[23] Thus the French school may have rejected atavism and insisted on the social milieu, but it hardly rejected biology in understanding the causes of crime.

Nevertheless, Lacassagne's statement, which he himself loved to repeat, expressed the resistance of French specialists to Lombroso, carving out a distinctly French approach.[24] While such biological theories of degeneracy had become somewhat passé in general criminological circles in the early twentieth century, Dr. Ernest Dupré incorporated them into his theories of "constitutional perversity." Historian Christian Debuyst notes Dupré imparted those theories to his disciple Georges Heuyer, who dominated the study of juvenile delinquency between the wars.[25]

One sign of the juvenile delinquency field's continued connection with the older school of criminal anthropology is the frequency with which scholars in the field referred to Lacassagne, even in the 1940s. At least four books published in the 1940s cited Lacassagne's statement, "Societies have the criminals they deserve."[26] André Gamet, a neuropsychiatrist from Lyons, noted in citing Lacassagne, "Here we have just about returned to the ideas of Jean-Jacques Rousseau."[27] In fact, as the above discussion clarifies, Lacassagne's views differed quite profoundly from those of Rousseau, but his aphorism lends itself to varied interpretations. The notion that societies deserve their criminals also poses a challenge. As it became clear in 1941 that the number of juveniles appearing in the courts was increasing at an alarming pace, experts invoked Lacassagne's statement to prod France, whose developmental delay had become more than an intellectual embarrassment. Perhaps France deserved what was happening and would continue to happen unless it accepted the reforms experts had been advocating. If the French considered themselves intellectual leaders in pediatric neuropsychiatry and child psychology, the country's institutional backwardness nevertheless left it ill equipped to handle the crisis of the war.

While three authors cited only the one phrase of Lacassagne's speech, Gamet included the rest of Lacassagne's statement, which expresses more clearly the French approach. "The social milieu is crime's cultural medium, the criminal is the microbe, an element that gains importance only when it finds itself in a medium that allows it to ferment."[28] French scholars thus viewed a person's behavior and character as reflecting an interaction of innate, biological tendencies with an environment that either suppressed or encouraged good or bad tendencies.

Nearly everyone in the field acknowledged both the importance of environment and the significance of heredity and biology. The debates centered on the relative importance of each factor. For example, psychologists sparred with neuropsychiatrists over the weight of what neuropsychiatrist Georges Heuyer labeled "hereditary constitutional tendencies." Gamet outlined the continuing debates in France, for example between the Freudian psychoanalytical approach that focused on the development of the ego, Freud's Oedipus complex, and Adler's inferiority complexes of early childhood. Renowned child psychologist Henri Wallon admitted that "the child bears in him dangerous potentialities" but argued that biology alone did not determine a child's future.[29] First, he said, not every person with a particular defect becomes a criminal; second, every person has both good and bad tendencies. Therefore, the environment we live in,

Wallon argued, determines which tendencies predominate.[30] René Le Senne, an educational psychologist at the Sorbonne, divided the question into one of character, which, "owing to the effects of hereditary Mendelian determinism, is anterior to the id," and personality, which is "acquired, changeable . . . a result of character and of events imposed from outside the individual."[31]

While Heuyer's neuropsychiatric school criticized the psychologists for denying the importance of hereditary tendencies, the Lyons neuropsychiatrist Gamet pointed out that neither psychologists nor psychiatrists still advocated the simplistic theory of the "born criminal." Gamet proposed that juvenile delinquency "is the result of a three-part family, social and individual current . . . The child is born with a certain baggage of character troubles linked to his heredity." Various early childhood pathologies then added their effects to the hereditary baggage, after which family and society "carve their marks."[32]

Specialists in law worked to reconcile the two approaches. André Perreau, for example, rejected the concept that character is an immutable "ensemble of innate dispositions." He argued that a person's innate qualities should be considered "tendencies and not definitive predispositions."[33] Yet he admitted that education's potential to influence a child's nature varied with the age of the child, from highly plastic infants to very influenceable young children to less easily reshaped adolescents. In other words, he said, "plasticity has its limits."[34] Legal expert Pierre Waquet devised a formula to express the dualistic approach: "vulnerability of the child + harmfulness of the milieu = measure of moral danger."[35]

The relative weight placed on biology or environment varied depending on the scholar and his or her background. Medical experts like Heuyer favored biology while admitting the influence of the environment. Conversely, psychologists and social workers weighted the environment heavily without denying the importance of biology.[36]

The Most Important Environmental Factor: The Family

In 1994, Richard J. Hernnstein and Charles Murray published *The Bell Curve*, renewing the argument that intelligence is genetically determined and plays a major role in a wide variety of social factors. The controversy they sparked makes clear that the debate over the relative importance of nature or nurture has hardly been resolved.[37] Unlike Hernnstein and Murray however, French experts in the 1940s firmly planted themselves in the middle, insisting that both nature and nurture played a role in the eti-ology of criminal behavior and devoting a large portion of their writings to environmental causes of crime. The child's family represented the most important environmental factor, they insisted. But how did they explain the relationship of family life to delinquent behavior by minors?

Some psychologists, such as Wallon and Le Senne, wrote about the complex interactions of the child with his or her parents, which they dis-cussed on a general theoretical level, usually not illustrating their theories with actual cases.[38] Most French studies, however, took a firmly empirical approach, especially favoring statistics gleaned from a large number of case studies. Their conclusions about the relationship between family life and crime provide an excellent example of how a series of limited studies echo through the literature and eventually emerge in the popular view as gospel.[39]

Guy Néron's 1928 doctoral thesis, a study of 450 dossiers from Heuyer's Clinique de neuropsychologie infantile, found that 64 percent of the minors came from "abnormal families" *(familles anormales).*[40] André Gamet, a student of Pierre Mazel in Lyons, published his thesis in 1942. Of the 1,000 cases involving minors he studied, 549 (over 50 percent) came from a "broken-up family environment."[41] The grand master of pediatric neuropsychiatry, Georges Heuyer, confirmed the importance of family. In 1942, *Pour l'enfance "coupable"* published the results of Heuyer's study of 400 dossiers about boys sent by the Seine Children's Court to his clinic. According to Heuyer, only 12 percent of these boys came from a "normally constituted family" leaving 88 percent from "bro-ken families" *(familles dissociées).*[42] Heuyer noted that a similar study un-dertaken in San Francisco found only 35 percent of the delinquent minors came from broken families. But rather than questioning the bias of his sample, Heuyer remarks, "The fact that our figure is so much higher may correspond to a much higher incidence of family breakdown in Paris."[43] Although many experts in the 1940s took Heuyer's study as proof of the dominant influence of the environment, sociologist Nadine Lefaucheur's excellent recent analysis of Heuyer's oeuvre astutely points out that the data from this particular study did not negate his views on heredity. Rather, Heuyer believed that the violence, alcoholism, early death, and di-vorce he found in these families resulted from the same hereditary "de-fects" that also caused the children's delinquency.[44] Still, Heuyer's article provided essential confirmation to those who considered broken families a pathological environment for children.

Heuyer advised Menut on his thesis study of 839 dossiers drawn from a Child Neuropsychiatric Center at the Paris Medical School's Mental Illness Clinic. Menut found 551 minors, or 66 percent, were "from a broken family."[45] By 1944 and through the end of the 1940s, most experts who wrote on juvenile crime proclaimed as fact that some 50 to 80 percent of juvenile delinquents came from what were variously referred to as "broken," "disunited," or "divided" families.[46] I shall use the term *broken families* as shorthand. Crémieux, Cotte, and Schachter undertook a study of nearly 3,000 dossiers, pulling together the findings of other experts, including Gamet, Néron, Heuyer, and even American psychiatrist William Healy. Averaging the results of all of the studies, they came up with an overall figure of 46.39 percent for the number of delinquent minors who came from "abnormal households" *(foyers anormaux)*.[47]

Nonresearchers gravitated to the highest figure. For example, a well-known Seine Department juvenile judge, Robert Chadefaux, stated in 1946, "This is a truth based on experience, 80 percent of the minors who appear in the Seine Children's Court come from households disorganized by divorce and separation or based on free union."[48] Chadefaux's conclusions derived not from research but from his personal anecdotal experience and from generally accepted wisdom, verified by the studies cited above. Similarly, Hélène Campinchi, a family law expert associated with the Seine court, wrote in 1945, "It would almost be too easy to prove and to recall, for example, that over 80 percent of the misbehavior of minors is due to a family deficiency."[49]

The coalescence of views around the upper boundary of 80 percent led experts in the 1940s to what seemed the ultimately logical conclusion about the rising curve of juvenile crime. If broken families led to delinquent behavior by minors, then the rapid tripling of the number of minors appearing in court between 1940 and 1942 must have resulted from the sudden removal of fathers from hundreds of thousands of families. Social worker S. Cotte's study of minors appearing in the Marseilles juvenile court found that the number of minors who appeared in court rose from around 200 minors a year in the 1930s to a peak of 722 cases in 1942. The high point, Cotte insisted, "coincides with the departure of fathers as prisoners of war, deportees, forced laborers in Germany."[50]

Many writers agreed with Cotte's conclusion, including Henri Joubrel, who argued that among the many wartime evils that caused the rising national curve of juvenile crime, the most important one "leaps to mind–lack of paternal authority." Too many fathers had been "retained in the army or in captivity," he said.[51] In 1948, Heuyer stated without hesitation that the increase in juvenile crime during the war could be explained by the following figures: 8 million men mobilized in 1940, 1.9 million captured, 1.6 million POWs absent for five years, 220,000 deportees, and 780,000 forced laborers.[52]

It should be noted that military captivity and divorce constitute qualitatively different experiences for families. While war captivity usually implies an unwanted and temporary separation resulting from military service to the country, separation and divorce are chosen by at least one of the parents. In addition, divorce involves different social attitudes and complicated legal restrictions. In the 1940s a divorce could be obtained only as a result of adultery, cruelty or abuse, or a spouse's conviction for a serious crime. In other words, the circumstances surrounding divorce implied serious emotional trauma and, at the least, fighting between parents. Furthermore, many people considered divorce a sign of personal failure and immorality. Because French society assigned women the critical role of guardian of the home, wives bore the brunt of the stigma of divorce, further complicating the lives of divorced mothers.

Yet our scholars insisted that the father's absence alone had serious repercussions for children. People writing about crime and delinquency in America today similarly blame single-parent families, by which they also really mean mother-headed families. Robert L. Maginnis's recent study, published by the Family Research Council, a conservative American think tank, concludes, "Children from single-parent families are more prone to commit crime . . . because unmarried mothers often lack the skills to support a family or to manage a household effectively."[53] Note how Maginnis shifts smoothly from the seemingly neutral term "single-parent families" to "unmarried mothers." Nancy Dowd, a legal expert, points out, "Single-parent families are regularly equated with poverty, family breakdown, juvenile delinquency, and crime . . . And while the connections are tied to a gender-neutral label, in reality we link these social problems to parenting by single *mothers*."[54]

The belief in the dangers of absent fathers was, if anything, stronger in 1940s France. Neuropsychiatrist Menut cited psychologist Lagache: "The father's absence is one of the most pathogenic conditions for the child." Assumptions about natural differences between the sexes implied a certain division of emotional labor within the family regarding child rearing. Mothers played an essential role in a child's moral upbringing. The caring, empathetic, nurturing nature of women allowed mothers to provide children with unconditional love. But when children misbehaved, fathers, because of men's natural authority and superior capacity for abstract moral reasoning, stepped in with discipline, which was often physical. Gamet pointed out that the absence of a father not only often led to economic hardship for the family, forcing the mother to work outside the home, but also meant the disappearance of the source of authority: "The father continues to be, no matter what anyone says, the leader . . . with his departure goes the threat of the 'salutary smack' [*claque salutaire*] that makes more than one child think twice before doing something wrong." While all authors considered the mother's role equally important, Joubrel explained that "a mother hardly ever has over her daughters, much less over her sons, sufficient educational influence. Never can the sweetness of affection replace the firm words of a father." Heuyer seconded Joubrel's analysis, pointing out that mothers who remained alone at home owing to the military service, captivity, deportation, or forced labor of their husband had to "acquire the distant father's authority, replace him" in shops or on farms. Heuyer concedes, "As a general rule, the French woman proved herself equal to the task. But she was not always able to exert enough authority over adolescents deprived of their fathers."[55]

Such conclusions rested on the clear assumption that a sizable number of the minors who appeared in court during the occupation were children of prisoners of war. Yet few authors included actual figures to justify their assumption. After years of searching, I uncovered only three studies authored by four scholars that explicitly counted children of POWs as a separate category in studying troubled minors. Gamet's 1941 study of 524 minors examined at the Triage Center at the Lyons School of Medicine and Pharmacy between July 1940 and July 1941 uncovered only 3 "POW sons" (*fils de p[risonnier de]g[uerre]*). Gamet's advisor, Pierre Mazel, cited the same figures in his article on the geographic distribution of delinquency in Lyons during the war. Mazel cautiously noted, "It would be too easy to excuse the current upsurge in juvenile delinquency by incriminating the considerable number of POWs." Yet he feared the future consequences "of such a breakup of the family milieu."[56] Pierre Flot's study of juvenile delinquency in Brittany, based on two private homes for delinquent youth in the years 1943 to 1945, found that 9 out of 200 residents (3 of 80 boys and 6 of 120 girls) had fathers who were POWs, or about 5 percent. Lafon's 1947 study of 100 girls at an observation center found only 1 girl whose father had been a POW.[57] The children of prisoners of war made up 1 to 5 percent of these samples. While surprised by the low number of POW children, less than 1 percent of his sample, Gamet had an explanation: most POWs would have been between the ages of twenty and thirty, therefore most POW children were probably younger than ten, and delinquent behavior usually did not manifest itself until age thirteen. Gamet concluded, "POWs' sons are 'potential' delinquent minors [en puissance]."[58]

Gamet raised a relevant point about the age of POW children between 1940 and 1942. Yet he and his fellow scholars sidestepped the logical conclusion. Given the small number of POW children in their population, the absence of POWs could not explain the threefold increase in the number of minors appearing in juvenile courts at that very same time, between 1940 and 1942. Minors appearing in court were real people, not Gamet's "potential" juvenile delinquents. Court statistics did not include "potential juvenile delinquents." Therefore the absence of POWs did not cause the rising curve of juvenile crime between 1940 and 1942. (Although the few samples that counted POW children might not have been particularly representative samples, experts drew all their conclusions from equally problematic samples.)

Why did experts in the 1940s overlook facts that completely invalidated the assumed connection between war captivity and juvenile delinquency? Surely the patriarchal assumptions that informed such conclusions were widely held and, notwithstanding Simone de Beauvoir, virtually unquestioned in France in this era. If anything, the Vichy regime's conservative propaganda only strengthened the outlook. However, beyond the reflexive anxiety about single mothers and absent fathers, close examination of writings from the 1940s on juvenile delinquency suggests another agenda that blinded the experts to inconsistencies in their analyses. By insisting loudly on the role of family breakdown, they successfully linked the issue of delinquency to a presumed family crisis that in fact preceded the war and that the war only aggravated. Juvenile reformers managed to pull the problem of minors who commit crimes, a group with little popular sympathy, into a mainstream political discourse not explicitly about crime.

Family, Demography, and Delinquency

France's preoccupation with family breakdown and the resulting decline of the French birthrate dates back at least to the mid-nineteenth century and was finally manifested in the Third Republic's Family Code of 1939 as well as in Vichy's laws against divorce, abortion, and married women's employment.[59] Miranda Pollard's work analyzes both continuities and discontinuities in Vichy's family policy. While Vichy maintained and executed many policies inherited from the Third Republic, it greatly amplified the propaganda, proved willing to use coercion to impose maternity on women, and placed family initiatives into a separate administrative structure for the first time, the General Commission on the Family (Commissariat générale à la famille, or CGF).[60] For those hoping to reform France's juvenile justice system, focusing on family breakdown as the cause of juvenile delinquency anchored the problem to this bigger, more popular cause. The breakdown of the French family was not just causing the birthrate to go down, it was also ruining the children who were born. Fernand and Henri Joubrel stressed the demographic importance of rehabilitating France's youth by citing Goethe: "To save a man is good, but saving a child is like saving a multiplication table."[61] By insisting that more than half of the children who appeared in courts came from broken families, delinquent youth could be portrayed as victims of selfish and hedonistic parents.

Scholars made it appear that one-half to four-fifths of delinquent minors were victims of such faulty families, by blurring, intentionally or unintentionally, certain key distinctions. In particular, authors in the 1940s incorporated, with virtually no discussion, the death of a parent, a critical factor, into the broken-family category. Chapter 3, which discusses court records from four juvenile courts, points out the striking number of minors who had lost one or both parents. The 1940s studies found similar rates. For example, Gamet's 1,000 cases included 549 minors who came from "broken families." But 258 of the 549 families had been "broken" by one parent's death. That number dwarfs the 44 cases of divorce or legal separation, and the 81 cases of de facto separation.[62] Judge Georges Epron described a social worker's study of minors appearing in the Grenoble Children's Court between 1936 and 1938. Of 167 cases, only 86 minors came from "complete" families, but among the 81 minors from "broken families," 44, more than half, had experienced the death of a parent. In both studies, nearly one-quarter of the minors in the total sample had lost a parent.[63]

Crémieux, Schacter, and Cotte's study of 2,964 delinquent minors included some 1,375 from "broken homes" (foyers dissociés). Of those, 743 minors had lost one or both parents—equaling 54 percent of the broken families and 25 percent of the total sample—while only 127 minors' parents were divorced or separated, representing 9 percent of the broken families and 4 percent of the total sample.[64] G. Kohler and Line Thevenin, from the Lyons Observation Center, reported on 294 children who had passed through the center between November 1943 and March 1945. Of the 129 minors from broken families, 35 cases involved the death of a parent, as compared with 14 cases of separated or divorced parents and 1 family experiencing "serious discord" *(mésentente grave)*. Yet Kohler concludes, "Thus, over 50 percent of the delinquents come from broken family environments."[65]

While the authors all mention the number of minors whose parents had died, only Menut's study tried to control for it. He compared his population of "emotionally disturbed" *(caractériels)* minors with a sample of nearly 13,000 children from regular Paris elementary schools. Both samples included children from broken families, but 71 percent of the general population's broken families involved death, in comparison to 56 percent of the emotionally disturbed children's families. Although the 15-percent difference could be significant, still more than half of the children he labeled disturbed were orphans. Also, Menut did not indicate which districts the Paris students came from, so in part he may have been measuring a class difference in divorce and separation rates.[66]

Still, Menut alone addressed the difference between death and separation. The fact that none of the other scholars considered orphans or half orphans a significant category worthy of separate analysis illuminates a number of critical problems with these studies. First, the object of study remains unclear. The profusion of terms signals the definitional confusion. The most common term, "broken families" *(familles dissociées)*, is used by Rey, Blancho, Kohler, Marcus-Jeisler, Heuyer, Lafon, Menut, and Gamet. Many terms are even more explicitly normative. Cotte writes about "irregular families" *(familles irrégulières)*, Chadefaux refers to "disorganized families" *(familles désorganisées)*, Robin uses the term "incomplete families" *(familles incomplètes)*, Pesle and Crémieux use "abnormal families" *(familles anormaux)*, and Kohler refers to "families with a structural defect" *(familles ayant un défaut de structure)*. Gamet, Pesle, and Mazel extended the moral judgment that shaped the category, including families in which the mother worked outside the home for a wage. Pesle's abnormal households included those with "working mothers leaving children abandoned" *(travaille de la mère laissant enfants abandonnés)*. Mazel similarly described some families as broken by "the mother's factory labor" *(travail de la mère à l'usine)*. Gamet asked, "How can such a household be normal?"[67]

The term *broken family* evokes action that deliberately breaks the marital bond. The tone of the writings, notwithstanding the information provided about orphans, implied that such families were broken by some act chosen by a parent—divorce, abandonment, separation. As Gamet stressed with boldfaced type, "More than 50 percent of delinquent minors come from a dwelling deserted by at least one of the parents." Having described families "deserted by a parent," Gamet lists in numerical order the causes, starting with the "death of one or the other parent."[68]

Certainly, both death and divorce entail increased financial hardship for custodial parents and both represent traumatic events in the life of a child or adolescent. But they are two different traumas. Including minors whose father or mother had died in the same category as the children of divorce and separation effectively doubled the percentage of juvenile delinquents from broken families. Combining the figures may have been intentional padding, but the normative language suggests, rather, that writers of the 1940s failed to see their own analytical sloppiness, owing to the strength of their assumptions about what constituted a "normal" family. The definition was unrelenting. A child had to have two living parents who were married and resided in the same household, with a mother who stayed at home. Menut illuminates the normative aspect in his summary of a normal family upbringing, which, in his view, required a "virile father, feminine mother."[69]

Some analyses discussed the emotional problems created for children by situations of parental conflict and divorce. Only one author, Judge Georges Epron in 1943, defined the normal family by considering not just the structure but also the quality of family life. Epron reported that 81 of his 167 minors came from single-parent families. But he did not use that figure to stand in for normality. Rather, in discussing normal and abnormal families, Epron examined reports on life at home and took into account such issues as parental conflict and the family's reputation in the community. He concluded that home life was reported to be normal for nearly 80 percent of the minors. Surprised by his own findings, Epron asked, "Where, then, are the great causes of juvenile delinquency denounced in all the studies that deal with the issue?" Contemporaries would have replied that Epron was looking at the wrong thing, the qualitative aspect of family life rather than the match between a child's family structure and a "normal family."[70] If the round hole was the two-parent, married, male-breadwinner family, then any family that did not have all those elements was a square peg and, by definition, "abnormal." The category of normal is inconsistently labeled, each study includes slightly different groups in it, and all studies merged categories that merited separate analysis, because experts were fixated on family structure, either downplaying the quality of family life or assuming that if the family structure fell outside the norm, the quality of family life would necessarily also be bad.

Furthermore, the studies in the 1940s were biased in ways that reduce their applicability to the total population of minors who appeared in juvenile courts. For example, Heuyer's study of 400 dossiers set the upper limit of 88 percent from broken families, a figure subsequently popularized at 80 percent. Yet all 400 cases involved boys examined at Heuyer's clinic at the Patronage des enfants et adolescents, hardly a random sample of boys appearing in juvenile courts. Judges sent boys to the Patronage either while a case was under investigation (preventive detention) or as a final placement. Both during and after an investigation, judges had wide discretion to leave the minor with his or her parents, to send the minor to a private charity like the Patronage, or to send the minor to a public supervised education house. Judges returned most minors to their parents. Thus boys who appeared in court from the Patronage did not represent a randomly selected group. Judges were more likely to return minors to families that on the surface did not present serious problems, and were more likely to send a minor to the Patronage in situations they took to signal trouble at home.[71] As sociologist Nadine Lefaucheur points out, the proper way to test the hypothesis that family breakdown caused delinquency would have been to set up a random sample of accused minors and a control sample of nondelinquent minors.[72]

The experts of the 1940s were intelligent and well educated. Such errors of analysis resulted from unquestioned assumptions about gender and family life, and from an agenda that, in another twist, had little to do with "family values." While a few studies considered ways of shoring up families, through stricter divorce laws, for example, or by requiring parent education classes, most analyses shifted gears as they moved from considering the causes of delinquency to recommending remedies. The experts of the 1940s wanted observation centers and scientific treatment in modern institutions, where minors would be removed from their families. They were engaged in the perennial struggle to build their own professional credibility and, more important, to exploit that credibility to gain power and authority over the population of delinquent and troubled youth. They worked hard, and succeeded to a large extent, at inserting themselves as experts into certain procedures and institutions that dealt with delinquent children. Chauvière argues that in the emerging and parallel maladjusted-children sector, the real leaders—technocrats, doctors, judges, and lawyers—maintained a profamily appearance by including certain family activists in their discussions while carefully guarding all real power over policy formation for themselves.[73]

Experts on delinquency blamed the family for a variety of reasons. They themselves held to patriarchal gender norms. In part they may have consciously amplified the family-breakdown rhetoric to win over the conservative moralists in power at Vichy. Primarily, however, blaming bad parents allowed the experts to avoid the conclusion I came to after studying court cases: the behavior of delinquent minors was essentially shaped by economic circumstances. Presenting delinquent minors as individuals responding in a rational way to economic cues would have favored a negative public view and justified retaining a punitive system to deter misbehavior. In France in the 1940s, blaming the family deflected censure from the minors themselves: minors who broke the law were victims of bad families. While juvenile delinquency reformers in the 1940s did not advocate fixing the families, neither did they propose punishing the minors more harshly. They believed they had the technology to repair the damage.

The war presented both danger and opportunity to those in the juvenile delinquency establishment who hoped to reform France's system. After the fall of France in 1940, as their part in the national search for what went wrong, delinquency experts pointed to France's inability to redeem its wayward children. The rapid rise in the crime rate could have provoked fear and anger against criminals, young and old. Both public officials and juvenile delinquency experts considered the situation by 1941 a crisis. Rey described delinquency as the "burning question of the day."[74] Experts, who had in fact been stressing the role of family breakdown for years, made good use of the opportunity presented by the public authorities' concern to increase their own authority and bring about change. The war and the resulting captivity of 1.6 million French POWs, which created 600,000 "fatherless" children, corresponded to an alarming rise in the juvenile crime rate. The war, in other words, seemed to prove that the experts had been right all along. As Néron explained, the war constituted an experience that "demonstrated . . . the importance of the father's absence in the genesis of character problems in the child."[75] Why, given such power, would juvenile delinquency experts have any motive for revising their basic analysis after discovering only a very small percentage of POW children in their samples? Reassessing the connection between captivity and delinquency would have meant rethinking the assumptions behind all their previous scholarship. Experts of the 1940s refused to see the inconsistencies in their own work because they simply had to be right.

Other Environmental Factors

Although for most specialists, their firm belief that family breakdown represented the most powerful environmental factor causing delinquency provided a tactically useful argument with conservative leaders, those who studied and wrote on delinquency in the 1940s also considered other environmental, community, and social causes that might contribute to delinquency. Unlike their empirical and statistical treatment of family breakdown, however, the experts contented themselves with describing other environmental factors rather than tabulating how many minors were in fact exposed to them. When considering social influences, the experts did not focus on class, income, or standard of living. Rather, they wrote in medicalized terms about unhealthy aspects of urban life, for example, slums, the crowding of families into small apartments, and the crowding of certain areas of cities, which lacked open space, parks, and other amenities.[76] In addition to being cramped and unsanitary, cities also presented unnatural, powerful temptations for young people, such as cafés, dance halls, and amusement parks. Writers concerned about the urban environment and juvenile crime often criticized department stores because they displayed luxury items in a tempting fashion to the longing eyes of France's youth, and flea markets because they provided easy outlets for stolen goods.[77] Experts worried also about the availability of cheap detective novels, for boys, and periodical literature, for girls. The Joubrels denounced women's magazines, pointing out that the 27 September 1940 issue of *Notre coeur* included "an apology for adultery, an apology for divorce, and an apology for suicide."[78]

However, nearly every book or article on juvenile crime singled out one especially dangerous environmental factor: the cinema. Doctors, lawyers, social workers, and religious activists alike decried the evil influence of films on the minds of France's youth. Three French specialists, Liévois, Lafon, and Crémieux, cited a single study published in a Portuguese journal, *Primo de Maio,* in 1938. The Portuguese authors had reviewed 1,810 recent films, counted the crimes depicted in them, and found 340 cases of armed robbery with or without murder, 74 cases of bribery, 254 cases of corruption of minors, 1,405 cases of adultery, and so on. They arrived at a grand total of 4,700 crimes and misdemeanors to which avid and impressionable young filmgoers would have been exposed.[79]

Beyond the medium's supposed glorification of criminal and immoral behavior, several authors worried about the very experience of attending the cinema. "In the darkness of an artificial environment . . . the child is impregnated with the film he sees, he is defenseless against it, and, aided by the spirit of imitation, he becomes entirely enmeshed in its atmosphere."[80] Liévois, Pesle, and Gamet also worried about more technical environmental issues—the dark, unventilated room; the stimulating bright lights emanating from the screen; the candy. Gamet cited Dr. Mario Bernarbei's medical study, which found that films maintained "the nervous system in a constant state of tension." Bernarbei demanded that the public authorities consider "the particular fragility of the not yet fully developed spinal-encephalo system of the child."[81]

Only Gamet actually counted the frequency with which juveniles went to the cinema. Of the 1,000 minors he studied, only 182 of them reported attending the movies at least once a week, hardly an overwhelming number.[82] As with our current concerns about violence on television, sex on the Internet, suicide and rock lyrics, MTV and illiteracy, the anxiety about film in the 1940s rested on deep fears about modern life. The mass culture of the cinema had only recently arrived in France. Contemporaries worried about their children being influenced by factors beyond the control of the family, churches, and schools. Much of the concern, particularly about Hollywood films, manifests another widespread French preoccupation of that era, fear of the United States and the modern, mass, popular culture it propagated.[83]

According to film historian Brett Bowles, Vichy officials agreed with delinquency experts that Hollywood films propagated a kind of hyperindustrial, hypercapitalist decadence; in other words, the exact opposite of the values the National Revolution promoted. The Vichy government disapproved of French children vegetating in dark, presumably insalubrious movie theaters, being tempted into all sorts of sexual debauchery. Until September 1942, Vichy acted on its concerns about the cinema, echoed in many prefects' reports, by requiring all foreign films to get prior approval (visa d'exploitation) from the Propaganda and Information Ministry and by using the process to ban objectionable American films. According to Bowles, the censure board essentially used moral criteria in its decisions. In a more radical move, in September 1942 Vichy pulled all "Anglo-Saxon" films from the theaters.[84] As for preventing delinquency, Pesle suggested a rather drastic solution: banning all children under age eighteen from cinemas.[85] However, most experts proposed a less extreme remedy that eventually was adopted—devising a rating system and prohibiting access to certain films for minors under a set age.

The Influence of Biology

Experts of the 1940s firmly believed that the environment, despite its powerful influence in shaping a child's behavior, constituted only half of the equation. Nature also played a critical role. A child was born with certain innate characteristics, somehow shaped by heredity, further manipulated by early childhood conditions and illnesses, upon which a healthy or unhealthy environment exerted its influence.

The idea of an inherited predisposition to criminal behavior could have fostered a negative view of delinquent minors. If delinquent youth were born bad, then rehabilitation would be useless and harsh punishment would be in order. Yet most French experts of the 1930s and 1940s, both deterministic about the conditions that caused misbehavior and optimistic about what they could accomplish with proper knowledge and equipment, maintained a benevolent view of the child criminal. In their view, it made no more sense to punish a child who committed a crime than it did to punish a child for catching pneumonia. In both cases, diagnosis and treatment constituted the appropriate response.

Most analyses of character thus began with the belief that the act by a minor of committing a crime or misdemeanor probably manifested some kind of condition or "character trouble" *(trouble de caractère)*. As Judge Chadefaux explained, "The criminal act passes to the second level, it remains only the first acute manifestation of serious problems."[86] At a training session for educators, one pediatric neuropsychiatrist warned his audience that nearly all children, as they develop, undergo various "character crises" *(crises de caractère)*. Having described in detail various "behavioral and intellectual problems" educators might encounter, he admonished them, "Do not imagine that you see abnormal cases everywhere."[87] But most specialists writing in the 1940s disregarded such caution.

Dr. Rey conceded that some juvenile delinquents might be normal, although he found not a single one of the recidivists he studied to be "exempt from character or intellectual troubles."[88] Most experts insisted that only about 20 to 30 percent of delinquent children could be considered normal. Social worker Cotte compared the findings from her study of

Marseilles to other studies and concluded that "the number of mentally insufficient among delinquents" oscillated between 75 and 82 percent."[89] Juvenile judge Georges Epron agreed that "80 percent of young delinquents concern the doctor or the psychiatrist." He advocated treating a delinquent minor as "a sick person who needs to be healed."[90]

Information from case files presented in Chapter 3 casts grave doubt on the validity of assertions that nearly 80 percent of delinquent youths suffered from serious emotional disturbances. Nevertheless, most specialists firmly believed that a very high proportion of juvenile delinquents suffered from some factor beyond their control and that, therefore, if France hoped to create a system to rehabilitate delinquent minors, the first step should involve diagnosis. Interestingly, experts writing on juvenile delinquency expressed little concern about how to determine what separated normal from abnormal children. First, the delinquent act itself both precipitated intervention and separated juvenile delinquents from other children, according to most specialists in the 1940s. More important, the nearly universal acceptance of mental and intellectual testing reassured experts that they could study these children objectively and scientifically.

Penal Administration inspector Jean Bancal advocated, in his highly influential 1941 book, that minors in the justice system be studied in the scientific spirit of a "chemist charged with analyzing a compound product."[91] Neuropsychiatrist Guy Rey promoted medical-psychiatric examinations for all minors charged with crimes, so that they could be "isolated, observed, catalogued." Perreau at first qualified that notion: "It would be too easy to believe that we can catalogue delinquent minors under numbered labels like a naturalist does with his brilliant insects or his rare butterflies." But, he continued, this was not because a child or adolescent should not be treated like an insect or a butterfly, but because the various psychiatric categories were difficult to separate out. Each child experienced the interpenetration of several conditions, leading Perreau to argue that "the dominant condition allows us to place them in one group rather than another."[92]

Observation Centers

Although they disagreed about the organization, control, and extent of testing, all authors insisted that France needed centers where minors could be observed and tested. Such centers, referred to as welcome centers (centres d'acceuil), observation centers (centres d'observation), or observation and triage centers (centres d'observation et de triage), and designed to receive minors charged with a crime while they awaited their trial, had been advocated in the 1930s.[93] But the demand became more insistent by late 1941, in part because of the dilemma facing judges who wanted to keep charged minors in custody without sending them to dangerously overcrowded adult facilities. Adult crime figures followed an upward curve similar to juvenile crime, but on a higher order of magnitude that nearly tripled the number of inmates. According to an April 1942 report, the number of adult prisoners had increased from 18,000 in September 1939 to 45,000 by April 1942. At the same time a number of prisons had been destroyed, evacuated, or requisitioned by the Germans, creating a serious prison-overcrowding crisis. The Fresnes pretrial detention center for minors was handling double the number it was meant to hold.[94]

Better than a pretrial detention center, an observation center would allow experts to observe, examine, and diagnose the delinquent minor while the investigating magistrate conducted his inquiry into the crime. Mazo, in her dissertation on observation centers, asked, "Why, up to now, have we not taken advantage of the investigation period prior to the child's court appearance to submit him to all the methods of inquiry with which modern science has provided us?" Bancal pointed out that the criminal investigation for a minor often took several months, since the expedited police and summary court procedure for adults caught in the act could not be used against a minor.[95] After their initial hearing, minors who appealed the court's decision could remain incarcerated for several more months. Thus minors often spent longer in custody prior to a final disposition than adults convicted and sentenced for the same offense.[96]

Bancal also lamented that even though minors remained in separate quarters, a detention center still felt like jail and minors often reacted by identifying with adult criminals and treating the authorities as enemies. Even minors sent to the best of reeducational facilities after pretrial incarceration arrived with an attitude that worked against efforts at rehabilitation. In addition, Bancal argued that lack of information about arriving minors handicapped the directors of supervised education houses. A "scientific procedure of psychological observation" would help the personnel determine appropriate treatment. Bancal insisted that France needed "scientifically equipped" observation and triage centers.[97]

Bancal and colleagues' concept of observation centers differed in significant ways from the idea of penal observation first proposed during the

Enlightenment. Jeremy Bentham's *Panopticon,* for example, placed prisoners in cells circling a central observer who could monitor and control every inmate. According to Bentham, "The more constantly the persons to be inspected are under the eyes of the persons who should inspect them, the more perfectly will the purpose of the establishment have been attained. Ideal perfection, if that were the object, would require that each person should actually be in that predicament, during every instant of time." Yet Bentham admitted that perfection could never be attained. Thus he advocated a system whereby a prisoner "at every instant, seeing reason to believe as much and not being able to satisfy himself to the contrary, he should *conceive*" himself to be observed at all times.[98]

The enlightened ideas of Bentham and Cesar Beccaria had a profound impact on systems of crime and punishment in the transition to the modern era. Michel Foucault and Michael Ignatieff have both written about the rise of the penitentiary in the early modern era as signaling the modern state's reflex to categorize, oversee, and control their populations. This impulse gave rise to a variety of disciplinary institutions, many of which Foucault wrote about: prisons, schools, and asylums. The rise of capitalism and modern structures of power created a need for systems that compelled individuals to internalize norms. The very term *penitentiary* indicates the modern prison's attempt not just to punish the body of the criminal but also to reform the soul. The desire to categorize and control is strongly reflected in twentieth-century writings both about child criminals and about all children who deviate from the norm. In a sense, observation centers would fill a gap that developed for children whom schools either could not discipline or no longer supervised because they were too old, once it became unacceptable merely to send such children to adult prisons.

The need to diagnose, the first step in categorizing and eventually controlling delinquent minors, inspired the advocates of observation centers in the 1940s. However, observation for diagnosis differed from Bentham's ideal of observation to reform, because it served not to correct behavior but to enumerate existing behaviors as the basis for diagnosis. The experts realized that minors who were being subjected to mental, intellectual, and psychological testing in observation centers would know they were being observed, and they worried that the totally artificial, medical environment of a testing center would not allow for a complete understanding of the observed subject. Therefore they wanted the centers to offer more natural environments—classrooms and workshops—where children would be unaware of the observation. Surprisingly, while they obsessively insisted on the need for observation centers, neuropsychiatrists in the 1940s wrote very little about treatment facilities or methods.

Delinquent and Maladjusted Youths: Separate Status or Universal System

Some juvenile reformers who advocated observation centers wanted them to triage only minors who had already attracted the state's notice by committing an offense. But efforts to reform the juvenile justice system paralleled a similar impulse under way before and during the war to create institutions to screen for and rehabilitate all children with physical or mental disabilities.[99] Thus many activists hoped to create general observation centers that would include juvenile delinquents and all children with behavioral problems. Such an approach involved essentially decriminalizing delinquent youth, removing them from the judicial and penal systems entirely, and merging delinquent youth into a broader category eventually designated "maladjusted children" *(enfants inadaptés)*.[100] Dr. Robert Lafon coined the term *maladjusted children*, a label he intended to sound neutral, nonpejorative, and medical.[101] As Chauvière points out, the term delineated a clear frontier between the normal and the pathological, one that could easily accommodate delinquent minors.

The question of whether juvenile delinquents should retain a separate status or merge into a broader category aroused fierce debate, both for intellectual reasons and for the practical interests at stake. The crux of the problem lay in the circularity of the interpretation. Nearly all minors who committed crimes were believed predisposed to do so by a mental or physical condition. While not every child with such a condition necessarily ended up committing a crime, nevertheless the logic of the accepted view dictated that all children with certain conditions were at risk for delinquent behavior. As Jean Fresneau explained, not all juvenile delinquents were "backwards" *(arriéré)* but "every backward child can one day become delinquent."[102]

Thus a truly effective, even preventive, response to delinquency would involve very early screening of all children, long before any of them came into contact with the law. Such early screening would both prevent crime and enable all children to receive the educational services and therapy they needed. Gamet, Fresneau, and Perreau advocated that a screening system of required medical exams be implemented in all elementary schools to, as

Fresneau explained, "detect bad tendencies." Family doctors could also be mobilized to screen for potential problems. Gamet insisted on the need for "medical exams to screen for children who are 'germ carriers.'" Social workers and workplace inspectors could also be enlisted in screening efforts.[103]

But under a system of positive law such as that in France, a person cannot be punished unless he or she actually commits an offense defined as such prior to the act. Even if experts could screen all children and determine those at high risk of becoming criminals, on what grounds would the state intervene? That is one reason observation centers appealed to the reformers. Observation centers were not prisons to punish criminals but scientific establishments to diagnose mental illness, emotional disorders, and criminal predilections. With the universal use of observation centers, rather than a criminal act's setting the punishment and rehabilitation process in motion, new diagnostic categories and labels would justify intervention beforehand. Waquet and others advocated incorporating delinquent minors into the category of children "in moral danger" *(en danger moral)*.[104] The ultimate consequence of such a system, however, would be that minors could be placed in custody not for something they did but for having a specified personality type.

"Predelinquent" children, the term used by Rey and Gamet, explicitly invoked future criminal behavior. One highly influential source defined predelinquency as "a mode of behavior that forecasts its eventual evolution into true delinquency." The signs of predelinquency included "a deficient family environment, inadequacies of aptitude or character, academic or occupational maladjustment." More developed predelinquent children would already have committed minor delinquencies like lying to or stealing from their parents, insubordination at school, or prostitution.[105]

Thus predelinquent and delinquent youth could fall under a broader rubric, children in moral danger, children at risk, or maladjusted children, for example.[106] Universalizing this sector required a screening system for all children that coordinated testing and remedial institutions on a national basis. In part because it threatened their control over significant institutional resources, the universal approach raised the hackles of some experts, particularly of many justice administration officials and policymakers. However, even they agreed on the immediate need during the occupation to open observation centers for delinquent minors. In fact, the Justice Ministry's rapid creation in 1943 of several observation centers specifically for delinquent minors might in part have been intended to pre-empt the attempts of other ministries, notably National Education and Family and Health, to create universal observation centers for maladjusted children that would include delinquents.

But the Justice Ministry's willingness to create observation centers raised another issue. Diagnosis required not just the mechanism but also agreement across a variety of fields on the definition of conditions and their symptoms. Neuropsychiatrist Georges Heuyer asserted, "It is, in fact, remarkable that most authors who write about delinquent children and children at risk do not agree on the meaning of the terms they use. We first had to undertake the huge task of providing valid definitions that all authors from our country would adopt."[107] The need for diagnostic categories accounts for the proliferation in this period of typologies, taxonomies, tables, diagrams, and lists that reveal an attempt by experts in the field to converge on certain categories.

Diagnostic Categories

The effort at classification came to fruition during the war. In 1943, Vichy established the Technical Council for Deficient and At-Risk Children (Conseil technique de l'enfance déficiente et en danger moral) with an ambitious mission, "to establish the status of deficient and at-risk children and to furnish for every situation where a child needs assistance, the techniques and methods that will allow us to ensure his screening, his observation, and his rehabilitation into social life."[108] The Technical Council invited the "most qualified" people to contribute their opinions on the medical, psychiatric, educational, and social problems of maladjusted youth. Not surprisingly, Chauvière points out, doctors constituted more than half, namely thirteen of the twenty-four most qualified people; the council included only three educators.

The Technical Council's first subcommittee, Nomenclature and Screening (Nomenclature et dépistage), proved to be vastly influential in shaping the future of France's treatment of children. Chaired by psychologist Daniel Lagache, the subcommittee included the usual experts, Heuyer, Dublineau, Girard, Préaut, and Wallon, and managed to draw up a standardized nomenclature that Heuyer proudly described as superior to those used in the rest of the world, a "monument of precision."[109] This nomenclature functioned for forty years like the American Psychiatric Association's *Diagnostic and Statistical Manual of Mental Disorders* does in the United States, as a widely accepted set of categories used to diagnose disorders. After the war, the first few issues of a new review, *Sauvegarde,* published the nomenclature in its entirety.[110] The nomenclature summarized a long discussion that had taken place over the previous decades, during which the basic categories were named and described. Its long-term success rested largely on the consensus that had already developed.[111]

Everyone agreed that certain medical conditions in the parents—syphilis, for example, or tuberculosis—could cause mental or behavioral problems in children. Experts in the 1940s also insisted on the importance of parental alcoholism, which they understood to cause inherited degeneracy, in contrast to our current view that alcohol creates a toxic fetal environment. Many experts continued looking for Lombroso's "degenerative signs" or the "stigmata of degeneracy," such as skull asymmetry, skin diseases, eyebrows that met, and ears with attached lobes, and "defects" like tattoos.[112] Most experts considered significant such early childhood "pathologies" as enuresis (bed-wetting), somnambulism (sleep walking), onanism (masturbation), convulsions, and head injuries.[113] The authors did not feel the need to explain precisely how bed-wetting and the like related to delinquent behavior; naming the behaviors satisfied them. Using medical terminology advanced their drive to create a scientific discipline with a technical language. Experts also considered "at risk" children with mental illnesses like depression, manic depression, and schizophrenia, which at the time probably included autism. Epilepsy was also considered a mental illness. Psychologists Wallon and Le Senne included psychosis and neurosis in their lists. Physically disabled or mentally handicapped children constituted another emerging category. As there was yet no accepted designation for mentally retarded children, authors referred to them variously as morons, feeble-minded *(débiles mentaux)*, mentally deficient, imbeciles, backwards *(arriérés)*, and idiots.

The group called the *"caractériels"*—which loosely translates as the emotionally disturbed—provides the most instructive category.[114] Discussion of character disorders, which were neither physical ailments nor mental handicaps nor mental illnesses, reveals the most about the agenda behind the thinking. Menut defined character disorders as "every case where there is maladjustment or abnormal reaction of the child vis-à-vis his milieu, every case, if you will, where there are behavioral problems."[115] If a behavioral problem indicated a character disorder, committing a crime was a behavioral problem and therefore prima facie evidence of "character trouble," which explains why so many juvenile delinquents fit into the category.

Emotional disorders was the hardest category to structure. The Technical Council's nomenclature committee resolved the problem by dividing *les caractériels* into three subgroups (the famous French three-part analysis): "character problems, morality problems, progressive character and behavioral problems."[116] Many experts weighed in on the discussion about character troubles, naming and describing the basic categories. Children with character problems could be overemotional, emotionally unstable, paranoid, depressed, apathetic, impulsive, or perverse.[117] Experts in the 1940s wrote about some categories that were positively poetic, like moral nonchalance, mythomania, and bovarysm.[118]

Gilbert Robin labeled "moral nonchalants" children with "a weak development in the moral sphere . . . [and] extreme moral carelessness." Morally nonchalant children made no effort at school and were passive even in their pleasure seeking. "Everything slides right over them," Robin wrote—advice, exhortation, and even punishment. "Indolent, spineless, suggestible, they let themselves be led." Robin nicely summarized their attitudes as "moral I don't care-ism" *(je m'en fichisme moral)*.[119] Rey elaborated that the morally nonchalant child had an elastic concept of honesty, was a fervent free rider who preferred to be left alone, and was prone to black market activities and thus responsible for the juvenile crime wave during the war. Pesle categorized the majority of juvenile delinquents as *abouliques,* from the verb *abouler,* which means "to hand over," the description of which sounds strikingly similar to that of Robin's moral nonchalants.[120]

Mythomaniacs, a category nearly every author discussed, were dreamers, imaginative tellers of lies who ended up believing many of them. Pesle insisted that mythomania "occurs more frequently in girls than in boys."[121] Rey explained that mythomaniacs lied not out of necessity but for the pleasure of inventing dramas with themselves in the starring role. In agreement with Pesle on gender and lying, Rey classified nine of the ten girls he examined as mythomaniacs.[122] According to Gamet, movies and women's magazines caused many cases of mythomania for girls. Boys who went to the movies and read detective novels risked a different condition, "bovarysm." Although it referred to boys, bovarysme, from Gustave Flaubert's novel *Madame Bovary,* indicated someone "pushed to spectacular or delinquent behavior by a refusal to accept his own inferiority and by a reality that seems too drab for him."[123]

The writers displayed no concern that the above personality traits and "conditions"—or at least elements of each—could probably be applied to nearly every adolescent. Defining the traits they found as *"troubles de caractère"* and providing scientific-sounding designations within a clear medical taxonomy removed the misbehaviors from the realm of free will and allowed for a therapeutic, as opposed to a punitive, response. "The criminal act is the external manifestation of a pathological conscience," wrote Robert Gautier.[124] Experts remained optimistic, however, because they believed that these conditions could, with proper techniques applied by properly trained personnel, be cured or at least mitigated.

Perverse and Perverted Children

One notable exception to that optimism troubled twentieth-century experts. Although they rejected the nineteenth-century's moral view of the "precociously perverted" child, they retained a similar category for inexplicably bad kids: "perverse children" *(enfants pervers)*.[125] Most writers divided them into children born perverse, the "constitutionally perverse" *(pervers constitutionnels)*, and children who had been perverted by their environment, the "perverted" *(pervertis)*. They understood and could hope to correct children perverted by a bad environment, but the constitutionally perverse aroused much anxiety and speculation. Perverse children, of normal intelligence and with no clearly discernible mental illness or physical or mental handicap, simply chose to act badly. They knew the difference between right and wrong—in other words, they acted with discretion—but they chose to do wrong and showed no remorse.

Rey referred to the constitutionally perverse as the superstars in the world of recidivist juvenile delinquents. His psychological profile of the perverse child included total anemotivity, lack of fear, cold-bloodedness. These minors were cynical, amoral, vain, and insensitive to sanctions.[126] Gautier explained that their rebelliousness derived from a "drive to compensate [for personality defects] by committing acts indicative of malice." The perverse child's emotional disequilibrium could lead either to active, aggressive instability and anger, or to passive indifference with apathy and laziness. Gautier listed four characteristics of the constitutionally perverse minor: "a perverse character nucleus, affective disequilibrium, perverse personality organization, and organization of instincts with toxic needs."[127] In other words, they were perverse!

Both Robin and Perreau wrote books about perverse children. Many of the experts cited above also addressed the topic. Perreau and Rey both cite Littré's definition of the perverse person as "he whose soul is turned toward evil."[128] Perreau characterized the constitutionally perverse as having an "arrested development of affectivity and of the moral sense, and the perversion of instincts, contrasting with the relative integrity of intellectual faculties, permanently determining antisocial reactions." The constitutionally perverse felt no emotion or affection *(anemotifs, inaffectifs);* they never cried, feared nothing, loved no one. We would probably label such a person a psychopath. But a child? Perreau asks, "There are some people whose nobility of character earns our admiration, why would there not be those whose perversion earns our despair?"[129]

Not only were girls considered more prone to mythomania, Perreau also noted that the percentage of "perverse minor girls seems to be higher than that of boys."[130] While Perreau neither explains nor illustrates that finding, his view rests on gendered definitions of perversity. Prostitution or even early sexual behavior was, for girls, considered prima facie evidence of perversion. Luckily, the experts reassured their readers, the truly perverse represented a small percentage, somewhere between 4 and 18 percent, of the total population of juvenile delinquents.[131]

Two critical facts about perverse children were less reassuring. First, they were contagious—they liked to "proselytize" and thus made natural gang leaders, using their wiles to attract the mentally retarded and morally nonchalant.[132] Second, "they are incorrigible and incurable," insisted Perreau. How, therefore, could society "achieve the antisepsis of the cultural milieu in which the bad seed might sprout?"[133] The perverse had to be located through screening, and then society "must isolate children who are contagious from a moral point of view," wrote Valet. Since reeducation could not work, perverse delinquents should not be included in the new therapeutic institutions the experts hoped to build. Rather, insisted Valet, "they must be detected as rapidly as possible and mercilessly eliminated."[134]

The term *elimination* had ominous overtones in the 1940s. But the five French authors who wrote most extensively about the perverse child all proposed and then rejected two possible eugenic solutions: prenuptial certificates and forced sterilization.[135] It was proposed that a medical prenuptial certificate, for which the perverse would be ineligible, be required for the issuance of a marriage license. However, all five authors acknowledged that prenuptial certificates could not prevent couples from having children out of wedlock. "It would be illusory to think that everyone would submit to the decisions of the trained man before perpetuating the species."[136]

The French experts noted and wrote about forced sterilization efforts undertaken in other countries, in particular Nazi Germany and the United States. Gamet cites one American eugenicist's recommendation that the government sterilize 10 percent of the total population. Perreau mentions experiments the state of Kansas had undertaken.[137] All five French authors concluded that forced sterilization represented an extreme solution that raised serious moral and religious objections. In the end, however, they rejected eugenic solutions not for moral but for scientific reasons. Despite the optimism of the group in general, they admitted they could never be completely sure of a diagnosis of perversity, and they conceded that they simply did not know enough yet about inheritance to advocate such an extreme measure. Perreau acknowledged, "From a medical point of view, we have remarked that the postulate on which sterilization rests, heredity, remains to be proven."[138] Why did perverse parents not always produce perverse children? Also, sterilization required an operation that was not always "benign." Gamet agreed: "Our knowledge of eugenics is still too imperfect to allow us to recommend such precise interventions for the entire nation."[139]

France's experts rejected eugenic solutions, converging instead on a solution that could be summarized as locking up the perverse and throwing away the key. But since the idea was to screen all children for perversity, what would happen if a child were diagnosed as perverse before he or she committed an illegal act? How could someone be incarcerated for life because he or she might commit a crime? Our experts devised a linguistic solution. Perverse minors would go not to jail but to a colony or an asylum. Perreau pointed out that it was not a matter of punishment but of the need to "remove [the perverse child] from society, where he could cause harm." Among those minors who had already committed a crime, it would be easy to screen out the perverse. Perreau recommended additionally, with great caution, that if their behavior revealed signs of perversity, and after proper medical-psychiatric testing, minors sent for a variety of reasons to either public or private institutions could be forwarded to institutions for the perverse.[140]

While all experts agreed in theory that the perverse child was incorrigible, they recommended leaving open the slight possibility of avoiding life-long incarceration. Both in the case of improper diagnosis and because the human potential for redemption occasionally reached even the perverse, Rey recommended a two-phase incarceration. A judge would set the minimum sentence for the perverse delinquent, based on the maximum sentence allowable for the crime or misdemeanor committed. After that time had been served, the perverse child's maximum sentence would remain indeterminate, varying with the behavior of the perverse person him or herself. The perverse, who were contagious, after all, would be released only if they were no longer "carriers" *(porteurs du germe)*. Rey and Perreau both quoted Dr. Grasset's recommendation that once the minimum sentence had been served, the perverse would go from being detained *(détenu)* to being retained *(retenu)*.[141]

Such a solution contradicted France's system of law based on having the punishment fit the crime. But experts in the 1940s denied that, for children, the system should base its response on the offense. The system should focus, as they put it, on the criminal child and not the crime, giving society its best chance at successful rehabilitation. Specialists and reformers preferred a system for delinquent minors based on "individualization of the penalty, postulating observation and classification of the convict."[142] The blend of nature and nurture produced a unique combination. The idea that it was more important to determine the character of the delinquent than the nature of the crime, or even the delinquent's criminal responsibility, had emerged long before the Vichy regime. Heuyer, for one, wrote in 1935, "In the presence of a guilty child, to avoid recidivism, it is more important to specify the character of the delinquent than the nature of the offense, in order to choose the best measure, be it medical treatment, moral correction, or even prolonged segregation."[143]

The juvenile delinquency establishment had converged on this general approach—individualized and character-oriented—but remained divided over key details. The bitterest controversies resulted from the conceptual tangle surrounding the interchangeability of various conditions with delinquency. Most delinquent minors, specialists in the field believed, had some condition, although not every delinquent child had a condition and not every child with a condition committed a crime. The idea that delinquent minors, those who actually committed an offense, should retain a separate legal status annoyed the group hoping to create a unified, national, therapeutic system for all maladjusted children, by which they meant children who were mentally ill, abused, disabled, troubled, in moral danger or at risk, predelinquent or delinquent. People in the fields of education, neuropsychiatry, and in some instances law, and especially administrators associated with the Ministries of National Education and Family and Health, advocated a unified system including delinquent minors. Such a system implied centralized control, or at least national coordination of elementary schools, family doctors, workplaces, training centers, observation centers, and an education or medical system, rather than leaving it to courts to handle minors who committed crimes. The ministry given control over such a unified system would coordinate public and private institutions for all maladjusted children, including juvenile delinquents.

Thus beyond the intellectual disputes, the press for a unified system provoked a power struggle over control of myriad interlocking institutions. Administrators from both the Family and Health Ministry and the National Education Ministry insisted that they should oversee the unified system. Education's authority over schools in France extended, it argued, to all public reeducational institutions. People from Education and Family and Health not only wanted to control the system themselves but they also desperately wanted to wrest control over juvenile delinquents and their facilities away from the Justice Ministry. Fresneau complained that the Justice Ministry's long-running but troubled efforts to reform supervised education houses had achieved so little that its promises no longer meant anything. The Ministry of National Education should take over the reeducation of delinquents, immediately setting up a "prophylactic" program of school screening. A young person with problems would be directed to a special orientation center rather than to juvenile court. Incorrigible minors who could not be reeducated would be interned until the expert opinion not of a judge but of a doctor pronounced them safe.[144]

The experts associated with the Justice Ministry and its subadministrations Penal Administration and Supervised Education fiercely resisted any solution that threatened to eliminate or even dilute their authority over juvenile delinquents. They argued that minors who committed crimes or misdemeanors had crossed an important line. Their position was strengthened by the fact that despite the popularity of developing a therapeutic system to replace the punitive one, few specialists working in the field of juvenile delinquency believed in eliminating punishment and incarceration entirely. Both Gamet and Valet, to justify retaining incarceration for perverse delinquents, cited an unattributed aphorism, "Fear of the police is the beginning of wisdom."[145] In effect, hardly anyone completely renounced the punitive alternative for the most incorrigible, perverse, hardened cases. Ultimately, retaining punishment, even for a tiny minority of delinquent minors, legitimized the Justice Ministry's attempt to maintain control over all juvenile delinquents.

Both during and after the war, such Justice Ministry administrators as Bancal, Ceccaldi, and Costa insisted that delinquent minors retain their separate legal status and separate court-affiliated observation centers and supervised education houses. Reformers conceded the need to sever the Supervised Education bureaucracy from Penal Administration but refused to consider allowing it to move out of the Justice Ministry entirely. They preferred setting up a new Directorate of Supervised Education within the Justice Ministry, no longer under Penal Administration, to run the state's supervised education houses for delinquent minors.

The war created a unique situation. The juvenile delinquency establishment fundamentally agreed on the etiology of delinquency, promoted the creation of observation centers, accepted the Technical Council's nomenclature, and concurred on the need to reform the existing system. While hundreds of thousands of fathers remained in POW camps, juvenile crime rates were rising, which, by confirming their warnings, empowered specialists in the field. In addition, the Justice Ministry urgently felt the need to react to rising juvenile crime rates without simply throwing delinquent minors into increasingly overcrowded prisons. Thus the state, as the next chapter will detail, played a critical role, forcing technocratic experts like neuropsychiatrists and jurists to work with lay reformers, bringing religious activists into the discussion, and muzzling education bureaucrats.

Although the Vichy government proved critical to these developments, people who wrote about juvenile delinquency during the occupation barely, if ever, mentioned Pétain or the French State at Vichy. They paid no lip service to Vichy's explicit ideological positions. They were happy to emphasize positions they held that overlapped with Vichy's worldview—the pathological impact of family breakdown, for example—but steered clear of racist or antidemocratic rhetoric. The authors noted relevant laws, decrees, and circulars, and served on public committees, but avoided reference to Vichy's explicit politicization of youth initiatives. One article mentioned Vichy's promotion of large families, only to reject it as unsound social policy. Heuyer's finding, based on his 400 dossiers, that many delinquent youths came from large families, led him to suggest in very guarded language that perhaps France should not promote large families at any cost. In typically eugenic language Heuyer concluded, "We must never overvalue the number, the quantity, and neglect the quality, of children." Gamet also noted the "impressive number of delinquent children" that came from large families. Unlike Heuyer, Gamet did not question the call for large families, but instead suggested more generous public assistance for large families.[146]

Most scholars continued to research, consult, and publish during the war. Activists and administrators ran their institutions, even undertaking reforms in boys' institutions, private ones like Ker-Goat, and public institutions like Saint-Maurice and Saint-Hilaire. Some authors who published books and articles just after the war, Blancho, Brauner, and Marcus-Jeisler, for example, carefully explored the impact of the war and the occupation on the lives of children. These studies, in addition to noting the usual, nonhistorically specific issues like family breakdown and character troubles, addressed the unique situation the war and occupation had created. They outlined the effects of unemployment, food shortages, the black market, evacuations, air raids, interrupted schooling, family separation due to the war, and the resulting breakdown of what they would call morality. Both Brauner and Marcus-Jeisler devoted attention to the tragic situation of Jewish children and considered the impact on adolescent boys of going underground, either to avoid forced labor in Germany or to join the Resistance.

Yet while some authors described the war's effects, they did not incorporate them into their basic analyses. Because war circumstances were both extraordinary and temporary, scholars avoided revising previous models. Developments during the war and occupation did not lead scholars to challenge the view of delinquent minors as victims of bad families or of psychological conditions. Doing so would have required them to portray delinquent minors as actively choosing crime in reaction to the circumstances, and to consider that, in this instance, crime might have been a somewhat rational response to economic breakdown. The low recidivism rate suggests that the war drew a larger group of adolescents into committing delinquent acts; it was not the same pool of delinquents committing more acts of delinquency. This conclusion also follows from the increase in the delinquency rate among young people. Giolitto, in his study of youth during the occupation, reports that in 1938 there were 1.94 juvenile delinquents per 1,000 young people. The rate peaked at 5.31 delinquents per 1,000 young people in 1942, before dropping back to 2.79 per 1,000 in 1945.[147] The prevailing medicalization of delinquency in the 1940s, the assumption that 80 percent of delinquents could be considered "abnormal," contrasts starkly with the fact that my study of four juvenile courts turned up very few cases of seriously troubled adolescents. Far from indicating an epidemic of emotional disturbances, most of the minors appearing in court had given in to passing temptation, inspired either by the opportunity to make money or by deprivation. The minors mostly stole, usually small quantities, sometimes for profit, sometimes to help out their families, sometimes to satisfy their urges.

Creating pathological categories like moral nonchalance and mythomania for lazy, weak-willed, easily tempted adolescents removed such behavior from the realm of free will and placed it in a therapeutic context. The results were clearly double edged. On the one hand, it set up an extremely intrusive system. Stealing ten peaches could unleash the police, an investigating magistrate, a social worker, and a psychiatrist on a family, whose every detail would be summarized in a series of reports. Shoplifting makeup and a blouse could land an adolescent first in an observation center for a range of medical and psychiatric tests and eventually, for up to seven years, in a state supervised education house. The "big brother" nature of the investigational and observational systems that eventually came to determine a delinquent minor's prospects hardly needs to be stressed. Yet on the other hand, French experts of the 1940s postulated a view of delinquency that led to a system that, by the end of the twentieth century, rarely incarcerates minors. A medicalized, technocratic vision that treats young people as chemical compounds or insects could be preferable to a moralistic view that treats them as dangerous predators and future adult criminals in need of ever-harsher punishment.

For the juvenile delinquency establishment, an extremely atypical political situation created by the convergence of military defeat, foreign occupation, a rising crime rate, and an authoritarian state fixated on family, youth, and moral regeneration gave free rein to ministries that competed with each other but did not have to answer to the public. This anomalous situation allowed in less than three years not just one but two major overhauls of a juvenile justice system that had been in place for thirty years and criticized for twenty years. Where the experts agreed, as on the need to create observation centers to avoid the pretrial detention of minors in jails, change took place. Although the system for juvenile delinquents remained separate, two ambitious parallel systems, one for delinquents and one for maladjusted children, emerged after the war and shaped the state's interaction with children and adolescents for at least the next forty years.

The intellectual struggle over the interchangeability of juvenile delinquents and maladjusted children both reflected and inspired political battles. Key administrators weighed in on the debates with books and articles of their own, and state administrators called on many leading experts, such as Heuyer, Donnedieu de Vabres, Spitzer, Guichard, Lagache, and Campinchi, to work on government committees considering legal and institutional reforms. So it is to the state that I now turn.

5

Progressive Change in an Authoritarian Regime: Vichy's Reforms

Developments in the various fields surrounding juvenile delinquency were critical to the changes that took place in the 1940s, but equally important were a number of actions taken by the Vichy regime. The post-liberation provisional government discarded some of Vichy's initiatives, but despite vehement denials, many Vichy-era provisions found their way into the system officially established in 1945. Thus, as with many other areas of policy, deep continuities were disguised by the political breaks in 1940 and 1944–45.

This chapter and Chapter 4 somewhat arbitrarily separate the academic, medical, social, and legal experts and activists in the field from government policymakers and administrators. In fact, the long-standing, continual, and close links between the groups from the 1930s through the war and beyond explain in part both why Vichy was able to advance reforms inaugurated by the Popular Front and why the postwar government was able to adapt what Vichy had set in motion. However, they remained separate groups. In France, the careers of trained specialists in the field, on the one hand, and public administrators, on the other, were symbiotic but followed separate paths that did not cross. The two groups trained at different schools and attained specialized degrees that qualified them for one or the other career path. Public administrators in charge of institutions that dealt with juvenile crime came from an administrative background and lacked academic training in relevant fields. Administrators relied on outside experts for validation. In turn, nongovernmental specialists and activists helped shape official policy; they offered advice, suggestions, and criticism, sometimes invited by the state, sometimes independently in publications. The relationship worked both ways. The experts wanted to play an advisory role in writing laws, informing judges, and reforming public institutions. They also relied on public funding for many of their initiatives. Thus, without the state's active role, little could have been attained.

Any system that deals separately with delinquent minors must include two parts: courts and institutions. Both parts of the system had been under attack before the war. Vichy compelled the solution of previously unresolved issues, created new institutions and reformed old ones, and ran training sessions for institutional personnel. These efforts forced not just an exchange of ideas but also the resolution of long-standing conflicts among activists, experts from many fields, and administrators. Vichy, with its proclerical orientation, required dialogue between secular and religious viewpoints. Vichy also, as Michel Chauvière astutely pointed out, muffled players who had been blocking certain changes. In particular, Vichy treated people connected to the Ministry of National Education as pariahs. To Vichy leaders, National Education served as a training ground for anticlerical zealots and republican proselytizers. Therefore Vichy reined in the ministry's territorial ambitions and muted its voice in discussions.

This chapter focuses primarily on how the 27 July 1942 law on delinquent youth came to be and on the legal and procedural changes it mandated. Many scholars in France continue to produce excellent work on the various state and private juvenile institutions.[1] Rather than repeating their efforts, I will instead briefly outline some key institutional changes that took place during the Vichy years.

The Supreme Council and the Proposed Law on Delinquent Children

Joseph Barthélemy, a professor and dean of the University of Paris Faculty of Law, took over as Vichy's minister of justice on 27 January 1941, replacing Raphaël Alibert, famous as the author of Vichy's anti-Semitic laws. According to historians Michael Marrus and Robert Paxton, the Germans blamed Alibert for the firing of head of government Pierre Laval on 13 December 1940 and forced him out.[2] Barthélemy, an old-fashioned right-wing conservative, adaptable and opportunistic, looked like a safe choice for Vichy.[3]

In the 1930s, Barthélemy played an infamous role in the correctional house scandals. He was the director of the Mettray agricultural colony's administrative council when Alexis Danan attacked it in the press. Despite the largely honorific nature of Barthélemy's position, historian Henri Gaillac argues that Mettray's administrative council knew how bad conditions at the school had become. In the mid-1930s, Barthélemy sued Danan for libel and won. But the court had been moved enough by the horrific descriptions of life at Mettray that it set damages at the symbolic figure of 1 franc. Documents from his years as Vichy minister of justice reveal Barthélemy's occasional outbursts of anger about the Mettray affair, still a sore point four years later. Nevertheless, his interest and experience in the field may explain his decision, shortly after his appointment, to tackle revision of the 1912 law.

In September 1941, Barthélemy stated that "of all the painful problems for which I carry the heavy responsibility, those of delinquent children occupy first place in my preoccupations. If you will, they make me feel the sharpest anguish. [Delinquency] is a social problem. It is a moral problem. It is a problem of justice. It is a problem of our future. It is, in the highest meaning of the word, a political problem."[4] In addition to his prior involvement in the field, Barthélemy's statement indicates his anxiety about the political ramifications of what was already evident, the alarming increase in the number of minors appearing in juvenile courts, up nearly 50 percent by 1941. Barthélemy's speech mentioned "something painful but a fact nonetheless, the constant inflation of juvenile criminality."[5]

To draft the new law, Barthélemy turned not to legal or psychiatric experts in the field but to two high-level administrators, Jean Bancal from Administrative Inspection Services, and Fernand Contancin, director of Penal Administration. Happily for Barthélemy, Vichy's authoritarian structure allowed him to proceed very differently from prewar ministers.[6] Under the Third Republic, the legislature initiated bills, and ministers had to gain parliamentary approval for measures they promoted. Committees formed to study the laws; deputies and senators engaged in lengthy floor debates and appealed to the public for support. The two-house legislature, the multiparty system in which a prime minister needed to keep unwieldy coalitions together, and the limited role of the presidency all left the Third Republic with weak executive leadership. The result had been short-lived governments and legislative gridlock.

Under Vichy, ministers no longer answered to an elected assembly and, consequently, had no immediate need to win over legislators or public opinion. Even Robert Paxton, highly critical of Vichy, points out that many legislative projects that had been in the works for years, even decades, quickly passed in the first few months of the Vichy government.[7] Eventually, interministerial conflicts would become as cumbersome as parliamentary ones had been, but in the meantime, rather than having to submit projects to an unwieldy legislative process, Barthélemy simply dictated the terms of the discussion and worked primarily with like-minded administrators of his own choosing.

After Bancal and Contancin had fully drafted the bill, Barthélemy appointed members to a Supreme Council of Penal Administration and Supervised Education Services (Conseil supérieur de l'Administration pénitentiaire et des Services de l'éducation surveillée), created a year earlier by the decree of 4 September 1940. The Supreme Council replaced three separate Justice Ministry advisory boards previously appointed to study the problems of penal administration and supervised education for minors. The single council, Barthélemy pointed out, was smaller, "easier to manage, thus more effective." Its mission was not to "speechify, discourse, hold forth and exchange ideas, memos, suggestions," but "to succeed."[8]

If the hands-off message did not get through clearly enough to the Supreme Council's members, in welcoming them to its first and only session, Barthélemy stressed his desire not to pull the busy members away from their normal occupations for too long. Rather, they would be presented with "very detailed plans that have been given much mature reflection by the various services, ready for publication, save the supreme reflection you are charged with providing."[9] Thus, in contrast to the time devoted to most legislation, even that produced by Vichy, the council was given only one day to discuss the law in its entirety, debate the articles, and approve the project. Archival records do not indicate that the council ever met again.

Having summoned the council to meet on 26 September 1941, Barthélemy explained that the proposed law, "pushed to the final stage of preparation and writing," had his full approbation and support. In closing, he informed the council that after a report on the bill, the session could begin with a general discussion, which he hoped would be conducted "with results in mind, rather than as a series of speeches." Barthélemy suggested that the council should not find the need for much discussion, then turned the meeting over to one of the bill's authors, Fernand Contancin, for a presentation of its basic ideas.[10]

The Supreme Council was heavily weighted with public officials: Penal Administration, Justice, Inspection Services, Civil Affairs, Budget, the General Commission on the Family, Youth, Technical Education, and Primary Education all were represented. The Supreme Council also included many key figures in the field: Henri Donnedieu de Vabres, professor of criminal law at the University of Paris Law Faculty; another law professor, named appropriately Alfred Légal, from the Faculty at Montpellier; Georges Heuyer, France's leading pediatric neuropsychiatrist; Mrs. Guichard, general secretary of Safeguarding Adolescence, one of the agencies that conducted case studies for the Seine Children's Court. Named to the council but not in attendance were Pierre de Casabianca, president of the Union des sociétés de patronage; Dr. Badonnel, an associate of Heuyer's from the clinic located at the girls' Supervised Education House at Fresnes; and Olga Spitzer, president of the Social Service for Children (SSE), another social service agency that conducted case studies for minors.[11]

Contancin admitted to this crowd of France's leading juvenile justice specialists and activists that he himself was no expert in the field. He had been summoned from the magistracy to work on a problem completely new to him. However, rather than a disadvantage, Contancin argued that his lack of knowledge left his mind open to study the problem, unhindered by preconceptions, the way a judge "goes through a judicial case file." He said he found in the vast material he read on the topic much idealism and generosity, and that he forced himself, despite the difficulty of the task, to succeed in reconciling grand theoretical ideas with the technical and practical problems posed by the real world.[12]

Contancin divided the problem of juvenile delinquency into two parts. First, what factors pushed a young person into delinquency? Contancin listed poverty, "the breakdown of households, debauchery." However, both Barthélemy and Contancin insisted that dealing with the causes of juvenile delinquency "escapes the competency" of the Justice Ministry and fell, rather, under the aegis of the Education, Youth, and Family administrations. Contancin defined the Supreme Council's mission as addressing not the causes of delinquency but the consequences of delinquent acts, which inevitably moved the problem into the Justice Ministry's sphere. Dealing with juvenile delinquency's consequences required reforming legislation, courts, and institutions created for delinquent minors.[13]

When Does a Juvenile Become an Adult?

The minutes of the discussion following Contancin's report are both extremely revealing and tantalizingly abbreviated, requiring a bit of reading between the lines. Criticism of the project revolved around two key issues, age and jurisdiction, each of which implied a number of subsidiary but equally controversial issues. In one of the project's most radical reforms, Contancin proposed reversing a change legislated in 1906 and lowering the age of penal majority from eighteen to sixteen. Donnedieu de Vabres opened the discussion by praising the broad outlines of the project but questioning the lowered age, which he asserted would deprive a very substantial group of young people of rehabilitative and reeducational services. He also pointed out that such a move went contrary to international trends, where increasingly the age of majority was being raised to eighteen. Even National Education had raised the age for taking the *baccalauréat* examination from sixteen to eighteen. Donnedieu de Vabres closed by upping the ante, proposing that they consider extending reeducational measures up to and even beyond the age of twenty-one.

Contancin justified his decision to lower the age. Based on his study, France had obtained excellent results in rehabilitating delinquent minors until the 1906 law increased the age to eighteen. The higher age limit had led to an influx into public institutions of older, "less reformable" minors whose presence "seriously compromised the recovery of other minors." Basically Contancin argued that by the age of sixteen, it was too late to reeducate someone. Bancal, coauthor of the bill, seconded Contancin, insisting that a minor entering an establishment in his or her eighteenth year "is not educable, it's too late. We cannot start the education of someone all over again that late in life."[14]

That statement baited Heuyer, who insisted that, "from a medical point of view," sixteen was far too early to treat people as adults, since puberty was not complete at that age. He insisted that sixteen- to eighteen-year-olds could benefit at the very least from the job training provided at reeducational institutions. He cited evidence from "a study of 400 juvenile delinquents" that found that 26 to 37 percent were between the ages of sixteen and eighteen (although it's not clear why the number varied by 11 percentage points). Heuyer asked if the council really wanted to let that many delinquent youths escape the system.[15]

The age issue was hardly a minor one. As Contancin explained, it emerged largely as a consequence of one of the bill's most radical changes, ending the question of "discretion" entirely for minors in juvenile courts. Lowering the age of majority meant that all sixteen- and seventeen-year olds would simply face adult courts and procedures and receive adult penalties without the attenuating excuse of age. Juvenile delinquency experts and activists could not abide having such a significantly large group completely escape their grasp. But maintaining the age at eighteen created a host of secondary problems, given the clear and shared assumption that the law should, somehow, treat sixteen- to eighteen-year olds differently. The assumption of total penal irresponsibility, which under 1912 law applied only to minors under age thirteen, could be extended to those under the age of sixteen, but no one really believed it should extend to the age of eighteen in every case. Interestingly, the group worked toward setting up a transitional system. Under most juvenile systems, a person goes from juvenile status to adult status in one day. Here the council groped its way toward procedures that created a two-year transitional period, leaving judges the choice of punitive or reeducational measures.

However, they were adamant about doing away with the pivotal determination of discretion for minors age thirteen to eighteen, by then one of the most criticized aspects of the existing system. Bancal and Contancin intended to end the needlessly complicated practice of judges determining discretion by, according to Barthélemy, "purely and simply" deleting the question. The 1912 law, by maintaining the discretion question, allowed legislators to harmonize competing humanitarian and repressive tendencies. But children's judges found that, to have recourse to what they felt was in the best interest of a minor's rehabilitation, they could use discretion as a tool. In other words, children's judges acquitted many minors who knew perfectly well that they had broken the law as having acted without discretion because the judges felt a reeducational institution in their case would be preferable to prison. The bill under consideration, Barthélemy proclaimed, "resolutely abandons the repressive concept. It proposes, in principle, that all measures must uniquely be measures of reeducation and rehabilitation." In theory, no one under the age of sixteen could be sent to an adult prison under any circumstances. In the event, however, the law did make an exception for minors under age sixteen found guilty of serious crimes—that is, murder, aggravated assault, or arson. They could be given a prison sentence that would be served not in an adult prison but in special quarters of a new type of institution the justice people hoped to create, a correctional colony.[16]

The bill's authors quickly gave in and kept the age of penal majority at eighteen. Since no one wanted the total presumption of penal irresponsibility to extend to age eighteen, the Supreme Council then had to devise a separate set of rules for minors sixteen to eighteen years old. Even Donnedieu de Vabres, who had sharply criticized the lowered age, admitted, "We must not submit minors sixteen to eighteen to the same regime." Camboulives, another representative of the Justice Ministry, proposed reinstating discretion for minors sixteen to eighteen. Donnedieu de Vabres again agreed, "We must maintain the idea of penal responsibility in the minds of young delinquents if we want good results." Attenuated penalties should only apply to minors under age sixteen, but Donnedieu de Vabres resisted reinstating discretion for minors sixteen to eighteen, a concept he hated.[17]

While most members of the council agreed that judges should have some flexibility to decide whether to apply reeducational or penal measures to minors between sixteen and eighteen, no one rallied to the idea of retaining discretion, a concept by then totally discredited. Pernot pointed out that the council needed to choose once and for all between "punishment" and an "educational system," to which Donnedieu de Vabres replied that "whipping was at one and the same time a penal and an educational method" whose passing he regretted. So much for progressivism. After discussion, the council voted unanimously to retain eighteen as the age of legal majority, but added a new article to the bill allowing minors sixteen to eighteen to be convicted and sentenced as adults, with no required attenuation of penalties. The council stated that it "leaves to the Chancellery the trouble of rewriting this provision more adequately," an omission that would have serious ramifications.[18]

None of these debates changed the basic fact that on the day of a person's eighteenth birthday, he or she reached the age of penal (not civil) majority and from then on would always be treated as an adult by the legal and penal systems. Once the council members had agreed on separate status and possible adult treatment for minors sixteen to eighteen without requiring attenuated sentences, a related dispute erupted over the makeup of the juvenile court. The Court for Children and Adolescents, which the bill established to hear cases for any person under the age of majority (eighteen), consisted under this bill of one judge from the Court of Appeals, assisted by three judges from the Courts of First Instance and an outside assessor. Contancin's bill proposed that the assessor be "of the female sex, chosen from among women particularly qualified by their behavior and by the services they have rendered to the cause of children."[19]

In fact, Mrs. Guichard, the only woman in attendance, twice asked the council why women could not sit as full members of the court. The minutes indicate that no one even bothered to respond to her question. Yet at a time when women did not have the right even to serve on juries, much less become judges, Contancin did propose requiring the Court for Children and Adolescents to include a woman in an advisory role. Judges were, he admitted, "sometimes presumed to be a bit harsh, somewhat insensitive to emotional considerations." Contancin asked Guichard for her opinion about requiring a female assessor, but either she never responded or the secretary did not record her response in the minutes. Guichard later made one barbed comment. During the discussion about how many judges should sit on the Courts for Children and Adolescents, Guichard quipped, "We should just have the female social worker and that's it." This comment, like her earlier questions, dropped into a void. Nothing Guichard said elicited any follow-up discussion.[20]

The question of how many people would sit on juvenile courts related directly to the age issue, because in cases of serious crimes committed by minors under the age of eighteen, the requirement that the Court for Children and Adolescents handle all cases made a jury trial impossible. In other words, sixteen- to eighteen-year olds who committed serious crimes could receive adult penalties without attenuation, up to and including capital punishment, if found guilty. However, unlike adults, juvenile defendants accused of capital crimes would not have had the right to a trial by jury. The council went back and forth on the question of including an outside lay assessor on the court. At one point the council approved a motion removing the required assessor, but at the end of the session, Camboulives pointed out that, as it stood, three juvenile judges alone had the "fearsome" power to condemn a minor to death. He argued in favor of two outside assessors, so that minors would have the same number of people judging them in capital cases as adults.[21] Pernot wondered aloud how the public would react when it discovered that three judges in closed session could condemn a minor to death. Eventually the council kept the number of judges at three and, for serious crimes, added two outside assessors.[22] However, the final version stated that the assessors had to fulfill the conditions for access to the civil service, which included women without requiring them. The minutes do not clarify exactly why the council dropped the requirement that at least one of the assessors be female. No further trace of discussion about gender appears in the minutes, save Guichard's occasional but unsuccessful attempts to interject it.

The possibility of capital punishment for minors shocked some people when the law appeared in France's *Official Journal*. In response, Joseph Magnol, dean of the Law Faculty in Toulouse, wrote to the Ministry of Justice. He explained that the 1942 law specifically abrogated Article 67 of the Penal Code, which attenuated capital punishment for minors, without replacing it. "Perhaps it was an oversight of the project's editor or a typographical error," Magnol suggested helpfully, never considering that the change might have been intentional. The 1942 law attenuated adult sentences for certain serious crimes but not for capital crimes. It meant that minors convicted of some crimes could get severe but attenuated penalties. However, since Magnol could not imagine that lawmakers really intended capital punishment for minors, judges could impose only reeducational measures and not attenuated adult sentences on minors guilty of the most serious, capital crimes. "Must I suppose," Magnol asks, "that minors could, under this hypothesis, be sentenced as adults?" Such an interpretation, Magnol insisted, ran counter to the overall spirit of the 1942 law.[23]

However, his worst-case assumption was correct. Pierre Ceccaldi, from Penal Administration, replied to Magnol that omitting the attenuation of the death penalty had been intentional. "Such criminal penalties in principle are applicable to minors who have incurred them, without any legal attenuation. The legislator wanted to maintain the weight of this threat over the most perverted children." Ceccaldi reassured Magnol that juvenile courts "would, however, never apply the criminal penalty."[24] The 1942 law provided an escape clause: for minors found guilty of serious crimes, a court would impose the adult penalty only "if the court deems it necessary."[25] In other words, minors would not be subject to mandatory sentencing rules under French criminal law, which stipulates a range of punishments that must be applied, although they can be suspended, for convictions of various crimes. The 1942 law allowed juvenile judges the discretion not to apply the harshest measures—death, deportation, banishment—even if those penalties were required for adults guilty of the same crimes.

In the end, the point was moot because the 27 July 1942 law never entered into effect. For the Supreme Council, the age issue opened a Pandora's box of secondary problems and brought the repressive tendencies of some participants to the surface. Ceccaldi's assurances must have rung hollow in a period when German military courts sentenced French minors to death and executed them for acts of resistance.

Universalizers versus Separatists

The second major area of controversy paralleled the dispute outlined in Chapter 4 between the universalizers, who wanted a single system that would include delinquent youth in the category of maladjusted children, and the separatists, who wanted delinquent minors to retain a distinct status. This intellectual division had real institutional ramifications. During the Supreme Council's meeting, representatives of each ministry or agency played out exactly their expected roles. Barthélemy and Pernot, Dayras, Camboulives from the Justice Ministry, Contancin from Penal Administration (a Justice subadministration), Bancal, Dequidt, and Pinatel from the Administrative Inspection Services fiercely defended their territory, insisting on a separate system for delinquent minors. Denis from

Family, Le Guen from Youth, and Froment with Joly from Education contested the Justice Ministry's control over juvenile delinquents. One thing was clear. The Supreme Council met in the Justice Ministry's territory and included a large number of Justice Ministry representatives. Justice held, at that point, almost all the cards, with one critical exception: money to fund its projects. Only the Ministry of Finance could allocate state funds, and thus it held absolute veto power over policy. The council's representative from the Budget Office, Richard, nearly scuttled the entire enterprise. At the crucial moment, however, almost everyone rallied against Richard to prevent the project from collapsing.

In the fight between universalizers and separatists, Justice Minister Barthélemy threw out the opening challenge. Other administrations, he said—Education, Youth, Family—should stick to dealing with the causes of juvenile crime. The Supreme Council needed to establish the necessary links between Justice and these other ministries. But once the various environmental or biological conditions had produced a delinquent act, then the juvenile fell under Justice's jurisdiction. While the courts and procedures for minors would differ from those for adults, judges had to remain at the center of the system for dealing with delinquency.[26] Contancin's report elaborated: "We must struggle against the causes [of juvenile delinquency] . . . We must help raise the delinquent child back up: *this is the problem that occupies us. A desire for clarity and realism demands that we treat each problem in its proper time and place.*" Clarity required distinguishing delinquent minors from other children who appeared in the courts, such as vagrants, abused or neglected children, and so on. It meant "carefully delineating the prerogatives of the Justice Chancellery, of the Family and Health Administration, of the General Youth Secretariat."[27]

Contancin conceded one point: Penal Administration and Supervised Education had to get a divorce. Drawing from the same personnel for adult prisons and juvenile institutions "cannot happen any more . . . *We absolutely must establish, once and for all, a rigorous, impenetrable barrier between the external service personnel from Penal Administration and those of Supervised Education.*"[28] He informed the Supreme Council that Justice administrators were then drawing up a statute to separate Penal Administration and Supervised Education personnel. Anyone wanting to work in an institution that housed minors would have to have the right attitude, a desire to educate youth, and also professional and pedagogical training that Supervised Education would provide after it became independent.[29]

Speaking for the universalizers, General Commission on the Family representative Denis denied that the system needed to retain a clear distinction between delinquent and other troubled minors. Rather, Denis insisted, "delinquent and predelinquent youth constitute a whole." Donnedieu de Vabres, although not officially attached to Justice, took Justice's side, saying, "Still, we must differentiate between the categories of minors."[30]

Discussion shifted to other issues, but at the first opportunity, CGF's representative Denis complained, "We cannot let the Justice Ministry have a monopoly" over delinquent minors, to which Contancin "repeated that there's no question of that." Denis pushed on, needling Barthélemy. Denis pointed out that Justice's efforts to reform institutions under its purview "had come in for criticism." This proved to be too much for Barthélemy, who, clearly annoyed, complained, "Whenever something is going wrong in the country, it's always the magistracy that gets blamed!"[31]

Paris judge Baffos tried to conciliate. He himself had visited several public juvenile institutions. "We must not speak ill of them," he said. Légal, the law professor from Montpellier, reminded the council that, in fairness to supervised education houses, courts sent them only the worst cases. To which, for reasons unclear, Contancin asked "not to become the object of systematic criticism. The personnel is not perfect; we are trying to improve it."[32] The defensiveness of Barthélemy and Contancin indicates how well the reform campaigns of the 1930s had hit their marks. Contancin maintained that the reforms they had undertaken "[had] been performed under the pressure of opinion, following various interventions and in an atmosphere of systematic and sometimes self-interested denigration." Justice administrators believed public criticism only complicated the task of reform.[33]

The bill's coauthor, Bancal, expressed similar irritation against the system's critics in his seminal book on the topic. He complained that proponents of the campaign against "so-called children's penal camps" had completely blown every little incident in public institutions out of proportion. The critics stopped at nothing, including publishing fake photographs. What did the truth matter, Bancal asked, "so long as shop girls fight over the sixth edition of the paper because of its huge, three column, stirring headlines!"[34] Justice administrators believed that Danan's press campaign in the 1930s against public juvenile institutions had only hampered their attempts at reform. Inside every supervised education house, denunciations and mutual recriminations flew among the personnel, creating a poisonous atmosphere not conducive to change. Seeing no value in public discussion and debate over the topic, Bancal insisted, in true technocratic terms, that such matters required instead "dispassionate study."[35] Neither Contancin nor Bancal nor Barthélemy seems to have considered the possibility that, by raising public sympathy for delinquent youth, the press campaigns made reforms politically possible. In the final outburst of the morning session, Barthélemy asked testily, "Does the Family Administration want to take over judging delinquent children?" Family representative Denis replied, "It's a quarrel over your monopoly," to which Contancin responded irritably, "Once again, no, no, and no."[36]

Perhaps because Justice Minister Barthélemy had called the meeting, appointed the members, convened the Supreme Council in the ministry's offices, and presumably provided the secretary who took the minutes, the reactions of representatives from Family, Youth, and National Education were either never fully aired or not completely reported in the minutes. However, the CGF had outlined its position on the bill in an undated, unsigned memo entitled "Observations on the Bill Labeled Code of Delinquent Youth Issued by Penal Administration Services." The memo insisted that the Penal Administration bill represented "a retreat in French legislation that is already backward." On the whole, it said, the bill represented a "return to repressive methods." First, under the pretext of simplification, the bill in fact increased the judicial mechanism's complexity and bureaucratic red tape. The new Courts for Children and Adolescents would be top-heavy with judges, who, notwithstanding their legal expertise, had no special training in childhood and adolescence. Neither did the bill require social service agencies to advise juvenile judges in every jurisdiction.[37] The memo's author complained that the bill's observation centers would be exclusively judicial centers, rather than being open to any family whose child manifested psychological, moral, or mental problems. Not only should observation centers serve all troubled children, they should fall under the aegis of Family and Health, not Justice. The memo criticized most severely the fact that the bill did not require a social worker's case study for every minor in the initial procedural phase. It was "intolerable and contrary to every principle of jurisprudence that the Chamber judge a child without having the assessment information that only a social case study and a medical psychiatric exam can furnish."[38]

While conceding some improvements over the 1912 law, the memo complained that the bill allowed judges, in exceptional circumstances, to send minors under investigation to adult detention centers, which should be absolutely forbidden. Rather, in the absence of observation center space, minors should be placed in institutions "run by the Family and Health or Youth administrations." The memo complained that the bill's triage procedure needlessly complicated the process, which should be concentrated in the hands of a single specialized jurisdiction. The memo also objected to a provision restricting appeals and criticized the fact that the bill's authors had clearly not read Family and Health's huge study of the problem of juvenile delinquency, which included responses from more than two hundred medical, legal, and pedagogical specialists. Nor had the bill's authors consulted France's world-renowned specialists Heuyer, Magnol, and Donnedieu de Vabres. Finally, the memo insisted that any new law on juvenile delinquency had to be reconciled with a legal project on children in moral danger, a project Family and Health was undertaking with National Education and Youth. Predelinquency and delinquency were not two distinct problems but two sides of the same coin. "It's about nothing less than serving minors deprived of an educational environment and thereby drying up delinquency at its sources."[39]

Since the broader issue of whether to create a single, universal system or two separate systems remained unresolved and entailed high stakes for both sides, the dispute inevitably erupted at the Supreme Council's session. Contancin commented on the predictable positions taken in the room. "The way this discussion is developing only reveals how much each party falls back on his particular point of view."[40] (He should have included himself.) But Justice held the upper hand, having convened the group. Justice exerted its power through its control of the meeting's timetable, discussion, and minutes. The Supreme Council had one day to complete its task, meaning that after Barthélemy's speech and Contancin's rather lengthy report, the council had only the remainder of the morning for general discussion. The afternoon session, run by Justice general secretary Dayras, began with Contancin's fairly lengthy response to points raised at that morning's meeting. The rest of the Supreme Council's afternoon discussion was limited to considering the bill's specific articles, each of which had to be amended or approved by the end of the session.

But Justice did not control everything, and the obvious dispute between Justice and the social ministries opened the door for the final power player, Richard, the representative from the Finance Ministry's Budget Office. The entire bill hinged on the creation of observation centers, because it stipulated that every minor referred on to the Court for Children and Adolescents had to be sent to an observation center. Before the new procedure could be instituted, there had to be enough observation centers to handle the demand. Thus Justice needed funding for the proposed centers or the entire project would fall apart. In the French government, the Finance Ministry was perhaps the most powerful executive ministry. At Vichy, the lack of public electoral pressure, combined with the extremely tight budgets resulting from the loss of nearly 60 percent of the state's revenues in occupation costs paid to Germany, only increased the Finance Ministry's power.[41]

However, in this case the political stakes were such that Richard from Budget could not simply refuse funding. Cleverly, he used the opening provided by CGF representative Denis's insistence on universal centers. Richard assured the Supreme Council that the Budget Office intended to "make a very large financial effort." But he needed guarantees that institutional precautions would avoid wasteful duplication. "It is necessary to avoid the parallel organization of three separate systems" by Justice, Youth, and Family. Richard asked for "a more thorough conciliation" before committing funds.[42]

Richard's comments provoked further disputes on the issue. Justice Minister Barthélemy insisted on the need for an "impenetrable barrier" *(cloison étanche)* between centers for delinquents and those for other troubled children. Still, Richard wondered why efforts could not be coordinated. Contancin admitted that he and Bancal had been concerned with keeping juvenile delinquency "under the prerogative of the Justice Ministry."[43] Richard continued to resist funding observation centers, asking peevishly who could prove to him that the CGF administration would not go ahead and create its own centers.[44] Why could a single observation center not serve all minors? Contancin lauded cooperation but insisted that there were limits. The observation centers they envisioned would have two separate areas, dormitories, where Contancin pointed out the dangers of mixing delinquent minors with other children, and technical sections whose laboratories, examining rooms, workshops, infirmaries, and classrooms could be shared with other services.

Richard then announced that since he felt it would take time for the Supreme Council to work out who could use the observation centers under what circumstances, he intended to hold up credits for another month. Faced with that threat, everyone else on the council, universalizers and separatists alike, rallied to save the bill. Many members of the council had been advocating observation centers for years. Despite their sharp disagreements over which administration should run them and which children would have access to them, at least this bill promised to create them.

The experts were in view of the Promised Land. Their disappointment at Richard's stalling comes through palpably in the minutes. Heuyer told Richard that England, Germany, Sweden, Belgium, and the United States all had good systems. "Only France has done nothing. We find ourselves here in the presence of a huge project that includes a new organization, but all the same, something can be done immediately. There's no risk of wasting the state's money!"[45]

By then, Richard had become attached to his ruse, insisting that the Budget Office would eventually come through with the money, but with what he now called a *minimum* delay of one month. The minutes then note that "a voice" yelled out, "This is a burial!" Barthélemy confined himself to criticizing the Budget representative for having "the worst kind of parliamentary methods." Trying to finesse Richard, Pernot pointed out that because of France's high inflation rates, delaying the project would only increase the final cost.[46]

Richard, probably expecting that the social ministries interested in controlling observation centers would rally to him, began to back down in the face of united opposition to his threatened funding delay. He accepted funding such centers in principle and asked only that the council postpone opening observation centers until an agreement had been reached on who could use them. Ceccaldi explained that once observation centers had opened, Justice could easily loan space to other administrations, and Contancin agreed that Justice would consent to sending delinquent minors to centers run by the CGF in certain circumstances. Still, Contancin insisted on the strict minimum of immediate funding for three centers. Richard again proposed postponing resolution of the debate to the next meeting of the council, to which Barthélemy exclaimed, "Do not always postpone everything, Mr. Finance Representative." The minutes then compress the remaining discussion of the issue to the dry statement: "The debate did not elevate itself much." The condensed minutes thus leave to the imagination exactly why Richard backed down. Surely the united pressure of the entire council, the knowledge that the current prison overpopulation crisis would cost money to fix anyway, and fear of the political fallout if Budget could be targeted as having single-handedly sabotaged the reform were factors. In any case, Richard promised the council, "You'll have your credits this afternoon," adding petulantly that he only wanted to prevent expensive institutional duplication. The morning session then adjourned.[47]

During the four-hour afternoon session, the council discussed and voted on every article, completing its work at eight o'clock in the evening. *Le Temps* carried the only publicity about the Supreme Council's single meeting, in a brief article published 30 September 1941, written by a reporter who summarized Barthélemy's opening speech. The article mentioned nothing about the debates. Once the council finished its session, the bill moved on to the Council of State (Conseil d'état), which approved it in December 1941. The law, dated 27 July 1942, appeared in the *Journal officiel*, the official record of laws, early in August 1942. Soon after, *Paris-Soir* published an article headlined, "From Now On, Criminal Children Will First Be Seen by Doctors and Then by Judges," with a brief two-column summary of the major provisions of the law.[48]

The Law of 27 July 1942 on Delinquent Children

Donnedieu de Vabres described the 1942 law, which completely replaced all previous laws pertaining to delinquent youth, as a "veritable Code of delinquent children."[49] Before 1942, juvenile offenders fell under Articles 66 to 69 of the Penal Code, modified by the laws of 1850 and 1912. In its key provision, maintained in the law of 2 February 1945 that replaced it after the war, the July 1942 law ended discretion as the pivot of the system. Instead, the new procedure established a two-tiered system. Arrested minors first appeared before a special preliminary court, the Advisory Chamber (Chambre du conseil), which determined either that the case should proceed or that the minor should be released. Contancin explained that it served no purpose to proceed with an imposing mechanism "to sanction simple facts that are not serious and that do not indicate any perversity in the child."[50]

The Advisory Chamber decided where to place minors awaiting hearings. The chamber's options included release to a parent's custody with or without probation, placement in a public or private institution, and, exceptionally, incarceration at a detention center. The investigating magistrate would collect information about the offense and would seek information about the minor's family, schooling, and habits. Based on the investigation, a second Advisory Chamber hearing would be held to determine whether to release the minor or to proceed. If the chamber decided not to release the minor, the case would be forwarded to the Court for Children and Adolescents, which this chapter will refer to as the Children's Court.

In the law's second major innovation, every minor whose case was forwarded to Children's Court would automatically be sent to an observation center, one of which would be available for each region's juvenile court. Thus the Advisory Chamber functioned as a triage point, eliminating the less serious cases from the Children's Court dockets. Serious cases could then be given greater attention, allowing for full testing and in-depth observation of each minor. A child or adolescent charged with a crime or misdemeanor thus received essentially two "trials," in the original meaning of the word, one on the alleged act, and one on the self in the observation center. Both trials determined the minor's final placement.[51]

In addition to doing away with discretion, the 1942 law included several significant changes in procedure once a case found its way to Children's Court. Despite the "progressive" intent of the reform, some of the procedural changes clearly reflected the authoritarian nature of the regime. First, for example, minors charged with crimes were no longer automatically appointed a defender. A law of 1897 had inaugurated the practice of appointing someone to defend minors. If charges went forward to the instructional phase, judges had to inform minors of their right to "choose a counselor from a list of lawyers . . . [or] one would be appointed automatically at the indicted party's request."[52] The 1912 law, rather than leaving the appointment of a defender to the minor's request, required the investigating magistrate to designate a defender for every minor under investigation. The 1942 law remained silent on that point but abrogated the 1912 law, meaning the 1897 law would again govern, and judges did not have to appoint a defender unless the minor requested one. One legal expert, Chassot, explained that, out of fear or ignorance, many minors refused even when informed of their right to counsel. Chassot labeled the change "clearly regrettable and bad."[53] The change did, however, conform to general trends in the legal system under Vichy, which increasingly diminished the rights of the accused.[54]

Second, the 1942 law eliminated two of the three ways minors could appeal their dispositions.[55] The 1912 law had not modified common law on appeals for juvenile court decisions. Minors could appeal just as adults could, with hearings in closed session. When a judgment was rendered "in absentia" *(par défaut)*, which happened regularly and usually led to a harsh judgment (see Chapter 3), "objections were accepted" *(l'opposition était admise)*. The minor or his or her parents could request another date to appear in the juvenile court and oppose the initial judgment. In most cases, when the minor and his or her parents opposed a juvenile court placement in a supervised education house, the judge changed the decision to a less drastic one. Finally, minors could contest a judgment "in cassation" (*recours en cassation:* appeals based on questions of law and procedure) before a criminal chamber. The 1942 law eliminated the first two options, normal appeals and objections, leaving only cassation open. Contancin and Bancal had argued for eliminating appeals and objections because, by the time a Children's Court made its final disposition, the case already would have had two investigations, by the investigating magistrate and the Advisory Chamber, guaranteeing serious examination of every case. Contancin had argued that limiting appeals simplified the judicial mechanism and prevented the multiplication of courts dealing with minors. Furthermore, the presence "of a member of the appeals court on the Children's Court bench" would "guarantee good justice."[56] Article 12 prohibited the judgment of minors in absentia; therefore they could no longer object to judgments made in their absence. As Donnedieu de Vabres pointed out, hearings "in absentia are poorly adapted to penal justice where the personality of the accused plays a dominant role."[57]

However, Donnedieu de Vabres's commentary highlighted one problem created by the elimination of normal appeals. What if, after the final Children's Court hearing, new facts emerged that established the minor's innocence? Cassation allowed for appeals based on circumstances only up to the moment of judgment. Only regular appeals allowed consideration of new evidence that emerged after the judgment. Donnedieu de Vabres recommended revising the law, although according to the minutes, he had not objected at the meeting to the article ending appeals.[58]

The possible imposition of capital punishment, the end of the automatic appointment of a defender, and the limits on appeals all represent repressive aspects of the 1942 law. Yet the basic objective had been to reduce the repressive nature of the juvenile justice system's treatment of minors. According to the 1942 law's preamble, the law definitively abandoned the correctional concept underlying the penal code and replaced it with "reeducation." Article 28 simply stated that the public institution for supervised education (*institution publique d'éducation surveillée,* or IPES) to rehabilitate minors would replace the supervised education house, giving the same type of facility its third designation in fifteen years. The preamble outlined two major changes in the state's relationship to remedial institutions. First, the new system would establish greater state control and coordination over the hundreds of private institutions operating in France. Furthermore, adding the word *public* to the renamed facilities signaled the state's desire to reverse the evolution of juvenile courts toward sending most minors to private institutions. Prior to 1850, nearly all minors considered in need of reform were sent to public institutions. But over the next century there had been a reversal. By 1940, four times more minors were placed in private institutions than in public ones. The 1942 law expressed the Supervised Education administration's renewed desire to assume a leading role in the field of rehabilitating youth.

Second, the 1942 law, without labeling them punitive, created "corrective colonies." Because the new, improved IPES would no longer be repressive in any way, special establishments were required for minors whose "degree of perversity makes them unreformable by ordinary supervised educational methods" and who, if mixed with less hardened minors, "could contaminate them."[59] Thus the Children's Courts could, on the basis of an observation center's report, send "minors whose perversity does not allow for correction by ordinary methods to . . . corrective colonies," where they would submit to firm discipline. Minors initially placed in an IPES could also be transferred to a corrective colony if their "misbehavior and perversity required exclusion." However, the system would not abandon hope for rehabilitation. After a minimum stay in a corrective colony, a minor transferred there from an IPES could be transferred back.[60]

While Article 28 simply named IPESs without describing them, the law's preamble outlined how the new institutions would operate. Although it is not signed, the preamble paraphrases a book published in 1941 by Jean Bancal, one of the 1942 law's two coauthors.[61] In particular, the description of the new reeducational system rested on Bancal's notion of the "pavilion system." Bancal recommended replacing large, prisonlike structures with a series of small pavilions to house and educate minors in a small-scale, family-like setting. A minor entering the school would start in a fairly Spartan pavilion that provided few amenities. As the minor improved, he or she would graduate to nicer and nicer pavilions with more and more amenities and privileges. Such a system rewarded good behavior, motivated students to want to improve themselves, and inspired them to emulate the institution's best, rather than its worst, pupils. While the state could require such a system only in its own institutions, the law also required all individuals and institutions that received minors to be accredited by the Justice Ministry.

In contrast to its stated renunciation of punitive measures, the 1942 law allowed judges, in cases of serious crimes, to apply criminal sanctions. As for attenuation for youth, the 1942 law stipulated attenuated sentences for minors ages sixteen to eighteen only if the disposition was temporary. Minors sixteen to eighteen facing final sentencing were subject to full adult penalties, up to and including death.[62] The Supreme Council's discussion of that provision primarily focused on the absence of a jury trial for minors accused of serious crimes. In the end, the council approved the article without amendment.

While purportedly establishing a completely new system, the 1942 law in fact maintained, with minor amendments, many of the 1912 law's provisions, such as probation, closed hearings, and strict limits on who could see juvenile records and what information the press could include in any coverage (no names or likenesses could be published, for example). The 1942 law did end the determination of discretion, however, and despite the declaration that the 1942 law ended once and for all the punitive treatment of minors, any minor committing a serious crime could receive an adult penal sentence. Harsher in this respect than the 1912 law, the 1942 law ended the required attenuation of penalties due to age for minors ages sixteen to eighteen. Furthermore, minors who emerged from their observational period labeled perverse were sent not to the new public institutions for supervised education but to corrective colonies, a return to the older system of penitentiary colonies. Some items, namely the observation centers and the reforms outlined for the IPES, did move away from a penal response and toward a therapeutic one. The punitive tendencies in the law can be attributed in part to Vichy's authoritarian nature, as revealed in similar procedural changes for adults restricting the rights of the accused and extending the state's power. However, similar contradictory tendencies also appeared in the postwar reform of the system, the law of 2 February 1945. Preference for therapeutic treatment did not imply, to those who worked in the field of juvenile delinquency, the complete renunciation of a punitive response in every single case for all young people under the age of eighteen.

The 1942 law could not take effect without an application decree (*décret d'application*). In France, a law outlines broad provisions but an application decree appropriates specific funds and establishes regulations for personnel and institutions, making possible the law's execution. The minutes from the Supreme Council meeting revealed why the Paris observation centers opened almost immediately, without an application decree, since the funds had been approved that day. But Vichy never passed an application decree allowing the 27 July 1942 law to enter into effect. Donnedieu de Vabres explains that until enough observation centers were available to handle every minor referred, the 1942 law's procedures could not be applied. In other words, the 1942 law "subordinated its own application to complicated and expensive installations that slowed down and eventually prevented that application."[63] In addition to the three Paris observation centers, several others centers opened in other parts of France during the occupation, usually the result of local collaboration among various public and private groups. Still, there was never enough space to hold every minor forwarded to Children's Court. Passage of an application decree for the 1942 law must also have been hindered by the departure of two key sponsors of the law. Barthélemy was replaced 16 March 1943 by Maurice Gabolde, and Contancin was fired, according to Chauvière, for refusing to turn over to the Germans Jews detained in Penal Administration prisons.[64]

Maladjusted Children

The 27 July 1942 law rejected the idea of a universal system decriminalizing delinquency and maintained a separate system for delinquent minors. However, movement continued on the other front. Just as Vichy acted as midwife in the birth of a new juvenile justice system, it also nurtured developments desired by the universalizers who had hoped to include juvenile delinquents in their systems but continued to work in behalf of maladjusted children. In this realm, a key factor impeding change had been the National Education Ministry's resistance. A 1909 law had given National Education control over the education of all "deficient children" *(enfants déficients)*. Therefore, the ministry had resisted any attempt by other administrations to set up schools for handicapped or mentally retarded children, jealously guarding its turf. But National Education suffered a serious loss of prestige and power during the Vichy years. Conservatives at Vichy considered the educational bureaucracy to be steeped in republicanism. The government believed schools had inculcated republican values, and the teaching profession, a hotbed of left-wing radicalism and Freemasonry, had corrupted generations of French youth. Thus, the Ministry of National Education, which ran the schools, lost considerable status in the new atmosphere. Education's reduced power allowed the Justice, Family and Health, and Youth administrations to take charge of various groups of handicapped children without obstruction.[65] A second key factor operating in favor of a universal system was that while Education lost power, religious activists gained power, owing to Vichy's support for greater coordination of religious institutions into a total system. During Vichy, for the first time, a "coherent, operational plan of rescue" for children who were "deficient and in moral danger," was established. The resulting system operated for the next fifty years.[66] (The American equivalent of the French category "children in moral danger" is "children at risk." Because it works better as an adjective, I shall use the term "at risk" for the remainder of this chapter.)

A law of 26 August 1942 gave Family and Health secretary Raymond Grasset the power to coordinate all services for all deficient or at-risk children and adolescents. Grasset worked with juvenile judge Jean Chazal to coordinate on a regional basis both private and public establishments for all deficient children, including juvenile delinquents. Because some areas of France were relatively unpopulated, rather than basing the new system on departments, Grasset and Chazal recommended dividing France into larger regions, each of which would have a central, specialized juvenile court, a universal observation center, and a coordinated, complete set of placement options, including reformatories, foster homes, camps, special schools, and halfway houses. A Regional Association for Safeguarding Deficient and At-Risk Children and Adolescents (*Association régionale de sauvegarde de l'enfance et de l'adolescence déficientes et en danger moral*, or ARSEA) was created by 1944 in each of ten pilot cities: Paris, Toulouse, Lyons, Nancy, Montpellier, Rennes, Clermont-Ferrand, Lille, Grenoble, and Orléans. The ARSEAs, although private, received subsidies from the Family and Health administration. Run by a local council that included public and private leaders in the field, each ARSEA's tasks included directly managing the regional observation center, coordinating regional services for all deficient children, and providing guidance and financial support to private charities and reeducation centers, which were to affiliate with the ARSEA.[67] Although the public institutions for supervised education could not legally affiliate with the ARSEAs, they could and did receive financial support from them.[68] ARSEAs were not mandated by law and thus had no legal basis to insist on affiliation, but they successfully asserted control over private organizations because, in conditions of penury, they had money without which many private charities could not survive. According to Chauvière, the postwar Departmental Councils for Children's Protection (Conseils départementaux de protection de l'enfance) were really renamed ARSEAs.[69]

The Technical Council

At the same time that the ARSEAs were being created, Vichy established, with the law of 25 July 1943, the Technical Council for Deficient and At-

Risk Children. In addition to the highly influential Nomenclature Sub-committee described in Chapter 4, the Technical Council included three other subcommittees: Reeducation, Occupational Therapy, and Jurisprudence and Prevention. Chazal published the report on all four committees. The Technical Council in 1943 had not given up hope on incorporating juvenile delinquents in the maladjusted children sector and thereby unifing testing, diagnosis, and treatment. Eventually the council's work resulted in passage of the law of 3 July 1944 on the protection of deficient and at-risk children. But the 27 July 1942 law creating a new system for delinquent minors had been passed a year prior to the Technical Council's creation. Having two different laws (27 July 1942 and 3 July 1944), in spite of the Technical Council's desires, reinforced the separate status of juvenile delinquents. The postwar revision in February 1945 of juvenile law maintained the separation for juvenile delinquents.

The Technical Council's subcommittee on Reeducation further divided itself into three groups. One of the "sub-subcommittees," headed by Dr. Leguillant, concerned itself with another obsession of the era, diagnosis and screening *(dépistage)*. His report recommended that family doctors screen children during regular medical visits and that schools hire medical inspectors to screen all students. Even classroom teachers could receive psychiatric training so they would recognize children in need of such testing.

Diagnosis and Screening, together with the Nomenclature Subcommittee, represented the Technical Council's two most successful groups. Both of them fell securely, as Chauvière points out, under the unchallenged domain of pediatric neuropsychiatry. Other committees were less successful. For example, the second Reeducation sub-subcommittee explored facilities and treatment programs. There, doctors clashed with education bureaucrats jealous of their turf. Chazal's report tactfully explained that it had been difficult to conciliate all the interests.[70] The Reeducation subcommittee's third group, which studied the recruitment and training of teachers and other reeducation personnel, aroused considerable friction among the various interests: doctors, representatives from Family and Health and National Education, special education teachers, monitors who worked with juvenile delinquents, and the religious teaching orders.[71] Chazal went so far as to admit that "conflicts, the word is not excessive, erupted."[72] The going must have been rough. Nevertheless, the Recruitment and Training sub-subcommittee managed to conduct two teacher-training sessions.

The Technical Council's Occupational Therapy Subcommittee, led by Dr. Préault, studied policies to end the social segregation of maladjusted children. Given the potential productivity of these children, the committee hoped eventually to end social prejudice against the handicapped so that France could make use of all available hands. The committee then listed various kinds of disorders and what people with those disorders might be fit to do; for example, the mentally retarded, whom the committee labeled submissive and faithful, made good skilled laborers.[73] The Technical Council's Jurisprudence and Prevention Subcommittee, run by Decugis and Chazal, wrote several proposed pieces of legislation, including the bill on the protection of deficient and at-risk children that became the law of 3 July 1944.

Although the Technical Council's work ultimately did not apply to juvenile delinquency, still it represented a major effort to unify France's treatment of all children considered outside the norm.[74] After France's liberation, various reformers raised again the possibility of decriminalizing juvenile delinquents and integrating them into the category and structures that dealt with all maladjusted children. But the universalist movement failed after the war to co-opt delinquent minors as, once again, the judicial branch reasserted its authority and independence.[75] The director of Supervised Education moved out from under Penal Administration in 1946 but refused to leave the Justice Ministry. Juvenile judges resisted having anyone take their place.

Public Institutions for Supervised Education during the War

The 1942 law suggested but did not legislate changes in the organization and operation of public facilities for juvenile delinquents, the supervised education houses, renamed public institutions for supervised education. However, the state of affairs at existing public institutions was hardly stagnant during the war.

The situation at public institutions quickly deteriorated over the summer and fall of 1940. First, a number of public facilities were evacuated or destroyed during the May–June 1940 fighting. Only one girls' preservation school, Cadillac, was left standing in the northern zone after the Battle of France. For boys, Eysses closed its doors 15 August 1940. Belle-Ile evacuated from the Brittany coast to Fontevrault, near Tours, in 1942. Furthermore, a law of 31 August 1940 reversed the rule prohibiting supervised education houses from hiring personnel from the Penal Administration, undoing a reform enacted in the late 1930s. Jacques Bourquin, a historian of supervised education, notes, "From early 1940 on, there was a return to penitentiary methods" in response to the war, defeat, exodus, and German occupation.[76]

The general mobilization order of September 1939 took the reforming director, François Dhallenne, and eighty members of his team away from the boys' supervised education house at Saint-Hilaire. Dhallenne's first replacement, Bardon, called out of retirement, lasted only until 2 November 1939. Bardon was replaced by Director Ulpat, who was nearing retirement as director of a girls' preservation school and had previously been in charge of the notoriously harsh boys' supervised education house at Belle-Ile. The new directors replaced monitors and educators mobilized into the army in 1939 with hastily hired substitutes and guards from adult prisons. Strictly banned by Dhallenne, billy clubs *(triques)* reappeared at Saint-Hilaire, along with brutal disciplinary methods. Students, already resentful about these policy reversals, were ripe for trouble by the time the Battle of France began. One of the fiercest fights of the battle in June 1940 took place only about three miles from Saint-Hilaire. On 19 June, after Pétain had requested armistice terms, German panzers reached Saumur on the Loire, site of a famous cavalry school. Rather than letting it fall without a fight, Saumur's cadets, using only training equipment, held the town's bridges for two days. Military historian Alistaire Horne designated this the one episode of the Battle of France that would "always leap forth from French history books in a blaze of glory."[77]

The experience proved less glorious for the wards of Saint-Hilaire. Hearing explosions, war planes overhead, and rumors that the Germans intended to shoot all prisoners, on 17 June one group of students refused orders to work in a beet field. In trying to defuse the situation, the assistant director apparently told the wards that if they wanted to leave, they would face serious dangers outside the school walls. That night, a large group of students insisted that the assistant director had promised them they could leave, and some 15 or so escaped in the confusion. The following day, as the school prepared to evacuate to a shelter, another group of 70 to 75 boys escaped after one boy grabbed an axe, opened the clothes room, grabbed civilian clothing, and then chopped down the exit door. More boys escaped during the move into the shelter. A total of 106 boys escaped over the two days. One boy drowned trying to cross a river, and 43 boys were never found. The rest of the escapees, some 62 boys, were apprehended in small groups and returned to Saint-Hilaire. Each time they found a group of escaped wards, the arresting police beat them before handing them over to school guards, who then followed suit. One guard used a blackjack to beat the boys, and tied their hands behind their backs tightly enough to cause bleeding. Journalist Jean Stève reported on the incident in a series of inflammatory articles that appeared in *Paris-Soir* in mid-December 1940. In response, the Penal Administration sent Bancal to investigate. By the time Bancal completed his investigation, in February 1941, Dhallenne, demobilized in August 1940, had resumed his position as director, quickly removed the worst of the offending guards, and threatened the rest with immediate termination at the first "error."[78]

While its experience was less dramatic, the events of 1939 and 1940 also reversed the minor prewar improvements undertaken at the supervised education house in Saint-Maurice. After the armistice, the Germans temporarily requisitioned the Saint-Maurice facility and relocated its wards to Aniane, near Montpellier. Aniane, the institution of last resort for the most difficult juveniles, had been completely untouched by any reform movement. In August 1941 the 240 wards of Saint-Maurice left Aniane and returned to their original setting.[79]

Halfway through the war, an unexpected and completely unrelated event resulted in major changes at the supervised education houses. In June 1942, Germany began demanding French labor. Initially Laval negotiated an arrangement that relied on French labor volunteers. By September 1942, faced with the failure of the voluntary program, Vichy passed a law requiring all able-bodied men and women to register for labor service. By then, persuasion had begun to mutate into coercion. Finally, in February 1943, a new law instituted the Obligatory Labor Service, or STO. However, workers could be exempted from the STO if they either joined the police or worked for the Penal Administration. As a result, many young men who never would have done so under other circumstances, lycée and university students, unemployed men with valued labor skills, flooded into the ranks of Supervised Education.

Historian Jacques Bourquin's interviews with Supervised Education personnel from that period uncovered the phenomenon. Bourquin found that many of the young men who chose to avoid the STO by joining Supervised Education rather than the police had been influenced by the widespread ideas about serving youth and by a variety of prewar and Vichy-era youth movements like scouting, the JOC, and the Chantiers de la jeunesse. Bourquin points out the similarities between supervised education houses and the Chantiers, both of which required uniforms, housed members in barracks, filled the day with patriotic songs and physical exercise, undertook community service, and inculcated a collective group mentality.[80] Bourquin's interviewees explained that information on the Supervised Education "hideout" *(planque)* passed by word of mouth. One former monitor recruited in Paris in 1943 alleged that Pierre Ceccaldi, assistant director of Supervised Education, encouraged his administration to hire young men trying to avoid forced labor in Germany. In any case, the STO led to an influx of new blood into institutions previously resistant to change.[81]

The new monitors, younger and dedicated to youth, created a very different atmosphere in the supervised education houses during the last two years of the war. In part, the smaller age gap between the wards and the new monitors facilitated closer relations between the two, also nurtured by a sense of shared hardship and insecurity created by the war. Bourquin argues that new monitors also identified more closely with their wards owing to the era's blurring of the line between acceptable and delinquent behavior, the new culture of legality. Nearly everyone took part in the illegal activities surrounding the black market. Furthermore, the monitors who applied for jobs with Supervised Education to avoid the STO were themselves skirting, if not breaking, the law. Under such circumstances, the monitors felt less of a sense of superiority over their minor wards, most of whom had committed petty thefts. According to one former monitor who worked at Saint-Hilaire during the war, "In 1943 we did not have any distractions. We concentrated our lives on the establishment, we lived on barracks time, we shared our joys with the kids, and they did not try to escape. There were the German police; events were such that we became very close."[82]

The new personnel and reform-minded directors at Saint-Maurice and Saint-Hilaire worked to end the penal atmosphere, to establish confidence between monitors and wards, and, despite local anxieties, to open up the institutions to their local communities. Unlike regular elementary or high school teachers, the monitor-teachers lived on site with the wards. Saint-Hilaire initiated a system based on scouting methods (troops, survival skills, back-to-nature projects). Saint-Maurice set up a representative council to make decisions about dividing up extra food or spending extra money.[83] However, the improvements brought about by the influx of new monitors avoiding the STO were of necessity short-lived. Few STO avoiders intended to make their career with Supervised Education. Once France was liberated, most of the new teachers left. Yet Bourquin argues that the experience provided models for what these institutions could become.

While several key leaders were concerned with improving things at supervised education houses for boys over thirteen, changes also took place at one institution for boys under thirteen. According to the 1912 law, a minor under thirteen could not be held responsible for his or her actions. Rather than the Children's Court, hearings for minors under thirteen took place in an Advisory Chamber, which could apply only educational and rehabilitative measures. There was one public rehabilitative institution for minors under thirteen. Théophile Roussel, in Montesson (Seine-et-Oise), had been created in 1902 for vagrant and delinquent children over the age of seven; the wards attended school to prepare for their Certificate of Primary Education (CEP) and undertook apprenticeships in gardening. In the 1930s Alexis Danan had criticized Théophile Roussel's excessively strict military nature. He referred to Director Maurice Journet as a "magnificent jailer."[84] Conditions under Journet had been dismal for many years. An inspection report concluded, "Numerous children at this school have been struck, sometimes violently, by the Director Mr. Journet, who beat them, either kicking them, hitting them with his fists or with a dog leash." Several wardens also engaged in violence against the boys.[85]

The Seine-et-Oise Department's public prosecutor investigated Théophile Roussel only after Danan's campaign culminated in an article *La Gerbe* published on 12 December 1940 describing the mistreatment of Théophile Roussel's wards. After the negative publicity and a resulting 21 December inspection, Director Journet attempted suicide on 23 December and again, successfully, on 25 December. Serge Huard, family director in the Family and Health administration, wrote to Minister of Justice Barthélemy, urging prosecution of several brutal wardens. "I especially call your attention to the importance I attach to this affair and to its urgent nature. It is absolutely necessary that the brutal methods still commonly used at Théophile Roussel disappear definitively from reeducational establishments." He added that the matter "thus far exceeds the particular case of an old supervisor and is destined to serve as a warning to all those who are guilty of a level of cruelty we can no longer tolerate."[86] Several wardens were prosecuted; four were convicted and sentenced to prison terms of five months to two years and charged sixteen-franc fines. Meanwhile a new reforming director, Jean Pinaud, took over Théophile Roussel in April 1941, cleaned up the worst abuses, and inaugurated a scouting system.[87]

Despite the interest shown from the mid-1930s in reforming boy's institutions, little interest developed in the 1930s in improving the situation at girls' institutions. The archetypal juvenile delinquent, to the public and to experts, was a boy. Public discourse about delinquent girls assumed sexual promiscuity. Reformers inadvertently, by posing the issue of reforming delinquents in terms of France's need for productive workers and soldiers, directed attention away from girls. Sophie Bourely studied the situation at one institution for girls, the Fresnes Supervised Education House, during the war. Although called a supervised education house, Fresnes was really a detention center where girls charged with crimes were sent while awaiting their final hearings. Thus most wards stayed only a few months. Although judges had been instructed to send a girl to Fresnes only as a last resort, the number of girls there doubled by 1941, and the facility reached four times its normal capacity by September 1942. Bourely compares the official regulations regarding diet, clothing, education, and activities to the reality, which not surprisingly usually fell short of the regulations. Despite its temporary nature, Fresnes still was supposed to provide the girls with schooling, very little of which took place.[88]

While neither clothing nor heat nor food met legal requirements, minors were better fed at Fresnes than its adult wards, leading Bourely to conclude that the minors lived in a secluded, hardly pleasant but privileged atmosphere in comparison to Fresnes's adult inmates. Rather than a truly rehabilitative institution, Fresnes was a "softened penitentiary."[89] On 1 October 1943, the Germans, in need of additional prison space, requisitioned Fresnes. The girls were evacuated to a private institution, Saint-Michel de Chevilly.[90] Chapter 6 will outline reform efforts that finally focused on public institutions for delinquent girls.

Vichy mandated one last, potentially disastrous institutional change that pertained to delinquent youth. In a final paroxysm, in response to German pressure, continual Allied air raids, the 6 June 1944 Normandy landing, and an increasingly militant domestic resistance movement, Vichy entered a supremely repressive phase. Among those who came to power, ultra-collaborationist Joseph Darnand had long been active in fascist groups. During the occupation Darnand created the Service d'Ordre légionnaire, which evolved in 1943 into the Milice française, an armed force that hunted down resisters, tried them in secret courts-martial, and executed them. Also in 1943, Darnand was named the general secretary for the maintenance of order, gaining control over the police. On 13 June 1944 he became minister of the interior. By that time, the Penal Administration, which still included Supervised Education, had been moved from the Jus-

tice Ministry into the Interior Ministry. The repressive potential for delinquent minors caused Louis Rollin, director of the Committee to Defend
Children in the Justice System, to write the minister of Family and Health
asking that Supervised Education move out of Interior to either Family
and Health or back to the Justice Ministry.[91] According to historian
Jacques Bourquin, several members of the Milice took over as regional
Penal Administration directors early in 1944. Interviews with former personnel indicated that on several occasions the Milice visited both Saint-
Maurice and Saint-Hilaire, searching, unsuccessfully, for Jewish children.[92]
In terms of articulating broad policy, Darnand seems not to have paid particular attention to the public institutions for minors under his control.
The only archival trace I found of Darnand's dealing with delinquent minors is a letter dated 13 May 1944 he sent to the Family and Health Ministry. Attached was a copy of a circular filled entirely with technical information about reimbursement procedures for minors placed in private or
public institutions under the 1912 law.[93]

While its four-year record vis-à-vis delinquent youth is mixed, Vichy's actions in this area left a number of legacies. First, the decision to write a revised code for delinquent youth in 1942, followed by the July 1944 law on
deficient children, solidified the division between the two overlapping sectors that continued after the war. The 27 July 1942 law on delinquent
youth stipulated a number of significant changes, throwing out the concept of discretion, for example, setting up a two-part process to winnow
out the serious cases, facilitating the observation and testing of minors
who moved on to the second phase. The French Committee of National
Liberation Committee (CFLN) rejected repressive aspects of the law, such
as not requiring attenuated sentences for minors sixteen to eighteen who
committed serious crimes, weakening provisions for the appointment of
defense counsel, and limiting avenues of appeal. Nevertheless many provisions similar to those in the 1942 law found their way into law after
the war.

During the war many new observation centers opened. After the war
the three Paris centers merged and moved to new headquarters in
Sauvigny-sur-Orge, a Paris suburb. At several public facilities for supervised education, reform-minded directors instituted improvements that
picked up speed with the influx of personnel after the imposition of forced
labor in Germany. While most of the new monitors moved on to other careers after 1944, they left behind an alternate vision for institutions that

had been operating as repressive penal systems for nearly a century. Finally, key administrators become aware of the unhealthy situation at public preservation schools for girls.

Vichy proclaimed the need to work for the moral regeneration of France's youth, but despite the potential for a repressive response to rising youth crime rates, power passed to reform-minded administrators and experts, resulting in the seeming contradiction of progressive change in a regressive state. Resistance leaders in Algiers rejected Vichy and everything it represented. Yet, as with family policy, the postwar leadership rescued or co-opted youth initiatives that had not been overtly politicized. Perhaps Vichy's actions vis-à-vis juvenile delinquency forced the hands of leaders in Algiers. Despite reservations about the 27 July 1942 law, the possibility of simply returning to the 1912 status quo had become unacceptable. If Vichy could overcome resistance to change, interministerial divisions, and professional rivalries to draw up a new code, then the new government in embryo realized it would have to prove itself capable of doing so as well. Work on a new law thus began in the spring of 1944 in Algiers. As Donnedieu de Vabres explained, the 1942 law "at least had the merit of creating a 'psychological shock,' of inciting a salutary emulation."[94]

6

The Victory of Juvenile Justice Reform, 1945 to the Present

After the war ended, few people in France expressed much interest in developments in the field of juvenile delinquency during the Vichy years. Over time, nearly everyone involved with juvenile delinquency and children's protection in France came to believe that the liberation of France represented a clean break. For example, a 1998 article on the juvenile justice system referred to the 2 February 1945 law as "the founding act of juvenile justice."[1] This version of events ignores the clear continuities that people involved in juvenile justice must have experienced at the time. No doubt, however, few experts involved had any interest in calling attention to their cooperation with the Vichy regime. They had no desire to contradict the postwar government's complete and total public renunciation of everything Vichy had done. Everyone shared an interest in concealing institutional, legal, and personal continuities.

Thus, even though the 27 July 1942 law on delinquent children never entered into effect, the provisional government of France, which took power after Vichy fell, officially rescinded it on 8 December 1944. Meanwhile, the courts—as they had before and during the war and during the occupation—continued to operate on the basis of Penal Code Articles 66 to 69 and the 1912 law. In September 1944, the post-liberation Justice Ministry had already appointed a committee, run by Helène Campinchi, an attorney at the Paris Court and Legal Council in the justice minister's office, to write the bill that eventually replaced the 1912 law.[2] Campinchi's committee worked quickly. A mere five months after the committee assembled, the law was passed, dated 2 February 1945. Such quick action resulted from the fact that work had begun on the project under the French Committee of National Liberation (Comité français de libération nationale) in Algiers.

François de Menthon, justice commissioner in Algiers and eventual minister of justice after the liberation, established a committee in April 1944 to study the problems of "guilty children." Regrettably, nearly all traces of this committee's work have disappeared. Years of searching at both the National Archives and Justice Ministry Archives turned up only a series of letters from de Menthon inviting people to sit on the committee, explaining its goals, and clarifying some critical points. He notified the group that he was creating two committees to study the problems surrounding youth crime—one to study reforming laws on delinquency in France, and one to study the situation in Algeria. One letter reveals that de Menthon had in fact studied Vichy's 27 July 1942 law. "The de facto authority calling itself the 'Government of the French State'" had achieved a total overhaul of juvenile legislation, he admitted. But, in his opinion, "Certain of its measures are technically acceptable, others more difficult to accept, certain ones impossible to put into practice." He wanted his committee to proceed quickly in the "useful and effective" reform of the 1912 law.[3]

De Menthon named Mr. Coste-Floret to chair the committee.[4] Each of the relevant bureaus, Justice, Education, Youth Services, Social Affairs, and the Provisional Consultative Assembly, named two representatives. The committee also included representatives from two private charities, one lay, one confessional, and a general secretary chosen by de Menthon. Aside from this letter, the file includes several letters inviting people to join the committee and a few formal acceptance letters. The committee drew from local circles in Algiers and included Mr. Viard, dean of the law school in Algiers, Vicar-General Emile Dauzon, and Dr. Porot, a professor of neuropsychiatry.[5]

Unfortunately, neither the minutes of this committee's meetings nor its final report could be found. Yet a postwar 1945 Justice report asserted that de Menthon's committee in Algiers had worked for four months and completed a final report favoring reform of the July 1912 law.[6] Jean-Louis Costa, postwar director of Supervised Education, in describing the situation in France at the time of the liberation, not only mentioned the work done in Algiers but also, without providing any names or details, claimed that a parallel, clandestine effort had taken place in Paris during the occupation, involving people from Supervised Education and the Paris Palais de Justice.[7] Not surprisingly, the clandestine group left no archival traces.

Most people in France accept the version of events proposed by the authors of the 1945 law, that the liberation of France wiped the slate clean and allowed them to create something entirely new. By the 1970s, the

1945 blank slate interpretation had become gospel to such an extent that nearly everyone in the field greeted Michel Chauvière's book, provocatively entitled *Enfance inadaptée: L'héritage de Vichy*, with shock, anger, and rejection. Chauvière argued that the political and institutional situation at Vichy represented a moment of rupture and innovation. While his book deals primarily with maladjusted children, a sector that tried but failed to incorporate delinquent minors, Chauvière also describes the 27 July 1942 law on delinquent children as a key event that capped ten years of effort and gave juvenile penal law its autonomy. "It took circumstances as exceptional as the war, occupation, and Vichy to break, at the same time, administrative habits and the traditions of private charities, eventually mixing them up under the banner of the interest of society and the superior interests of children."[8]

At the time the authors of the 2 February 1945 law, rather than pointing up similarities, excoriated the 1942 law, denying that it had any useful or progressive elements. For example, in a 1945 article Helène Campinchi argued that Vichy's 1942 law, rather than significantly improving the 1912 law, marked "a double setback."[9] Under the 1912 law, social case studies of the child and the family were required for all minors under age thirteen and were optional for minors thirteen to eighteen. The 1942 law made social case studies and medical-psychiatric exams optional even for minors under age thirteen. The second setback, according to Campinchi, was that the 1942 law reversed the 1912 law's appointment of lay people with experience and interest in children to juvenile courts. And although the 1942 law was intended to end the preventive detention of minors in adult jails, Campinchi complained that the reality fell far short. In 1942, many of the 2,224 minors placed under preventive detention ended up in prisons like Fresnes and Les Tourelles, owing to the lack of space in alternative institutions.[10]

The Ministry of Information's 1945 study of juvenile delinquency during the war is even more critical than Campinchi's article and labels the 27 July 1942 law a "stillborn text . . . heavy with pretensions." Rather than improving on the 1912 law, the 1942 law introduced "the most harmful" innovations, such as limiting avenues for appeal. The report further points out that two-thirds of the 1942 text created "on paper incontestably attractive organisms for the most part, but whose essential, widespread defect was not to exist, even in outline or embryonic form." By announcing such promising changes, the 1942 law misled the public into thinking things had changed, "whereas only decorative names" had been given to the same "sometimes sordid" institutions commonly known as children's penal camps. The report concludes that "by disguising the existing evil, Vichy aggravated rather than abolished it."[11]

The lack of documentation on the 1945 law committee's work prevents the kind of analysis possible for the 1942 law, allowing only guesswork as to how carefully its authors had read the 1942 law, how the final text emerged, and what compromises it represented. Clearly the Campinchi committee rejected repressive aspects of the 1942 law regarding the appointment of a defender, the limits on avenues for appeal, and the attenuating excuse of minority. However, both texts reflect impulses, ideas, and critiques of the 1912 law that had emerged over the previous two decades. Whether the Campinchi committee adopted some aspects of the 1942 law or whether both laws simply reflected the widespread consensus of the 1940s, a number of striking similarities, along with some critical differences, emerge upon comparison of the 1942 and 1945 texts.

The Laws of 2 February 1945 and 27 July 1942

Both laws discarded the concept of discretion entirely, asserted complete penal irresponsibility, and privileged education over repression. Article 2 of the 1945 law states that the "Children's Court will pronounce measures of protection, assistance, supervision, education, or reform that it deems appropriate to each case." In theory, the 1945 law established the complete penal irresponsibility of all minors, an assumption many of today's French scholars and experts in the field of delinquency repeat like a mantra. However, like its 1942 predecessor, the 1945 law continued to allow judges the possibility of imposing criminal penalties. Children's Courts could, when the circumstances and the personality of the delinquent "seem to the judge to require it," convict and sentence minors thirteen to eighteen under Penal Code Articles 67 and 69. Furthermore, although minors sixteen to eighteen retained the attenuating excuse of age, Article 2 of the 1945 law allowed the Children's Court, with written justification, to deny the attenuating excuse of minority, making it possible for minors sixteen to eighteen to receive full adult penalties.[12]

The 1945 law is somewhat less repressive in this instance than the 1942 law only because it comes at the issue of punishment from the opposite direction. The 1945 version favors protection but allows judges to punish, with justification, whereas the 1942 version established punishment for older minors but allowed judges to avoid it. The 1942 law denied the attenuating excuse of minority for minors sixteen to eighteen involved in serious crimes.[13] In final sentencing, minors thirteen to eighteen could incur the full adult penalty, up to and including capital punishment. In his 1945 commentary, Donnedieu de Vabres considered this restriction "so remarkable that one could, with some appearance of reason, attribute it to an error."[14] However the 1942 law provided juvenile court judges with sentencing flexibility, rather than requiring them to impose full adult sentences. The 1945 law, by extending the minority excuse to minors up to age eighteen, reflected, according to Donnedieu de Vabres, a "spirit of benevolence." But judges could, with written justification, deny the attenuation.[15]

Under both the 1942 and 1945 laws, the most severe penalties would be applied only to the tiny minority of juvenile offenders who were at least sixteen and were involved in the most serious of crimes. The vast majority of juvenile cases involved very petty offenses. Although the people concerned with reforming France's system believed that even petty offenses could, for some delinquent minors, signal serious underlying family or personality problems, invoking the full investigational mechanism for every single minor arrested or charged would be unwieldy. Thus both revisions, 1942 and 1945, tried to create a system that would winnow out potentially serious cases for full treatment. The 1942 law set up a two-phase process, separating out the more serious cases so that less serious ones could be disposed of rapidly; minors charged with a crime or misdemeanor first appeared before the Advisory Chamber, which quickly disposed of the simpler cases and sent only more serious cases on to the Courts for Children and Adolescents. The 1945 law also established a two-phase process, but instead of the Advisory Chamber, the 1945 law created a completely new kind of magistrate, the children's judge *(juge des enfants)*.

The 1945 law's new system, "more effective, quicker, and well-adapted to simple cases," not only reduced the number of judges from three to one in the preliminary stage but also combined two previously separate judicial functions.[16] The magistracy in France had always been strictly divided between judges on the bench and investigating magistrates. The children's judge combined both functions. The 1945 law required each Court of First Instance (Tribunal de première instance), or District Court, to appoint at least one specially trained children's judge for a three-year term. The children's judge functioned as the triage point, quickly handling the least serious cases. Like an investigating magistrate, the children's judge also had the power to question the people involved, collect information about the case, request a case study of the family or a medical-psychiatric examination of the minor. Under the 1945 law, the children's judge had to justify forgoing medical exams and family studies. Interestingly, Article 8 allowed children's judges also to forgo the "required investigation" *(instruction obligatoire)* of the crime or misdemeanor. The law's preamble explained that since many minors were caught in the act or confessed their misdeeds, the "manifestation of reality poses no problems."[17] In other words, the 1945 law placed the investigation of the minor on a par with, if not above, the investigation of the crime.

The new system rested heavily on the children's judge, who was given a series of options. He or (eventually) she could close a case if the infraction "has not been established." Otherwise the children's judge could admonish the child; return him or her to a parent, guardian, tutor, or other person "worthy of confidence,"[18] with the option of probation to the age of twenty-one; request further social or medical studies; place the minor in an observation center for an in-depth examination; or send the case to another investigating magistrate for further investigation of the crime. Finally, the children's judge could forward the case to the Children's Court (Tribunal pour enfants). The 1945 law separated the parties in cases involving both minors and adults, sending all minors to the children's judge. Article 10 stipulates that in cases forwarded to the full Children's Court, parents could choose someone to defend their child or a defender would automatically be appointed. Thus Article 10 reversed a highly criticized aspect of the 1942 law, which had made appointment of a defender contingent on the minor's request.[19]

During the investigation phase, the children's judge could provisionally return minors to their parents, or send them to a welcome center, a private charity, Public Assistance, a hospital, or a public educational or occupational training center. The judge could provisionally place the minor in an observation center run by the Justice Ministry. In addition, the children's judge could supplement any of the measures with probation. Minors and their families could, for their part, appeal all placement decisions. Unlike under the 1942 law, placement in an observation center could precede the initial hearing. When children's judges forwarded a case to the Children's Court, they could place the minor in an observation center, but they were not required to do so as under the 1942 law. Making observation center placements optional allowed the 1945 law to enter quickly into effect.

Finally, the 1945 law revised but did not entirely eliminate one of the most criticized provisions of the 1912 law: preventive detention, by which judges could send minors to adult jails *(maisons d'arrêt)* during the investigation phase. Article 11 of the 1945 law states that neither a children's judge nor an investigating magistrate can place minors over thirteen in jail provisionally, unless they deem such a measure indispensable or if it is impossible to take any other measure; under such circumstances, there must be separate quarters for juvenile detainees. Judges must justify in writing sending any minors under thirteen to jail prior to their hearing. Legal scholar Donnedieu de Vabres asserted that, under Article 11, the preventive detention of minors in adult jails, "the deplorable consequences of which for children are known," would become truly exceptional.[20]

Thus the children's judge alone handled simple cases, or he sent cases on to the full Children's Court. The appointment of at least one children's judge in each judicial district *(tribunal d'arrondissement)* simplified and accelerated the preliminary investigation. Eliminating the requirement that a three-judge panel hear all juvenile cases eased the shortage of magistrates that France faced just after the war. It also encouraged something many critics had long advocated, the creation of a truly specialized corps of judges to handle young offenders.

In another interesting innovation, the children's judge not only handled all cases in the preliminary phase, he or she also sat on the full Children's Court. The issue of judicial rank had posed a long-standing problem for the system prior to 1945. Judges who served on the Courts for Children and Adolescents, which under the 1912 law were only special sessions of District Courts, held a fairly low rank in the judicial hierarchy. Juvenile judges either had to abandon their specialty in children to advance their career or sacrifice any hopes of advancement to continue serving youth. That anomaly prevented a truly specialized magistracy, since most judges served on a Court for Children and Adolescents for only a few years. The 1945 law remedied that situation by creating a unique organizational structure for the Seine Judicial District in and around Paris, France's largest judicial district. Children's judges could be drawn from the Appeals Court, a higher rank than magistrates from District Courts. Donnedieu de Vabres explained that Children's Judges could thereby advance to the Appeals Court while continuing to serve in the juvenile justice system, allowing the development of a truly specialized and dedicated corps.[21]

The creation of the children's judge thus resolved a number of problems. Recent critics have argued that assembling in the hands of one children's judge the formidable powers to investigate, judge, and sentence violates the human rights of the accused.[22] However, in 1945 and even in 1942, reformers recognized the dangers of concentrating too much power in the hands of judges, especially in cases involving serious crimes in which, under both the 1942 and the 1945 laws, minors sixteen to eighteen could be sentenced to criminal penalties without the attenuating excuse of minority. In France, unlike the United States, criminal juries for adults have always included magistrates who deliberate alongside private citizens. Both laws attempted to create a panel for minors charged with serious crimes similar to that of a jury for adults, equalizing the number of people on the judicial panel for minors and including lay outsiders. Vichy's 1942 law supplemented the three judges on the Court for Children and Adolescents with lay assessors. The 1945 law stipulated that the Children's Court always include two nonjudicial assessors, who were appointed for three-year terms by the Justice Ministry and were persons of either sex, over age thirty, of French nationality, notable for their interest in children's issues, and sworn to secrecy.[23] The 1945 law, by explicitly mentioning "persons of either sex," placed women on an equal footing with men. Donnedieu de Vabres pointed out that the opportunity for women to serve as lay assessors on the Children's Court coincided with their finally gaining the franchise, access to elected office, and access to criminal juries in 1944.[24]

The 2 February 1945 law maintained the practice of closing juvenile court hearings to the public. All three laws, 1912, 1942, and 1945, prohibited the publication of juvenile court proceedings in books or newspapers, radio publicity, and fictionalized representations in films. Similar restrictions applied to reproducing any portrait or illustration of a minor. Only witnesses, close relatives, members of the bar, officials of relevant private groups and charities, and probation delegates could attend Children's Court sessions. The Children's Court could even waive the minor's appearance in favor of a representative such as a lawyer, parent, or guardian. Another interesting provision, Article 14, allowed judges to dismiss minors from the courtroom after questioning them. Donnedieu de Vabres explained that this provision was meant to prevent the "unfortunate impact" of a child's hearing testimony that might weaken the parents' moral authority in the child's eyes. The Children's Court could then openly and honestly discuss family problems and also "prevent the embarrassment to parents" of exposing their children to critical evaluations of the family.[25] However, the Children's Court rendered its final judgment in a public hearing. The media could report on final hearings but could present only factual summaries and identify the minor only with an initial.

If the children's judge sent a case on to the Children's Court and an investigation determined the minor's guilt, the 1945 law limited the court's options. Minors under thirteen could be returned to their parents; sent to a private institution or to Public Assistance; or placed in a public educational, job-training, or "medico-pedagogical" institution. In cases involving minors over thirteen, judges could also order placement in what the law referred to as "Public Institutions of Professional, Supervised, or Corrective Education" until the minor reached the age of twenty-one. Donnedieu de Vabres noted that this terminology only loosely corresponded to existing state institutions for delinquent minors—former penitentiary colonies, renamed supervised education houses in 1927, renamed public institutions for supervised education in 1942. Judges could also determine that the best measure for a minor thirteen and older would be a criminal penalty: a fine, prison, or both. For all measures, judges could also order probation to age twenty-one or provisional probation, with a final decision to be made after one or two trial periods.

The 1945 law created three kinds of probation: provisional probation during the investigation phase, accessory probation ordered as part of the final ruling, and prejudicial probation ordered before the Children's Court hearing, renewable at the judge's discretion. Prejudicial probation eliminated the bottleneck that the 1942 law created in mandating placement in an observation center for all minors while their cases awaited adjudication by the Court for Children and Adolescents.[26] The 1945 law, in another original measure, enabled judges to include probation for minors placed in public institutions or even sent to prison. Probation empowered children's judges to intervene and modify placements even after a final ruling.

To avoid lengthy procedural delays, the 1942 law had imposed serious restrictions on appeals of juvenile court rulings, allowing only appeals in cassation, challenges based on legal or procedural issues. The 1912 law had allowed minors or their parents to lodge an appeal through the usual channels, and to lodge an objection to the court's decision and receive a new court date to make their case. The 1942 law eliminated normal appeals based on evidence that came to light after the trial as well as posthearing objections. Articles 22 and 23 of the 1945 law retained all three avenues, objections, appeals, and cassation, for rulings of both the children's judge and the Children's Court.[27]

Article 27 of the 1945 law set out the conditions for judicial revision of measures of protection, assistance, education, or reform. One year after the judge's placement order, a minor's family could request the restoration of custody and return of the child. If the judge rejected that request, the family could try again after another year. In cases of probation violations, the children's judge could, on his or her own authority or based on a request by the public authorities, the minor, the parents, or the probation officer, modify all placements and rule in all probation violations or requests for restoration of custody. The Children's Court had the same powers, but only the full court, not the children's judge alone, had the power to remove a child from his or her family or guardians and revoke custody. Only the full Children's Court could place a minor in a public reeducational, professional, or corrective institution.

The 1945 law also further closed the criminal records of minors, which had been made available to certain public authorities and to the local police. "In order to remove all obstacles to the [minor's] possible subsequent recovery," under the 1945 law Children's Court dispositions would not become a part of the minor's permanent record. Children's Court decisions were forwarded only to judicial authorities, and not to the police or any other public authority. After five years, the Children's Court could expunge the record entirely (in which case the court had to notify the local police).[28]

Donnedieu de Vabres wrote the commentary in the leading legal review for both the 1942 and the 1945 law. His 1945 comments on the 27 July 1942 law are much more openly critical than his 1942 commentary on that same law had been. Nevertheless, Donnedieu de Vabres lauded the 1942 law's attempt to provide a complete and unified code for delinquent youth that replaced all previous laws: Articles 66 to 69 of the Penal Code, the law of 5 August 1850 on the education and patronage of young detainees, and the 1912 law. In contrast, the 2 February 1945 law had more limited goals, modifying rather than replacing the Penal Code in line with the new system being instituted, rescinding only Article 68, which sent minors thirteen to sixteen with adult accomplices to adult courts in cases of serious crimes.

To establish greater control over the variety of private charities handling delinquent minors, the 1945 law required all such persons and charities to receive prior authorization from the prefect, even if the charity had official status as an establishment "of public utility" or if it had been operating under the 1912 law's provisions. Donnedieu de Vabres expressed regret that the 1850 law remained in effect, whereas the 1942 law had rescinded it and included new dispositions for public supervised education institutions. The term *professional education institutions* in Article 16 referred obliquely to the work of reformers at Saint-Maurice and a new public institution that opened after the liberation, Saint-Jodard. Donnedieu de Vabres described them as model institutions where specialized educators and monitors applied such new methods as scouting and occupational training, and he insisted on the urgency of adopting new methods in all public institutions. He even went so far as to recommend studying the relevant sections of the 27 July 1942 law.[29]

Analysis of the 2 February 1945 Law

The series of reforms that took place in 1945 represented the culmination of many trends. Criticism of certain provisions of the Penal Code and the 1912 law, and in particular the concept of discretion, dated at least to the 1920s, as did criticism of public institutions for young offenders. Serious efforts to reform specific public institutions began in the mid-1930s in response to Alexis Danan's press campaigns, and intensified after the arrival in power of the Popular Front. Reformist impulses inspired key figures in the Popular Front cabinet, like Marc Rucard (Justice, then Health) and Cécile Brunschwig (undersecretary of National Education), to try replacing penal personnel in juvenile institutions with trained educators.

The Popular Front's efforts had met heavy resistance within the institutions, and had run completely out of steam as the Popular Front coalition fell apart and the nation's attention turned increasingly to the rising German threat. Thus the Vichy years represented a watershed in every area of the system. Reforming impulses that had nearly disappeared by 1939 revived, with the encouragement of certain people in Vichy's inner circles. Major changes in placement options and in institutional operations laid the foundation for the 1945 law. The critical moment occurred at the September 1941 meeting called by Justice Minister Barthélemy to review the bill that eventually became the 27 July 1942 law. At that meeting both the universalizers, who wanted one system for "maladjusted children" that included delinquents, and the separatists, who wanted delinquents to be treated separately, rallied to save the reform bill they were drafting from the Budget Office's threat to cut off funding. The threat forced reformers on both sides of the issue to compromise their positions in order to realize their commitment to reform, and ultimately sealed the separation of juvenile delinquents and other maladjusted children into two sectors.

Michel Chauvière believes that the unification of the two systems re-emerged as a possibility briefly just after the liberation, but the Justice Ministry continued to resist ceding control over delinquent minors, a substantial population involving significant resources. Confirming Chauvière's analysis, Pierre Ceccaldi, assistant director of Supervised Education, complained in a 1947 article about being "threatened by new tendencies manifesting themselves in favor of unification with services for maladjusted children."[30] The opening in 1942 and 1943 of three observation centers in the Paris area preempted the creation of "universal" centers for both delinquent and maladjusted youth by the competing ministries, Education and Health. The very existence of these observation centers in 1945 helped Justice retain control over this sector, even though the universalizers had also made huge strides during the war. Family and Health and National Education had sponsored the creation of observation centers in ten pilot regions of France. In those regions a new kind of public-private agency, the Regional Association for Safeguarding Deficient and At-Risk Children (ARSEA), coordinated public and private institutions for maladjusted children. As for delinquent minors, the 27 July 1942 law ended the pivot of discretion, outlined the new system for public institutions for supervised education, and established the principle of coordination of private institutions by public authorities. Reforms undertaken by the Popular Front, temporarily suspended in the crisis of 1940, resumed at public institutions for boys during the war. The Technical Council for Deficient and At-Risk Children started work in 1943, eventually publishing the 1946 nomenclature that reshaped and unified French diagnostic methods and categories for children and adolescents (see Chapter 5). Toward the end of the war, Dominique Riehl inaugurated reforms at a public girls' institution.

Thus, despite the strident rejection of everything that had happened prior to 1945, postwar reforms built on efforts undertaken during the war. Even the highly significant innovation of the children's judge was, in some ways, a modified, simplified version of the Advisory Chamber system the 1942 law mandated to clear the juvenile court docket of less serious cases. An inventive idea in 1945, the children's judge continues to function as the central figure in France's current juvenile justice system, determining which minors undergo testing, which cases will be forwarded to the Children's Court, and, currently, centralizing information and access to a wide range of social services.

Another postwar accomplishment that had been called for since the 1930s and advocated by Jean Bancal, a key author of the 1942 law, was that the Supervised Education Administration, formerly under the Penal

Administration, gained its long-sought independence in 1945 through elevation to the status of a department *(direction)*, an autonomous bureau in the Justice Ministry. Once freed from Penal Administration, Supervised Education could recruit, train, promote, and fire the personnel working in juvenile institutions. The law of 1 September 1945 that established its independence assigned to the new Supervised Education Department a series of tasks beyond running public institutions: studying the problem of children in the courts; determining the observational and reeducational methods used in public establishments; controlling all private social service agencies that conducted investigations for the Children's Courts; overseeing all institutions that received either delinquents or runaways; directing all measures relating to the probation system for minors.[31]

The first director, Jean-Louis Costa, appointed 11 December 1945, divided Supervised Education into three bureaus. The first bureau managed public institutions, recruited and trained personnel, and determined reeducation methods. The second bureau oversaw private institutions. The third bureau, a judicial service, maintained relations with the Children's Courts and probation services. In January 1946 Costa created an inspectorate within Supervised Education, whose mandate included not just inspecting institutions but also pursuing legislative and institutional reforms, as well as intensifying efforts to recruit and train new personnel. The Supervised Education inspector also sat on the Interministerial Committee to Coordinate Services for Maladjusted Children, ensuring links between the two systems. The inspectors visited and reported on several hundred public and private institutions, examining everything from the physical state of the facilities to meal plans to the pedagogical and rehabilitative methods employed. Based on their reports, the inspectorate put together a series of reform recommendations. It also sponsored publication of a serious journal, *Education surveillée,* to serve as liaison and information source for judges, educators, social workers, and others involved in the system. In 1947, *Education surveillée* merged with one of France's premier journals in the field, *Sauvons l'enfance,* the postwar incarnation of *Pour l'enfance "coupable,"* signaling the spirit of cooperation and desire for expertise in this branch of public administration.[32] The Supervised Education Department also created and continues to sponsor a group of researchers, currently led by Jacques Bourquin, from a variety of disciplines—history, psychology, sociology—who are interested in juvenile delinquency, children's protection, and institutional developments in Supervised Education.

Given that the 1945 reforms represented the fruition of trends dating to the early twentieth century, an interesting question is whether similar changes would have taken place without the war and the Vichy regime. A new system probably would have emerged eventually as a natural development of the trends, although in a slower and more piecemeal fashion. The war and Vichy proved critical to the rapid creation of a total system, for many reasons. The shock of the defeat and collapse of the Third Republic, by validating criticism of the previous system, made throwing out old systems conceivable, even necessary. The situation created by the war and the occupation—shortages, the black market, a growing wage-price gap—contributed to the huge increase in the number of minors who got in trouble with the law, something bound to worry a regime pinning much of its hope of remoralizing France on the younger generation and obsessed by the size and health of France's population. Concern in the conservative media about rising youth misbehavior focused not on delinquent minors but on the countercultural *zazous*. The general public, deeply implicated in the *système D,* could no longer judge harshly the petty thievery and swindling carried out by delinquent youths. Thus, rising juvenile crime rates did not provoke an outcry for increased repression, but they did prod the Justice Ministry to undertake reforms. The Vichy government, notwithstanding its regressive, racist, and repressive nature, paved the way for deep reforms. Its authoritarian structure removed the roadblock of parliamentary debate and public criticism. Out of mistrust, Vichy also pushed a powerful player in the field, National Education, to the sidelines. Vichy's clerical impulses forced the integration of Catholic and other religious experts and institutions with the secular authorities and social service agencies. The very fact that Vichy succeeded in writing a new juvenile justice code in 1942 provided major incentive to the Resistance authorities to prepare their own reforms even before France was liberated. The provisional government felt the need to act quickly to repair the damage done to France's children by the war.[33] As the preamble to the 1945 law explained, "The question of guilty children is one of the most urgent problems of the present period." The preamble also expressed an idea that continues to reverberate to the present, "France is not rich enough in children that it should have the right to neglect any child that might become a healthy being."

The Immediate Impact of the 1945 Reforms

To gain a sense of the 2 February 1945 law's impact on the operation of the juvenile courts, I looked at several cases from the period in 1946 when the new procedures actually came into effect. My goal was not to compile information about the minors, their crimes, and the court's judgments, as in Chapter 3. Rather, I wanted to see if the courts began to operate in an entirely different manner. The cases from 1946, however, showed great continuity in the court's operation. The makeup of the bench changed in accordance with the law, from three judges to two judges and two assessors. But the names of the judges in the Paris court did not change. At least some of the same judges who had served on the Seine Court for Children and Adolescents during the war continued to serve in 1946. This continuity in personnel explains to a certain extent the continuity in the court's operation. The language changed in accordance with provisions of the 1945 law; courts no longer judged—that is, acquitted or convicted— minors but "decided" their fate, reflecting the notion of the penal irresponsibility of minors. However, the judge's options had not really changed much. Judges could return minors to their parents or guardians, to a charitable person or institution, or to the renamed public institutions. While they no longer asked and answered the discretion question, judges could decide whether the court "must apply penal law to the minor."[34]

The operation of the courts hardly changed once the 1945 law entered into effect, because long before 1945 the judges had taken matters into their own hands. One thing emerged clearly from studying court records: prior to 1946, judges did not take the discretion question seriously. They no longer really considered whether a minor had acted with discretion and should face penalties, or without discretion and should be acquitted. Rather, judges determined what they thought the best outcome would be. Should a minor be returned to his or her family or sent to a private institution, a state institution, or prison? Then they used discretion as a tool. Whether or not a minor in fact had acted with discretion, a judge who deemed that a particular minor required rehabilitation, remediation, or reeducation simply acquitted that minor as having acted without discretion, enabling the court to choose the preferred outcome. If a judge thought a brief stay in jail would be salutary in a particular case, then he convicted the minor as having acted with discretion. Thus judges acted in fact on the principles laid out in both the 1942 and 1945 laws. In other words, the courts had, certainly by the late 1930s, subverted Articles 66 to 69 of the Penal Code from within, reflecting the twentieth century's changed ideas about why children committed crimes and how society should respond. By the 1930s most people involved in the field had moved from the bipolar model of the nineteenth century that separated criminal children into victims and villains *(enfance victime/enfance coupable)* deserving of either pity or punishment, reflected in both the Penal Code and the 1912 law, to attributing the misbehavior of minors to a wide range of external environmental or internal biological causes. Parents and adults, blamed in the nineteenth century for actively perverting children and leading them into crime, now could be at fault for creating a psychological disturbance, for example by divorcing. Furthermore, most experts believed that the great majority of young people who appeared in the courts also suffered from a range of emotional or mental disorders that both reduced their responsibility for their actions and justified substituting a therapeutic response for a punitive one.

Although juvenile courts adopted the new procedures of the 1945 law in 1946, the first ever national training session for children's judges was held in Paris beginning on 1 December 1947.[35] The session, run by Supervised Education, lasted two weeks and covered six topic areas: judicial, medical, psychological, pedagogical, administrative, and social issues. The sessions included visits to local institutions, practical training, and lectures on such topics as adolescent psychology.[36]

As for the ten or so institutions under the direct responsibility of the Supervised Education Department, boys' institutions had been the target of reform efforts for ten years by 1946. Henri Joubrel, long-time advocate for delinquent minors, visited Saint-Hilaire after the war. Under the pen name Victor Lapie, Joubrel published a fictionalized description. The title, *Saint-Florent-la-Vie* or Saint-Florent the Living, clearly, for people in these circles, played on Saint-Hilaire's unofficial nickname, Saint-Hilaire the Dead (la Mort).[37] The novel follows the life of a boy at Saint-Florent before and after reform. Dr. Le Guillant, an expert in the field, wrote a glowing review of the book. "Before, it was a children's penal camp: 'Saint-Florent the Dead.'" Le Guillant judged the book's portrait of the institution prior to reform "very realistic," even though it "might perhaps seem exaggerated to those who never knew the atrocious situation that the internal cycle of sanctions and revolts condemned incarcerated adolescents to suffer."[38] Joubrel describes how reformers rendered the institution both open and reeducational. "True professional training, but especially the methods and spirit of scouting, operated this transformation."[39]

Joubrel also reported in nonfictional form on a 1948 visit to Saint-Maurice, calling the excellent reputation of Saint-Maurice's professional school well deserved. Many of Saint-Maurice's students passed the test for a Certificate of Professional Aptitude, he said, leaving them better prepared for life in the real world. Saint-Maurice's atmosphere was agreeable, the buildings were freshly painted, "bright and pleasant." Saint-Maurice had adopted the pavilion system, which Jean Bancal had long advocated. Boys began their stay in a "trial section," sleeping in "locked rooms." With good behavior, a boy could move up to a transitional section, dormitory rooms with more amenities and, as Joubrel pointed out, decorated in either an aviation or naval motif. After continued good behavior, a boy could be promoted to the merit section, where each student had a room of his own. Finally, those on the verge of leaving could live in the halfway house, where residents furnished their own very pleasant rooms. Saint-Maurice had soccer fields, a swimming pool, a theater group, and a chorus. Once in the merit section, boys were allowed to leave the premises, for example to attend a movie or even a dance. Every twenty-four students shared a radio, a set of books, and some games. The school newspaper allowed the students free expression. One article described a soccer match between the Saint-Maurice team and the local police. "It was a great game, one that allowed us to sympathize with the worthy defenders of the law who, for once, did not get their men."[40]

Reform Reaches Girls' Institutions

The glowing reports of outside observers like Joubrel and Donnedieu de Vabres may not have corresponded to what the wards who lived in the institutions experienced, but by the late 1940s and early 1950s institutions for boys were certainly in better physical condition and were clearly less repressive than public institutions for girls. The ten-year gap in awareness of the need to reform institutions serving delinquent girls versus those serving boys reflected gendered interpretations of behavior. Sophie Bourely's study found that nearly half of the girls at Fresnes were sent there under provisions of the 1935 law that, in theory, decriminalized vagrancy. After 1935 judges were not to take penal measures against the behaviors that fell under the rubric of vagrancy, which for girls often included prostitution, but only to determine which reeducation measures should be applied. But for the girls at Fresnes, the difference must not have been discernable. Society judged harshly disobedient behavior like running away or sexual promiscuity in girls that threatened not just the patriarchal control of their fathers but also their future status as wives and mothers.

The 1930s press paid hardly any attention to girls' institutions even as it bitterly denounced excesses at boys' institutions. Ironically, the language reformers used to advocate change for boys reduced the visibility of the plight of girls in public preservation schools. Mistreatment of boys represented, in conditions of demographic crisis, the waste of potentially productive citizens. At that time, however, the concept of the productive citizen was exclusively masculine, centering on men's roles as workers and soldiers. Girls of course also had an essential future role, but their misbehavior seriously compromised, in the traditional view, the likelihood that they would contribute healthy babies to the French population. Once crossed, the line between virtue and promiscuity for girls was considered nearly impossible to cross back over. This view of the slippery slope for girls reflected more than just public norms. One pediatric neuropsychologist wrote that premature sexuality in girls in and of itself signaled constitutional perversion.[41]

Sociologist Béatrice Koeppel paints a grim picture of the two state-run girls' institutions, Clermont and Cadillac, on the eve of the war, and by 1943, according to Koeppel, the treatment of delinquent girls had undergone "an upsurge of severity that proved to be inhuman, indeed even absurd."[42] The war had forced Clermont to close. Cadillac attracted the attention of reformers only in 1943, after a series of visits by two Supervised Education administrators, Pierre Ceccaldi and Paul Lutz. The buildings resembled prisons, with supervisors in prison-guard uniforms. The girls still slept in "chicken cages" (metal mesh cubicles). On entering Cadillac their hair was cut Joan of Arc style, they were given plain black frocks to wear, and they were required to maintain total silence. Girls spent most of their time doing laundry or sewing, they received hardly any schooling, and they were not provided with books. Ceccaldi and Lutz, horrified, reported their findings to Daniel Lagache, an expert in the field and a psychology professor at the University in Clermont-Ferrand. Lagache sent his assistant, Dominique Riehl, a psychologist and former scout leader, for a follow-up visit. She, too, was appalled, "scandalized," by her visit to Cadillac, and she accepted the task, after negotiating full hiring and firing power, of reforming the place.[43]

Riehl attributed the grim situation and the lack of a reforming impulse on behalf of girls in state institutions to the prevailing wisdom that the better of the delinquent girls were sent to private charities—one of the Catholic Bon Pasteurs.[44] Judges placed only girls considered truly perverted and impossible to rehabilitate in public institutions. Riehl hoped, once she was given the job of reforming Cadillac in 1944, to create a new climate, one that did not rest on the assumption that the girls were all "unreformable constitutionally perverse."[45]

Riehl published an article about her efforts in 1946. She wanted to do away with the harsh disciplinary approach, break the population down into small teams to foster more of a family atmosphere, encourage closer relations between monitors and wards, institute scouting, and set up psychological services. She faced two major obstacles. First, the existing prisonlike buildings hampered the new internal organization that Riehl hoped to initiate. Second, as Riehl put it, the state institution had in fact gotten only the "failures" or worst cases.[46] Riehl dedicated most of her efforts to creating a brand new public institution of supervised education that opened after the war at Brécourt. Cadillac stumbled along until it was rocked by a scandal involving the suicide of a girl, Marguerite B., in 1948. The suicide scandal eventually led to Cadillac's closure in 1951.[47]

That same year, a new center to train educators to work with delinquent youth in public institutions opened at Vaucresson, outside of Paris. By then, the Paris area observation centers had merged into one center at Sauvigny-sur-Orge, just outside Paris. By the late 1950s, Children's Courts were sending some 20 percent of minors sixteen to eighteen whom they adjudicated to public institutions, although by then most such institutions were halfway houses, small group homes where minors lived but left to go to jobs or apprenticeships during the day, returning in the evening for schooling or counseling.[48] At that time, the state had 2,000 places in its institutions, supplemented by 20,000 places in private institutions.[49]

Long-Term Developments in Juvenile Justice

In spite of the reforms that had supposedly taken place, Jacques Lerouge, arrested for stealing a coffee grinder, described his life in the late 1950s in what he called a correctional house *(maison de correction)*, a term that had long been out of official use. Lerouge described the setting as a children's penal camp *(bagne d'enfants)*. Although he attempted suicide, he was never sent to a doctor or a psychiatrist. He also hints that one educator sexually abused the boys. His two years of juvenile detention, he said, provided him only with a "pass key for later entry into all your prisons!"[50]

In the 1970s, public institutions were renamed again, becoming special institutions of supervised education *(institutions spéciales d'education surveillée,* or ISESs). Children's Judge Jean Chazal asserted that neither public nor private institutions resembled in any way the former correctional houses or penal colonies. Staffed by specialized educators, under the direction of "psychopedagogical and pediatric neuropsychiatric technicians," the ISESs, Chazal insisted, placed delinquent minors in a family atmosphere with a liberal system open to the outside world. Treatment was based on confidence in the students, the value of the group, and student self-government. Special institutions also provided serious occupational training.[51]

Whether or not the reality matched Chazal's glowing descriptions, one trend seems to repeat itself. No matter how high-minded the reformers and how successfully they remake the institutions, over time institutions for delinquent minors tend to regress. The zeal of the reformers is rarely carried forward by their successors, public attention wanes, and people in supervisory positions can be tempted to abuse their authority over the wards, who, as both minors and detainees, have little power and no voice. In recognition of such tendencies, France in the postwar decades moved increasingly away from the incarceration of delinquent minors.

Deinstitutionalization

Through the 1950s, 1960s, and 1970s, the percentage of minors sent to public institutions declined from 19 percent in 1959 to about 3 percent in 1973, according to Marc Ancel.[52] In 1975 a study commission chaired by Costa, by then chief justice at the Cassation Appeals Court, proposed "the abolition of all incarceration—preventive detention and prison sentences alike," for minors under age sixteen.[53] Although Costa's proposed abolition never came to pass, by 1982 courts sent only about 1 percent of delinquent minors to institutions.[54] In 1989 there were only two detention centers for incarcerated juvenile delinquents left in France, and only one of them a closed facility. Alternative placement options included observation centers, resident training centers, after-care centers, and halfway-house educational action centers.[55]

The binary choice of either institutional placement or leaving a minor at home frustrated many judges. Probation had its limits, even though professional social workers and educators increasingly replaced unpaid volunteers as probation officers. A 1958 law instituted an intermediate option, educative assistance. Increasingly in the 1960s and 1970s judges ordered what is called a measure of educational action in an open setting, or an AEMO *(action éducative en milieu ouvert)*. In such cases, minors are left with their family and are assigned a multidisciplinary team, usually headed by a social worker. The AEMO team evaluates the minor and the family, draws up a plan, and helps the minor to implement it. The social worker works directly with the minor and the family and also serves as intermediary between the minor and the courts, schools, and other establishments and social service agencies. An AEMO team of six or seven people might include special educators, psychologists, and household consultants to provide psychological and educational support and family counseling. The AEMO team has access to a variety of open settings—professional training centers, educational action houses, halfway houses, and foster families—where the minor may participate in weekend programs, art classes, sports, nature activities, and summer camps.[56] AEMO teams can be assigned to both delinquent and at-risk minors, in an ultimate victory for the universalizers.

In the late 1980s, the Justice Ministry once again initiated a series of reforms. In 1987, a new law prohibited the provisional detention of minors thirteen to sixteen.[57] The number of minors incarcerated, using a single date for comparison, declined from nearly 1,000 in 1986 to about 500 in 1989.[58] That same year, Supervised Education was renamed Judicial Protection of Youth (Protection judiciaire de la jeunesse), highlighting the increased emphasis on protection.[59] Then-Justice Minister Pierre Arpaillange instructed a team to look into reforming the 1945 law in two ways: by improving procedural guarantees of the "right to forget the incident once the young person has become an adult" and the right to a defender, and by maintaining specialized jurisdictions. Arpaillange insisted that he had no intention, despite his nod in the direction of harsher treatment, of reopening what he called "closed centers" *(centres fermés)*. Instead, he wanted a variety of placement options—institutions, foster families, a "network of places"—available for judicial authorities who needed quickly to remove a child from the home.[60]

Currently if a minor commits a crime or misdemeanor, it is considered a sign of a disturbance, a serious episode in the ongoing and accepted crisis of adolescence. Although the universalizers in the 1940s wanted to move delinquent minors out from under the control of the Justice Ministry and merge them with other maladjusted and at-risk children, in effect the movement went in the other direction. Judicial Protection of Youth also handles children at risk, which the French now refer to as "minors in danger" (previously "children in moral danger"). In fact, in 1995 the system handled four times as many minors in danger (205,815) as delinquent minors.

Noële Herrenschmidt and Antoine Garapon in 1995 published an annotated book of sketches done at the Palais de Justice in Paris. Garapon, a former children's judge, refers to the children's judge as the "originality of the French system," combining the tasks of protecting at-risk children and judging delinquent minors. Most of the procedures involving minors take place in the informal setting of the children's judge's chambers. The judge does not wear a robe, sits at a desk, and, rather than interrogating the parties involved, attempts to establish a dialogue, listening to as well as questioning the minor, parents, and other interested parties. The children's judge, in conjunction with social workers, acts at a critical moment of life, "when destiny is still flexible."[61] Many of the judges in these sketches are women, who work to gain the confidence of the minors but also invoke the authority of their position to admonish minors if needed. The children's judge undertakes the criminal investigation; orders social, psychological, and family studies; and integrates social, educational, occupational, medical, and psychological services for the minor and even for the entire family. One of the sketches describes a children's judge meeting a group that included parents, teachers, and the director of a halfway house; another sketch shows her meeting with the minor alone. One day Garapon and Herrenschmidt observed a young adult woman who returned of her own volition to see "her" judge, the one who had followed her for five years, for advice on personal problems. Only the most serious cases are forwarded to the full Children's Court, an experience that Garapon argues will "provide the minor with a sense of his responsibilities by having him confront the cold world of the law." Given the court's location in the center of Paris at the imposing Palais de Justice, Garapon notes that often a single appearance in Children's Court produces good results, but only so long as this ultimate and symbolic resource is used sparingly, preventing it from becoming common. At the Children's Court, the children's judge is still assisted by two nonprofessional assessors. Educators may attend hearings to present information about the adolescents. Also included are prosecutors and a clerk who records the proceedings.

Yet at the end of the twentieth century, just as the protective, therapeutic vision seems to have triumphed, the juvenile justice system in France finds itself pulled in the opposite direction, by developments in the field, by the new circumstances of juvenile crime, and by global movements. Over the past two decades, juvenile crime rates have risen in France, as they have in other Western industrial nations. According to a Ministry of Justice brochure, in 1995 the juvenile justice system handled 51,933 delinquent minors.[62]

Developments in the 1990s

Recently, for the first time in many years, a series of incidents involving minors triggered serious questioning of the very foundations of France's juvenile justice system. In May 1997 two teenagers stabbed a fifteen-year-old boy to death in Bondy, a working-class area outside of Paris, for refusing to turn over his watch. Later that year a gang of adolescent boys raped a fourteen-year-old girl in Strasbourg.[63] Intense media coverage of these incidents raised fears in France of increasingly violent minors. In 2001, the media intensively covered the case of the so-called Longwy torturers. From September 1999 to January 2000, six of the ten students in the junior class of Longwy's technical high school had singled out one of their classmates for abuse. Starting with insults and demands, the group graduated to blows, burns, and a game called "punching ball." The case's magnetism owes something to its similarities with the bullying that apparently resulted in the 1999 Columbine High School massacre in Colorado. Beyond that, the idea that six teenage boys engaged in such intense and increasingly violent bullying of a classmate again raised the specter of constitutionally perverted, evil, monstrous youths who take pleasure in tormenting the weak. In covering the final disposition of the case, however, the press turned around and slew the monsters it had created, stressing the tearful remorse and contrition that all of the boys demonstrated as they begged the court, the victim, and his family for forgiveness.[64]

The therapeutic impulse is now deeply rooted in France and may limit how far the French system will move in a punitive direction. Still, the rising incidence and increasingly violent nature of juvenile crime have inspired demands for a harsher response. While Arpaillange's instructions in the late 1980s on reforming the 1945 law focused primarily on improving protection and civil rights, he also articulated a notion increasingly popular in the 1980s: the system needed to develop "ways for minors to make reparations for the damages caused."[65] Until most recently, France's concession to "get tough" policies involved trying to ensure that delinquent minors accept responsibility and in some way repay society for the damage they have done, rather than lengthening prison sentences or treating more minors as adults.[66] In a conversation, Jacques Bourquin noted that public opinion in France increasingly called for the juvenile justice system to put more emphasis on restitution. As of June 1983, judges could order minors to perform community service, or "work of a general interest." Refining that idea, a law passed in January 1993 introduced a new option: minors can be ordered to perform "a measure or activity of help [*aide*] or reparation with regard to a consenting victim, or in the interest of the community." According to law professor Jean-François Renucci, reparation encourages delinquent minors to accept responsibility for their acts and to be aware of the consequences of their behavior. While admitting that such a response includes a punitive aspect, Renucci stresses its educational nature and its avoidance of incarceration, "whose noxious effects are real."[67]

The harsher response to youth crime has caused the number of minors sentenced to prison, which declined precipitously after 1987 and 1989 restrictions on the preventive detention of minors under sixteen, to climb again in the 1990s. There are two ways to count the number of minors serving penal sentences, using either the number of minors in detention over an entire year, or using the number of minors in detention on a given date. Unlike in the United States, where sentences are usually set in years, in France the two figures vary widely, because the average length of detention for minors, although up from 2.2 months in 1997, was only 3.6 months in 1999. Either way, however, the number of minors in detention has increased: over a year, from 2,368 in 1993 to 4,326 in 1999; on a given date, from a low of 395 on 1 January 1991 to 672 on 1 January 2000. More recently, the figures might indicate a reversal: on 1 January 2001 the number of minors in prison had declined to 602.[68]

The evidence suggests that in France today, strong mechanisms—intellectual, political, and institutional—resist abandoning the therapeutic approach for a repressive one, in spite of pressures in that direction. On the "get tough" side, in May 1998 Jean-Pierre Chevènement, then minister of the interior, sent a confidential letter to Prime Minister Lionel Jospin calling for a major overhaul of the 1945 law. Chevènement advocated separating the protective and punitive functions of children's judges, repealing the 1987 prohibition of provisional detention, and reopening punitive institutions for certain delinquents. The letter fell into the hands of the left-wing daily *Libération*, which published it, sparking a lively public debate among representatives from the Ministries of Justice, Social Affairs, and Interior. Minister of Justice Elisabeth Guigou, when appointed, had vigorously defended the 1945 law, arguing that its principles were "not outdated."[69] Chevènement's proposals thus unleashed powerful forces from within the juvenile justice system, starting with Guigou, who mobilized resistance to his ideas. Minister of Social Affairs Martine Aubry, together with a large group calling themselves "children's professionals," rallied to Guigou's point of view.

In the midst of the debate, *Le Monde* published the results of a study by sociologist Sophie Body-Gendrot and political scientist Nicole Le Guennec. While their research confirmed that minors increasingly committed certain kinds of serious crimes, Body-Gendrot and Le Guennec attributed the change to economic problems, political disempowerment, lack of social integration, and the culture of the street. The public's anxiety centered on France's growing suburban slums, which faced high unemployment and poverty and were populated by poorly integrated adolescents, often children of immigrants.[70] Body-Gendrot and Le Guennec warned against adopting the increasingly repressive and punitive policies of Britain and America, which they consider shortsighted, given the resulting high recidivism rates. "Besides," they said, "labeling young people who come from minority groups as potential criminals is disastrous for the civic spirit of a nation."[71] In the end, Prime Minister Jospin resolved the dispute between those advocating a return to punitive methods and the system's defenders by ordering a study of the 1945 law with a view to improving on it but not ending it.

Yet, increasingly, specialists on delinquency have found many of their assumptions about delinquency as an episode in the personal crisis of adolescence challenged by the new situation in the suburban slums that surround most large cities in France. As Denis Salas, an expert on the justice system, notes, the accepted view that delinquency represents a period of initiation, a symptom of psychic distress, or an index of risk no longer accords with the rising adolescent violence generated by the creation of a poor, ethnically differentiated underclass. The reaction of these young people is increasingly viewed as a revolt against their "situation of exclusion" and a sign of their "distance" *(eloignement)* from and lack of integration into the broader society. Salas warns against solutions that do not take this reality into account.[72]

Thus, from an approach that focused on the individual adolescent experiencing a transitional crisis, French scholars, officials, and delinquency specialists are moving back toward a social milieu interpretation, minus the biology of the earlier version. This response to the new, socially generated delinquent behavior directs attention not just to delinquent youth but also to the broader social problem. France has in fact begun experimenting with a mixture of policies designated the "politics of the city" *(la politique de la ville).* Constructed around prevention, the new policies focus on security and on deeper social problems. Neighborhood policing programs are implemented alongside attempts to mobilize the community itself.[73]

An article in *Libération* in March 1999 described one successful attempt to apply the new "politics of the city" to Tarterêts, outside Paris, which had become a hub for car theft, chop shops, gangs, and drug dealing. Anger between the local, primarily Muslim and immigrant community and the police reached a boiling point. Fires were set in trashcans to attract the fire department and rocks were thrown to draw in the police, who reacted with increased militancy. Finally the department's prefect intervened, withdrew the police, and prepared both the community and the police for big changes. He met with a local youth group, promising an end to "helmeted, booted, muscular operations" so long as the police were not harassed. He divided the area into three zones, assigning three cops on foot to patrol each zone. The police, who volunteered for this assignment, got special training. Prosecutors targeted and jailed a few of the worst offenders. An infrared camera installed in a garage known to house a major chop shop put an end to its business. Many young people had reacted against the escalation of gang violence, which had resulted in several deaths. According to one local resident, "The generation that created this fucked up mess has truly matured. They have taken too many blows." In the final piece of the puzzle, a local Muslim Association was established, and it appealed to fathers to join. About 70 to 80 men began regularly taking part, increasingly joined by their sons. As a sign of improved relations, the association invited the prefect and the chief of police to a dinner celebrating the end of Ramadan, something that would have been inconceivable months earlier. The police and municipal authorities now consult with the community before making policy changes or implementing urban renewal programs. Finally, funds are available to support programs like the local soccer team and a hip hop group that works with the area's schoolchildren over the summer. Crime has fallen 18 percent and continues to fall, each month's rate half the rate of the same month the previous year.[74]

Even the most punitive option in France manifests therapeutic tendencies. Minors in detention by law must be kept separate from adults, usually serving their time in centers for youth detainees (*centres de jeunes détenus,* or CJDs). The largest CJD, Fleury-Mérogis, located outside Paris, in the 1990s experienced increasingly dangerous gang violence, culminating in riots in 1998. Fed up, in March 1999 the medical and teaching teams at

Fleury-Mérogis wrote to the government denouncing the situation and calling for reforms. "What a paradox," they wrote, "our society incarcerates young people more and more often for problems of violence and then lets them become victims of these same offenses inside the prison. In such conditions, can the penalty make any sense to these young people? We don't think so. For many, the CJD generates hatred of society."[75] In response, early in 2000 Penal Administration Director Martine Viallet undertook a major reform of Fleury-Mérogis that, ironically, resembles the pavilion system Jean Bancal advocated in 1941. The inmates are now divided into small groups of twelve to fifteen, and each group is assigned twenty-two supervisors who volunteered for the position and have undergone special training. Two supervisors are assigned to each minor, and it is hoped that they will forge a personal relationship with their charges, encouraged by the frequent contact at meals and in the courtyards. After spending their first several days in an arrival quarter, the young wards are sent, based on their behavior, to units with varying regimes. The Structured (Encadrement) Unit does not allow any leisure activities; the Basic Unit offers two hours per day of activities like video games and sports, in addition to school and professional training; and the Liberal Unit permits continuous access to the activity rooms. According to the press, the level of violence in the center has declined greatly since Viallet introduced the reforms. Thus penal sanctions do not, in France, preclude a therapeutic response. According to the press, Fleury-Mérogis's supervisors and wardens work closely with educators, doctors, and psychiatrists.[76]

Children's Protection or Children's Rights?

In the modern era, responses to juvenile crime, over time and from place to place, have oscillated between the punitive and the therapeutic. Frieder Dünkel's essay comparing juvenile justice systems across Europe defines the opposing systems as the welfare model, which corresponds to the therapeutic approach, and the justice model, or punitive approach. The welfare model, characterized by the central role of the juvenile judge, emphasizes education and individualized treatment involving social workers and psychologists. Procedures are relatively informal, and the system handles both delinquent and at-risk minors. The justice model replaces individualized, indeterminate, educational measures with penalties, determinate and proportional, that are imposed by judges. Procedures are more formal, prosecutors and defense attorneys play a large role, and criminal sanctions can be imposed, usually at an age of criminal responsibility lower than in the welfare model.[77] In reality, most systems fall in between these two ideal types. Clearly France falls on the welfare side of the spectrum, although its system includes elements of the justice model.

A larger, global movement now taking place adds a new dimension to the welfare versus justice debates. Since the 1980s, the concept of human rights has expanded to include children. The idea that human rights should not be denied because of a person's young age, that children have the right to upkeep, education, culture, and religion, that they should not be subject to arbitrary detention or economic exploitation, has been enshrined in the 1989 United Nations Convention on the Rights of the Child. While appealing in theory, the notion of children's rights can clash headlong with another governing idea, that parents, unless it can be proved otherwise, speak in the best interests of their own children. In the United States, children's rights have been asserted in cases involving custody disputes and Christian Scientists' refusal of medical treatment for their children. However, the harmful potential of elevating children's rights over the wishes of a parent became clear in watching Elián González, the six-year-old Cuban boy rescued in November 1999 from the seas; he was deluged by his Miami relatives with chocolate milk and video games and paraded in front of television cameras while he parroted their demand that he be allowed to stay in the United States, disregarding his father, who wanted Elián returned to him in Cuba.

Since the establishment of children's protection in the nineteenth century, parents' rights over their children have not been absolute. The state can supersede parents in cases of neglect and abuse. The left-wing proponents of children's rights who view the idea as empowering children may not adequately consider how the concept also serves right-wing desires to hold young people fully responsible for their acts. As Nicholas Queloz, an associate of the United Nations Crime and Justice Research Institute, points out, demands for the legal rights of children to due process and due treatment often lead to calls for the right to equal punishment.[78] To Queloz, the legal model has drifted furthest off course in the United States.

The United States: Birth and Resting Place of Juvenile Courts?

At the dawn of the twentieth century, the United States was a magnet, attracting French admiration and jealousy, and inspiring attempts to emulate the juvenile justice system pioneered on this side of the Atlantic. As the twenty-first century begins, the United States has become a repellent example of what can go wrong if the punitive impulse is not bridled, serving usefully as a line that France, so far, refuses to cross. The situation for juveniles varies from state to state, but after a move toward leniency and deinstitutionalization during the first two-thirds of the twentieth century, crowned by the Juvenile Justice and Delinquency Prevention Act of 1974, the trend reversed. In the 1980s the United States experienced a frightening crime wave, supposedly fueled by the epidemic of crack cocaine that hit the inner cities at that time. Between 1965 and 1985, the number of minors arrested for violent felonies doubled.[79] In response, over the course of the 1980s many states and localities adopted a get-tough approach, which became apparent as one state after the next reduced the age at which juvenile offenders could be removed from juvenile court jurisdiction and tried as adults. By 1997, forty-five states had passed laws making it easier to transfer minors from the juvenile into the adult criminal system.[80] In Harris County, Texas, which includes Houston, some thirty-three juveniles were certified to stand trial as adults in 1993. In 1996, after the adult certification age was lowered from fifteen to fourteen, some 178 minors were certified as adults.[81] Minors certified for trial in adult courts in the United States, unlike in France, benefit from no attenuation of penalties based on age. In Florida, two recent cases make clear how harsh the adult system can be for minors. Lionel Tate, now fourteen, was convicted of first-degree murder and sentenced to life without parole for beating to death a six-year-old playmate. He claimed to have been imitating the wrestlers he had seen on television. Nathaniel Brazill, also fourteen, shot and killed a teacher who would not let him return to class after his suspension. He was convicted and sentenced to twenty-five years to life.[82]

Minors in the United States are not even spared capital punishment, since the U.S. Supreme Court has ruled that executing people who were minors when they committed their crimes does not constitute cruel and unusual punishment. A special issue in 1989 of one of France's leading dailies, Le Monde, on children's rights included a highlighted box that explained that in the United States more than thirty minors had been sentenced to death for crimes committed before the age of majority, and that one had been executed in 1985, two in 1986. With understated horror, the segment closed, "Must we remind you that laws in Montana and Mississippi authorize the execution of children twelve or thirteen years old?"[83] Not to be outdone, in 1998, Texas state legislator Jim Pitts proposed the death penalty for children as young as eleven, a proposal firmly rejected by then-governor George W. Bush.[84] By 1998 some 143 people in the United States had been executed for crimes they committed as minors.

In the early 1990s, the crescendo of fear about crime in general and juvenile crime in particular continued to grow. By 1993 the number of minors arrested for violent felonies was triple the 1965 figures.[85] Few people pointed out the reassuring fact that the vast majority of juveniles, some 95 percent, were arrested for nonviolent offenses. Instead, experts like James Q. Wilson, a professor at the University of California, Los Angeles; John DiIulio, then professor of politics at Princeton University; and James Alan Fox, dean of the College of Criminal Justice at Northeastern University, heightened the alarm. Noting that the vast majority of violent crimes are committed by older adolescents and young adult males, they warned of a growing generation of superpredators, former crack babies living in the inner cities, raised by single mothers, addicted to drugs, who would bring about a crime wave of biblical proportions. The 1994 case of two boys, ten and eleven years old, who threw a five-year-old boy out a window in one of Chicago's most notorious housing projects, seemed to confirm those fears.[86]

One element of the anxiety went unspoken for the most part, or was expressed in coded language, the question of race. Young African-American males, whose rates of imprisonment far exceed those of any other population group, once again came to be feared as an out-of-control, criminal underclass. (This view has deep roots in the United States, dating back at least to the nineteenth century.) The race factor became explicit only in an egregious case. Dehundra Caldwell, a black teenager with no prior record, was sentenced to three years in prison for having stolen twenty dollars' worth of ice cream bars. Outraged critics charged racism, eventually his case was reopened, and his sentence was reduced to twelve months' probation with community service.[87]

For the most part, the racism of the juvenile justice system's treatment of young African-American males has gone unchallenged, the huge numbers involved serving only to confirm social anxieties and prejudices. In the face of widespread fear about juvenile superpredators, a radical idea germinated. As one headline explained, "With Juvenile Courts in Chaos, Critics Propose Their Demise."[88] While it has not yet taken place, juvenile courts could disappear in the nation that invented them, owing to a strange marriage of right- and left-wing critiques. To the law-and-order side, juvenile courts only indulge young criminals, whose heinous acts deprive them of any consideration of their youth. In proposing new legislation in 1996, Republican senator Orin Hatch stated, "We've got to stop coddling these violent kids like nothing is going on."[89]

Ironically, right-wing demands to end the separate system for young people have been echoed by left-wing scholars and activists, whose criticism rests on entirely different foundations. Michel Foucault's critiques of disciplinary institutions have powerfully influenced scholars of crime and deviance. More prominent in the United States, however, Thomas Szasz lobbed the most explosive bomb at the therapeutic state with his 1961 book, *The Myth of Mental Illness,* which insisted, "Mental illness is a myth whose function is to disguise and thus render more palatable the bitter pill of moral conflicts in human relations." Szasz also charged, "The classification of (mis)behavior as illness provides an ideological justification for state-sponsored social control." In Szasz's view, the therapeutic state re-presses (cures) disapproved thoughts, emotions, and actions through pseudo-medical interventions. Szasz disliked the undermining of individual responsibility and the coercive paternalism of the therapeutic response. His work helped inspire a successful drive to deinstitutionalize the mentally ill, the effects of which continue to be felt in American cities.[90] In addition to left-wing and libertarian thinkers' aversion to the therapeutic approach, juvenile courts have also been attacked on the basis of children's rights. Left-wing legal scholars like Barry Feld, for example, a professor of law at the University of Minnesota, denounce the lack of constitutional safeguards for minors in the informal juvenile court system and its indeterminate sentencing. Thus groups across the political spectrum in the United States have chipped away at the American therapeutic model of juvenile justice. The problem is that abandoning therapy and protection has hardly led to increased personal freedom or to benign responses to juvenile crime.

Pointing out the unpleasant alternatives, legal scholar Irene Rosenberg, who has worked as a defense attorney in juvenile court, takes up the thankless task of defending the system. In an article fittingly titled "Leaving Bad Enough Alone," Rosenberg argues strongly against the abolition of juvenile courts. First, she concedes all the shortcomings of the juvenile justice system but strongly denies that the disparity in procedural and constitutional safeguards between adult and juvenile courts is significant enough to opt out of juvenile justice. A 1967 Supreme Court ruling spelled out constitutional safeguards for minors. *In re Gault,* 387 U.S. 1

(1967), specified that juveniles have the right to notice of the charges, assistance of counsel, cross-examination and confrontation, and the privilege against self-incrimination.[91] Second, Rosenberg describes as "romantic" the idea that all adults accused of crimes benefit from the right to trial by jury. Rosenberg points out that 90 to 95 percent of accused adults give up their right to a jury trial, using it rather as a chip in "plea bargaining poker." Finally, Rosenberg strongly doubts that adult criminal courts will take the immaturity and vulnerability of children into account adequately in assessing culpability and determining sentences, a point the recent cases in Florida confirm.[92]

A case in Chicago starkly highlighted the dangers faced by children in the adult system. At first, the news aroused much hand-wringing, as it involved very young boys accused of a gruesome murder. On 9 August 1998, two boys, ages seven and eight, both African American, were arrested in Chicago. After police questioned them, they confessed to killing an eleven-year-old girl, Ryan Harris, because they wanted her bicycle. The press, in a feeding frenzy whetted by an announced police press conference, thronged the loading dock to see the boys as they were transferred to the Cook County Juvenile Justice Center. "The press was waiting to see the demons," according to Chicago *Tribune* reporter Maurice Possley, but reporters were shocked to see two gangly boys, one missing baby teeth, dazed and red-eyed from crying. The two boys had been taken into police custody and questioned for hours, without their parents present. Even adults have been known to confess to crimes they did not commit under the pressure of police interrogation. Children under stress are even more prone to distortion. Prosecutors wanted to keep the boys in custody. Attorneys R. Eugene Pincham and Andre Grant, hired by one of the boys' parents, fought hard for their release, backed by two therapists who testified that the boys posed no danger to the community. However, only Pincham's leaking of police report information implicating an adult pedophile changed the tenor of press coverage from deploring the savagery of the boys to questioning the interrogation procedures. Eventually the boys were completely cleared by the crime lab report that semen was present on the victim's underwear. Because medical experts described the possibility of semen coming from boys seven and eight as highly remote, prosecutors dropped the charges against the boys. Three weeks later, the crime lab found that the DNA in the semen matched that of an adult convicted sex offender. The Chicago police have done little soul-searching about their methods, and prosecutors have yet to charge the pedophile, who is serving time for another crime. Still, the case attracted widespread national attention and, for many people, has functioned as a "cautionary tale," in the words of Franklin Zimring, professor of law at the University of California, Berkeley.[93]

In fact, this case and other signs could indicate that the punitive trend in the United States is finally running out of steam. The wave of school shootings in 1998 and 1999 might have fed the demands for an even harsher system. Certainly there has been harsh punishment meted out and little interest expressed in the rehabilitation of those responsible. But the fact that the young males involved were white, suburban, and often came from two-parent, middle-class families, something widely remarked by the press, challenged assumptions about where danger lurks.

Perhaps the most significant factor reducing the demand for harsher punishment is the fact that for every year since 1992, crime rates have fallen. As this trend became apparent, the experts who had warned of a superpredator crime wave first maintained their position, pointing out that the population of older adolescent and younger adult males—the group that commits most crimes—was then at a temporary ebb. With the baby boom generation's children about to come of age, experts like Fox and DiIulio continued to cite ominous trends. DiIulio, for one, pointed specifically to the growth in population of black males age fourteen to twenty-four, which was increasing at a faster rate than the white male population that age. He argued that, if history holds true, "young blacks will be responsible for a disproportionate share of violent crimes when compared to whites." Yet by the turn of the twenty-first century, the predicted crime wave had failed to materialize, and violent youth crime was at a ten-year low.[94] Even DiIulio, whom President George W. Bush named in 2001 to head the new White House Office of Faith-Based and Community Initiatives, has not only retracted but even come to regret his earlier positions.[95]

Some conservatives have argued that the very solutions they promoted, tougher treatment, more aggressive policing, longer stays in adult prisons, have reduced the crime rates.[96] Others point to efforts to keep guns out of the hands of juveniles. French observers have long pointed to the ready availability of guns in explaining American crime trends. While the powerful National Rifle Association denies that connection, research in juvenile crime confirms it. Between 1989 and 1993, the number of homicides among juveniles involving handguns increased fivefold, and some 80 percent of juvenile homicides were committed with guns.[97] In a 1998 study

Howard Snyder, research director at the National Center for Juvenile Justice in Pittsburgh, confirmed the significance of handguns in the increased number of juvenile homicides in the late 1980s.[98] Policies cracking down on the sale of handguns to minors have been remarkably successful at reducing juvenile homicide. The Boston Police Department, by directing a massive and well-publicized effort at keeping guns out of the hands of juveniles, almost miraculously reduced the juvenile homicide rate 80 percent between 1990 and 1995. In 1996, not a single juvenile homicide took place in Boston.[99]

Snyder also challenges the theory that teenagers are becoming more violent in nature. As it turns out, much of the overall increase in violent crime figures resulted from a new classification that police and the FBI adopted. Until the late 1980s, the police ignored or at least did not report altercations between minors as violent crimes. In the late 1980s, similar fights were redefined as aggravated assaults, a violent felony. According to Zimring, the reclassification of juvenile fights as aggravated assaults created "a completely artificial crime wave."[100] In fact, despite worries about superpredators, Zimring describes the average case of juvenile violence as "becoming less serious every year . . . youth in 1998 are no more prone to violence than were teens 20 years ago."[101] Even in 1994, when the rate of violent offenses committed by minors reached its peak at three times the 1965 figure, according to Vincent Schiraldi, director of the Justice Policy Institute, some 94 percent of juvenile arrests were for nonviolent offenses and only one-half of 1 percent of juvenile arrests were for violent offenses.[102]

Jerome G. Miller, former commissioner of youth corrections in Massachusetts and Pennsylvania, editorialized against the "drumbeat of demand for harsher laws." In the 1970s, Miller worked to deinstitutionalize juvenile justice systems in those states. Republican Governor Frank Sargent replaced all reform schools in Massachusetts with 200 different nonprofit programs and group homes, along with individual intensive treatment for the worst cases. Often one caseworker supervised no more than two young people. Miller points out that reducing the harshness, rather than increasing crime, had positive results. Ten years after closing its institutions, Massachusetts's recidivism rate was much lower than that of states relying on reform schools and prisons. Measuring the number of juveniles reincarcerated within three years of their release, in 1989 Massachusetts had a 24 percent recidivism rate, Texas a 43 percent rate, and California a 62 percent rate.[103] Barry Krisberg, president of the National Council on

Crime and Delinquency, concurs. He says that transferring juveniles to an adult criminal system increases recidivism.[104]

In comparing figures across Europe, Frieder Dünkel finds that lenient systems do not increase juvenile crime. Raising the age of criminal responsibility in Norway from fourteen to fifteen, and decriminalizing petty offenses by those under age fifteen in Austria had no negative consequences on the crime rates in those countries. Dünkel notes similar findings for the use of noncustodial alternatives, arguing that custodial sanctions should be reserved as a last resort. When prison is used, sentences should be short and proportional to the crime. Diverting minors from custodial institutions reflects what he terms the episodic involvement of most juveniles and the petty nature of most juvenile offenses.[105]

Harsher systems have not proven more effective. Even the best of juvenile institutions tend to degenerate into brutal holding pens. Finally, there is simply no questioning the vulnerability of minors in adult systems. Adult prisons are dangerous places. Minors imprisoned with adults in the United States are five times more likely to be sexually assaulted and eight times more likely to commit suicide than children in juvenile facilities.[106] While the notion of children's rights has usefully led to a reassertion of certain procedural safeguards for children, still, children are not the same as adults. They are dependent on adults for the provision of their basic needs. Intellectually, they develop over time. Parents, schools, churches, and society in general progressively impose a prevailing morality. Children often have difficulty separating fantasy from reality. Few children understand the finality of death. There is no inborn sense that taking something desirable that belongs to someone else is bad; any parent of a two-year-old realizes this idea must be taught. Children are especially susceptible to pressure from their peers. Morally, children move from being entirely self-centered at birth to gaining an awareness of others and finally to developing a sense of responsibility to others. And notwithstanding romantic notions of childhood innocence, children are capable of committing heinous acts—but without an adult sense of right and wrong.

The therapeutic response to juvenile crime takes more of these factors into consideration, although it too has its flaws. Fairly minor acts can trigger a massive apparatus. Diagnostic categories label behavior that nearly everyone manifests at some time. In France, scholars like Jacques Donzelot and Philippe Meyer have extended Foucault's critiques of disciplinary systems to the twentieth-century treatment of children, when the state, via the new "priests" of the scientific era—doctors, psychiatrists, social workers—extended its power into the supposedly once private sphere of the family. Meyer considers children's activists and reformers mere instruments of the state. "In the war waged by the State against irregular families . . . the child is no more than a pretext and a hostage."[107] While Donzelot and Meyer challenge a naively positivist view of reformers as entirely unselfish and humanitarian, their analyses imply that, prior to such changes, families were free of outside intervention. Scholars of medieval and early modern family life, such as Lawrence Stone and Natalie Zemon Davis, have richly documented the many ways that neighbors, church authorities, and local leaders continuously and vigorously intruded to regulate family life. The therapeutic state thus substitutes for older systems a secular, impersonal intervention that, in democratic systems, is ultimately susceptible to public pressure. Furthermore, critics of the therapeutic state's paternalism, coercive power, and tendency to medicalize social reality might do well to look at the United States and consider the alternatives. The punitive response of the last two decades has proven the extreme vulnerability of children and adolescents in adult systems. Practically, it has been less successful at stopping certain behaviors than therapeutic systems and has incarcerated and stigmatized large numbers of primarily minority youths. Could therapy really be worse?

Interestingly, developments in the United States and France have often moved in opposite directions over the twentieth century. Perhaps current differences stem from the contrasting visions both of capitalism and of children. American capitalism opts for unbridled individualism with a minimum of state intervention. France prefers capitalism with a state presence to protect the vulnerable and assure a minimum level of welfare. More important, however, the two societies manifest profoundly different political attitudes toward children. The United States, for now the only remaining superpower, with a huge population, a powerful economy, and a massive military, has no fear that it will not have enough babies. In fact, the opposite idea is expressed, both by left-wing environmentalists, who promote zero population growth to help preserve scarce resources and curb urban sprawl, and by right-wing antiwelfare forces. Differential birth rates between whites and various minority and immigrant communities, and census data showing that "whites" are becoming a minority, only increase the sense that the wrong people are having children—and too many of them at that. The decision to have children, rather than being defined as a contribution to the nation's future worthy of the nation's support, is defined as an individual act. Racism, cloaked by supposedly neutral social-scientific theories like the ones DiIulio until recently promoted, further dilutes any identification with or sympathy for delinquent minors.

France, for all the wrong reasons, by 1900 defined its declining population growth rate as a crisis. By 1940, decades of propaganda had drummed in the idea that children are the most important part of the national patrimony. At the end of the twentieth century, generous prenatal medical benefits and family leave policies reinforce that idea. Children are the responsibility not just of the individual family but also of the community and the state. The preamble of the 1945 law, "France is not rich enough in children that it should have the right to neglect any child that might become a healthy being," is cited often in works on juvenile justice in France. Juvenile reformers in the 1930s deliberately linked the issue of delinquent youth to the broader demographic issue, a strategy that paid off during the Vichy regime and continues to operate decades later.

Thus in spite of recent French concerns about rising juvenile crime rates and perceptions of increasing youth violence, the punitive reaction against juvenile delinquents has been much milder than in the United States. The shift to a harsher system in France primarily involves restitution. While Children's Courts have sentenced an increasing number of minors to prison, the rate is still only .008 youths in detention per 10,000 people, whereas in the United States, it is 2.5 per 10,000. The United States has five times more people than France, but sixteen times more minors in jail.[108] France's juvenile justice system is extremely, intrusively therapeutic. Doubtless such intervention exhibits the usual tendencies, empowering white, middle-class judges, social workers, and doctors to intrude into, supervise, and attempt to control immigrant and working-class families. But France's experts had, and continue to have, no doubt about which direction they prefer. As early as the 1920s, juvenile delinquency specialists and activists saw clearly what they hoped to accomplish. Capitalizing on the publicized scandals of the 1930s and the crisis of defeat, working steadily in the same direction before, during, and after the war, they achieved major goals in the decade surrounding World War II. The system has evolved considerably, but the 1945 law, still in effect, determined the direction of that evolution, one that most experts in the 1940s envisioned. The treatment of juvenile delinquents in France is embedded in a state and a society that places tremendous value on its children and young people. Combined with France's positivist tradition, a continuing strong faith in science and technology, and a long-standing and widespread acceptance of state activism in social fields, this has resulted in a French juvenile justice system that matches perfectly its worldview.

Appendix: Informational Sheet

This is a translation of the informational sheet *(bulletin de renseignements)* that investigating magistrates sent to local authorities in cases of juvenile crime. The 1912 law required courts to investigate not just the crime but also the minor's background. While only about one-third of the Paris case files included a report from a social worker, every case file in the four departments I researched included these sheets (see Chapter 3).

About the minor named_____
who was under the age of 18 at the time of the events.

A. The minor

1. Last name, first name.
2. Date and place of birth (to be documented). Nationality.
3. Is he a legitimate child, legitimized by marriage, natural, or acknowledged?
4. Where or with whom does he really live?
5. Is he a full orphan, or has he lost just his father or just his mother?
6. Is he a ward of the nation (which department?), or does he have the right to be?
7. What is his religion?
8. What is his degree of instruction? (Is he completely illiterate? Can he read and write? Does he have his Certificate of Primary Education?)
9. Does he attend or has he attended a primary or professional school? What are the teachers' opinions of him, or what do they remember about him?
10. Has he completed an apprenticeship, and if so, where? Who were his employers, and what is their opinion of him?
11. Does he have a trade? Which one? What occupation does he intend to enter? Does he have special aptitudes or personal preferences?
12. Was he contributing a salary to his family's upkeep?
13. How is his health? Has he had any serious illnesses? Does he have any physical or mental infirmities that could influence his discretion?
14. Describe the character, morality, habits, and tendencies of the accused.
15. With whom does he usually spend time? Are his friends older, and do they seem more perverted than he?
16. Could we suppose that the minor could have been incited to commit the

235

crime or misdemeanor by his parents, or his superiors, or other persons with authority over him?

17. Has he been arrested or prosecuted prior to the current case? For what?
18. Has he been detained by way of paternal correction?
19. Does he seem susceptible to improvement? If so, based on all the information gathered, what measures would best ensure his moral recovery?

B. The parents

1. Names, first names, profession, current and former home addresses, nationality of the parents of the accused (or of the guardian or of the people with whom he lives).
2. Are both his parents deceased? Just one of them? From what illness?
3. Are they married or are they cohabiting? Are they separated, divorced, remarried?
4. How is their relationship with the accused?
5. How many children live with them? Are some of them step-siblings?
6. Describe their conduct, their morality, their reputation. Have they ever been convicted? For what crimes or misdemeanors? Are they inclined toward drunkenness, laziness, or habitual misconduct?
7. How well do they fulfill their parental duties to educate and provide for their children? Have any of their other children been abandoned, prosecuted, or legally removed from their custody?
8. Do they work at home or outside the home? Are they capable of taking care of their children and of providing effective supervision?
9. What are their expenses and their resources? How much do they earn? Do they receive any financial help? Could they afford to pay a monthly pension, and how much?
10. What do they want to happen in this case?
    a. That the child be returned to them, or that he be returned to a region near them or near some other person?
    b. That he be sent to a penitentiary colony until he reaches the age of majority?
    c. That he be placed with Public Assistance (if he is under 16 and qualifies)?
    d. That he be placed in the custody of a charitable person or institution?
11. Do the parents provide sufficient guarantees of morality and firmness to allow their child to be returned to them, and do they promise to undertake every effort to return him to the straight and narrow? How do they plan to fulfill those intentions?
12. In case of placement, do they want to remain in contact with their child, or have they completely lost interest?

C. Miscellaneous declarations

D. Justified opinion of the Police Commissioner (or of the Justice of the Peace in rural counties)

Notes

Introduction

1. Milos Sebor, *La Délinquance juvénile actuelle* (Paris: Imprimerie nationale, 1947), p. 7.
2. *Journal officiel, Débats,* Assemblée constituante provisoire, session of 22 March 1945, p. 683.
3. Hugh Cunningham, *Children and Childhood in Western Society since 1500* (New York: Longman, 1995), pp. 61–78, 134–162.
4. Michel Foucault, *Discipline and Punish,* trans. Alan Sheridan (New York: Vintage, 1979).
5. Robert Nye, *Crime, Madness and Politics in Modern France* (Princeton: Princeton University Press, 1984).
6. Christian Debuyst, "Les différents courants psychiatriques et psychologiques en rapport avec les savoirs criminologiques." In Christian Debuyst et al., *Histoire des savoirs sur le crime et la peine* (Montréal: Les Presses de l'Université de Montréal, 1998). Laurent Mucchielli edited and contributed several chapters on the history of criminology to *Histoire de la criminologie française* (Paris: L'Harmattan, 1994), which also includes a chapter by Debuyst, "L'oeuvre d'Etienne De Greef," pp. 335–349, and one by another leading scholar, Philippe Robert, "Le renouveau de la sociologie criminelle," pp. 429–447.
7. Jacques Donzelot, *The Policing of Families,* trans. Robert Hurley (New York: Pantheon, 1979); Philippe Meyer, *The Child and the State: The Intervention of the State in Family Life,* trans. Judith Ennew and Janet Lloyd (New York: Cambridge University Press, 1983).
8. Michel Chauvière, *Enfance inadaptée: L'héritage de Vichy* (Paris: Les Editions ouvrières, 1980); Jacques Bourquin, "De l'éducation corrective à l'éducation surveillée," in *Enfants et prison* (Paris: Editions Eshel, 1990); Bourquin, "Sur la trace des premiers éducateurs de l'Education surveillée: 1936–1947," in "Deux contributions à la connaissance des origines de l'Education surveillée," *Cahiers du Centre de recherche interdisciplinaire de Vaucresson* 2 (October 1986), hereinafter cited as *Cahiers du CRIV.*
9. Béatrice Koeppel, *Marguerite B.: Une jeune fille en maison de correction*

(Paris: Hachette, 1987), and "Les Temps forts de la rééducation des filles (de Cadhillac à Brécourt): 1935–1950," *Cahiers du CRIV* 2 (October 1986): 61–94. In October 2000 the review *Le Temps de l'histoire* published an issue titled *L'Enfant de justice pendant la guerre et l'immédiat après-guerre.* Unfortunately I received notice of this publication too late to incorporate its excellent and very germane essays into my analysis. See *Le Temps de l'historie* 3 (October 2000).

10. Pierre Pedron, *La Prison sous Vichy* (Paris: Les Editions de l'Atelier/Editions ouvrières, 1993); Jean-Marc Berlière, *Le Monde des polices en France* (Brussels: Complexe, 1996); Simon Kitson, "The Police in the Liberation of Paris," in H. R. Kedward and Nancy Wood, *The Liberation of France: Image and Event* (Oxford: Berg, 1995); Alain Bancaud, "La Magistrature et la répression politique de Vichy ou l'histoire d'un demi-échec," *Droit et société* 34 (1996): pp. 557–574.

1. From Child Criminals to Juvenile Delinquents

1. Paul Griffiths, *Youth and Authority: Formative Experiences in England 1560–1640* (Oxford: Clarendon Press, 1996).

2. Jean-Marie Mayeur and Madeleine Rebérioux, *The Third Republic from Its Origins to the Great War, 1871–1914*, trans. J. R. Foster (Cambridge: Cambridge University Press, 1987), p. 330. For an outstanding study of population politics and the rise of demography in nineteenth-century France, see Joshua Cole, *The Power of Large Numbers: Population, Politics, and Gender in Nineteenth-Century France* (Ithaca: Cornell University Press, 2000).

3. Only recently have a few voices begun to question the tough approach in the United States. See Margaret Talbot, "The Maximum Security Adolescent," *New York Times Magazine,* 10 September 2000, pp. 40–47; according to journalist Elizabeth Becker, John J. DiIulio, Jr., former professor of politics at Princeton University, in 2001 head of White House Office of Faith-Based Initiatives, regrets propagating the theory of juvenile offenders as "superpredators." "For an Office with a Heart, a Man with a Change of One," *New York Times,* 9 February 2001 (hereinafter cited as *NYT*).

4. Ralph Lepointe, *Le Vagabondage des mineurs* (Paris: Maurice Lavergne, 1936), pp. 47–48.

5. Kathleen Nilan, "Hapless Innocence and Precocious Perversity in the Courtroom Melodrama: Representations of the Child Criminal in a Paris Legal Journal, 1830–1848," *Journal of Family History* 22 (July 1997): 251–285.

6. Nilan, "Innocence and Perversity," p. 252.

7. Henri Gaillac, *Les Maisons de correction 1830–1945* (Paris: Editions Cujas, 1970), p. 40.

8. Patricia O'Brien, *The Promise of Punishment: Prisons in Nineteenth-Century France* (Princeton: Princeton University Press, 1982), pp. 129–130. See former New York State chief justice Sol Wachtler on the cruelty of solitary confinement, *NYT,* March 10, 1996.

9. For more theoretical discussion of theories of confinement and their relationship to structures of power, see Michel Foucault, *Discipline and Punish*, trans. Alan Sheridan (New York: Random House, 1977); Jacques Donzelot, *The Policing of Families*, trans. Robert Hurley (New York: Pantheon, 1979); Philippe Meyer and Michael Ignatieff, *A Just Measure of Pain: The Penitentiary in the Industrial Revolution, 1750–1850* (London: Macmillan, 1978); Robin Evans, *The Fabrication of Virtue: English Prison Architecture 1750–1840* (Cambridge: Cambridge University Press, 1982); O'Brien, *The Promise of Punishment*.

10. Nilan agrees that many social observers worried about the evil effects of urbanization on France's children. "Innocence and Perversity," pp. 260–262.

11. Gaillac, *Maisons de correction*, p. 97.

12. O'Brien, *Promise of Punishment*, p. 131; Chris Leonards's talk, "Border Crossing: The Genesis of a New Concept of the 'Criminal Child' in European Discourses on Juvenile Care in the Nineteenth Century," delivered at a conference in Cambridge (9–10 April 1997, "Becoming Delinquent: European Youth, 1650–1950"), described international movements for juvenile penal reform in the nineteenth century.

13. Lee Shai Weissbach, *Child Labor Reform in Nineteenth-Century France* (Baton Rouge: Louisiana State University Press, 1989); Rachel Fuchs, *Abandoned Children: Foundlings and Child Welfare in Nineteenth-Century France* (Albany: State University of New York Press, 1984); Antony M. Platt, *The Child Savers: The Invention of Delinquency* (Chicago: University of Chicago Press, 1969).

14. Gaillac, *Maisons de correction*, p. 100.

15. Weissbach, *Child Labor Reform*; Fuchs, *Abandoned Children*; Colin Heywood, *Childhood in Nineteenth-Century France* (Cambridge: Cambridge University Press, 1988), pp. 260–286; Platt, *The Child Savers*.

16. Jan Goldstein, *Console and Classify: The French Psychiatric Profession in the Nineteenth Century* (New York: Cambridge University Press, 1987); see chap. 5 for development of "legal medicine" through the use of alienists to determine sanity under Article 64 of the Penal Code, beginning in the 1820s.

17. Christian Debuyst, "L'Ecole française dite du 'milieu social,'" in Christian Debuyst et al., *Histoire des savoirs sur le crime et la peine* (Montreal: Les Presses de l'Université de Montréal, 1998), p. 304.

18. Robert Nye, *Crime, Madness and Politics in Modern France: The Medical Concept of National Decline* (Princeton: Princeton University Press, 1984), p. 170.

19. Nye, *Crime, Madness and Politics*, pp. 90–91.

20. Debuyst, "Les Différents Courants psychiatriques et psychologiques en rapport avec les savoirs criminologiques," in Debuyst et al. *Histoire des savoirs*, pp. 420–427. I am glossing over, here, a very rich discussion about how various figures—Lombroso, Tarde, Durkheim, Dupré, Heuyer—interacted and created the field of criminology. In addition to Debuyst's collection, see

Philippe Robert and Marc Renneville in Laurent Mucchielli, ed., *Histoire de la criminologie française* (Paris: L'Harmattan, 1994).

21. Nye, *Crime, Madness and Politics,* pp. 78–95.

22. Sylvia Schafer, *Children in Moral Danger and the Problem of Government in Third Republic France* (Princeton: Princeton University Press, 1997).

23. John Neubauer, *The Fin-de-Siècle Culture of Adolescence* (New Haven: Yale University Press, 1992), agrees that Compayré was "more interested in adolescents' social lives and souls than in their sexuality," p. 147.

24. Kathleen Alaimo, "Shaping Adolescence in the Popular Milieu: Social Policy, Reformers, and French Youth 1870–1920," *Journal of Family History* 17, no. 4 (1992): 423.

25. Schooling was compulsory from age seven to age thirteen, but children who attained their Certificate of Primary Education before age thirteen could leave school (although few children got this exemption). See Antoine Prost, *L'Enseignement en France, 1800–1967* (Paris: Armand Colin, 1968), p. 193. Many thanks to Barry Bergen and Sharif Gemie for information about schooling. See Sharif Gemie, *Women and Schooling in France, 1815–1914: Gender, Authority and Identity in the Female Schooling Sector* (Keele, England: Keele University Press, 1995).

26. Barry Bergen, "Molding Citizens: Ideology, Class and Primary Education in Nineteenth-Century France," Ph.D. diss., University of Pennsylvania, 1987.

27. Alaimo, "Shaping Adolescence," pp. 422–423.

28. Neubauer, *The Culture of Adolescence,* chap. 9.

29. Alaimo, "Shaping Adolescence," p. 432.

30. Cities in Wisconsin, New York, Ohio, Maryland, and Colorado followed suit in 1903; juvenile courts in Denver and Boston opened in 1905. Other countries were also inspired by the United States: England created juvenile courts in 1908 and Germany did in 1910. Hugh Cunningham, *Children and Childhood in Western Society since 1500* (New York: Longman, 1995), p. 149; Neubauer, *The Culture of Adolescence,* p. 181; Eric C. Schnieder, *In the Web of Class: Delinquents and Reformers in Boston, 1810s–1930s* (New York: New York University Press, 1992), pp. 148–169.

31. Owings, remarkably, not only played a critical role in the creation of children's welfare institutions in France but also completed a doctorate in France under Durkheimian sociologist Paul Fauconnet. Owings's dissertation, *Etude sur le traîtement de l'enfance délinquante en France* (Paris: Presses universitaires de France, 1923), describes the operation of juvenile courts. See also Marie-Antoinette Perret, "L'Enquête social (loi 1912): Les services sociaux près le Tribunal pour enfants de la Seine à Paris dans l'Entre-deux-guerres," mémoire de maîtrise d'histoire, Paris VII, 1989; Evelyne Diebolt, *A l'origine de l'association Olga Spitzer: La Protection de l'enfance hier et aujourd'hui, 1923–1939* (Paris: Association pour la recherche appliquée, 1993).

32. Lepointe, *Le Vagabondage des mineurs,* p. 25.

33. Michele Perrot, "Des Apaches aux Zoulous . . . ou de la modernité des

Apaches," in *Enfance délinquante, enfance en danger: Une question de justice* (Paris: Ministère de la Justice, Direction de la protection judiciaire de la jeunesse, 1996), pp. 49–54.

34. Gaillac, *Maisons de correction*, pp. 252–253.

35. This theme emerged in a number of papers presented at a conference on delinquency titled "Becoming Delinquent: European Youth 1650–1950," held at the University of Cambridge in April 1999 (Pamela Cox, "On the Margins of Justice: Policing Girls in Twentieth-Century Britain"; Franca Iacovetta, "Gossip, Contest and Power in the Making of Suburban Bad Girls: Toronto, 1940s–1950s"; Heike Schmidt, "Risky Girls and Girls at Risk: Correctional Education and Girls in Imperial Germany"; Astri Andresen, "'Reformed' Youth: Norway, 1900–1945").

36. According to Lepointe, girls twelve to sixteen arrested for prostitution could be held under administrative detention for a maximum of two months. As adults, prostitutes were required to obtain official recognition, in the form of a prostitute's card. Lepointe, *Le Vagabondage*, p. 29.

37. René Luaire, *Le Rôle de l'initiative privée dans la protection de l'enfance délinquante en France et en Belgique* (Paris: Librairie générale de droit et de jurisprudence, 1936), p. 38.

38. Françoise Lièvois, *La Délinquance juvénile* (Paris: Presses universitaires de France, 1946), p. 37.

39. See Nilan, "Hapless Innocence and Precocious Perversity."

40. Alaimo, "Shaping Adolescence," p. 432.

41. Michel Chauvière, *Enfance inadaptée: L'heritage de Vichy* (Paris: Les Éditions ouvrières, 1980), pp. 12–16; see also Debuyst, "Les Différents Courants," p. 427.

42. The explanation shifted from the nineteenth century's focus on poverty, family stability, and parental morality to psychological factors. Family life was examined less for class or morality and more for family interrelationships and their impact on personality. O'Brien, *Promise*, p. 147.

43. Françoise Tétard, "Resumé: Délinquance juvénile: Stratégie, concept ou discipline?" unpublished paper available at the Centre de recherche interdisciplinaire de Vaucresson, call number 44312; Tétard argues that "delinquent youth" was not subsumed into the *enfance inadaptée* sector because the term "juvenile delinquency" itself defined its own institutional and intellectual boundaries. But some people in the juvenile delinquency sector favored merging.

44. After the war, *Pour l'enfance "coupable"* changed its title. The Joubrels' book title went further, *L'Enfance dite "coupable"* (So-called "Guilty" Children).

45. In November 1947 it merged with the *Revue de l'education surveillée* to become *Rééducation*. The inaugural issue of *Rééducation* includes on the first page a very interesting discussion of the title choice and various options the editors considered. The editors considered *"jeunesses inadaptées,"* for example but noted "we touch on an issue of nomenclature," p. 1.

46. Pierre Videau, *Trois Maisons de relèvement du ressort de la cour d'appel de*

Besançon et de quelques suggestions nouvelles en matière de rééducation des mineurs délinquants (Gap: Imprimerie Louis-Jean, 1938), p. 21.

47. Chauvière attributes the progress in cross-disciplinary collaboration to the national committee, whose first meeting established the unifying theme of children "at risk" *(en danger moral)*. Chauvière, *Enfance inadaptée,* p. 24; André Beley, *De la prophylaxie de l'acte anti-social chez les mineurs instables* (Paris: Les Éditions Végan, 1933).

48. Chauvière, *Enfance inadaptée,* pp. 23–24.

49. René Fugeray (abbé), *Mère Anjorrant et son oeuvre: L'Institut de Jésus-Christ Bon-Pasteur et de Marie-Immaculée,* vol. 1: *L'Ere des fondations* (Paris: G. Beauchesne, 1928); Abbé P. Bordarrampé, *Le Vénérable Louis-Edouard Cestac, fondateur de Notre-Dame du Refuge (Anglet, près Bayonne) et la congrégation des servantes de Marie: Sa vie, son oeuvre* (Bayonne: Imprimerie de Porché Frères et cie., 1928); Father Daniel-Antonin Mortier, *Bonne mère, ou la Révérende Mère Chopin, fondatrice de la Congrégation de Notre-Dame-de-Grâce, Châtillon-sous-Bagneux (Seine)* (Paris: Desclée, de Brouwer, et cie., 1926).

50. Thanks to Jacques Bourquin for allowing me to view photographs from the era's preservation schools.

51. Luaire, *Le Rôle de l'initiative* privée, p. 4.

52. Luaire, *Le Rôle de l'initiative privée;* Pierre de Casabianca, *Les Nouveaux Tribunaux pour mineurs en Italie* (Agen: Imprimerie moderne, 1934); Henry Toubas, *Les Institutions pénitentiaires pour mineurs délinquants: Etude comparée avec certains pays étrangers, projets de réformes* (Nimes: Imprimerie Azémard, 1936); Henry Van Etten, *Une enquête internationale sur quelques établissements pénitentiares* (Paris: Gaston Doin, 1932).

53. Eric Schneider, *In the Web of Class: Delinquents and Reformers in Boston, 1810s–1930s* (New York: New York University Press, 1992), p. 149.

54. Videau, *Trois maisons de relèvement,* p. 187.

55. Gaillac, *Les Maisons de correction,* p. 348.

56. Roger Albernhe, *La Nécessité d'un personnel spécialisé pour s'occuper des enfants en justice* (Montpellier: Imprimerie du Progès, 1938).

57. Henri Danjou, *Enfants du malheur: Les bagnes d'enfants* (Paris: A. Michel, 1932); Germain Despres, *Bagnes d'enfants* (Paris: Imprimerie de Moif et Paxcaly, n.d.); Henri Wallon, *Une plaie de la société: Les Bagnes d'enfants* (Bourges, Secours ouvrier international, 1934).

58. Gaillac, *Les Maisons de correction,* pp. 288–289; Marianne Oswald, *One Small Voice* (New York: McGraw-Hill, 1945), p. 287. Apparently a film about the incident, based on the Prévert-Oswald version, was supposed to be filmed at Belle-Ile in 1945. For reasons unexplained, the film was never produced; Gaillac, *Les Maisons de correction,* p. 300.

59. *Détective,* 23 January 1935.

60. *Journal de la femme,* 13 April 1935; "Enfants martyrs!" *Le Figaro,* 10 January 1936.

61. *Le Populaire*, 2 December 1935.

62. According to Philippe Bernard and Henri Dubief, *The Decline of the Third Republic 1914–1939*, trans. Anthony Forster (Cambridge: Cambridge University Press, 1985), *Paris-Soir*, with a circulation of 1.75 million, dwarfed all other Paris dailies. Only *Le Petit Parisien* came close, with a daily circulation of 1 million, the paper with the next highest circulation, *Le Journal*, stood at 410,000, and even the influential *Le Temps* sold only 70,000 copies a day, p. 263.

63. *Paris-Soir*, 6 April 1937, p. 1.

64. Gaillac, *Les Maisons de correction*, p. 292.

65. *Paris-Soir*, 8 April 1937, p. 1.

66. Luaire, *Le Rôle de l'initiative privée*, p. 419.

67. Gaillac, *Les Maisons de correction*, p. 351.

68. The law of 28 June 1904 modified paternal correction by setting up provisions for assuming authority over minors with behavioral problems. Prior to both these legal modifications, in 1881 paternal correction accounted for only 2 percent of all incarcerated minors. Significantly, three-quarters of paternal correction cases involved girls; 1 of every 5 incarcerated girls fell into the category, whereas only 1 in 100 boys did. O'Brien, *Promise of Punishment*, pp. 118–119.

69. Lepointe, *Le Vagabondage*, pp. 51–52; Hélène Campinchi's 1945 article confirms these figures, "Le Statut de l'enfance délinquante et la loi du 27 juillet 1942," in Louis Hugueney et al., eds., *Etudes de science criminelle et de droit pénal compare* (Paris: Sirey, 1945), p. 163.

70. Lepointe, *Le Vagabondage*, p. 98.

71. Lepointe, *Le Vagabondage*, p. 96.

72. Geneviève Mazo, *Le Centre d'observation et la loi du 27 juillet 1942 relative à l'enfance délinquante* (Paris: H. Van Etten, 1944), p. 25.

73. Linda Clark, *Schooling the Daughters of Marianne: Textbooks and the Socialization of Girls in Modern French Primary Schools* (Albany: State University of New York Press, 1984), pp. 98–99.

74. Vincent Auriol proposed a law on the reform of delinquent minors: Archives nationales (AN), F60 427 E 11 A, 26 July 1938. Rucard wrote about his desire to create an entirely new system "relative to the protection of children in the justice system": AN, F60 608 S1 F, 3 February 1937 (Archives nationales hereinafter cited as AN).

75. Monique Charvin et al., *Recherche sur les juges des enfants: Approches historique, démographique, sociologique* (Paris: Conseil de la recherché du Ministère de la Justice, 1996), p. 37.

76. On the Popular Front, see Julian Jackson, *The Popular Front in France Defending Democracy, 1934–1938* (Cambridge: Cambridge University Press, 1988); Joel Colton, *Léon Blum: Humanist in Politics* (New York: Knopf, 1966); Jacques Kergoat, *La France du Front populaire* (Paris: La Découverte, 1986).

77. See the first part of Mathias Gardet and Françoise Tétard, eds., *Le Scoutisme et la rééducation dans l'immédiate après-guerre: Lune de miel sans lendemain?* Document de l'Institut national de la jeunesse et de l'éducation populaire 21 (June 1995), pp. 13–70.

78. Jacques Bourquin has noted that the 1937–38 reforms primarily adopted educational approaches, following Henry Wallon, rather than building on the neuropsychiatric theories of Georges Heuyer. This is hardly surprising, since at the time the medical and neuropsychiatric circles concerned themselves almost exclusively with the screening, diagnosis, and elaboration of pathologies, and hardly at all with spelling out treatment options corresponding to the various disorders they elaborated. Jacques Bourquin, "Enfant de justice pendant la guerre," report on seminar of 25 January 1996, pp. 1–2.

79. C. Brunshwig, 16 November 1936, Sous-Sécretaire d'état, Education Nationale, AN, F60 427 E 11 A.

80. Gaillac, *Les Maisons de correction,* p. 373.

81. In French, an "ensemble de maqueraux, de voleurs, pantins, d'insignifiants." AN, CAC 760175/15, letter dated 28 May 1938.

82. Gaillac, *Les Maisons de correction,* pp. 309–310.

83. Ibid., p. 313.

84. AN, F60 608 S 1 F. Henri Sellier is best known for his role in creating low-cost public housing, originally called habitation à bon marché.

85. *Paris-Soir,* 8 April 1938, p. 1, "Mettray condemned, Eysses reformed. M. Henri Sellier declares Mettray a dirty and impossible house. For having dared to publish the same opinion about that house, *Paris-Soir* is being sued by Mettray for 300,000 francs in damages." Interestingly, this front-page headline was coupled with continuing coverage of Roger Abel's death at Eysses.

86. Gaillac, *Les Maisons de correction,* p. 290.

2. The Experience of World War II for Children and Adolescents

1. Raymond Ruffin, *Journal d'un J3* (Paris: Presses de la Cité, 1979), p. 28.

2. Gilles Ragache, in his excellent study of childhood during the war, points out that schoolbooks during the occupation, facing German censorship and Vichy restrictions, used the metaphor of a storm rather than writing directly about the war, and that this must have shaped childhood memories. *Les Enfants de la guerre: Vivre, survivre, lire et jouer en France 1939–1949* (Paris: Perrin, 1997), pp. 25–29.

3. Joel Blatt edited a volume of *Historical Reflections/Réflexions historiques* (no. 1, Winter 1996 22) reassessing the French defeat of 1940 in articles by Nicole Jordan, Carole Fink, Omer Bartov, William Irvine, Robert Young, John Cairns, Martin Alexander, Stanley Hoffmann, and others.

4. W. D. Halls, *The Youth of Vichy France* (Oxford: Clarendon Press, 1981), p. 4.

5. François Pakonyk, *1940–1945, Les enfants de l'exode* (Paris: La Pensée universelle, 1984), p. 23; also letter of 22 November 1985 to the author.

6. The records never report her as dead, although no further information about her appears even in much later documents. Archives départementales (AD) du Nord, 1125 W 367. (Archives départementales hereinafter cited as AD).

7. Alfred Brauner, *Ces enfants ont vécu la guerre* (Paris: Les Editions sociales françaises, 1946), pp. 206–207.

8. Halls, *Youth of Vichy France*, p. 3.

9. *Les Jeux interdits* also portrays the bizarre, sporadic, and at times profound intrusion of the war into the lives of people removed from the battlefront. The peasant family's eldest son, enticed to pursue a horse whose fleeing owners either abandoned it or were killed, sickens and eventually dies of injuries sustained while trying to capture it. Despite the lost girl, the dead son, and another son who narrowly escapes capture in the Battle of France, this family's daily life, farming and feuding with neighbors, goes on as usual.

10. Jean-Pierre Levert et al., *Un lycée dans la tourmante: Jean-Baptiste Say 1934–1944* (Paris: Calmann-Lévy, 1994), p. 68.

11. Archives départementales de Paris (ADP) D1U6 3656. (Archives départementales de Paris hereinafter cited as ADP).

12. Ibid., D1U6 3656.

13. AD Indre-et-Loire, 127 W 230.

14. AD Gard, 6U 10/262.

15. Most cases involving violent crime were unrelated to the war; the few involuntary homicides involved fatal bicycle or automobile accidents; several cases of assault involved scuffles between boys.

16. ADP, D1U6 3680.

17. Ibid., D1U6 3680. In Tours an adult yelled at an officer, "I say shit to you assholes . . . You don't belong here, you should be over there. I have yet to see a gendarme at the war front!" AD Indre-et-Loire, 127 W 228.

18. For more on this complicated series of events, see Jean-Pierre Azéma, *From Munich to the Liberation, 1938–1944* (New York: Cambridge University Press, 1984); Marc Ferro, *Pétain* (Paris: Fayard, 1987); Jean-Paul Cointet, *Pierre Laval* (Paris: Fayard, 1993); Robert Paxton, *Vichy France* (New York: Columbia University Press, 1982).

19. Philippe Pétain, *Discours aux français, 17 juin 1940–20 août 1944* (Paris: Albin Michel, 1989), p. 57.

20. Paxton, *Vichy France*, pp. 52–54, Germany allowed Vichy to pay lower occupation costs from 10 May 1941 (a concession in exchange for the Protocols of Paris allowing Germany access to French military bases in Syria, p. 118) through 11 November 1942, pp. 143–144; Azéma, *From Munich to the Liberation*, pp. 45–46.

21. Paxton, *Vichy France*, pp. 144, 361–362.

22. The large numbers resulted primarily from mistakes made by the French High Command, both in overall strategy and in not attempting to remove

large numbers of soldiers before they were surrounded (for example, from the Maginot Line and Belgium). See Sarah Fishman, "Grand Delusions: The Unintended Consequences of Vichy France's Prisoner of War Propaganda," *Journal of Contemporary History* (April 1991), and Yves Durand, *La Captivité: Histoire des prisonniers de guerre français 1939–1945* (Paris: Fédération nationale des combattants prisonniers de guerre et combattants d'Algérie, Tunisie, Maroc, 1982), pp. 34–43.

23. Vichy negotiations led to about 200,000 POW repatriations by late 1944. See Sarah Fishman, *We Will Wait: Wives of French Prisoners of War 1940–1945* (New Haven: Yale University Press, 1991), p. 34.

24. Paxton, *Vichy France*, p. 369; Edward L. Homze, *Foreign Labor in Nazi Germany* (Princeton: Princeton University Press, 1967), p. 195.

25. Paxton, *Vichy France*, p. 144.

26. Essay by Gisèle Bertrand, Huguette Foulquier, Eliette Lastenouse, Louise Fillol, and Claudine Doudiès, ages ten to thirteen. *Les Ecoliers de Tournissan 1939–1945* (Toulouse: Editions Edouard Privat, n.d.), p. 122.

27. A metric ton is very close to an American ton—.98 of one, to be exact. The equivalent for milk would be 308 million gallons. Having compared the figures, Robert Paxton claims that France supplied more food to Germany than even Poland, Paxton, *Vichy France*, pp. 144, 360; see also Yves Durand, *La France dans la deuxième guerre mondiale* (Paris: Armand Colin, 1989), p. 65.

28. Azéma, *Munich to the Liberation*, p. 234, n. 32; Michel Cépède, *Agriculture et alimentation en France durant la IIe guerre mondiale* (Paris: Editions M.-Th. Génin, 1961), p. 69; the Germans requisitioned and bought with inflated marks some 10,400,000 hectoliters of wine during the occupation, Durand, *La France*, p. 65.

29. Micheline Bood, *Les Années doubles: Journal d'une lycéenne sous l'Occupation* (Paris: Editions Robert Laffont, 1974), p. 70.

30. *Les Écoliers de Tournissan*, p. 83.

31. In 1940, official rations provided about 1800 calories per person per day, gradually declining to 1700, then 1500. Late in 1942, adults received 1220 calories a day, workers in strenuous jobs 1380, and the elderly only 850 calories a day. From Cèpède, *Agriculture*, p. 151; Paxton, *Vichy France*, p. 360; Arthur Marwick, *War and Social Change in the Twentieth Century* (New York: St. Martin's Press, 1974), p. 193; Henri Amouroux, *La Vie des français sous l'occupation* (Paris: Fayard, 1983), pp. 131–151; Azéma, *Munich to the Liberation*, n 35, p. 234; Durand, *La France*, p. 77.

32. *Les Écoliers de Tournissan*, p. 120.

33. Dominique Veillon, *Vivre et survivre*, pp. 101, 112, 116.

34. Ibid.; Hanna Diamond, *Women and the Second World War in France, 1939–1948* (London: Longman, 1999); Fishman, *We Will Wait;* Paula Schwartz, "The Politics of Food and Gender in Occupied Paris," *Modern and Contemporary France* 7, no. 1 (February 1999): pp. 35–46.

35. Ruffin, *Journal d'un J3*, pp. 70–71.

36. See Deborah Reed-Danahy, *Education and Identity in Rural France: The Politics of Schooling* (Cambridge: Cambridge University Press, 1996), p. 212; she discusses the meaning of the verb *se débrouiller* in the context of local peasant resistance to the national systems and rules, but agrees that the term implies cleverness, resourcefulness, rather than simple effort.

37. *Journal officiel*, 19 March 1942, p. 1076; see also Emmanuelle Rioux, "Les Zazous: Un phénomène socioculturel pendant l'Occupation," mémoire de maîtrise, Paris-X Nanterre, 1987, p. 122.

38. Brauner, *Ces enfants ont vécu la guerre*, p. 208.

39. Roger-Ferdinand, *Les J3: Ou la nouvelle école* (n.p.: Imprimerie de Sceaux, 1944), pp. 7–8.

40. Ragache, *Les Enfants de la guerre*, p. 38.

41. Another city cited in this study, Saint-Etienne, found that of 2,500 children in 1940–41, 18 percent had lost weight, 9 percent had stayed the same. The worst off were children aged thirteen and fourteen, 20 to 29 percent of whom were deficient. *Children in Bondage: A Survey of Child Life in the Occupied Countries of Europe and in Finland* (New York: Longmans, Green and Company, 1942), pp. 38–40.

42. Twenty-two percent of the girls and 28 percent of the boys in the Montpellier study were under the normal height; 12 percent of all the children were underweight, Alfred Sauvy, *La Vie économique des Français de 1939 à 1945* (Paris, 1978), pp. 199–200; Cépède, *Agriculture et alimentation*, pp. 410–411.

43. The study also found that boys were an average of 3.5 centimeters and girls 2.2 centimeters shorter in 1945 than in 1935. *L'Enfance et la Croix rouge française* (Paris: Librairie J. B. Baillire, 1946), p. 30.

44. Veillon, *Vivre et survivre*, p. 227, from *L'Oeuvre*, 17 July 1942.

45. Philippe Pétain, speech of 13 August 1940, in *Discours aux français*, p. 77.

46. *Children in Bondage*, p. 44.

47. Paxton, *Vichy France*, p. 376.

48. Sauvy, *La Vie économique des Français*, p. 204.

49. *Les Ecoliers de Tournissan*, p. 126.

50. In the prewar period, about 30 percent of women entered the labor force. Fishman, *We Will Wait*, pp. 57–59.

51. For a full discussion of POW children, see ibid., pp. 70–74, 157–159.

52. Veillon, *Vivre et survivre*, p. 223, from Pétain, "Message à la jeunesse de France," 29 December 1940, *La France nouvelle* (Montrouge: Draeger, 1941), p. 94.

53. Veillon, *Vivre et survivre*, p. 225, from *Ames vaillantes*, 19 October 1941.

54. Jean-Michel Barreau, "Vichy, Idéologue de l'école," *Revue d'histoire moderne et contemporaine* 38 (1991): 592; "Marshal, Here We Are" ("Maréchal, nous voilà") was the title of a song glorifying Pétain that Vichy distributed to all the schools.

55. Chevalier's laws of 6 December 1940 and 6 January 1941 introduced op-

tional religious instruction into the public schools and allowed public support of private religious schools. For more on Chevalier and Carcopino, see Halls, *Youth of Vichy France,* pp. 20–32; Pierre Giolitto, *Histoire de la jeunesse sous Vichy* (Paris: Perrin, 1991), pp. 97–123; Stéphane Corcy-Debray, "Jérôme Carcopino, du triomphe à la roche tarpéienne," *Vingtième siècle* 58 (April–June 1998): 70–82.

56. Barreau, "Vichy, Idéologue," pp. 590–91; Giolitto, *Histoire de la jeunesse,* pp. 124–158; Eric Jennings, "'Reinventing Jeanne': The Iconology of Joan of Arc in Vichy Schoolbooks, 1940–44," *Journal of Contemporary History* 29 (1994): 711–734 (Jennings also discusses the general rewriting of school texts).

57. Ragache, *Les Enfants de la guerre,* see pp. 114–118 on school texts, pp. 122–133 on race.

58. Halls, *Youth of Vichy France,* p. 113 ff.; Giolitto, *Histoire de la jeunesse,* p. 129.

59. Barreau, "Vichy, Idéologue," pp. 590–591; Giolitto, *Histoire de la jeunesse,* pp. 124–158.

60. Giolitto, *Histoire de la jeunesse,* p. 137.

61. Ibid., p. 141.

62. Halls, *Youth of Vichy France,* p. 114; Giolitto, *Histoire de la jeunesse,* pp. 136–137.

63. Simone de Beauvoir, *La Force de l'âge* (Paris: Gallimard, 1960), p. 532; Jean Guéhenno wrote in his *Journal des années noires* on 7 August 1941, "Stupidity abounds. For the fourth time today I had to swear on my honor that I am neither Jewish nor a Freemason." Cited by Giolitto, *Histoire de la jeunesse,* p. 137; see also Claude Singer, *Vichy, l'université et les juifs* (Paris: Pluriel/ Les belles lettres, 1996), p. 102; Jean-Pierre Levert et al., *Un lycée dans la tourmente: Jean-Baptiste Say 1934–1944* (Paris: Calmann-Lévy, 1994) includes photocopies of the actual forms from the lycée's archives, pp. 88–89, 94.

64. Marcel Ophuls, *The Sorrow and the Pity,* trans. Mireille Johnston (New York: Outerbridge and Lazard, 1972), p. 75; Giolitto, *Histoire de la jeunesse,* pp. 141–142.

65. Vichy justified its measures against employed women simply with reference to the high unemployment rate. Nevertheless, the law rested on the patriarchal assumptions that men had a higher claim to jobs; that married women did not need to earn an income; that all married women could return to a home supported by a male breadwinner. For an excellent and very thorough discussion of the 11 October 1940 law, see Miranda Pollard, *Reign of Virtue: Mobilizing Gender in Vichy France* (Chicago: University of Chicago Press, 1998), chap. 6; also Fishman, *We Will Wait,* pp. 44–45.

66. Linda L. Clark, *The Rise of Professional Women in France: Gender and Public Administration since 1830* (Cambridge: Cambridge University Press, 2001), pp. 244–253; Pollard, *Reign of Virtue,* p. 162.

67. Giolitto, *Histoire de la jeunesse,* p. 141. Evidence about how children reacted to anti-Semitic policies targeted at their schoolmates will be discussed later in this chapter.

68. For comparison, although both countries are smaller than France, Austria lost 640 schools, Poland 6,152; Thérèse Brosse, *L'Enfance victime de la guerre* (Paris: UNESCO, 1949), pp. 45–46.

69. Eugen Weber, *The Hollow Years: France in the 1930s* (New York: W. W. Norton, 1994), p. 209; Barry Bergen, "Molding Citizens: Ideology, Class and Primary Education in Nineteenth-Century France," Ph.D. diss., University of Pennsylvania, 1987.

70. See AN, Police générale: F7 15146, on German opposition to a single French youth movement; Michel-A. Bernard, "Pas de dissolution! Pas de mouvement unique!" in *Aujourd'hui* 25–26 July 1942. On youth movements, in addition to Halls and Giolitto, an excellent collection of articles edited by Michel Chauvière appears in a special issue of the journal *Les cahiers de l'animation* 49–50 (1985): "Education populaire: Jeunesse dans la France de Vichy 1940–1944."

71. See Giolitto, *Histoire de la jeunesse,* p. 551; Rioux, "Les Zazous," p. 35.

72. See Halls, *Youth of Vichy France,* pp. 286–287.

73. Ibid., p. 269.

74. I found sixteen cases of minors sent to Centres de jeunesse by juvenile judges in Paris. ADP, D1 U6 3786, 3812, 3839, 3890, the last one in September 1944. "Centres de jeunesse," *Paris-Soir* 4 September 1942.

75. René Duverne, "Menace sur les Centres de jeunesse," *Pour l'enfance "coupable"* 63 (March–April 1946).

76. Giolitto, *Histoire de la jeunesse,* pp. 514–525.

77. *Children in Bondage,* p. 45; Giolitto, *Histoire de la jeunesse,* p. 501.

78. *Quinze conférences sur les problèmes de l'enfance délinquante* (Paris: Editions familiales de France, 1946), p. 7.

79. Giolitto, *Histoire de la jeunesse,* p. 499, argues that while scouting shared with the National Revolution the veneration of leadership, discipline, and rural virtue, and so supported the Vichy government at first, scouts were neither racist nor collaborationist and resisted the dissolution of the Jewish scouting movement, the Eclaireurs israélites, ordered 29 November 1941 by Darquier de Pellepoix, p. 502.

80. W. D. Halls, *Politics, Society and Christianity in Vichy France* (Oxford: Berg Publishers, 1995), p. 295.

81. The word *maquis* refers to the thick brush of the Corsican countryside, where people fleeing the authorities often hid.

82. See H. R. Kedward, "The Maquis and the Culture of the Outlaw," in R. Kedward and R. Austin, *Vichy France and the Resistance* (London: Croom Helm, 1985), and his excellent book, *In Search of the Maquis: Rural Resistance in Southern France 1942–1944* (Oxford: Oxford University Press, 1993).

83. Rioux, "Les Zazous," pp. 56, 52.

84. Ibid., pp. 13, 29, 41.

85. Irene Guenther, "Nazi 'Chic'? Fashioning Women in the Third Reich," Ph.D. diss., University of Texas at Austin, 2001, discusses the irony of the work most women undertake to appear "natural."

86. Rioux, "Les Zazous," pp. 15–29.

87. Dominique Veillon, *La Mode sous Vichy* (Paris: Payot, 1990), pp. 236–239; Jean-Pierre Rioux, "Survivre," *L'Histoire* 80 (1985): 94. Raymond Ruffin cites a lexicon that circulated in his lycée during the war, "La Nation: A.B.C. (*abaissée*/debased); La République: D.C.D. (*décédée*/deceased); La Gloire: F.A.C. (*éffacée*/erased); Les Provinces: C.D. (*cédés*/ceded); Le Peuple: E.B.T. (*hébété*/stupified); La Justice: H.T. (*achetée*/bribed), La Liberté: F.M.R. (*éphemère*/ephemeral); *Journal d'un J3*, p. 96.

88. Rioux, "Les Zazous," pp. 171–172, 192, 168.

89. Pierre Ducrocq, "Swing qui peut," *La Gerbe* (4 June 1942): 7; "Qu'est-ce qu'un zazou-zazou?" *Au Pilori*, 11 June 1942; Max Davigny, "En descendant le Boul 'Mich,'" *Jeunesse* 2 (February 1941); *L'Illustration* (28 March 1942). See also Rioux, "Les Zazous," p. 96; Jean-Claude Loiseau, *Les Zazous* (Paris: Le Sagittaire, 1977).

90. "Le Zazou," *Au Pilori* 3 September 1942; see Rioux, "Les Zazous," p. 88.

91. Jean Bosc, clipping in AN, Police générale, F7 15146, dated 12 October 1942.

92. Anglo-Americans demonstrated a similar hostility to this youth culture. Los Angeles experienced what were dubbed the "zoot-suit riots," from 3 to 6 June 1943, when servicemen attacked, beat, and stripped Mexican-American boys targeted as zoot suiters and juvenile delinquents, while, according to Janis Appier, the Los Angeles police stood by and watched. See Janis Appier, "Juvenile Crime Control: Los Angeles Law Enforcement and the Zoot-Suit Riots," *Criminal Justice History: An International Annual* 11 (1990): 147–167. Luis Alverez's research reveals that some Los Angeles police officers, on and off duty, answered calls by forming their own "Vengeance Squad" that took part in the violence against minority youth in East LA; Luis Alverez, "The Power of the Zoot: Race, Community and Resistance in American Youth Culture, 1940–1945," Ph.D. diss., University of Texas at Austin, May 2001.

93. "Sing Song Touamotou," *Gringoire,* 3 July 1942, p. 3; Rioux, "Les Zazous," p. 81.

94. "Zazouismus: Umriss einer Franzosischen Nachkriegsbewegung," *Pariser Zeitung,* 24 August 1942, AN, Police générale, F7 15146.

95. Ruffin, *Journal d'un J3,* p. 110.

96. Claudine Vegh, *Je ne lui ai pas dit au revoir: Des enfants de déportés parlent* (Paris: Gallimard, 1979), p. 107.

97. Ibid., p. 33.

98. Ibid., p. 113.

99. Michael Marrus and Robert Paxton, *Vichy France and the Jews* (New York:

Basic Books, 1981); see also André Kaspi, *Les Juifs pendant l'occupation* (Paris: Seuil, 1991).

100. After the war, Laval and Xavier Vallat, leader of the Commissariat général aux questions juives, claimed that Vichy protected many French Jews. Marrus and Paxton soundly disproved that argument in their exhaustively researched book *Vichy France and the Jews*.

101. Marrus and Paxton, *Vichy France and the Jews*, p. 245, from Lucien Steinberg, "La Collaboration policière, 1940–44," unpublished paper, 1978, p. 28.

102. Marrus and Paxton, *Vichy France and the Jews*, pp. 251–252.

103. Vegh, *Je ne lui ai pas dit au revoir*, p. 108.

104. Ibid., pp. 59–62.

105. Marrus and Paxton, *Vichy France and the Jews*, p. 263.

106. Ibid.

107. Ibid., pp. 265–269.

108. Deborah Dwork, *Children with a Star: Jewish Youth in Nazi Europe* (New Haven: Yale University Press, 1991), p. 65.

109. See Philip Gourevitch, "The Memory Thief," *New Yorker*, 14 June 1999.

110. Robert Vivier, *L'Indre-et-Loire sous l'occupation allemande, 1940–1944* (Tours: Comité d'histoire de la deuxième guerre mondiale, 1965), table 1.

111. Vegh, *Je ne lui ai pas dit au revoir*, p. 36.

112. Ibid., pp. 52–53.

113. Ibid., p. 57.

114. Ibid., p. 75.

115. Ibid., p. 116.

116. Pierre Laborie, *L'Opinion française sous Vichy* (Paris: Seuil, 1990), p. 279.

117. Octave Merlier, ed., *Rédaction sujet: La drôle de guerre, l'occupation, la libération racontées par des enfants* (Paris: Juilliard, 1975), pp. 51–52.

118. Marrus and Paxton, *Vichy France and the Jews*, pp. 271, 276; Laborie, *L'Opinion française*, pp. 279–280, 343.

119. Brauner, *Ces enfants ont vécu la guerre*, p. 209.

120. One former POW wife recalls that her husband, repatriated from a POW camp for health reasons, joined the Resistance. In 1944 she and her children witnessed his rearrest by the Gestapo. Deported to Neuengamme, he never returned. Interview with Marie-Louise Mercier, January 1985.

121. Brauner, *Ces enfants ont vécu la guerre*, pp. 209–210.

122. Ibid., p. 211; this effect is similar to what Robert Coles found in studying African-American children and adolescents who risked their safety in the civil rights struggle in the 1960s. *Children of Crisis: A Study of Courage and Fear* (Boston: Little, Brown, 1964).

123. Laborie, *L'Opinion française*, p. 285; Philippe Burrin, *La France à l'heure allemande 1940–1944* (Paris: Seuil, 1995), p. 592, n. 13.

124. Ruffin, *Journal d'un J3*, p. 229.

125. Paula Schwartz, "*Partisanes* and Gender Politics in Vichy France," *French Historical Studies* 16, no. 1 (Spring 1989): 126–151.

126. S. Marcus-Jeisler, "Réponse à l'enquête sur les effets psychologiques de la guerre sur les enfants et jeunes gens en France," *Sauvegarde* 9 (March 1947): 23.

127. "Va te faire enculer," ADP, D1U6 4209.

128. AD Gard, 6 U 10 400 and 401. Nearly all of these cases were labeled *"non lieu,"* or unsolved (no suspects).

129. Ministère de la Justice, *Compte général de l'administration de la justice civile et commerciale et de la justice criminelle 1944 à 1947* (Melun: Imprimerie administratif), pp. xviii, xxiii.

130. Robert Zaretsky, *Nîmes at War* (State College: Pennsylvania State University Press, 1994), p. 240.

131. One POW explained that France could not have been spared, "given the number of shops working for the war." Another exhorted his family, "You must hang on, this is not the time to weaken . . . buck up, it won't be long." Contrôles techniques, AN, F7: 14934, survey of April 1944; AN, F7: 14927, June 1944, July 1944.

132. Merlier, *Rédaction*, pp. 85–86.

133. See map of destruction by region in Cépède, *Agriculture et alimentation*, p. 419.

134. Veillon, *Vivre et survivre*, pp. 264–265.

135. Colin Dyer, *Population and Society in Twentieth-Century France* (London: Hodder and Stoughton, 1978), p. 127.

136. Brosse, *L'Enfance victime*, p. 24 *L'Enfance en danger (Problèmes de Poitou)* (Poitiers: Oudin, 1946), p. 5; there were 12.5 million people under the age of twenty during the war, about 29 percent of the total French population.

137. Megan Koreman, *The Expectation of Justice: France 1944–1946* (Durham, N.C.: Duke University Press, 1999), p. 8.

138. Jill Sturdee, "War and Victimization through Children's Eyes: Caen—Occupation and Liberation," in H. R. Kedward and Nancy Wood, eds., *The Liberation of France: Image and Event* (Oxford: Berg Publishers, 1995), p. 297.

139. Ibid., pp. 298–299.

140. Brauner, *Ces enfants ont vécu la guerre*, p. 219.

141. Sarah Farmer, *Martyred Village: Commemorating the 1944 Massacre at Oradour-sur-Glane* (Berkeley: University of California Press, 1999).

142. Merlier, *Rédaction*, pp. 30–31.

3. The Wartime Juvenile Crime Wave as Manifested in the Courts

1. Milos Sebor, *La Délinquance juvénile actuelle,* Session Internationale de Police Criminel 15 (Paris: Imprimerie nationale, 1947), p. 1.

2. Ministère de la Justice, *Compte général de l'administration de la justice civile et commerciale et de la justice criminelle: Années 1944 à 1947* (Melun: Imprimerie administrative, 1953), p. xxii.

3. Ministère de la Justice, "Rapport quinquennal sur l'application de la loi du 22 juillet 1912 sur les Tribunaux pour enfants et adolescents et sur la liberté surveillée," *Journal officiel*, Annexe administrative, 16 April 1946, p. 2.

4. Justice, *Compte général*, pp. xx, xxii.

5. From 1937 to 1939, 57 cases involved repeat offenders, compared with 52 between 1940 and 1942, when Lyons's total number of juvenile cases went from 778 to 1,273. Guy Rey, *Contribution à l'étude de l'enfance coupable: Les mineurs délinquants récidivistes* (Lyons: Bosc, 1942), pp. 20, 59; Pierre Mazel et al., "Deux aspects du problème social de l'enfance coupable: La recrudescence actuelle et la cartographie lyonnaise de la délinquance juvénile," *Journal de médecine de Lyon* 528 (5 January 1942): 47.

6. The one scholar, Pierre Flot, whose study specifically considered the father's captivity, found only 4 to 5 percent of juvenile offenders were POW children. Pierre Flot, *Constatations médicales et sociales relatives à la délinquance juvénile en Bretagne* (Paris: R. Foulon, 1945), pp. 17, 21, 22.

7. For full discussion of this issue, see Chapter 4.

8. Philippe Robert, "Le Renouveau de la sociologie criminelle," in Laurent Mucchielli, ed., *Histoire de la criminology française* (Paris: L'Harmattan, 1994), pp. 438–440.

9. Although the Germans wanted the harshest possible treatment for resisters, relying on French police and courts to handle crime in France reduced Germany's administrative workload. Alain Bancaud's work on French magistrates uncovered the high-level policy struggles over the justice system between France and Germany and describes how French judges reacted to the situation. Alain Bancaud, "La Magistrature et la répression politique de Vichy ou l'histoire d'un demi-échec," *Droit et société* 34 (1996): 557–574.

10. Only entering every single name into a database, a massive undertaking, would allow a computer to generate a truly random sample. I tried to choose as randomly as possible by opening the book and letting my finger drop onto about ten cases from each register.

11. A. Crémieux, M. Schachter, and S. Cotte, *L'Enfant devenu délinquant* (Marseilles: Comité de l'enfance déficiente, 1945), p. 41; see also André Gamet, *Contribution à l'étude de l'enfance coupable: Les facteurs familiaux et sociaux* (Lyons: E. Vitte, 1941), p. 79; Aimée Racine, *Les Enfants traduits en justice: Etude d'auprès trois cents dossiers du Tribunal pour enfants de l'arrondissement de Bruxelles* (Paris: Sirey, 1935), p. 34; the Justice Ministry report of 1946 found that from 1939 to 1943, 21 percent of the minors appearing in the courts were girls, Justice, "Rapport quinquennal," pp. 2, 3; a report from 1951 found that from 1946 to 1949, 17 percent of the minors in juvenile courts were girls, La Documentation française, "La Délinquance juvénile en France," *Notes et études documentaires* 1423 (19 January 1951): p. 4.

12. Justice, *Compte général*, pp. xx, xxii; see also Justice, "Rapport quinquennal," p. 2.

13. Of 165 cases from 1942 through 1944, Crémieux found 116 theft cases (70

percent), and Henri Van Etten's survey claimed that 72 percent of the cases in the Paris Children's Courts in 1942 involved theft. Crémieux, *L'Enfant devenu délinquant,* p. 27. Henri Van Etten, "Au tribunal pour enfants de la Seine, Statistique 1942," *Pour l'enfance coupable* 53 (March–April 1944): 7.

14. After the war, in 1949, Moral Assistance, Safeguarding Adolescence, and the SSE merged their functions into the Service to Safeguard Youth (Service de sauvegarde de la jeunesse), funded by the Justice Ministry. Marie-Antoinette Perret, "L'Enquête sociale (Loi 1912): Les services sociaux de la Seine à Paris dans l'entre-deux-guerres," maître d'histoire, Paris-VII, 1989, p. 144.

15. SSE case reports from the war years have been placed at the Paris Departmental Archives; according to archivist Philippe Grand, access remains entirely closed. The SSE, now known as the Association Olga Spitzer, celebrated its seventieth anniversary in 1993. An overview of the agency's history claimed that the SSE conducted very few social investigations for the courts before 1949.

16. A published guide to judicial holdings by department indicated that not every department had juvenile court records from the period 1936–1946. Letters went out to the thirteen departmental archives that looked promising for juvenile court records. Seven archivists returned positive responses and one sent a negative response. Jean-Claude Farcy, *Guide des archives judiciaires et pénitentiaires 1800–1958* (Paris: CNRS, 1992).

17. I have more Paris cases because I spent ten days researching those records and only five days in each provincial archive. I collected information on more cases in the Nord in those five days because the archivists had culled minors' dossiers from the rest of the files, whereas in Indre-et-Loire, the Seine, and the Gard, cases involving minors were mixed in with adults and filed by date, which slowed down the process of finding the minors.

18. According to Timothy Baycroft, although people in the region retained their Flemish cultural identity, their French national identity was only strengthened in the interwar years. See Paul Lawrence, Timothy Baycroft, and Carolyn Grohmann, "Degrees of Foreignness and the Construction of Identity in French Border Regions during the Inter-War Period," *Contemporary European History* 10, no. 1 (2001): 59–63.

19. Robert Zaretsky, *Nîmes at War* (State College: Pennsylvania State University Press, 1994), p. 77.

20. Ibid., chap. 4, pp. 89–124.

21. In archives where I was likely to come across resistance cases because files for minors were mixed in with adult files (Seine, Indre-et-Loire, and the Gard), the Gard files show the most evidence of resistance activity in comparison to other regions. However, Seine case files include only 1943, so it would be wrong to draw any conclusions about the dearth of resistance-related cases there.

22. Chinon, in the Indre-et-Loire, had summary tables that noted only the minor's name, age, the charge, and the court's final decision. The information

was so minimal that I did not include the 36 cases from Chinon in my comparisons, but since the Chinon tables indicate the court's final decision, I added these to the 107 complete provincial files for a total of 143 in comparisons of leniency.

23. Jean-Marc Berlière, *Le Monde des polices en France* (Brussels: Complexe, 1996), see his entire chapter on the Vichy years, "1940–1944: Une police prise au piège?" On this law as the extension and fulfillment of Third Republic policies, see pp. 163–171.

24. The Paris police merged with the National Police in 1966.

25. Christine Horton, *Policing Policy in France* (London: Policy Studies Institute, 1995), pp. 7–13.

26. Philip John Stead, *The Police of France* (New York: Macmillan, 1983), p. 147.

27. Simon Kitson, "The Police and the Deportation of Jews from the Bouches-du-Rhône in August and September 1942," *Modern and Contemporary France* 5, no. 3 (1997): 309–317.

28. Berlière, *Le Monde des polices*, p. 192.

29. ADP, 221/73/1/0047.

30. ADP, 221/73/1/0001.

31. The fiancé received a sentence of two years and the doctor got six months and revocation of his medical license, but the minor was acquitted as having acted without discretion and was returned to her parents. AD Indre-et-Loire, Tours 127 W 231.

32. Pierre Waquet, *La Protection de l'enfance* (Paris: Dalloz, 1943), p. 113; "Les Assistantes de police," *Pour l'enfance coupable* 47 (March–April 1943).

33. Berlière's book discusses in detail how police investigators questioned adult suspects, moving from a process nicknamed *"la cuisine"*—a combination of repeated questioning, persuasion, wearing down, offering free meals or wine coupons—to threatening or using actual violence, known as the *"passage au tabac,"* named for the pack of cigarettes awarded to police officers who obtained confessions. Berlière does not mention whether juvenile suspects came in for similar treatment. Berlière, *Le Monde des polices*, pp. 50–51.

34. AD Gard, Uzès 8 U 8 127.

35. AD Indre-et-Loire, Tours 127 W 272.

36. AN, BB 18 3353, 4226.

37. Yvonne Knibiehler, *Nous, les assistantes sociales* (Paris: Aubier, 1980); Bonnie Smith, *Ladies of the Leisure Class: The Bourgeoises of Northern France in the Nineteenth Century* (Princeton: Princeton University Press, 1981); Pierre Waquet, *La Protection de l'enfance* (Paris: Librairie Dalloz, 1943) p. 115; Hyancinthe Dubreuil, *A l'image de la mère: Essai sur la mission de l'assistante sociale* (Paris: Edition sociale française, 1941), pp. 1–28.

38. ADP, 221/73/1/0008.

39. ADP, 221/73/1/0007.

40. ADP, 221/73/1/0008, 0001.

41. ADP, 221/73/1/0008, 0004.

42. ADP, 221/73/1/0009.
43. ADP, 221/73/1/0043.
44. ADP, 221/73/1/0015.
45. We also learn that he was bottle fed, had his first tooth at six months, talked at thirteen months, walked at nineteen months, toilet trained early. ADP, 221/73/1/0015.
46. ADP, 221/73/1/0045.
47. ADP, 221/73/1/0014.
48. ADP, 221/73/1/0004.
49. ADP, 221/73/1/0043.
50. ADP, 221/73/1/0045.
51. Perhaps because the father's company provided the apartment and a large garden for free. ADP, 221/73/1.
52. ADP, 221/73/1/0008.
53. ADP, 221/73/1/0008.
54. ADP, 221/73/1/0015.
55. ADP, 221/73/1/0014.
56. ADP, 221/73/1/0004.
57. Sentences that regularly appear include: "My son gives me complete satisfaction; he regrets his mistake; I promise to supervise him better."
58. Working-class districts include the fourth and tenth to fifteenth arrondissements, which had significant working-class populations, and the heavily working-class seventeenth through twentieth arrondissements, which alone accounted for 30 percent of the cases.
59. ADP, 221/73/1/0004.
60. ADP, 221/73/1/0008.
61. AD Nord, Lille, not catalogued.
62. ADP, 221/73/1/0001.
63. AD Nord, 1125 W 367.
64. *"Inconnu"* or *"non dénommé."* One mother was listed as unnamed. Less reliably reported, 30 of the 667 cases (4.5 percent) from the Paris penalty registers listed fathers as unknown.
65. ADP, 221/73/1/0008.
66. ADP, 221/73/1/0001.
67. ADP, 221/73/1/0043.
68. Bancaud, "La Magistrature et la répression politique de Vichy," pp. 557–574. See also Alain Bancaud, "Les Magistrats face à la lutte armée," in François Marcot, ed., *La Résistance et les Français: Lutte armée et maquis: Colloque international de Besançon* (Paris: Les Belles Lettres, 1996), pp. 183–192.
69. The youth received a two-month suspended sentence. AD Nord, 1125 W 367.
70. AD Indre-et-Loire, Tours 127 W 261.

71. AD Nord, 1125 W 368. I should like to thank Charles Closman for his help in this instance.

72. D. ran away from the Patronage in September 1944 and turned up at home. Despite his father's request that he be allowed to stay at home, D. was returned to the Patronage. AD Nord, 1125 W 368. See Sylvia Schafer, *Children in Moral Danger* (Princeton: Princeton University Press, 1997). She argues that under the 1898 law courts readily took children's misbehavior to indicate a bad family environment.

73. M. got a one-month suspended sentence. AD Indre-et-Loire, Tours 127 W 266. I should like to thank Pierrette Hernandez for this translation. The misspelling of *heure* as *buere* completely threw me off!

74. AN, F60 519 J1A sd10, 1 July 1941.

75. AN, F60 519.

76. Bancaud, "La Magistrature et la répression politique," p. 565.

77. Bancaud, "Les Magistrats face à la lutte armée," pp. 183–192; and Bancaud, "La Magistrature et la répression politique de Vichy," pp. 557–574.

78. Justice, "Rapport quinquennal," p. 2.

79. Justice, *Compte général,* pp. xxi–xxii.

80. Henri and Fernand Joubrel, *L'Enfance dite "coupable"* (Paris: Bloud et Gay, 1946), pp. 10–11.

81. Ibid., p. 121.

82. Miranda Pollard, *Reign of Virtue: Mobilizing Gender in Vichy France* (Chicago: University of Chicago Press, 1998), p. 174; this chapter focuses on Vichy and abortion politics.

83. Justice, *Compte général,* p. xx.

84. Ibid., p. xvii.

85. "La Répression des dénonciations anonymes," *Le Temps,* 28 February–1 March 1942, p. 2.

86. Eight of the twenty-one complainants employed the minors charged with theft.

87. ADP, 221/73/1/0015.

88. AD Gard, 6U 10 385.

89. According to Henry Van Etten's study of the Seine Children's Court in 1942, 54 percent of those judged were returned to their families, slightly more than half with probation, 14 percent were sent to a private charity, and only 7.3 percent were sent to a supervised education house. It is not clear what happened to the remaining 25 percent. "Au Tribunal pour enfants de la Seine," p. 7.

90. In other words, 82 of 531 boys were sent to a supervised education house, in comparison to 14 of 135 girls.

91. 37 of 135 girls, 93 of 531 boys.

92. ADP, 221/73/1/0009.

93. In percentages, 2 percent of fourteen-year-olds, 7 percent of fifteen- and six-

teen-year-olds, and 23 percent of seventeen-year-olds were convicted as acting with discretion.

94. In 18 cases neither the parents nor the minor appeared; in 2 cases the parent was absent but the minor appeared. Of the 45 minors in the entire sample whose parents did not appear, 20 were sent to a supervised education house.

95. Two of 3 in December 1943; 2 of 3 in January 1944; 5 of 5 in May 1944; 2 of 4 in November 1940; all 7 in April 1943; 1 of 2 in October 1943; 3 of 3 in November 1943; all the absent minors were sent to supervised education houses in January, April, July, and August 1945 and April 1946.

96. Irene M. Rosenberg and Yale L. Rosenberg, "The Legacy of the Stubborn and Rebellious Son," *Michigan Law Review* 47, no. 6 (May 1976): 1104–1106; see also Irene M. Rosenberg, "The Constitutional Rights of Children Charged with Crime: Proposal for a Return to the Not-So-Distant Past," *UCLA Law Review* 27, no. 3 (February 1980): 656–721; Irene M. Rosenberg, "Leaving Bad Enough Alone: A Response to the Juvenile Court Abolitionists," *Wisconsin Law Review* 1993, no. 1, pp. 163–185.

97. The Justice Ministry issued another circular 22 September 1942 underlining the urgency of opening Observation Centers and demanding a report by 1 December from all jurisdictions, outlining what they had accomplished. AN, CAC 760175/63.

98. ADP, 221/73/1/0045.

99. ADP, 221/73/1/0004, 0015.

100. ADP, 221/73/1/0043.

101. ADP, 221/73/1/0001.

102. ADP, 221/73/1/0001.

103. ADP, 221/73/1/0015.

104. P. spent the 3,000 francs he made on movies and other "miscellaneous pleasures" *(plaisirs divers)*. ADP, 221/73/1/0047.

105. ADP, 221/73/1/0012.

106. ADP, 221/73/1/0015.

107. ADP, 221/73/1/0045, 0009, 0045.

108. Rousseau would have been proud! ADP, 221/73/1/0001.

109. ADP, 221/73/1/0006.

110. AD Indre-et-Loire, Tours 127 W 230.

111. ADP, 221/73/1/0008.

112. ADP, 221/73/1/0015.

113. ADP, 221/73/1/0015.

114. "Fumiers, salauds!! C'est des enculés comme vous que représente l'ordre nouveau." He was returned to his parents. ADP, D1 U6 3993.

115. "Enculés, salopes, fumiers à Pétain." He was sentenced to 15 days and charged 30 francs in fines. ADP, D1 U6 4117.

116. The court ordered the anti-Vichy housekeeper to undergo psychiatric testing to determine whether she was in full possession of her mental faculties! AD Gard, Nîmes, 6 U 10 354.

117. AD Nord, 1125 W 367.

118. AD Gard, Nîmes 6 U 10 370.

119. ADP, 221/73/1/0009.

120. ADP, 221/73/1/0045.

121. ADP, 221/73/1/0045.

122. ADP, D1 U6 4034.

123. 31 percent of cases from provinces, 33 percent from Paris case files listed one or both parents as deceased.

124. Jean-Pierre Rioux, "Survivre," *L'Histoire* 80 (1985): 96.

125. Jean Chazal, *Les Bandes asociales d'enfants et leur réintégration dans les cadres* (Paris: UNESCO, 1949), p. 48.

4. The Juvenile Delinquency Establishment during the War

1. Michel Chauvière, *Enfance inadaptée: L'héritage de Vichy* (Paris: Les Editions ouvrières, 1980).

2. Heuyer ran the Clinique de neuropsychiatrie infantile that began operation in 1925 at Rollet's Patronage de l'enfance et de l'adolescence, but moved during the war to the Hôpital des enfants malades. Roubinovitch and H. Badonnel ran the Laboratoire médico-psychiatrique at the Fresnes Supervised Education House, and Paul-Boncour ran the Laboratoire médico-psychiatrique at La Roquette. Dublineau, Heuyer's assistant, became general secretary of the Medico-Psychological Society.

3. Marc Renneville, "La Réception de Lombroso en France," in Laurent Mucchielli, ed., *Histoire de la criminologie française* (Paris: L'Harmattan, 1994), p. 111.

4. Henri Wallon, *Une Plaie de la société: Les bagnes d'enfants* (Bourges: Secours ouvrier international, 1934).

5. Lagache was evacuated from Strasbourg and went to the Psychiatric Hospital in Clermont-Ferrand for the duration of the war.

6. Henri Donnedieu de Vabres served as a judge in the Nuremberg war crimes trials after the war. His son Jean joined Charles de Gaulle, eventually serving as chargé de mission in de Gaulle's cabinet from 1944 to 1946.

7. AN, F60 1677 B 2800/3, Vichy press release on the Service de la protection des mineurs, dated 2 December 1943.

8. De la Morlais also served as director of a private institution for delinquent boys in Brittany, Ker-Goat.

9. It has not been possible to find given names for all of these women.

10. Philippe Rey-Herme, *Quelques aspects du progès pédagogique dans la rééducation de la jeunesse délinquante* (Paris: J. Vrin, 1945), pp. 3–4.

11. I do not know if he was related to Adolphe Crémieux, a famous Jewish republican leader and politician active in the nineteenth century. In any case, Albert was likely to have been Jewish.

12. There is a letter signed by Olga Spitzer dated 24 March 1941 in AN, CAC

760175/63. The Justice dossier on Edmond Spitzer contained documents from August 1941 through January 1942, AN BB 18 3304/1370/41; Olga Spitzer's absence was noted 26 September 1941. AN, BB 30 1711/11.

13. Alfred Brauner, *Ces enfants ont vécu la guerre* . . . (Paris: Les Éditions sociales françaises, 1946); "Assemblée générale, Service social de l'enfance, 29 June 1945," report by Desmaret.

14. Henri Joubrel, *Ker-Goat: Le Salut des enfants perdus* (Paris: Les Editions familiales de France, 1947), p. 6.

15. *Pour l'enfance "coupable"* 45 (November–December 1942).

16. Chris Leonards, "Border Crossings: The Genesis of a New Concept of the 'Criminal Child' in European Discourses on Juvenile Care in the Nineteenth Century," paper presented at the conference Becoming Delinquent, European Youth 1650–1950, University of Cambridge, 9–10 April 1999.

17. Geneviève Mazo's study of observation centers notes that a professor from the University of Moscow first proposed the idea in 1900 and mentions the session devoted to observation at the 1905 Budapest International Penitentiary Congress. Geneviève Mazo, *Le Centre d'observation et la loi du 27 juillet 1942* (Paris: H. Van Etten, 1944), p. 29.

18. Raymond Valet, *Contribution à l'étude du traitement et de l'assistance de l'enfance anormale: Le problème de l'adaptation sociale des enfants irréguliers* (Lyons: Bosc Frères, 1942), p. 15.

19. Mazo, *Le Centre d'observation*, p. 7.

20. André Perreau, *Le Mineur pervers de constitution* (Lyons: Bosc Frères, 1942), pp. 94, 98; see also Georges Heuyer, *Délinquance et criminalité de l'enfance* (Paris: Masson, 1935), p. 6; Georges-Dominique Pesle, *L'Enfance délinquante vue d'un Centre de triage* (Paris: R. Foulon, 1945), p. 10; Joubrel, *Ker-Goat*, pp. 68, 117.

21. Marc Renneville, "La Réception de Lombroso en France," in Mucchielli, *Histoire de la criminologie*, pp. 107–111.

22. Ibid.; Laurent Mucchielli, "Hérédité et 'milieu social': Le faux antagonisme franco-italien, la place de l'Ecole de Lacassagne dans l'histoire de la criminologie," in Mucchielli, ed., *Histoire de la criminologie*, pp. 189–214.

23. Renneville, "La réception de Lombroso," p. 125.

24. Ibid., p. 112.

25. Christian Debuyst, "Les Différents courants psychiatriques et psychologiques en raport avec les savoirs criminologues," in Christian Debuyst et al., *Histoire des savoirs sur le crime et la peine* (Montreal: Les Presses de l'Université de Montréal, 1998), p. 422.

26. Mario Carrasco-Barrios, *Théories sur les causes de la criminalité infantile et juvénile, étude critique* (Paris: Jouve, 1942), p. 151; Pierre Mazel, Paul F. Girard, André Gamet, "Deux aspects du problème social de l'enfance coupable: La recrudescence actuelle et la cartographie lyonnaise de la délinquance juvénile," *Le Journal de médecine de Lyon* 528 (5 January 1942): 48; Guy Rey, *Les Mineurs délinquants récidiviste* (Lyons: Bosc Frères, 1942), p. 14;

André Gamet, *Contribution à l'étude de l'enfance coupable: Les facteurs familiaux et sociaux* (Lyons: E. Vitte, 1941), p. 17.

27. Gamet, *Les Facteurs familiaux et sociaux,* p. 17.

28. Lacassagne, cited in ibid.

29. Henri Wallon, "Milieu familial et délinquance juvénile," *Pour l'enfance coupable* 32 (January–February 1940): 4. "Tendances héréditaires constitutionnels"; "l'enfant porte en lui des virtualités dangereuses."

30. Ibid., p. 4.

31. René Le Senne, "Caractérologie et enfance délinquante," *Educateurs,* July–August 1946, p. 263. He devised a wonderful schema for labeling people, based on a letter system: E = *émotifs,* nA = *inactivité,* S = *secondarité,* so a sentimental personality would be EnAS, and so on, p. 269.

32. Gamet, *Les Facteurs familiaux et sociaux,* pp. 18–22.

33. André Perreau, *Le Mineur pervers,* pp. 10–11, 15; Perreau found "a bit sterile" the concept that character is an immutable "set of innate aptitudes."

34. Ibid., pp. 10–11, 15.

35. Pierre Waquet, *La Protection de l'enfance: Etude critique de législation et de science sociale* (Paris: Dalloz, 1943), p. 92.

36. Erwin Frey, *L'Avenir des mineurs delinquents* (Paris: Imprimerie Réaumur, 1947), p. 15; juvenile judge Frey listed heredity as the first factor in predicting delinquency and stated that "environmental factors do not play the most important role as a cause of recidivism." In fact, his study focused on repeat offenders, a small fraction of the total population of minors in the courts.

37. Richard Hernnstein and Charles Murray, *The Bell Curve: Intelligence and Class Structure in American Life* (New York: Free Press, 1994).

38. Henri Wallon, "Milieu familial"; René Le Senne, "Caractérologie et enfance délinquante." Le Senne refers instead to renowned artists and intellectuals, such as Rimbaud, Verlaine, Mallarmé, Leconte de Lisle, pp. 264, 268.

39. For example, recently two Danish researchers uncovered how medical science had landed on the widely accepted idea that 35 percent of patients on placebos improve. This figure has long been used in evaluating new drug therapies. But when they tracked down published studies on the placebo effect, they found that the studies all ultimately rested on one paper published in 1955, whose conclusions the researchers found problematic. Gina Kolata, "Placebo Effect Is More Myth than Science," *NYT,* 24 May 2001.

40. Cited in Heuyer's preface to G. Menut, *La Dissociation familiale et les troubles de caractère chez l'enfant* (Paris: Editions familiales de France, 1944), p. 5; Menut also cites Néron's dissertation on p. 23 but claims that 70 percent of the minors were from abnormal families. Néron did not publish his thesis as a book until 1952, at which point he cited Joly's study of 400 dossiers from the Patronage des enfants et adolescents that found some 86 percent came from "conspicuously defective family situations" and ended by claiming that his 1928 thesis found "similar figures," although 64 percent is

21 points lower than 85 percent. Guy Néron, *L'Enfant vagabond* (Paris: Presses universitaires de France, 1952), p. 67.

41. Gamet, *Les Facteurs familiaux et sociaux,* p. 25.

42. Georges Heuyer, "Enquête sur la délinquance juvénile: Etude de 400 dossiers," *Pour l'enfance "coupable,"* 1942.

43. Ibid., p. 4; Gamet, *Les Facteurs familiaux et sociaux,* p. 23.

44. Nadine Lefaucheur, "Dissociation familiale et délinquance juvénile ou la trompeuse éloquence des chiffres," in Michel Chauvière et al., eds., *Protéger l'enfant: Raison juridique et pratiques socio-judiciaires, XIXe–XXe siècles* (Rennes: Presses universitaires de Rennes, 1996), p. 129.

45. Menut, *La Dissociation familiale,* p. 23; his sample was drawn from Heuyer's Annexe de neuropsychiatrie infantile, Cliniques de malades mentales, Faculté de médecine, Paris.

46. The terms in French are *dissocié,* from the verb *se dissocier,* which means to split or break up; *désagrégé,* which also means to break up or disintegrate; *désunis,* which means divided or disunited.

47. Albert Crémieux, M. Schachter, and S. Cotte, *L'Enfant devenu délinquant* (Marseilles: Comité de l'enfance déficiente, 1945), p. 22.

48. Robert Chadefaux, "Les Causes sociales de la délinquance juvénile," *Educateurs,* July–August 1946, p. 246. Interestingly, Chadefaux describes families broken by divorce or separation, whereas the actual studies did not limit themselves to those factors.

49. Hélène Campinchi, "Le Statut de l'enfance délinquante et la loi du 27 juillet 1942," in Louis Hugueney, H. Donnedieu de Vabres, and Marc Ancel, eds., *Etudes de science criminelle et de droit pénal comparé* (Paris: Sirey), p. 175.

50. S. Cotte, "Rapport sur l'enfance délinquante et en danger moral, d'après l'expérience marseillaise" *Pour l'enfance "coupable"* 60 (July–September 1945): 2. That same sentence is repeated word for word in Crémieux et al., *L'Enfant devenu délinquant,* p. 154.

51. Henri and Fernand Joubrel, *L'Enfance dite coupable* (Paris: Bloud et Gay, 1946), p. 21.

52. Georges Heuyer, "Psychopathologie de l'enfance victime de la guerre," *Sauvegarde* 17 (January 1948): 5.

53. Robert Maginnis, "Single-Parent Families Cause Crime," in A. E. Sadler, ed., *Juvenile Crime: Opposing Viewpoints* (San Diego: Greenhaven Press, 1997), p. 64.

54. Author's italics, Nancy E. Dowd, *In Defense of Single-Parent Families* (New York: New York University Press, 1997), p. xii.

55. Menut, *La Dissociation familiale,* p. 27; Gamet, *Les Facteurs familiaux et sociaux,* p. 31; Joubrel, *L'Enfance dite coupable,* p. 21; Heuyer, "Psychopathologie de l'enfance," pp. 4–6.

56. Mazel, "L'Enfance coupable," p. 48.

57. Gamet, *Les Facteurs familiaux et sociaux,* p. 27; Mazel's 1942 study, based on what must have been the same sample, since it involved 524 cases from

the Lyons region and Mazel was Gamet's thesis advisor, repeated that there were 3 POW children. Mazel, "L'Enfance coupable," p. 48; Pierre Flot, *Constatations médicales et sociales relatives à la délinquance juvénile en Bretagne* (Paris: R. Foulon, 1945), from the Centre d'acceuil du Service social de sauvegarde de l'enfance et de l'adolescence d'Ile-et-Vilaine and the Bon Pasteur de Saint-Cyr de Rennes, p. 21; Robert Lafon, "La 'Famille coupable,'" *Sauvons l'enfance* 70 (May–June 1947): 4.

58. Gamet, *Les Facteurs familiaux et sociaux,* p. 27.

59. There is now a vast and growing literature on France's demographic obsession and its profound impact on political culture, feminism, and the development of French social and welfare policies. See, for example, Joshua Cole, *The Power of Large Numbers: Population, Politics and Gender in Nineteenth-Century France* (Ithaca: Cornell University Press, 2000); Karen Offen, "Depopulation, Nationalism, and Feminism in Fin-de-Siècle France," *American Historical Review* 89, no. 3 (June 1984): 648–676; Angus McClaren, *Sexuality and Social Order: The Debate over the Fertility of Women and Workers in France, 1770–1920* (New York: Holmes and Meier, 1983); Susan Pedersen, *Family, Dependence and the Origins of the Welfare State: Britain and France, 1914–1945* (Cambridge: Cambridge University Press, 1993); Mary Louise Roberts, *Civilization without Sexes: Reconstructing Gender in Postwar France, 1917–1927* (Chicago: University of Chicago Press, 1994); Elinor Accampo, Rachel G. Fuchs, and Mary Lynn Stewart, eds., *Gender and the Politics of Social Reform in France, 1870–1914* (Baltimore: Johns Hopkins University Press, 1995); Alisa Kraus, "Depopulation and Race Suicide: Maternalism and Pronatalist Ideologies in France and the United States," in Seth Koven and Sonya Michel, eds., *Mothers of a New World: Maternalist Politics and the Origins of Welfare States* (London: Routledge, 1993), pp. 188–212; Sarah Fishman, *We Will Wait: Wives of French Prisoners of War, 1940–1945* (New Haven: Yale University Press, 1991); Marie-Monique Huss, "Pronatalism in the Inter-War Period in France," *Journal of Contemporary History* 25, no. 1 (January 1990): 39–68; Cheryl Koos, "'On les aura!' The gendered politics of abortion and the Alliance nationale contre la dépopulation, 1938–1944," *Modern and Contemporary France* 7, no. 1 (February 1999): 21–34; James F. McMillan, *Housewife or Harlot: The Place of Women in French Society, 1870–1940* (New York: St. Martin's Press, 1981); William H. Schneider, *Quality and Quantity: The Quest for Biological Regeneration in Twentieth-Century France* (Cambridge: Cambridge University Press, 1990); Françoise Thébaud, "Le Mouvement nataliste dans la France de l'entre-deux guerres: L'Alliance nationale pour l'accroisement de la population française," *Revue d'histoire moderne et contemporaine* 32 (April–June 1985): 276–301.

60. Miranda Pollard, *Reign of Virtue: Mobilizing Gender in Vichy France* (Chicago: University of Chicago Press, 1998).

61. Joubrel, *L'Enfance dite coupable,* p. 14.

62. Gamet, *Les Facteurs familiaux et sociaux,* p. 26; 133 minors had lost a father, 125 a mother.

63. Georges Epron, "Réflections au sujet de quelques enquêtes relatives à des mineurs délinquants," *Pour l'enfance "coupable"* 50 (September–October 1943): 5; 30 minors had lost a father, 14 a mother.

64. Crémieux, *L'Enfant devenu délinquant,* p. 23; 431 minors had lost fathers, 231 had lost mothers, and 81 were full orphans. Menut's total of 839 dossiers included 36 percent who were either half or full orphans, 19.5 percent whose parents had either separated or divorced, *La Dissociation familiale,* p. 26. Flot found that 37 percent of the girls and 30 percent of the boys had lost a parent, 25 percent of the girls and 13.7 percent of the boys had divorced or separated parents, *Constatations médicales,* p. 211.

65. G. Kohler and Line Thevenin, "Le Centre polyvalent d'observation de Lyon. *Sauvegarde* 11 (May 1947): 1; 18 had lost a father, 12 a mother, 5 both parents. See also Robert Lafon, "La Famille coupable"; of 100 girls from his Centre d'observation Olivier, 18 had lost a mother, 17 a father (for a total of 35 orphans), while 15 had parents who were separated and 9 had parents who were divorced (24 total), p. 4.

66. Menut, *La Dissociation familiale,* p. 26; in calculating orphans, Menut omitted the 12 percent who were full orphans from the delinquent group, so he claimed it was 71 percent versus 43.5 percent, not 71 percent versus 56 percent. Perhaps this was because his central concern was the evil effects on children of remarriage by divorced or widowed parents, something full orphans could not experience.

67. Pesle, *L'Enfance délinquante,* p. 30; Mazel, "L'Enfance coupable," p. 45; Gamet, *Les Facteurs familiaux et sociaux,* pp. 26–27; 7 percent had working mothers.

68. Gamet, *Les Facteurs familiaux et sociaux,* p. 25.

69. Menut, *La Dissociation familiale,* p. 103.

70. Epron, "Mineurs délinquantes," pp. 6–7.

71. See Lefaucheur, "Dissociation familiale," p. 125.

72. Ibid., p. 129.

73. Chauvière, *Enfance inadaptée,* p. 55.

74. Rey, *Les Mineurs délinquants récidivistes,* p. 11. Blancho calls the numbers shocking *(effarantes);* Pierre Blancho, *Esquisse sur l'enfance après la guerre de 1940 à 1945: Etude médico-sociale* (Paris: R. Foulon, 1948), p. 12.

75. Néron, *L'Enfant vagabond,* p. 72.

76. Gamet, *Les Facteurs familiaux et sociaux,* p. 16; Mazel, "L'Enfance coupable," p. 51.

77. Gamet, *Les Facteurs familiaux et sociaux,* p. 66; Mazel, "L'Enfance coupable," p. 45.

78. Joubrel, *L'Enfance dite coupable,* p. 31.

79. Françoise Liévois, *La Délinquance juvénile: Cure et prophylaxie* (Paris: Presses universitaires de France, 1946), pp. 151–152; Liévois cites as her source for

the Portuguese study an article by Robert Lafon ("Le Problème actuel de l'hygiène mentale des enfants et adolescents"), but does not provide the journal title or publication date; the same study is cited in Crémieux, *L'Enfant devenu délinquant*, p. 89.

80. Pierre Blancho, *Esquisse sur l'enfance après la guerre*, p. 24.

81. Gamet, *Les Facteurs familiaux et sociaux*, p. 97.

82. Ibid.

83. Fear of the evil effects of movies on young people was not merely in keeping with Vichy's moralism and mistrust of America, it was a constant theme that both predated and followed the war. See Céline Lhotte and Elisabeth Dupeyrat, *Le Jardin flétri: Enfance délinquante et malheureuse* (Paris: Bloud et Gay, 1939); P. Nobécourt and L. Babonneix, *Les Enfants et les jeunes gens anormaux* (Paris: Masson, 1939); E. Le Gal, *L'Enfance moralement déficiente et coupable* (Paris: Les Publications sociales agricoles, 1943), p. 31; Rey, *Les Mineurs délinquants récidivists*, pp. 39–40; Gamet, *Les Facteurs familiaux et sociaux*, pp. 94–95; Pesle, *L'Enfance délinquante*, p. 1; Valet, *Enfants irréguliers;* Crémieux et al., *L'Enfant devenu délinquant;* Perreau, *Le Mineur pervers*, p. 126; Daniel Parker, "Influence de la presse enfantine et du cinéma sur la délinquance juvénile," in *Quinze conférences sur les problèmes de l'enfance délinquante* (Paris: Editions familiales de France, 1946); Liévois, *La Délinquance juvénile*, 151–152; Michel Le Bourdellès, "Notes sur le cinéma et la délinquance juvénile," *Rééducation* 8 (July 1948): 24; Blancho, *L'Enfance après la guerre*, p. 24; Claude Kohler, "Le cinéma et les enfants," *Revue de criminologie et de police technique* 3, no. 1 (January–March 1949): 48–54; and Gilbert Robin, *L'Education des enfants difficiles* (Paris: Presses universitaires de France, 1948).

84. On 10 September 1942 Vichy's newly created Comité pour l'organisation de l'industrie cinématographique (COIC) and Emile Galey, director of La Cinematographie nationale, made the decision to ban so-called Anglo-Saxon films, a decision sparked by pressure from the Germans that also reflected the hardening ideological collaboration of Vichy-German relations just prior to and following the Allied landing in North Africa. Many thanks to Brett Bowles for this information. See also his article, "Screening *les Anneés Noires:* Using Film to Teach Vichy," *French Historical Studies* 25, no. 1 (Winter 2002).

85. Joubrel also wanted to limit youths' exposure to illustrated magazines, which he found equally objectionable for children, and to ban children from cafés; Joubrel, *L'Enfance dite coupable*, p. 31.

86. Cited by Judge Frey, *L'Avenir des mineurs délinquants*, p. 16; from Chadefaux's article "Application pratique de l'ordonnance du 2 février 1945" in the *Revue d'education surveillée* (no date or page; pre-1947).

87. Cited in Joubrel, *Ker-Goat*, p. 120.

88. Rey, *Les Mineurs délinquants récidivists*, p. 40.

89. Pesle reported only 37 percent of his subjects as "normal," without character

problems, and compared his findings to Heuyer's figure of 30 percent and Guichard's figure of 20 percent normal. Pesle, *L'Enfance délinquante vue d'un Centre de triage,* p. 19. "Insuffisants mentaux parmi les délinquants," S. Cotte, "Rapport sur l'enfance délinquante," *Pour l'enfance "coupable"* 60 (July–September 1945): 2.

90. Georges Epron, "Réflexions sur l'ordonnance du 2 Février 1945 sur l'enfance délinquante," *Pour l'enfance "coupable"* 62 (January–February 1946): 1.

91. Jean Bancal, *Essai sur le redressement de l'enfance coupable* (Paris: Sirey, 1941), p. 56.

92. Rey, *Les Mineurs délinquants récidivists,* p. 55; Perreau, *Le Mineur pervers,* p. 52.

93. See M. Taton-Vassal, *Exposé sur les décrets-lois du 30 octobre 1935* (Cahors: Imprimerie Coueslant, 1935); P. Nobécourt and L. Babonneix, *Les Enfants et les jeunes gens anormaux* (Paris: Masson, 1939), pp. 300–301.

94. Minister of Justice Joseph Barthélemy, "Le Surpeuplement des prisons," memo dated 21 May 1942, AN, F60 519 J1A1sd14; and Georges F. Boudier, report to the Comité de défense des enfants traduits en justice de Paris, November 1940, AN, CAC 760175/63.

95. Adults caught in flagrante delicto, or in the act, could be brought immediately before the court, which could dispose of the case that same day under provisions of the criminal code. However, the 1912 act required all cases involving minors to have a full investigation of the crime and of the minor's background. See Roy Ingleton, ed., *Elsevier's Dictionary of Police and Criminal Law, English-French and French-English* (New York: Elsevier, 1992), p. 430; Martin Weston, *An English Reader's Guide to the French Legal System* (London: Berg, 1991), p. 122.

96. Mazo, *Le Centre d'observation,* p. 9: "Procédé scientifique d'observation psychologique." Bancal, *Le Redressement de l'enfance coupable,* p. 37.

97. Bancal, *Le Redressement de l'enfance coupable,* pp. 37, 44, 45.

98. Jeremy Bentham, *Panopticon; or, The Inspection House* (London: T. Payne, 1791), p. 40.

99. Chauvière, *Enfance inadaptée,* pp. 1–146.

100. Ibid., p. 96.

101. Ibid., pp. 96–97, from Robert Lafon, "Recherche sur les critères d'inadaptation," *L'Enfance inadaptée,* special issue of *Revue de droit sanitaire et social* 28 (October–December 1971).

102. Jean Fresneau, *Orientation et adaptation sociale des mineurs délinquants et des enfants déficients* (Paris: Union française universitaire, 1945), p. 2.

103. Ibid., pp. 3; Gamet, *Les Facteurs familiaux et sociaux,* p. 91; see also Perreau, *Le Mineur pervers,* pp. 106–107.

104. Pierre Waquet, *La Protection de l'enfance* (Paris: Dalloz, 1943), p. 100.

105. Ibid.; Rey, *Les Mineurs délinquants récidivists,* p. 54; Daniel Lagache, "Nomenclature et classification des jeunes inadaptés," *Sauvegarde* 4 (October 1946): 18.

106. Chauvière, *Enfance inadaptée*.

107. Georges Heuyer, "Le Conseil technique de l'enfance déficiente ou en danger moral: Son fonctionnement, ses travaux," in Jean Chazal, *L'Enfance et l'adolescence déficientes ou en danger moral*, 1944, p. 24.

108. Cited from *Journal officiel*, 25 July 1943; Chauvière, *Enfance inadaptée*, p. 73.

109. Heuyer, "Le Conseil technique," p. 24; Lagache, "Nomenclature," *Sauvegarde* 2, 3, 4 (June, July, October 1946). In its key accomplishment, this subcommittee created a catchall term, *enfance inadaptée* (maladjusted children), which experts used for the next forty years to indicate abandoned, orphaned, retarded, difficult, at-risk *(en danger moral)*, criminal, delinquent, and predelinquent children. Michel Chauvière argues that the Technical Council instituted an entire "maladjusted children's sector" (*Enfance inadaptée*, p. 96), a public and private network of testing centers, schools for children, and schools to train teachers.

110. *Sauvegarde* 2, 3, 4 (June, July, October 1946).

111. The nomenclature's classificatory scheme included three basic divisions: *les malades, les déficients*, and *les caractériels*, Lagache, *Sauvegarde* 2 (June 1946): 2.

112. I would like to thank my student Richard Terry for pointing out that the similarities between tattoos and forms of body marking in so-called primitive cultures in Africa might explain why experts in the early twentieth century viewed them as signs of atavism or deevolution.

113. Flot, *Constatations médicales et sociales*, pp. 27–31. Pesle, *L'Enfance délinquante*, p. 23; Rey, *Les Mineurs délinquants récidivistes*, p. 35.

114. Henri Wallon, "Milieu familial et délinquance juvénile"; René Le Senne, "Caractérologie et enfance délinquante," *Educateurs*, special issue, July–August 1946; Frey, *L'Avenir des mineurs délinquants*, p. 19.

115. Menut, *La Dissociation familiale*, p. 14.

116. Lagache, *Sauvegarde* 4 (October 1946): 15.

117. Flot's list included hyperemotionality, instability, mythomania, and perversity; Pesle listed "émotifs, instables, paranoiques, mythomanes, pervers, abouliques, déprimés"; Joubrel catalogued "apathiques, hyper-émotifs, instables, cyclothymiques [bi-polar], impulsifs, paranoiques, mythomanes, schizoides and pervers." Flot, *Constatations médicales et sociales*, pp. 37–38; Pesle, *L'Enfance délinquante*, pp. 16–18; Joubrel, *L'Enfance dite "coupable,"* p. 36.

118. Rey, *Les Mineurs délinquants récidivists*, p. 42; Gilbert Robin, "Il y a pervers et pervers," *Pour l'enfance "coupable"* (November–December 1937): 2; Gamet, *Les Facteurs familiaux et sociaux*, pp. 102–103.

119. Gilbert Robin, *Enfances perverses* (Paris: La Vulgarisation scientifique, 1945), pp. 38–39.

120. Rey, *Les Mineurs délinquants récidivists*, p. 40; Pesle describes *abouliques* as apathetic boys who were dirty, lazy, lacked will power and character, and who followed their peers even into crimes; *L'Enfance délinquante*, p. 18.

121. Pesle, *L'Enfance délinquante,* p. 18. Dr. Ernest Dupré first wrote about mythomania in 1905.

122. Rey, *Les Mineurs délinquants récidivists,* p. 42.

123. Gamet, *Les Facteurs familiaux et sociaux,* pp. 102–103; Lagache, "Nomenclature," *Sauvegarde* 4 (October 1946): 7.

124. Robert Gautier, "Le Pervers constitutionnel," *Rééducation* 3 (January 1948): 27.

125. On the nineteenth century, see Kathleen Nilan, "Hapless Innocence and Precocious Perversity in the Courtroom Melodrama: Representations of the Child Criminal in a Paris Legal Journal, 1830–1848," *Journal of Family History* 22 (July 1997): 251–285.

126. Rey, *Les Mineurs délinquants récidivists,* p. 45.

127. Gautier, "Le Pervers constitutionnel," pp. 27–28.

128. Rey, *Les Mineurs délinquants récidivists,* p. 45; Perreau, *Le Mineur pervers,* p. 27.

129. Robin, "Il y a pervers et pervers"; Robin, *Enfances perverses;* Perreau, *Le Mineur pervers,* pp. 2, 13, 17, 29–32; Rey, *Les Mineurs délinquants récidivists,* p. 2.

130. Perreau, *Le Mineur pervers,* p. 47 n. 13. Heuyer mentions among qualities of the "hystériques" that they are "mythomanes suggestibles" (*Délinquance et criminalité,* p. 19), which suggests why mythomania is associated with girls.

131. Rey, *Les Mineurs délinquants récidivists,* p. 20; Perreau, *Le Mineur pervers,* p. 47.

132. Valet, *Enfants irréguliers,* p. 18; Perreau, *Le Mineur pervers,* pp. 35–37; Rey, *Les Mineurs délinquants récidivists,* p. 45.

133. Perreau, *Le Mineur pervers,* pp. 37–39, 54.

134. Valet, *Enfants irréguliers,* p. 45.

135. Gamet, *Les Facteurs familiaux et sociaux,* p. 115; Perreau, *Le Mineur pervers,* p. 134.

136. Perreau, *Le Mineur pervers,* p. 134.

137. Gamet, *Les Facteurs familiaux et sociaux,* p. 115; Perreau, *Le Mineur pervers,* p. 134 (he probably meant Indiana).

138. Perreau, *Le Mineur pervers,* p. 134.

139. Ibid., pp. 115, 134.

140. Georges d'Heucqueville, *Souvenirs de médecin-légiste* (Paris: Peyronnet, 1946), section entitled "Faut-il éteindre les familles de criminels?" pp. 86–91; Valet, *Enfants irréguliers,* pp. 45 ff.; Perreau, *Le Mineur pervers,* p. 118–199.

141. Rey, *Les Mineurs délinquants récidivists,* p. 55; Perreau, *Le Mineur pervers,* p. 121. This idea resembles the current thinking about sex offenders. Some states in the United States can transfer sex offenders they determine present a continuing danger to the community to a mental facility after they have served their full prison sentence. The U.S. Supreme Court in June 1997 upheld one state's version of that law.

142. Pierre Ceccaldi, "Origines et perspectives de l'éducation surveillée," *Sauvons l'enfance* 69 (March–April 1947): 1.

143. Heuyer, *Délinquance et criminalité,* p. 15.

144. Fresneau, *Mineurs délinquants,* pp. 4–5; see also E. Le Gal, *L'Enfant moralement déficient et coupable* (Paris: Les Publications sociales agricoles, 1943).

145. Gamet, *Les Facteurs familiaux et sociaux,* p. 122; Valet, *Enfants irréguliers,* p. 21.

146. Heuyer, "Enquête sur la délinquance juvénile," p. 4; Gamet, *Les Facteurs familiaux et sociaux,* pp. 47–49.

147. Pierre Giolitto, *Histoire de la jeunesse sous Vichy* (Paris: Perrin, 1991), p. 41; Giolitto does not define the criteria on which he based his figures for delinquent minors (number arrested? number appearing in court?), nor does he clarify the precise age group (presumably ages thirteen to eighteen), nor does he cite his source.

5. Progressive Change in an Authoritarian Regime

1. In addition to Henri Gaillac's classic account, *Les Maisons de correction,* and Michel Chauvière's *Enfance inadaptée: L'héritage de Vichy* (Paris: Les Editions ouvrières, 1980), see also Chauvière's "L'Emergence de l'éducation surveillée en France vers 1945," in Michel Chauvière, Pierre Lenoël, and Eric Pierre, eds., *Protéger l'enfant* (Rennes: Presses universitaires de Rennes, 1996), pp. 149–166; Jacques Bourquin, "Saint-Maurice, colonie pénitentiaire agricole," *Le Journal de Sologne* 83 (January 1994): 42–49; Eric Pierre, "Les Premières générations de juges des enfants et le scoutisme," and Françoise Tétard, "Le Métier d'éducateur: Scout's connection," both in Mathias Gardet and Françoise Tétard, eds., *Le Scoutisme et la rééducation dans l'immédiat après-guerre: Lune de miel sans lendemain?* (Marly-le-Roi: Institut national de la jeunesse et de l'éducation populaire, 1995); Béatrice Koeppel, "Les Temps forts de la rééducation des filles (de Cadhillac à Brécourt): 1935–1950," *Cahiers du CRIV* 2 (October 1986); Francis Bailleau, *Les Jeunes face à la justice pénale* (Paris: Syros, 1996).

2. Michael Marrus and Robert Paxton, *Vichy France and the Jews* (New York: Basic Books, 1981), p. 75.

3. Before the war, Barthélemy denounced a decree of 12 November 1938 revoking naturalizations of Jewish immigrants and defended a number of Jews and antifascist Italians. Marrus and Paxton point out that "time, defeat, and the office of Minister of Justice under Vichy were to change Barthélemy's views." In a 1941 speech, Barthélemy compared the Jewish problem to a cancer in need of surgery. Marrus and Paxton, *Vichy France and the Jews,* p. 56.

4. Ministère de la Justice, AN, BB 30: 1711/11, 26 September 1941, p. 4; notwithstanding this claim that juvenile reform took first place in Barthélemy's preoccupations, in his 600-page memoir it merited only a brief mention in a

footnote added by the editors, his son Jean Barthélemy and Arnaud Teyssier. Joseph-Barthélemy, *Ministre de la Justice, Vichy 1941–1943* (Paris: Pygmalion, 1989), p. 286.

5. *Le Temps,* 30 September 1941, p. 2.
6. Ministère de la Justice, AN, BB 30: 1711/11, 26 September 1942, p. 3.
7. Robert Paxton, *Vichy France: Old Guard and New Order* (New York: Columbia University Press, 1982), p. 137. Paxton notes that it had taken some 200 bills to pass an income tax, and the Republic's attempt to pass an old-age pension law had failed twenty-four times since 1936.
8. Ministère de la Justice, AN, BB 30: 1711/11, 26 September 1942, p. 3.
9. Ibid.
10. Ibid., p. 4.
11. Spitzer was apparently in hiding, as her husband, Edmond, had been anonymously denounced as Jewish in August 1941. See Chapter 4.
12. Ministère de la Justice, AN, BB 30: 1711/11, 26 September 1942, p. 6.
13. Ibid., pp. 4, 6, 8.
14. Ibid., pp. 21–23.
15. Ibid., p. 23.
16. Ibid., p. 10.
17. Ibid., pp. 24, 35.
18. Ibid., p. 36.
19. Ibid., p. 13.
20. Ibid., pp. 33, 42.
21. Ibid., p. 44.
22. H. Donnedieu de Vabres, "Loi du 27 juillet 1942, Commentaire," *Recueil critique 1943: Législation,* Notebook 1 (Paris: Dalloz, 1943), p. 35. Donnedieu de Vabres's commentary on the resulting law of 27 July 1942 noted that in matters of serious crimes, minors were deprived of the "guarantee that the participation of jurors constitutes for adults." Yet during the council's discussion, he twice argued against reducing penalties for minors sixteen to eighteen.
23. Ministère de la Justice, AN, BB 30: 1711/11, letter from Magnol, 2 October 1942.
24. Ibid., response to Magnol from Ceccaldi, n.d.
25. Donnedieu de Vabres, "Commentaire," p. 36.
26. Ministère de la Justice, AN, BB 30: 1711/11, 26 September 1941, p. 4.
27. Ibid., pp. 6–7.
28. Ibid., p. 18.
29. The issue of separating personnel predated the war. A decree of 17 August 1938 officially separated Penal Administration and Supervised Education's personnel, but the links were restored by a decree of 31 August 1940. Jacques Bourquin, "Sur la trace des premiers éducateurs de l'Education surveillée: 1936–1947," in "Deux contributions à la connaissance des origines de l'Education surveillée," *Cahiers du CRIV 2* (October 1986): 23.
30. Ministère de la Justice, AN, BB 30: 1711/11, 26 September 1941, p. 24.

31. Ibid., pp. 27–28.
32. Ibid., p. 28.
33. Ibid., p. 18.
34. Jean Bancal, *Essai sur le redressement de l'enfance coupable* (Paris: Sirey, 1941), p. 8.
35. Bancal, *Essai sur le redressement,* p. 9.
36. Ministère de la Justice, AN, BB 30: 1711/11, 26 September 1941, p. 30.
37. Etat français, AN, 2 AG 605 cm 19 D.
38. Ibid.
39. Ibid.
40. Ministère de la Justice, AN, BB 30: 1711/11, 26 September 1941, p. 26. For more on this dispute, see Michèle Becquemin-Girault, "La Loi du 27 juillet 1942 ou l'issue d'une querelle de monopole pour l'enfance délinquante," in *Le Temps de l'histoire* 3: *L'Enfant de justice pendant la guerre et l'immédiat après-guerre* (October 2000): 55–76.
41. Paxton, *Vichy France,* pp. 53, 144.
42. Ministère de la Justice, AN, BB 30: 1711/11, 26 September 1941, pp. 24–25.
43. If other administrations had appropriate institutions ready to go, Justice could "limit its role exclusively to arbitration." But since the other administrations had nothing on the table, Justice felt compelled to continue playing a role in the reform of delinquent minors. Ibid., p. 26.
44. Ibid., p. 27.
45. Ibid., p. 29.
46. Ibid.
47. Ibid., pp. 30–31.
48. "Désormais les enfants criminels comparaîtront: D'abord devant des médecins ensuite devant des magistrats," *Paris-Soir,* 18 August 1942.
49. H. Donnedieu de Vabres, "Loi du 2 février 1945, Commentaire," *Recueil critique 1945: Législation,* Notebook 1 (Paris: Dalloz, 1945), p. 178.
50. Ministère de la Justice, AN, BB 30: 1711/11, 26 September 1941, p. 11.
51. See preamble of 27 July 1942 law, *Journal officiel,* 27 July 1942.
52. M. Chassot, "Les conséquences pénales et civiles de l'infraction commise par le mineur," thesis, University of Dijon, 1943, pp. 27–28.
53. Ibid., p. 28.
54. Jean-Louis Halpérin, "La Législation de Vichy relative aux avocats et aux droits de la défense," *Revue historique* 579 (July–September 1991): 143–156.
55. See Chassot, "Les Conséquences," chap. 3, pp. 68–98.
56. Ministère de la Justice, AN, BB 30: 1711/11, 26 September 1941, p. 13.
57. Thanks to Roger Wiesenbach, editor of the Law-France website, for explaining these procedures. Donnedieu de Vabres, "Commentaire" (1942), p. 34.
58. Donnedieu de Vabres, "Loi du 27 juillet 1942, Commentaire," p. 34; Ministère de la Justice, AN, BB 30: 1711/11, 26 September 1941, p. 41.
59. Ministère de la Justice, AN, BB 30: 1711/11, 26 September 1941, p. 16.

60. *Journal officiel,* 27 July 1942.

61. Bancal, *Essai sur le redressement.*

62. Donnedieu de Vabres, "Loi du 2 février 1945, Commentaire," p. 178.

63. Ibid., p. 175.

64. Michel Chauvière, "L'Emergence de l'éducation surveillée en France vers 1945," p. 159; Pierre Pédron does not mention a cause for Contancin's dismissal: *La Prison sous Vichy* (Paris: Les Editions de l'atelier, 1993), p. 158.

65. Chauvière, *Enfance inadaptée,* p. 82.

66. Ibid., p. 9.

67. Chauvière points out that the ARSEA structure mirrored the corporatist model Vichy hoped to impose on the economy, *Enfance inadaptée,* p. 72.

68. Chazal, *Coordination des services de l'enfance déficiente ou en danger moral: Buts, activités, réalizations* (Paris: Ch. A. Bédu, 1944), p. 12; Chauvière, *Enfance inadaptée,* pp. 55–58.

69. They were later renamed Children's Protection Institutes (Instituts de protection de l'enfance).

70. Chazal, *Coordination,* p. 27

71. Chauvière, *Enfance inadaptée,* p. 96.

72. Chazal, *Coordination,* p. 28

73. Chauvière, *Enfance inadaptée,* p. 105.

74. Ibid., p. 77.

75. Ibid., pp. 163–167, and Pierre Ceccaldi, "Origines et perspectives de l'Education surveillée, Suite," *Sauvons l'enfance* 70 (May–June 1947): 9. See also J. L. Costa, postwar director of Education surveillée, *Le Phénomène de la délinquance juvénile: Rapport annuel à M. Le garde des Sceaux* (Melun: Imprimerie administrative, 1947).

76. Bourquin, "Sur la trace," p. 33.

77. Alistaire Horne, *To Lose a Battle: France 1940* (London: Penguin Books, 1969), p. 632.

78. Inspection générale des services administratifs, AN, F1a 3656, report of 4 February 1941 by Jean Bancal; this is a remarkable, very detailed, and evenhanded report. Notwithstanding Bancal's anger at *Paris-Soir* and his tendency to find excuses for the administration, he comes down on the students' side, particularly crediting their accounts of brutality.

79. Jacques Bourquin, "Le Temps de la réforme: 1934–1936–1950," *Journal de Sologne* 83 (January 1994): 44. Many thanks to Mr. Bourquin for providing copies of his articles and spending time showing me photographs and even a video documentary filmed at Mettray with two former wards. The Centre national de formation et d'études de la Protection judiciaire de la jeunesse group at Vaucresson is doing excellent and very important work on these institutions.

80. Bourquin, "Sur la trace," p. 33.

81. Ibid., p. 34. Bourquin could not determine if Jews and others wanted by the authorities also could be protected by employment in Supervised Education. Both Saint-Maurice and Saint-Hilaire took in Jewish minors to prevent their

deportation, with the knowledge of F. Dhallenne, Saint-Hilaire's director (p. 36).

82. Ibid., p. 39.

83. Inspection générale des services administratifs, AN, F1a 4656; "mutiny of June 1943" is misdated: the documents describe the events of June 1940.

84. Michel Blondel-Pasquier, "Le Cas de Montesson, une école de cadres 1943–1953," in Documents de l'Institut national de la jeunesse et de l'éducation populaire 21: Le Scoutisme et la rééducation dans l'immédiat après-guerre: Lune de miel sans lendemain? (June 1995): 84.

85. AN, BB 18, 3281, 20/41, letter dated 26 January 1941.

86. Ibid., letter dated 17 January 1941.

87. Blondel-Pasquier, "Le Cas de Montesson," pp. 84–85.

88. Sophie Bourely, "Les Filles mineures dans les prisons de Fresnes entre 1939 et 1943," Mémoire de Maîtrise, Paris, 1992, pp. 58, 142.

89. Ibid., p. 177.

90. Ibid., p. 58.

91. Ministère de la Santé, AN, CAC 760175/16, letter of 19 November 1943.

92. Jacques Bourquin, "L'Education surveillé, d'un mouvement à une institution 1937–1945," report of seminar entitled "L'Enfant de justice pendant la guerre," Paris, 3 December 1996, p. 1.

93. Ministère de la Santé, AN, CAC 760175/16.

94. Donnedieu de Vabres, "Loi du 2 février 1945, Commentaire," p. 175.

6. The Victory of Juvenile Justice Reform

1. The article calls it "l'ordonnance fondatrice . . . qui affirme la primauté de l'éducation sur la répression." Le Monde, 29 May 1998, p. 8; see also Anne Chemin, "La Justice des mineurs a cinquante ans," Le Monde, 7 February 1995, and, from a 1995 Sorbonne colloquium in honor of the 1945 law, Enfance délinquante, enfance en danger: Une question de justice (Paris: Ministère de la Justice, 1996). Christian Rossignol disputes the notion of a postliberation clean break; see "La Législation 'relative à l'enfance délinquante': De la loi du 27 juillet 1942 à l'ordonnance du 2 février 1945, les étapes d'une dérive technocratique," Le Temps de l'histoire 3: L'Enfant de justice pendant la guerre et l'immédiat après-guerre (October 2000): 17–54.

2. Ministère de la Justice, "Le Douloureux Problème de l'enfance délinquante," Cahiers français d'information de la documentation française 5 (16 March 1945): 19. I have no idea if Hélène is related to César Campinchi, the radical deputy who proposed legislative reforms in 1937.

3. Comissariat à la Justice (Algiers), AN, BB30: 1729, Correspondence, 10 May 1944.

4. J. L. Costa, Le Phénomène de la délinquance juvénile: Rapport annuel à M. Le garde des Sceaux, Ministère de la Justice, Direction de l'Education surveillée (Melun: Imprimerie administrative, 1947), p. 15.

5. Others on the committee included Mr. Laugier, rector of the Algiers Acad-

emy; Mr. Bendjelloul; Mr. Fajon; Samuel Lebar (Lebhar in some documents); Mr. Mouchino, labor inspector; Mr. Sabatie, director of primary instruction; and Dr. Tzanck, coordinator of youth services, sports, and school hygiene. Comissariat à la Justice (Algiers), AN, BB30: 1729.

6. Ministère de la Justice, "Le Douloureux Problème de l'enfance délinquante," p. 19.

7. Costa, *Le Phénomène*, p. 15.

8. Michel Chauvière, *Enfance inadaptée: L'héritage de Vichy* (Paris: Les Editions ouvrières, 1980), pp. 18, 42–43, 141, 144–145.

9. Helène Campinchi, "Le Statut de l'enfance délinquante et la loi du 27 juillet 1942," in Louis Hugueney, Henri Donnedieu de Vabres, and Marc Ancel, eds., *Etudes de science criminelle et de droit pénal comparé* (Paris: Sirey, 1945), p. 176.

10. Ibid., p. 178.

11. Ministère de l'Information, "Le Délinquance juvénile en France," *Notes documentaires et études* 173 (29 October 1945): 4.

12. *Journal officiel*, 4 February 1945.

13. The 1942 law attenuated only temporary penalties for minors sixteen to eighteen.

14. Since Donnedieu de Vabres sat on the Supreme Council that deliberated on the 1942 law, either the final version varied from the one he saw, or he did not notice the provision at the time. Ceccaldi's letter to Magnol, cited in the previous chapter, denied that this provision was an accident. Henri Donnedieu de Vabres, "Loi du 2 février 1945, Commentaire," *Recueil critique 1945: Legislation*, Notebook 1 (Paris: Dalloz, 1945), p. 178.

15. Ibid.

16. *Journal officiel*, 4 February 1945.

17. Ibid.

18. Ibid.

19. Ibid.

20. Donnedieu de Vabres, "Commentaire," p. 173; de Vabres argued that a decision to send any minor under eighteen, not just minors under 13, to an adult prison should require a "justified order."

21. Ibid., p. 171. The 1942 law had also attempted to remedy the rank problem by creating a smaller number of larger jurisdictions for juvenile courts, something that France eventually adopted.

22. Dominique Charvet, "Préface," in Antoine Garapon and Denis Salas, eds., *La Justice des mineurs: Evolution d'un modèle* (Paris: Librairie génerale de droit et de jurisprudence, 1995), p. xiii.

23. Donnedieu de Vabres, "Commentaire," p. 175.

24. Ibid., p. 173; referring to laws of 17 November 1944 and 21 April 1944. The 1942 bill had initially stipulated that the two outside assessors had to be women, a requirement removed from the final version.

25. Ibid., p. 174. Exposé de motifs, Ordonnance du 2 février 1945, *Journal officiel*, 4 February 1945.

26. Donnedieu de Vabres, "Commentaire," p. 175.
27. Ibid., p. 176. *Journal officiel*, 4 February 1945.
28. Donnedieu de Vabres, "Commentaire," p. 179.
29. Ibid., pp. 170, 174.
30. Pierre Ceccaldi, "Origines et perspectives de l'Education surveillée, suite," *Sauvons l'enfance*, May–June 1947, p. 9.
31. Costa, *Le phénomène*, p. 19.
32. Ibid., pp. 20–21.
33. Mathias Gardet and Yvonne Le Goïc, "Les enfants perdus et le scoutisme de Ker Goat à La Prévalaye," in Mathias Gardet and François Tétard, eds., *Le Scoutisme et la rééducation dans l'immédiat après-guerre: Lune de miel sans lendemain?* document de l'Institut national de la jeunesse et de l'éducation populaire 21 (Paris, June 1995), p. 204.
34. ADP, D1 U6 4345.
35. As the French say, there was a *"décalage"* (lag) between the law and its application.
36. Pierre Ceccaldi, "La Première session d'études des Juges des Enfants," *Rééducation* 3 (January 1948): 5–6.
37. Victor Lapie, *Saint-Florent-la-Vie* (Paris: Vigot Frères, 1947).
38. Dr. Le Guillant, "Review of Victor Lapie, *Saint-Florent-la-Vie*," *Sauvegarde* 7 (January 1947): 38.
39. Ibid.
40. Henri Joubrel, "L'Ecole professionnelle de Saint-Maurice," *Rééducation* 8 (February 1948): 36, 37.
41. Perreau, *Le Mineur pervers de constitution* (Lyons: Bosc Frères, 1942), p. 47, n. 13.
42. Béatrice Koeppel, "Les Temps forts de la rééducation des filles (de Cadhillac à Brécourt): 1935–1950," *Cahiers du CRIV* 2 (October 1986): 69.
43. Koeppel, "Les Temps forts," p. 80.
44. Founded in Orléans in 1852, by 1950 there were more than 350 Bon Pasteurs for girls. Koeppel, "Les Temps forts," p. 69.
45. Jacques Bourquin, "La Patrouille des renards dans les cages à poules: L'Education surveillée 1937–1950," in Gardet and Tétard, eds., *Le Scoutisme et la rééducation dans l'immédiate après-guerre*, p. 104.
46. E. Riehl, "L'Institution publique d'education surveillée de Cadillac," *Sauvons l'enfance* 64 (May–June 1946): 2.
47. Béatrice Koeppel, *Marguerite B.: Une jeune fille en maison de correction* (Paris: Hachette, 1987).
48. Jean Chazal, *L'Enfance délinquante*, 11th ed., Que sais-je 563 (Paris: Presses universitaires de France, 1983), p. 88; Robert Allée, *Education en milieu ouvert* (Paris: Publications du Centre technique national d'études et de recherches sur les handicaps et les inadaptations, 1982), p. 36.
49. Chazal, *L'Enfance délinquante*, p. 54.
50. Jacques Lerouge, *Le Condamné à mort* (Paris: Stock, 1996), p. 121.
51. Chazal, *L'Enfance délinquante*, pp. 91–92.

52. Cited in ibid., pp. 120–121.
53. Ibid., p. 124; Allée, *Education en milieu ouvert,* p. 36.
54. The Justice Ministry reports that the number of delinquent minors sent to institutions declined from 2.3 percent in 1976 to 1 percent in 1984. Ministère de la Justice, *Bilan statistique de l'évolution de l'activité des juridictions de la jeunesse 1976–1984 et de l'incarceration des mineurs 1976– 1985,* n.p., n.d., p. 12.
55. George Thomas Kurian, *World Encyclopedia of Police Forces and Penal Systems* (New York: Facts on File, 1989), p. 135.
56. On the new version of probation, see Allée, *Education en milieu ouvert,* pp. 181–204.
57. *Le Monde,* 29 May 1998.
58. Ibid., 7 February 1995.
59. Agathe Logeart, "Mineurs délinquants," in "Dossiers et documents," *Le Monde* 168, special issue (July–August 1989): p. 8.
60. Ibid.
61. Antoine Garapon, *Carnets du Palais: Regards sur le Palais de Justice de Paris* (Paris: Albin Michel, 1995).
62. *La Protection judiciaire de la jeunesse* (Paris: Ministère de la Justice, Direction de la Protection judiciaire de la jeunesse, n.d.), p. 3.
63. *Libération,* 23 May 1997; John-Thor Dahlburg, "Youths without Hope Shake the French," *Los Angeles Times,* 27 February 1998.
64. *Le Monde,* 19 April 2001, 24 May 2001.
65. Logeart, "Mineurs délinquants." "Dossiers et documents."
66. Conversation with Jacques Bourquin, June 1994.
67. Jean François Renucci, *Le Droit penal des mineurs,* 3rd ed. (Paris: Presses universitaires de France, 1998), pp. 99–104.
68. *Le Monde,* 22 May 2001, and *Enfants en prison* (Lyons: Observatoire international des prisons, 1998), p. 167.
69. *Le Monde,* 29 May 1998.
70. Ibid., 27 May 1998.
71. Ibid.
72. Denis Salas, "L'Enfant paradoxal," in Antoine Garapon and Denis Salas, eds., *La Justice des mineurs: Evolution d'un modèle* (Paris: Librairie générale de droit et de jurisprudence, 1995), pp. 52–53.
73. Jacques Faget and Anne Wyvekens, "Bilan de la recherche sur le crime et la justice en France de 1990 à 1998," in Lode van Outrive and Philippe Robert, eds., *Crime et justice en Europe depuis 1990* (Paris: L'Harmattan, 1999), p. 152.
74. Olivier Bertrand, "La Délinquance chute aux Tarterêts: La cité s'apaise," *Libération,* 8 March 1999.
75. Cited in *Le Monde,* 23 March 1999.
76. Ibid., 22 May 2001.
77. Frieder Dünkel, "Legal Differences in Juvenile Criminology in Europe," in

Tim Booth, ed., *Juvenile Justice in the New Europe* (Sheffield: Joint Unit for Social Services Research, 1991), p. 5; in the same collection, see also Nicholas Queloz, "Protection, Intervention and the Rights of Children and Young People," pp. 32–33.

78. Queloz, "Protection, Intervention," p. 38.

79. Alex Kotlowitz, "The Unprotected," *The New Yorker,* 8 February 1999, p. 51.

80. William Glaberson, "Rising Tide of Anger at Teen-Aged Killers," *NYT,* 24 May 1998; Office of Juvenile Justice and Delinquency Prevention, 1999 Report.

81. Stefanie Asin, "More Juveniles Certified to Stand Trial as Adults," *Houston Chronicle,* 19 January 1997.

82. Editorial, *NYT,* 23 May 2001.

83. R. S., "Condamnés à mort," "Dossiers et documents," *Le Monde* 168, p. 6.

84. Same Howe Verhoven, "Texas Legislator Proposes the Death Penalty for Murderers as Young as 11," *NYT,* 18 April 1998.

85. Kotlowitz, "The Unprotected," p. 51.

86. Editorial, *NYT,* 6 February 1996.

87. "Youth Avoids Prison in Theft of Ice Cream Bars," *NYT,* 30 September 1994. On nineteenth-century fears of black youth, see Roger Lane, *Roots of Violence in Black Philadelphia, 1860–1900* (Cambridge, Mass.: Harvard University Press, 1986).

88. Fox Butterfield, "With Juvenile Courts in Chaos, Critics Propose Their Demise," *NYT,* 21 July 1997.

89. Fox Butterfield, "Republicans Challenge the Notion of Separate Jails for Juveniles," *NYT,* 24 June 1996.

90. Jacob Sullum, "Curing the Therapeutic State: Thomas Szasz on the Medicalization of American Life," *Reason Online,* July 2000; although horrific, overcrowded institutions have been closed, deinstitutionalization swelled the ranks of the homeless in the 1980s; see Thomas Szasz, *The Myth of Mental Illness* (New York: Hoeber-Harper, 1961), and his website, www.szasz.com.

91. The Gault case involved a fifteen-year-old sentenced in Arizona to five years in a juvenile facility for making an obscene phone call to a neighbor. Irene Rosenberg, "Leaving Bad Enough Alone: A Response to the Juvenile Court Abolitionists," *Wisconsin Law Review* 1 (1993): 166, n. 12.

92. Ibid., pp. 164–173; see also "With Juvenile Courts in Chaos, Critics Urge That They Be Scrapped," *NYT,* 31 July 1997.

93. Kotlowitz, "The Unprotected," pp. 42–53.

94. Jacques Steinberg, "The Coming Crime Wave Is Washed Up," *NYT,* 3 January 1999; see also *NYT,* 24 December 1999.

95. Elizabeth Becker, "For an Office with a Heart, a Man with a Change of One," *NYT,* 9 February 2001.

96. "The Mystery of New York: The Suddenly Safer City," *NYT,* 23 July 1995;

Fox Butterfield, "Crimes of Violence among Juveniles Decline Slightly," *NYT,* 9 August 1996.

97. Fox Butterfield, "Grim Forecast Is Offered on Rising Juvenile Crime," *NYT,* 8 September 1995.

98. Fox Butterfield, "Guns Blamed for Rise in Homicides by Youths in 80s," *NYT,* 10 December 1998.

99. "When Jail Doesn't Work," *NYT,* 22 May 1997.

100. Butterfield, "Guns Blamed."

101. Ibid.

102. Vincent Schiraldi, letter to the editor, *NYT,* 29 July 1997.

103. Jerome G. Miller, "Juvenile Justice, Facts vs. Anger," *NYT,* 15 August 1998; Joseph B. Treaster, "Beyond Probation: Breaking the Cycle of Juvenile Arrests," *NYT,* 12 December 1994; see also Laura Cohen's letter to the editor, *NYT,* 3 August 1998.

104. Evelyn Nieves, "California Proposal Toughens Penalties for Young Criminals," *NYT,* 3 June 2000.

105. Dünkel, "Legal Differences," pp. 2–4.

106. Schiraldi, letter to the editor; for a compelling portrait of minors in adult prisons, see Margaret Talbot, "The Maximum Security Adolescent," *New York Times Magazine,* 10 September 2000, pp. 40–47.

107. Philippe Meyer, *The Child and the State: The Intervention of the State in Family Life,* trans. Judith Ennew and Janet Lloyd (New York: Cambridge University Press, 1983), p. 11; Jacques Donzelot, *The Policing of Families,* trans. Robert Hurley (New York: Pantheon, 1979).

108. *Enfants en prison,* pp. 153, 167.

Bibliography

Interviews

Marie-Louise Mercier, January 1985
Georges d'Heuqueville, June 1989
Jacques Bourquin, June 1994
Jeanne Decker, July 1994

Archival Sources

Archives nationales, Fontainebleau

Direction générale de la Santé, Sous-direction de la Famille, de l'Enfance et de la Vie sociale, Bureau FE3: Enfance et jeunesse. 760175/11, 15, 16, 68, 120

Archives nationales, Paris

Chef de l'Etat
  Archives du Cabinet civil
    2AG 440 c.c.3, a, b, c, d, e, f, g, h, i, j, k, l, m, n, o, p, q, r, s
  Archives du Cabinet militaire, Service médical, Protection de l'enfance
    605 cm 19 d
  Dossiers sur le Conseil national constitués au Secrétariat général du Premier Ministre
    654 308A
Ministère de l'Intérieur, Délégation en zone occupée
  Justice
    F1a 3656
Ministère de la Justice
  Correspondance générale de la Division Criminelle
    BB 18 3281 20/41, 3304, 3320—2113 A 41, 3331—2649 A41, 3358—4226 A41
  Régime de Vichy
    BB 30 1711/11

279

Commissariat à la Justice d'Alger
  BB 30 1729
Police générale
Archives du Service de sécurité allemand en France
  F7: 15145–6
Sûreté Nationale, Contrôles techniques
  F7: 14927, 14934
Secrétariat générale du gouvernement et Services du Premier Ministre, Documentation
  Education nationale (426–436)
    F60 427 E11/A
  Enfance
    F60 608 S1 F
  France Libre et Gouvernement provisaire de la République française, Documentation, Gouvernement de Vichy
    F60 1677 B2800/2, 8
  Etablissements pénitentiares
    F60 519 J1A sd10, 14

Archives départementales de Paris

D1 U6 3390, 3391, 3411, 3431, 3440, 3451, 3460, 3494, 3507, 3544, 3570, 3583, 3594, 3609, 3624, 3641, 3642, 3656, 3668, 3680, 3692, 3705, 3706, 3719, 3733, 3744, 3757, 3768, 3785, 3786, 3798, 3812, 3825, 3839, 3853, 3854, 3867, 3868, 3890, 3891, 3892, 3904, 3905, 3919, 3920, 3934, 3935, 3944, 3951, 3964, 3965, 3978, 3979, 3998, 4005, 4019, 4020, 4033, 4034, 4044, 4056, 4069, 4070, 4082, 4083, 4087, 4091, 4103, 4116, 4117, 4131, 4144, 4157, 4168, 4177, 4186, 4196, 4205, 4209, 4218, 4227, 4236, 4242, 4248, 4255, 4261, 4273, 4284, 4288, 4297, 4306, 4315, 4331, 4363, 4404

Archives départementales de Paris, Dépot annexe de Villemoisson-sur-Orge

221/73/0001, 0003 bis, 0004, 0006, 0007, 0008, 0008 bis, 0010, 0011, 0012, 0013, 0014, 0015, 0044, 0045, 0046, 0047, 0048, 0049

Archives départementales du Gard

Nîmes 6 U 10 258, 259, 260, 262, 268, 272, 283, 300, 310, 320, 322, 353, 354, 358, 360, 369, 370, 384, 385, 401
Uzès 8 U 8 115, 120, 125, 127

Archives départementales du Nord

Lille, nonclassified dossiers
Cambrai 1125W 355, 356, 361, 368, 369, 370, 373

Archives départementales d'Indre-et-Loire

Chinon 1246 W 179
Tours 127 W 228, 230, 231, 232, 234, 246, 249, 252, 256, 261, 264, 266, 271, 272, 275, 278, 316, 317, 318

Primary Sources

Actes du congrès international du Patronage des libérés et des enfants traduits en justice: Paris 22–24 Juillet 1937. Cahors: Imprimerie A. Coueslant, 1937.

Albernhe, Roger. *La nécessité d'un personnel spécialisé pour s'occuper des enfants en justice.* Montpellier: Imprimerie du Progès, 1938.

Amor, M. *Statistique pénitentiaire pour l'année 1945.* Melun: Imprimerie administrative, 1947.

Archambault, Paul. *Le Problème familial.* Paris: Editions familiales de France, n.d.

Assistance publique. *Administration générale de l'assistance publique à Paris . . . Année 1940: Services des enfants assistés et de la protection des enfants du premier âge du département de la Seine.* Paris: Assistance publique, 1941.

———. *Administration générale de l'assistance publique à Paris . . . Année 1941: Services des enfants assistés et de la protection des enfants du premier âge du département de la Seine.* Paris: Assistance publique, 1943.

———. *Administration générale de l'assistance publique à Paris . . . Année 1942: Services des enfants assistés et de la protection des enfants du premier âge du département de la Seine.* Paris: Assistance publique, 1943.

———. *Administration générale de l'assistance publique à Paris . . . Année 1944: Services des enfants assistés et de la protection des enfants du premier âge du département de la Seine.* Paris: Assistance publique, 1946.

"Les Assistantes de police." *Pour l'enfance "coupable"* 47 (March–April 1943).

Bancal, Jean. *Essai sur le redressement de l'enfance coupable.* Paris: Sirey, 1941.

Barbizet, Georgette. "L'enfance en danger moral et la guerre." *Pour l'enfance "coupable"* 6 (January–February 1940).

———. "Assistantes de police." *Pour l'enfance "coupable"* 8 (January–February 1942).

———. "L'Oeuvre libératrice." *Pour l'enfance "coupable"* 9 (July–August 1943).

Barthélemy, Joseph. *Ministre de la Justice, Vichy 1941–1943: Mémoires.* Paris: Pygmalion, 1989.

Beley, André. *De la prophylaxie de l'acte anti-social chez les mineurs instables.* Paris: Les Editions Végan, 1933.

Bentham, Jeremy. *Panopticon; or, The Inspection House.* London: T. Payne, 1791.

Bernard, Michel-A. "Pas de dissolution! Pas de mouvement unique!" *Aujourd'hui* (25–26 July 1942).

———. "Travail—famille—patrie." *Aujourd'hui* (19 September 1942).

Bize, D. R. "Sur l'esprit d'observation." *Rééducation* 8 (July 1948): 24–29.

Blancho, Pierre. *Esquisse sur l'enfance après la guerre de 1940 à 1945: Etude médico-sociale.* Paris: R. Foulon, 1948.

Bordarrampé, P., Abbott. *Le Vénérable Louis-Edouard Cestac, fondateur de Notre-Dame du Refuge (Anglet, près Bayonne) et la congrégation des servantes de Marie: Sa vie, son oeuvre.* Bayonne: Porché Frères, 1928.

Bossy, L. *L'Enfance dans les fers.* Paris: Presses Alpha, 1938.

Bourrat, L., P. F. Girard, and R. Pellet. *L'Enfance irrégulière: Psychologie clinique.* Paris: Presses universitaires de France, 1946.

Brauner, Alfred. *Ces enfants ont vécu la guerre . . .* Paris: Les Editions sociales françaises, 1946.

Brosse, Thérèse. *L'enfance victime de la guerre: Une étude de la situation européenne.* Paris: UNESCO, 1949.

Brunschvicg, C. "Comment lutter contre le désoeuvrement de la jeunesse?" *Pour l'enfance "coupable"* 6 (January–February 1940).

Campinchi, Hélène. "Le Statut de l'enfance délinquante et la loi du 27 juillet 1942." In Louis Hugueney, Henri Donnedieu de Vabres, and Marc Ancel, eds. *Etudes de science criminelle et de droit pénal comparé.* Paris: Sirey, 1945, pp. 161–214.

———. "L'Enfance délinquante devant la loi." *Educateurs* (July–August 1946): 292–308.

Carbuccia, Horace de. *Sauvons les enfants de France.* Corbeil: Imprimerie Crété, 1943.

Carrasco-Barrios, Mario. *Théories sur les causes de la criminalité infantile et juvénile: Étude critique.* Paris: Jouve, 1942.

Casabianca, Pierre de. *Les Nouveaux tribunaux pour mineurs en Italie.* Agen: Imprimerie moderne, 1934.

Ceccaldi, Pierre. "Origines et perspectives de l'Education surveillée." *Sauvons l'enfance* 69 (March–April 1947): 1–5.

———. "Origines et perspectives de l'Education surveillée." *Sauvons l'enfance* 70 (May–June 1947): 9–11.

———. "La Première session d'études des juges des enfants." *Rééducation* 3 (January 1948): 5–6.

Chadefaux, Robert. "Application pratique de l'ordonnance du 2 février 1945." *Revue d'Education surveillée* (1946).

———. "Les Causes sociales de la délinquance juvénile." *Educateurs,* special issue (July–August 1946): 245–251.

Chassot, Maurice. *Les Conséquences pénales et civiles de l'infraction commise par un mineur à la suite de la loi du 27 juillet 1942 sur l'enfance délinquante.* Dijon: Imprimerie Darantière, 1943.

Chazal, Jean. *Coordination des services de l'enfance déficiente ou en danger moral: Buts, activités, réalisations.* Paris: Ch. A. Bédu, 1944.

———. *L'Enfance et l'adolescence déficientes ou en danger moral: Coordination et réalisations.* Paris: Ch. A. Bédu, 1944.

———. *Les Enfants devant leurs juges.* Paris: Editions familiales de France, 1946.

———. "La Formation et la spécialisation du juge des enfants." *Rééducation* 8 (July 1948): 20–24.

————. *Les Bandes asociales d'enfants et leur réintégration dans les cadres*. Paris: UNESCO, 1949.

Children in Bondage: A Survey of Child Life in the Occupied Countries of Europe and in Finland. New York: Save the Children Fund, Longmans, Green and Co., 1942.

"Comment est née *Rééducation*." *Rééducation* 1 (November 1947).

Costa, Jean-Louis. *Plan de réforme des services de l'Education surveillée et des institutions protectrices de l'enfance en danger moral: Ministère de la Justice, Direction de l'Education surveillée*. Melun: Imprimerie administrative, 1946.

————. *Le Phénomène de la délinquance juvénile*. Melun: Imprimerie administrative, 1947.

Cotte, S. "Rapport sur l'enfance délinquante et en danger moral, d'après l'expérience marseillaise." *Pour l'enfance "coupable"* 60 (July–September 1945).

Crémieux, Albert, M. Schacter, and S. Cotte. *L'Enfant devenu délinquant*. Marseilles: Comité de l'enfance déficiente, 1945.

Danan, Alexis. *L'Epée du scandale*. Paris: R. Laffont, 1961.

————. *Maisons de supplices*. Paris: Denoel et Steele, 1936.

Danjou, Henri. *Enfants du malheur: Les bagnes d'enfants*. Paris: A. Michel, 1932.

Dargent, R. "Les Services de protection de l'enfance au Palais de Justice et plus particulièrement au Parquet." *Pour l'enfance "coupable"* 3 (September–October 1937).

Davigny, Max. "En descendant la Boul 'Mich.'" *Jeunesse* (2 February 1941).

Deligny, Fernand. *Graine de crapule: Conseils aux éducateurs qui voudraient la cultiver*. Paris: V. Michon, 1945.

"La Délinquance juvénile en France." *La Documentation française*. Notes et études documentaires 1423 (19 January 1951).

Delpeuch, Germain. *Un service auxiliaire du Tribunal pour enfants: La Protection Toulousaine de l'enfance*. Toulouse: Imprimerie régionale, 1935.

Demoisy, M. "Les Effets de la crise et du chômage sur l'enfance et l'adolescence." *Pour l'enfance "coupable"* 2 (September–October 1936).

"Désormais les enfants criminels comparaîtront: D'abord devant des médecins ensuite devant des magistrats." *Paris-Soir,* 18 August 1942.

Despres, Germain. *Bagnes d'enfants*. Paris: Imprimerie de Moif et Paxcaly, n.d.

D'Heucqueville, Georges. *Né sans famille*. Paris: Hachette, 1945.

"Documentation: Quelques extraits de lettres de pupilles de maisons d'Education surveillée." *Pour l'enfance "coupable"* 38 (September–October 1941).

"Documents, mouvement de la délinquance des jeunes dans les dernières années." *Rééducation* 8 (July 1948): 32.

Dominique, Marie. "Réflexions sur le problème des sanctions dans la rééducation des enfants difficiles et délinquants." *Pour l'enfance "coupable"* 54 (May–June 1944).

Donnedieu de Vabres, Henri. "Le Code de la famille et la répression de l'avortement." *Pour l'enfance "coupable"* 6 (January–February 1940).

———. "Loi du 2 février 1945, Commentaire," *Recueil Critique 1945: Législation,* notebook 1. Paris: Dalloz, 1945.

———. "Loi du 27 juillet 1942, Commentaire," *Recueil Critique 1943: Législation,* notebook 1. Paris: Dalloz, 1943.

———. "Où en est la réforme du statut de l'enfance délinquante?" *Pour l'enfance "coupable"* 52 (January–February 1944).

"Le Douloureux problème de l'enfance délinquante." *Cahiers français d'information de la documentation française* 5 (March 1945): 19.

Ducrocqu, Pierre. "Swing qui peut." *La Gerbe,* 4 June 1942, p. 7.

Duverne, René. "Menace sur les centres de jeunesse." *Pour l'enfance "coupable"* 63 (March–April 1946).

"Enfance coupable? Non, société coupable!" *Le Populaire,* 2 December 1935.

"L'Enfance délinquante: Données actuelles, causes, préventions, observation." *La Santé de l'homme* 58 (January–February 1950).

L'Enfance en danger (problèmes de Poitou). Poitiers: L'Association poitivine pour le relèvement et la protection de l'enfance déficiente ou en danger moral, 1946.

L'Enfance et la Croix-rouge française. Paris: Librairie J. B. Baillière, 1946.

"Les Enfants Martyrs." *Détective,* 23 January 1935.

E. P. "Le Centre de M. Centre féminin spécialisé pour difficultés caractérielles." *Pour l'enfance "coupable"* 47 (March–April 1943).

Epron, Georges. "La composition du Tribunal pour enfants." *Pour l'enfance "coupable"* 39 (November–December 1941).

———. "La Compétence du juge des enfants." *Pour l'enfance "coupable"* 41 (March–April 1942).

———. "Réflexions au sujet de quelques enquêtes relatives à de mineurs délinquants." *Pour l'enfance "coupable"* 50 (September–October, 1943).

———. "Réflexions sur l'ordonnance du 2 février 194 sur l'enfance délinquante." *Pour l'enfance "coupable"* 62 (January–February, 1946).

Fatou, Raymond. "A propos du rôle des visiteurs de prison dans le patronage des pupilles des maisons d'éducation surveillée." *Pour l'enfance "coupable"* 28 (March–April 1939).

Favre, Henry. *La Maison d'éducation surveillé d'Eysses.* Toulouse: Privat, 1933.

Flot, Pierre. *Constatations médicales et sociales relatives à la délinquance juvénile en Bretagne.* Paris: R. Foulon, 1945.

Foulquié, Paul. *Les Droits et la liberté de l'enfant.* Paris: Editions Spes, 1946.

La France nouvelle. Montrouge: Draeger, 1941.

Fresneau, Jean. *Orientation et adaptation sociale des mineurs délinquants et des enfants déficients.* Paris: Union française universitaire, 1945.

Frey, Erwin. *L'Avenir des mineurs délinquants.* Paris: Les Cahiers de sauvegarde, 1947.

Fugeray, René. *Mère Anjorrant et son oeuvre. L'Institut de Jésus-Christ Bon-Pasteur et de Marie-Immaculée.* Vol. 1: *L'Ere des fondations.* Paris: G. Beauchesne, 1927; 2nd ed., 1939.

Gamet, André. *Contribution à l'étude de l'enfance coupable: Les facteurs familiaux et sociaux.* Lyons: E. Vitte, 1941.

Gautier, Robert. "Le Pervers constitutionnel." *Rééducation* 3 (January 1948): 27–34.

Godard, Victor. *Vingt-cinq années au service de l'enfance déficiente en Bretagne: L'Ecole de rééducation de Dinon.* St.-Brieuc: Les Presses Bretonnes, 1947.

Heuyer, Georges. *Délinquance et criminalité de l'enfance.* Paris: Masson, 1935.

———. *Enquête sur la délinquance juvénile: Etude de 400 dossiers.* Paris: Pour l'enfance "coupable." 1942.

———. "Le Conseil technique de l'enfance déficiente ou en danger moral, son fonctionnement, ses travaux." In Jean Chazal, *L'Enfance et l'adolescence déficientes ou en danger moral,* p. 24.

———. "Psychopathologie de l'enfance victime de la guerre." *Sauvegarde* 17 (January 1948): 3–46.

Hossenlop, Marianne. *Essai psychologique sur les bandes de jeunes voleurs.* Clermont-Ferrand: Imprimerie générale, 1944.

Huguenin, Elisabeth. *Les Tribunaux pour enfants.* Paris: Delechaux et Niestlé, 1935.

Joubrel, Fernand. "Le Centre de rééducation du Hinglé." *Pour l'enfance "coupable"* 45 (November–December 1942).

Joubrel, Henri. "Promenade à travers les maisons d'enfants de l'Administration pénitentiaire." *Pour l'enfance "coupable"* 53 (March–April 1944).

———. "Va-t-on nationaliser les oeuvres privées?" *Sauvons l'enfance* 66 (September–October 1946).

———. *Ker-Goat: Le salut des enfants perdus.* Paris: Editions familiales de France, 1947.

———. "L'Ordonnance du 2 février 1945 est-elle appliquée?" *Sauvons l'enfance* 70 (May–June 1947): 8–9.

———. "L'Ecole professionnelle de Saint-Maurice." *Rééducation* 8 (July 1948): 36–37.

———. *Saint-Florent-la-Vie,* see Lapie, Victor.

Joubrel, Henri, and Fernand Joubrel. *L'Enfance dite coupable.* Paris: Bloud et Gay, 1946.

Jouhy, E., and V. Shentoub. *L'Evolution de la mentalité de l'enfant pendant la guerre.* Paris: Delachaux et Niestle, 1949.

Journal officiel: Débats. Provisional Constituent Assembly, session of 22 Mars 1945.

Junck, Robert. "Génération perdue de l'Europe." *Educateurs* (July–August 1946): 356–359.

Kohler, Claude. "Le Cinéma et les enfants." *Revue de criminologie et de police technique* 3, no. 1 (January–March 1949): 48–54.

Kohler, G., and Line Thevenin. "Le Centre polyvalent d'observation de Lyon." *Sauvegarde* 11 (May 1947): 11–19.

La Morlais, Anne-Marie de. *Science et technique de la rééducation des mineurs délinquants: Dix cours.* Paris: Editions pour l'enfance coupable, 1943.

——. "Etude sur l'enfance coupable allemande et l'enfance nazie." *Sauvons l'enfance* 67, 68 (November–December 1946, January–February 1947).

Lafon, Robert. "La 'Famille coupable.'" *Sauvons l'enfance* 70 (May–June 1947): 1–8.

——. "Recherche sur les critères d'inadaptation." *L'Enfance inadaptée,* special issue of *Revue de droit sanitaire et social,* vol. 28 (October–December 1971).

Lagache, Daniel. "Nomenclature et classification des jeunes inadaptés." *Sauvegarde* 2, 3, 4 (June, July, October 1946).

Lalère, M. "Les Infractions au rationnement." In Louis Hugueney, Henri Donnedieu de Vabres, and Marc Ancel, eds., *Etudes de Science criminelle et de droit pénal comparé.* Paris: Sirey, 1945.

Lapie, Victor (pseud. of Henri Joubrel). *Saint-Florent-la-Vie.* Paris: Vigot frères, 1947.

Le Bourdellès, Michel. "Notes sur le cinéma et la délinquance juvénile." *Rééducation,* 8 July 1948.

Le Gal, E. *L'Enfant moralement déficient et coupable.* Paris: Les Publications sociales agricoles, 1943.

Le Moal, Paul. "Les Causes médico-psychiatriques de la délinquance." *Educateurs,* special issue (July–August 1946): 252–261.

Lepointe, Ralph. *Le Vagabondage des mineurs.* Paris: Maurice Lavergne, 1936.

Le Senne, René. "Caractérologie et enfance délinquante." *Educateurs,* special issue (July–August 1946): 262–270.

Levade, Maurice. "L'Ordonnance du 2 février 1945 relative à l'enfance délinquante." *Pour l'enfance "coupable"* 63, 64 (March–April, May–June 1946).

——. "L'Ordonnance du 2 février 1945 relative à l'enfance délinquante." *Sauvons l'enfance* 66 (September–October 1946): 10–11.

——. "L'Ordonnance du 2 février 1945 relative à l'enfance délinquante." *Sauvons l'enfance* 68 (January–February 1947): 6–11.

Lhotte, Céline, and Elisabeth Dupeyrat. *Le Jardin Flétri: Enfance délinquante et malheureuse.* Paris: Bloud et Gay, 1939.

Liévois, Françoise. *La Délinquance juvénile: Cure et prophylaxie.* Paris: Presses universitaires de France, 1946.

Luaire, René. *Le Rôle de l'initiative privée dans la protection de l'enfance en France et en Belgique.* Paris: Librarie générale de droit et de jurisprudence, 1936.

Lutz, Paul. "La Rééducation des jeunes délinquants." *Educateurs,* special issue (July–August 1946): 337–347.

——. "Les Idées du mois: Le gout du sensationnel." *Rééducation* 8 (July 1948): 3–4.

Magnol, Joseph. "De l'exécution des peines prononcés contre les mineurs de 13 à 18 ans." *Rééducation* 8 (July 1948): 5–13.

Mangé, Geneviève. *L'Enquête sociale et le droit des mineurs.* Bordeaux: E. Taffard, 1952.

Marcus-Jeisler, Simone. "Réponse à l'enquête sur les effets psychologiques de la guerre sur les enfants et jeunes gens en France." *Sauvegarde* 8, 9 (February, March 1947): 3–23, 3–18.

"Martyrs d'enfants. Assez!" *Journal de la femme,* 13 April 1935.

Mauco, Georges. "Le Centre psycho-pédagogique de l'Académie de Paris au lycée Claude-Bernard." *Sauvegarde* 15–16 (November–December 1947): 56–65.

Mauriac, François. "Enfants martyrs!" *Le Figaro,* 10 January 1936.

Mazel, Pierre, Paul F. Girard, and André Gamet. "Deux aspects du problème social de l'enfance coupable: La recrudesence actuelle et la cartographie lyonnaise de la délinquance juvénile." *Le Journal de médicine de Lyon* 528 (January 1942): 45–51.

Mazo, Geneviève. *Le Centre d'observation et la loi du 27 juillet 1942 relative à l'enfance délinquante.* Paris: H. Van Etten, 1944.

———. "Les Centres d'observation: L'Ordonnance du 2 février 1945 relative à l'enfance délinquante." *Pour l'enfance "coupable"* 54 (May–June 1944).

Menant, Guy. "La revue de *l'Enfance coupable* reparaît." *Pour l'enfance "coupable"* 60 (July–September 1945).

Menut, G. C. *La Dissociation familiale et les troubles de caractère chez l'enfant.* Paris: Editions familiales de France, 1944.

Mestrel Combremont, Pierre de. *Réadaptation sociale et rééducation des mineurs et des adultes: Vers une synthèse de la psychologie, de la pédagogie et du droit.* Paper presented at the eleventh International Patronage Congress, Paris, 22–24 July 1937. Cahors: A. Coueslant, 1938.

Ministère de l'Information. "La Délinquance juvénile en France." *Notes documentaires et études* 173 (October 1945).

———. "La Situation démographique et sanitaire de la France." *Notes documentaires et études* 172 (1945).

Ministère de la Justice. "Le douloureux problème de l'enfance délinquante." *Cahiers français d'information de la documentation française* 5 (16 March 1945): 19.

———. *Rapport quinquennal sur l'application de la loi du 22 juillet 1912 sur les Tribunaux pour enfants et adolescents et sur la liberté surveillée.* Melun: Imprimerie administrative, 1946.

———. *Direction de l'Education surveillée: Rapport annuel à M. le Garde des Sceaux.* Melun: Imprimerie administrative, 1947.

———. *Compte général de l'administration de la justice civile et commerciale et de la justice criminelle, Années 1944 à 1947.* Melun: Imprimerie administrative, 1953.

———. *Direction de d'Education surveillée: Bureau des études et programmes–K4: Bilan Statistique de l'évolution de l'activité des juridictions de la jeunesse 1976–1984 et de l'incarceration des mineurs 1976–1985.* n.p. n.d.

Miquel, René. "L'Adolescence sans foi ni loi." *Le Matin,* 3, 4, 5 February 1943.

Morlhon, J. Fabre de. "Dans quels lieux doivent se tenir les audiences des juridications pour enfants?" *Rééducation* 9 (August 1948): 5–10.

Mortier, Daniel-Antonin. *Bonne mère, ou la Révérende Mère Chopin, fondatrice de la Congrégation de Notre-Dame-de-Grâce, Châtillon-sous-Bagneux (Seine)*. Paris: Desclée de Brouwer, 1926.

Neron, Guy. *L'Enfant vagabond*. Paris: Presses universitaires de France, 1952.

Nobécourt, P., and L. Babonneix. *Les enfants et les jeunes gens anormaux*. Paris: Masson, 1939.

"Notes et information, région Parisienne." *Pour l'Enfance "Coupable"* 48 (May–June 1943).

Oswald, Marianne. *One Small Voice*. New York: McGraw-Hill, 1945.

Owings, Chloe. *Le Tribunal pour enfants: Etude sur le traitement de l'enfance délinquante en France*. Paris: Presses universitaires de France, 1923.

Parker, Daniel. "Influence de la presse enfantine et du cinéma sur la délinquance juvénile." *Quinze conférences sur les problèmes de l'enfance délinquante*. Paris: Editions familiales de France, 1946.

Péan, Charles. *L'Enfance déficiente et en danger moral*. Paris: Imprimerie du labourer, 1945.

Perreau, André. *Le Mineur pervers de constitution*. Lyons: Bosc frères, 1942.

Pesle, Georges-Dominique. *L'Enfance délinquante vue d'un centre de triage*. Paris: R. Foulon, 1945.

Pétain, Philippe. *Discours aux français*. Paris: Albin Michel, 1989.

Philippon, Odette. *La Jeunesse coupable vous accuse: Les causes familiales et sociales de la délinquance juvénile (enquête mondiale)*. Paris: Sirey, 1950.

Pinatel, Jean. "La Méthode de l'éducation surveillée et la loi du 27 juillet 1942." In Louis Hugueney, Henri Donnedieu de Vabres, and Marc Ancel, eds., *Etudes de science criminelle et de droit pénal comparé*. Paris: Sirey, 1945.

———. "Science pénitentiaire et criminologie juvénile." *Revue de criminologie et de police technique* 3, no. 1 (January–March 1949): 33–47.

"Qu'est-ce qu'un zazou-zazou?" *Au Pilori*, 11 June 1942.

Quinze conférences sur les problèmes de l'enfance délinquante. Paris: Editions familiales de France, 1946.

Racine, Aimée. *Les Enfants traduits en justice: Etude d'après trois cents dossiers au Tribunal pour enfants de l'arrondissement de Bruxelles*. Paris: Sirey, 1935.

"La Réforme de la législation de l'enfance délinquante." *Le Temps*, 13 August 1942.

"La Répression des dénonciations anonyms." *Le Temps* (28 February–1 March 1942.

Rey, Guy. *Contribution à l'étude de l'enfance coupable: Les mineurs délinquants récidivistes*. Lyons: Bosc frères, 1942.

Rey-Herme, Philippe. *Quelques aspects du progrès pédagogique dans la rééducation de la jeunesse délinquante*. Paris: Librairie philosophique J. Vrin, 1945.

Richard, Marthe. *Mon fils Gil*. Paris: SLIM, 1948.

Riehl, E. "Etude résumée sur la rééducation en internats spécialisés." *Pour l'enfance "coupable"* 56 (September–December 1944).

———. "L'Institution publique d'éducation surveillée de Cadillac." *Sauvons l'enfance* 64, 65 (May–June, July–August 1946): 2–4, 6–9.

Riffier, Roger. "Méthode active de Ker-Goat." *Rééducation* 9 (September 1948): 5–10.

Robin, Gilbert. "Il y a pervers et pervers." *Pour l'enfance "coupable"* 21 (November–December 1937).

———. *Enfances perverses*. Paris: La Vulgarisation scientifique, 1945.

———. *L'Education des enfants difficiles*. Que sais-je 323. Paris: Presses universitaires de France, 1948.

Roger-Fernand. *Les "J3" ou la nouvelle école*. Sceaux: Imprimerie de Sceaux, 1943.

Ruby, Pierre. *L'Enfance coupable*. Marseilles: Sémaphore de Marseille, 1936.

Scholoesing, D. "Coup d'oeil sur un Patronage." *Pour l'enfance "coupable"* 2 (April 1936).

Sebor, Milos. *La Délinquance juvénile actuelle*. Paris: Imprimerie nationale, 1947.

Service sociale de l'enfance. Report on general assembly held 29 June 1945.

"Sing Song Touamotou." *Gringoire*, 3 July 1942, 3.

Sinoir, G. "Nature et fonctionnement du Centre d'observation de mineurs délinquants." *Sauvons l'enfance* 65, 66 (July–August, September–October 1946): 1–4.

———. "Les Temps d'observation." *Educateurs* (July–August 1946): 283–291.

Spitzer, Olga. *Le Service social de l'enfance en danger moral 1923–1942*. Paris: Crété, 1945.

Taton-Vassal, M. *Exposé sur les décrets-lois du 30 octobre 1935*. Cahors: Imprimerie Coueslent, 1935.

Toubas, Henry. *Les Institutions pénitentiaires pour mineurs délinquants: Étude comparée avec certains pays étrangers, projets de réformes*. Nîmes: Imprimerie Azémard, 1936.

Valet, Raymond. *Contribution à l'étude du traitement et de l'assistance de l'enfance anormale: Le problème de l'adaptation sociale des enfants irréguliers*. Lyons: Bosc frères, 1942.

Van Etten, Henri. *Une enquête internationale sur quelques établissements pénitentiaires*. Paris: Gaston Doin, 1932.

———. *Ce qu'il faut savoir du problème de l'adolescence coupable*. Paris: Pour l'enfance "coupable," 1937.

———. "La Religion au service de la lutte contre la délinquance juvénile." *Pour l'enfance "coupable"* 38 (September–October 1941).

———. "L'Ecole Théophile-Roussel de Montesson (Seine-et-Oise)." *Pour l'enfance "coupable"* 40 (January–February 1942).

———. "Au Tribunal pour enfants de la Seine (Statistique 1942)." *Pour l'enfance "coupable"* 53 (March–April 1944).

———. "Au Tribunal pour enfants de la Seine (Statistique 1944)." *Pour l'enfance "coupable"* 61 (October–December 1945).

Ventré, Y. "Le Scoutisme à l'IPES du Saint-Hilaire." *Pour l'enfance "coupable"* 61 (October–December 1945).

Videau, Pierre. *Trois maisons de relèvement du ressort de la cour d'appel de Besançon et de quelques suggestions nouvelles en matière de rééducation des mineurs délinquants*. Gap: Imprimerie Louis-Jean, 1938.

Wallon, Henri. *Une plaie de la société: Les bagnes d'enfants*. Bourges: Secours ouvrier international, 1934.

———. "Milieu familial et délinquance juvénile." *Pour l'enfance "coupable"* 32 (January–February 1940).

Waquet, Pierre. *La Protection de l'enfance: Etude critique de législation et de science sociale*. Paris: Dalloz, 1943.

Wolf-Machoel, J. *La Réadaptation de la jeunesse et des déracinés de guerre*. Boudry: Editions de la Baconnière, 1945.

"Le Zazou." *Au Pilori*, 3 September 1942.

"Zazouismus: Umriss einer Französischen Nachkriegsbewegung." *Pariser Zeitung*, 24 August 1942.

Personal Testimonies, Edited Writings, Memoirs

Beauvoir, Simone de. *La Force de l'âge*. Paris: Gallimard, 1960.

Bood, Micheline. *Les Années doubles: Journal d'une lycéene sous l'occupation*. Paris: Robert Laffont, 1974.

Bruneteau, Pierre. *J'ai deux enfants: Récits*. Paris: René Debresse, 1941.

Cazals, Rémi, E. *Les Ecoliers de Tournissan 1939–1945*. Toulouse: Editions Edouard Privat, 1978.

D'Heucqueville, Georges. *Souvenirs de médicin-légiste*. Paris: Peyronnet, 1946.

Denoen, Emile. *Rue des enfants abandonnés: Récit*. Paris: J. Vigneau, 1945.

Les Ecoliers de Tournissan 1939–1945. Toulouse: Editions Edouard Privat, n.d.

François, Claude. *Enfants victimes de la guerre, une expérience pédagogique, le Renouveau*. Paris: Bourrelier, 1949.

Guéhenno, Jean. *Journal des années noires*. Paris: Gallimard, 1947.

Jean-Hubert. *Adolescents aux yeux ternis*. Paris: Albin Michel, 1945.

Léger, Raoul. *La Colonie agricole et pénitentiaire de Mettray: Souvenirs d'un colon 1922–1927*. Paris: L'Harmattan, 1997.

Levert, Jean-Pierre, Thomas Gomart, and Alexis Merville. *Un lycée dans la tourmante: Jean-Baptiste Say 1934–1944*. Paris: Calmann-Lévy, 1994.

Limouzin, René. *Le Temps des J3: Une adolescence paysanne pendant la guerre de 1939–1945*. Treignac: Editions "Les Monédières," 1983.

Merlier, Octave, ed. *Rédaction sujet: La drôle de guerre, l'occupation, la libération, racontées par des enfants*. Paris: Julliard, 1975.

L'Occupation et la libération vues par des écoliers ardennais. Mézières: G. Bouche, 1946.

Ophuls, Marcel. *The Sorrow and the Pity*, trans. Mireille Johnston. New York: Outerbridge and Lazard, 1972.

Pakonyk, François. *1940–1945, Les enfants de l'exode*. Paris: La Pensée universelle, 1984.

Pierquin, Bernard. *Journal d'un étudiant parisien sous l'occupation (1939–1945)*. N.p.: Bernard Pierquin, 1983.

Ruffin, Raymond. *Journal d'un J3*. Paris: Presses de la cité, 1979.

Solente, R. *L'Enfance délinquante: Vie vécue et documentation*. Pont-Levoy: n.p., 1947.

Vegh, Claudine. *Je ne lui ai pas dit au revoir: Des enfants de déportés parlent*. Paris: Gallimard, 1979.

Ziolkowski, Jean. *Les Enfants du Sable, Récit*. Bainville-sur-Mer: L'Amitié par le livre, 1957.

Newspapers and Journals, 1930s and 1940s

Aujourd'hui
Au Pilori
Educateurs
Le Figaro
La Gerbe
Gringoire
L'Illustration
Jeunesse
Le Journal de la femme
Le Journal de médecine de Lyon
Le Matin
Pariser Zeitung
Paris Soir
Le Populaire
Pour l'enfance "coupable"
Rééducation
Revue de criminologie et de police technique
Revue de droit sanitaire et social
Santé de l'homme
Sauvegarde
Sauvons l'enfance
Le Temps

For a bibliography of secondary works, please visit the author's website at http://vi.uh.edu/pages/FAC/fishman/fishman.html.

Index

abnormal children designation, 28, 29, 136. *See also* maladjusted children

abnormal families. *See* broken families in psychological analysis

adolescence, conceptual developments, 9, 22, 24, 33

adolescents: adult ambivalence about, 11; social interaction needs, 17; internal experience of war for, 45–50; economic deprivations of war, 48–50, 52–60; and Vichy regime, 50–52, 60–66; and forced labor program, 66–67; *zazou* youth culture, 67–69; Resistance activity, 75–78; adult status for, 169–174

adult certification age, lowering of United States, 225

adult status for older adolescents, 169–174

AEMO (measure of educational action), 216–217

age issue for juvenile status, 14, 21–22, 24, 169–174, 231

agricultural youth colonies, 17–18, 36–37

agriculture, German plundering of, 53, 54, 246n27

Alaimo, Kathleen, 22

Albright, Madeleine, 73

Alibert, Raphaël, 62, 70, 166

Allied operations to liberate France, 78–81

American culture and *zazous*, 68, 69

Ancel, Marc, 216

Aniane public supervised education house, 191

anti-Semitism, 61–62, 69, 70–75, 269n3

appeals, judicial, 178, 182–183, 205

apprenticeships, reform uses of, 22, 40, 64–65

armistice with Germany, 49, 50–52

Arpaillange, Pierre, 217

ARSEA (Regional Association for Safeguarding At-Risk Children and Adolescents), 187, 208

atavism theory, 133

at-risk children, 29, 152–164, 174–181, 186–187

attenuated sentences, 184–185, 200

Aubry, Martine, 220–221

Auriol, Vincent, 39

Azéma, Jean-Pierre, 52

Baden-Powell, Sir Robert, 40

Bailleau, Francis, 11

Bancal, Jean: education focus of, 42, 208–209; on diagnosis of children, 149, 150; and delinquent children law (1942), 167–168, 171, 176–177, 184

Barbizet, Georgette, 129

Barreau, Jean-Michel, 61

Barthélemy, Joseph: libel suit against *Paris-Soir*, 43; and delinquent children law (1942), 166–168, 171, 175–177, 179–180, 186; anti-Semitism of, 269n3

Battle of France, 45, 46–50

Beauregard, Paul, 26

Beauvoir, Simone de, 62

Beccaria, Cesare, 15, 151

Belgium, juvenile justice reforms in, 32, 41, 131, 132

Belle-Ile correctional school, 35, 189

Benjamin, René, 61

Bentham, Jeremy, 151

Béranger, René, 26

Bernarbei, Mario, 147

Bertillon, Jacques, 12

Bessis, Georges, 129, 130

Bianqui, Pierre, 129

Binet, Alfred, 28